UNDERSTANDING
EDUCATIONAL REFORM
IN GLOBAL CONTEXT

REFERENCE BOOKS IN
INTERNATIONAL EDUCATION
(General Editor: Edward R. Beauchamp)
(Vol. 22)

GARLAND REFERENCE LIBRARY
OF SOCIAL SCIENCE
(Vol. 663)

Reference Books in International Education

Edward R. Beauchamp
General Editor

UNDERSTANDING EDUCATIONAL REFORM IN GLOBAL CONTEXT
Economy, Ideology, and the State

Mark B. Ginsburg
Editor

GARLAND PUBLISHING, INC. • NEW YORK & LONDON
1991

Library of Congress Cataloging-in-Publication Data

Ginsburg, Mark B.
    Understanding educational reform in global context : economy,
ideology, and the state / Mark B. Ginsburg.
        p.   cm. — (Garland reference library of the social science ; vol.
663. Reference books in international education ; vol. 22)
    Includes bibliographical references (p.   ) and index.
    ISBN 0-8240-6896-3 (alk. paper)
    1. Educational change—Case studies. I. Title. II. Series.
Garland reference library of social science ; vol. 663.
III. Series: Garland reference library of social science. Reference
books in international education ; vol. 22.
LA217.2.G56   1991
370—dc20   91–3812
                                                                  CIP

Printed on acid-free, 250-year-life paper
Manufactured in the United States of America

TABLE OF CONTENTS

vi

SERIES EDITOR'S FOREWORD

This series of scholarly works in comparative and international education has grown well beyond the initial conception of a collection of reference books. Although retaining its original purpose of providing a resource to scholars, students, and a variety of other professionals who need to understand the role played by education in various societies or regions of the world, it also strives to provide up-to-date information on a wide variety of selected educational issues, problems, and experiments within an international context.

Contributors to this series are well-known scholars who have devoted their professional lives to the study of their specialization. Without exception these men and women possess an intimate understanding of the subject of their research and writing. Without exception they have not only studied their subject in dusty archives, but they have also lived and travelled widely in their quest for knowledge. In short, they are "experts" in the best sense of that often overused word.

In our increasingly interdependent world, it is now widely understood that it is a matter of survival that we not only understand better what makes other societies tick, but that we also make a serious effort to understand how others, be they Japanese, German, or Chilean, attempt to solve the same kinds of educational problems that we face in North America. As the late George Z.F. Bereday wrote: "[E]ducation is a mirror held against the face of a people. Nations may put on blustering shows of strength to conceal public weakness, erect grand façades to conceal shabby backyards, and profess peace while secretly arming for conquest, but how they take care of their children tells unerringly who they are" (*Comparative Methods in Education*, New York: Holt, Rinehart & Winston, 1964, page 5).

Perhaps equally important, however, is the valuable perspective that studying another education system (or its problems) provides us in understanding our own system (or its problems). To step outside of our own limited experience and our commonly held assumptions about schools and learning in order to look back at our system in contrast to another places it in a very different light. To learn, for example, how the Soviet Union or Belgium handles the education of a multilingual society; how the French provide for the funding of public education; or how the Japanese control admissions into their universities enables us to understand that there are alternatives to our own familiar way of doing things. Not that we can often "borrow" directly from other societies; indeed, educational arrangements are inevitably a reflection of deeply rooted political, economic, and cultural factors that are unique to a society. But a conscious recognition that there are other ways of doing things can serve to open our minds and provoke our imaginations in ways that can result in new approaches that we would not have otherwise considered.

Since this series is intended to be a useful research tool, the editor and contributors welcome suggestions for future volumes as well as ways in which this series can be improved.

Edward R. Beauchamp
University of Hawaii

AUTHORS

N'Dri Thérèse Assié-Lumumba has been teaching and coordinating of a graduate program in education at Centre Interafrican de Recherche et d'Etudes Supérieures en Science de l'Education based in Togo. She is currently a resident fellow at UNESCO International Institute for Educational Planning in Paris. In 1991 she will be a Fulbright Fellow at Cornell University. She has taught and done research in several institutions, including the University of Houston, Vassar College and Bard College. Her teaching and research interests include comparative and international education, social change in Third World countries, women and gender issues in development.

John M. Barrington is a reader in Education at Victoria University of Wellington, New Zealand. He teaches courses on policy studies and race relations. His current research interests include educational reform in New Zealand and internationally, with a particular focus on issues of governance and teachers.

Susan F. Cooper, former administrator at the University of Liberia, is a doctoral student in the International and Development Program at the University of Pittsburgh. Her dissertation is on the selection and organization of knowledge at the University of Liberia in national and world-system context.

Peter Darvas is a research associate at the Hungarian Institute for Educational Research. He is currently a Graduate Student in sociology at New York University. His teaching and research interests are in educational policy analysis and comparative educational sociology.

Sara Morgenstern de Finkel earned her Licenciada en Educación from Buenos Aires University, Argentina, and her M.A. and Ph.D. in Sociology from Essex University, England. She is a lecturer in Sociology at the Universidad Nacional de Educación a Distancia, Spain. Her professional interests are in sociology of education and sociology of work.

Mark B. Ginsburg is the Director of the Institute for International Studies in Education and Professor in the Department of Administrative and Policy Studies and of Sociology at the University of Pittsburgh. His scholarship focuses on the work, political action, and preparation of educators in relation to contradictory class, gender, and race relations. He published *Contradictions in teacher education and society: A critical analysis* (Falmer Press) in 1988.

Esther E. Gottlieb is a senior lecturer in social and comparative analysis of education at State Teachers College Seminar Hakibbutzim, Tel Aviv, Israel. She received her Ph.D from the University of Pittsburgh, where she studied in the international development education program. Currently she teaches qualitative research, social and comparative analysis of education, and policy analysis. Her ongoing research involves the study of the discursive construction of knowledge in education, reform rhetoric, and the professionalization of teaching. She has participated in a series of policy analyses for the Israeli Ministry of Education, and is currently co-editing the first issue of a new journal of teachers education (in Hebrew).

Tukumbi Lumumba-Kasongo has been teaching in the Program in Africana Studies and the Department of Political Science at Vassar College. He has taught and conducted research in several institutions, including the University of Liberia, where he served as the chair of the Department of Political Science; the University of

Houston; Wellesley College; and the Council for Development of Economic and Social Research in Africa CODESRIA (Dakar, Senegal). His teaching and research interests include political economy of Third World countries, social and political movements in Africa, educational policy and politics of education, international politics and questions related to philosophy and ideology of social progress. He is the author of *Nationalist ideologies, their policy implications and the struggle for democracy in African politics*, Edwin Mellen Press, Forthcoming.

Don Martin is an associate professor in the Department of Administrative and Policy Studies, School of Education at the University of Pittsburgh. His professional and research interests are in the areas of the history of education, politics of education, critical theory, and work/reform and education.

Henry D. R. Miller is a lecturer in Sociology in the Organizational Studies and Applied Psychology, division of Aston Business School at Aston University in Birmingham, England. He teaches courses on culture and communication, the problems of management in a changing environment and the social context of personnel work as well as policy and management in education. His research interests include change in higher education, the education training interface and the relationship of professionalism to trade unionism, particularly among teachers.

Rolland Paulston is a professor of International and Development Education in the School of Education at the University of Pittsburgh. His current research examines representations of educational reform, education in social movements, and explanations of social and educational change.

Rajeshwari Raghu, a native of India and former teacher and civil servant, is a doctoral student in the Social and Comparative Analysis in Education program at the University of Pittsburgh. Her research interests include how preservice teachers develop conceptions of gender relations and how they orient themselves to act "politically" on issues of gender relations in classrooms, schools, and communities.

xi

Susan Rippberger is a doctoral student in the International and Development Education Program at the University of Pittsburgh. Her current research interests are in the areas of interpretative studies in bilingual bicultural education and social change in Mexico and historical analyses of educational trends in Nicaragua.

Susan L. Robertson is a lecturer in the Department of Education Studies and senior researcher in the International Institute for Policy and Administrative Studies, Western Australian College of Advanced Education, Perth. Her teaching and research focus on educational sociology, politics and the policy process in Australia.

Carlos Alberto Torres holds a licentiate and teaching credential degrees from the Universidad del Salvador in Argentina, a masters in Political Science from the Latin American Faculty of Social Science (FLASCO) in Mexico, and a masters and Ph.D. in Education from Stanford University in the United States. He is currently an assistant professor at the Graduate School of Education, University of California, Los Angeles. He has taught in universities in Argentina, Mexico, the United States and Canada. He is the author of *Politics of nonformal education in Latin America* (Praeger, 1990) and coauthored with Daniel Morales-Gomez *The state corporatist politics and education policy making in Mexico* (Praeger, 1990). In addition, he has published a number of books and articles on political sociology of education, nonformal education, comparative education, and critical pedagogy.

George E. Urch is a professor of comparative and international education in the Center for International Education at the University of Massachusetts School of Education. He has been involved in research and has worked with educators on the African continent for the past twenty-five years. Recently he directed a three year project in Tanzania designed to strengthen the teaching of English, Mathematics, and Science in the secondary schools. He holds a Ph.D. degree from the University of Michigan.

Roger R. Woock has held senior academic positions in both Canada, the United States and Australia. His writing has focused on comparative aspects of educational systems and the sociological aspects of educational policy development and critical practice. He is currently the Deputy Dean of the newly established Institute of Education at the University of Melbourne, Australia.

Hugo Zegarra, a former professor of sociology in Peru, completed his masters degree in political science and is now enrolled in the Social and Comparative Analysis in Education doctoral program at the University of Pittsburgh. His research interests focus on the state, world capitalist economy, social movements, and educational reform.

PREFACE

Mark B. Ginsburg

This book represents a collective effort to understand educational reforms as processes of ideological and social struggles. These struggles can be seen to take place in the context of contradictory economic, political, and cultural dynamics at the local, national, and world-system level. The book, however, not only represents an attempt to clarify a number of issues related to educational reform and to describe and analyze the contexts and processes associated with educational reform. It also constitutes an intervention in the ideological struggle over how education and human experience, more generally, needs to be reformed or, more appropriately, transformed.

The set of national case studies presented in this volume represent a range of societies in terms of both the region of the world in which they are located and the ideology and organization of their political economies. We do not claim that they constitute a representative sample of nations, but they clearly provide us with a sense of the range of experiences, in the past and present, in "reforming." As you will see, there are both similarities and differences across the various cases, and these we use to seek an understanding of educational reform in global context.

The origins of this collective project can be traced to work that colleagues and I undertook in England beginning in 1976 (e.g., Ginsburg, Meyenn, and Miller 1979; Ginsburg, Wallace and Miller

1988). In a sense that work undertaken, while I was on the faculty at the University of Aston in Birmingham, is symbolic of the project on which this volume is based. We began an ethnographic study of five middle schools and their communities (Ginsburg, et al. 1977). The development and implementation of the concept of middle schools was initially seen as a case of reforming the organization of schooling in the context of other "reform" rhetoric and action under the banner of the comprehensivization of secondary schooling in England, but also elsewhere in Europe and other regions of the world. But for us what began as an examination of the experience of an organizational innovation in education--middle schools-- evolved as a study of the experience of educators during a period punctuated by cuts in educational expenditure, "debates" about the "problems" in education, and proposals for and efforts to implement other "reforms" in education.

We were thus encouraged to understand the experience of these middle school teachers, headmasters, students, and their parents in relation to broader dynamics than at least I initially envisioned that we could. Given that then Prime Minister James Callaghan launched the "Great Debate on Education" during a time of economic and fiscal crisis and at a point where his Labour government was coming under increasing criticism on the economy and a range of other issues, it made it relatively easy for us to see this local case of middle school teachers in "Midland County" as connected to national level dynamics. However, although colleagues and I considered the notion of a global economic dynamics--a world system level approach, this did not figure very strongly in our early analyses of our field work.

Within a few years after returning to the United States to work at the University of Houston in 1979, I thought I was having a dream (actually nightmare would be a more appropriate term) when then President Ronald Reagan launched what he termed a "Great Debate on Education" in 1983. As time moved on and I became more aware of dynamics in other societies, I increasingly sought to understand what was taking place in education on a global scale. During this period I also became more interested in and concerned about the need for teachers and other workers/citizens to be involved in struggles to build a more just, equitable, peaceful world (see Ginsburg 1987, 1988 and 1990).

Both my intellectual and political concerns come together in the project represented in this volume. This project more specifically can be seen to have commenced during discussions that took place during a two-session panel I organized on "Restructuring State-Profession Relations in the Face of World Economic Crisis" at the 1988 meeting of the Comparative and International Education Society in Atlanta, 17-20 March. As an outgrowth of the dialogue that occured during and after that conference, colleagues and I decided to pull together a series of national case studies which could be used to address a number of theoretical and political issues. To focus the discussion and to stimulate further debate I worked with a group of graduate student colleagues at the University of Pittsburgh, where I had moved in the Fall of 1987 to become Director of Institute for International Studies in Education. The initial product of this effort was presented at the annual meeting of the Comparative and International Education Society at Harvard, 30 March - 2 April, 1989. A revised and extended version of this work was published in the *Comparative Education Review* (Ginsburg et al. 1990) and a further modified version appears as the first chapter of this volume.

A draft of this critical review of existing literature on "educational reform" and a copy of an earlier published discussion of the English case study (Ginsburg, Wallace, and Miller 1988) were distributed to a group of colleagues in preparation for an authors' conference hosted at the University of Pittsburgh, "Understanding Educational Reform in International Context: The Dialectic of Human Agency, Ideology, Economy, and the State," 21-23 June 1989. These very stimulating and productive days of dialogue were followed by many of the participants convening in Montreal, 26-30 June 1989, to present and further discuss their work at the World Congress of Comparative Education. Subsequent to these meetings drafts of chapters have been circulated to and commented on by other members of the group involved in this project.

Thus, this book represents a collective effort, one that we invite you, the reader, to join. All the authors of chapters in this volume welcome your comments, criticisms, advice, and involvement in trying to understand and struggle in relation to educational reform in global context. We hope we have made a modest contribution through our collective project, and look forward to working with you and others to further develop it.

I would like to acknowledge the financial support provided by a University of Pittsburgh School of Education Research Team Grant. The funds for this grant come from generous support from Buhl Foundation and the School of Education alumni. This grant facilitated hosting the authors' conference in Pittsburgh, as well as communication with authors as the chapters were being written.

A project such as this obviously also involves the contribution of many other people besides those who appear as chapter authors. First, I would like to mention others who participated in the discussions on which this book was based. This includes a number of colleagues who originally planned, but were unable for a variety of reasons, to develop a case study as a chapter for this book in the time frame I set: Don Adams, Khalipha Bility, David Berman, Michael Chen, Susan Cooper, Bill Dinello, Astrid Fischel Volio, John Hawkins, Tom La Belle, Raj Pannu, David Plank, and Chris Ward. I would also like to thank the other people who participated and contributed to the discussions at the authors' conference in Pittsburgh: Naseem Ahmed, Louise Brennen, Nezahat Coskun, Nick DeFigio, Ichemkhou Eleyou, Margaret D'Eramo, Noreen Garman, Charles Gorman, Helen Hazi, Joseph Lagana, Rajeshwari Raghy, Ladji Sacko, HyungSok So, Seth Spaulding, Monte Tidwell, and John Weidman.

Appreciation is also expressed to Ed Beauchamp, Janice Gibson, and Thomas La Belle, who provided encouragement and support at key phases of this book project.

I am indebted as well to Lesah Johnson and Yvonne Jones for their tireless and outstanding effort in wordprocessing the book manuscript. Susan Cooper also performed admirably as my editorial assistant throughout the period of work on this book. I also want to thank Donnie Booker and Shannon Gallagher, respectively, Administrative Secretary and Financial Bookkeeper for the Institute for International Studies in Education, for all their efforts in making this project and this book possible.

Finally, I wish to thank my spouse, Barbara; my children, Jolie, Kevin, and Stefanie; my parents, Norman and Blance Ginsburg, my parents-in-law, Milton and Doris Chasin; my Grandfather, Fred Burg; and other members of my extended family.

This volume is dedicated to the educators, parents, and other citizen/workers who continue to struggle for a better world.

REFERENCES

Ginsburg, M. 1987. Contradictions in the role of Professor as Activist. *Sociological Focus*, 20, 2: 111-22.

Ginsburg, M. 1988. What is to be done? Critical praxis by educators of teachers. In *Contradictions in teacher education and society: A critical analysis*, by M. Ginsburg, 199-220. New York: Falmer Press.

Ginsburg, M. 1990. El proceso de trabajo y la accion politica de los educadores: Un analisis comparado (The labor process and political action of educators: A comparative analysis). *Revista de educación* (Extraordinario): 317-345.

Ginsburg, M., Cooper, S., Raghu, R., and Zegarra, H. 1990. National and world system explanations of educational reform. *Comparative Education Review*, 34, 4: 474-499.

Ginsburg, M., Meyenn, R., and Miller, H. 1979. Teachers, the 'Great Debate,' and education cuts. *Westminister Studies in Education*, 2: 5-33.

Ginsburg, M., Meyenn, R., Miller, H., and Ranceford-Hadley, C. 1977. *The role of the middle school teacher*. Birmingham, England: University of Aston Educational Enquiry Monograph Series.

Ginsburg, M., Wallace, G., and Miller, H. 1988. Teachers, economy and the state: An English example. *Teaching and Teacher Education*, 4, 4: 317-37.

Understanding
Educational Reform
in Global Context

EDUCATIONAL REFORM: SOCIAL STRUGGLE, THE STATE AND THE WORLD ECONOMIC SYSTEM[1]

Mark B. Ginsburg, Susan Cooper, Rajeshwari Raghu, and Hugo Zegarra

Since the mid-1970s in every region of the world we have witnessed extensive rhetoric and activity identified as "educational reform" in nations characterized as "developed" and "developing," as "capitalist" and "socialist," and as "democratic" and "totalitarian" (Gumbert 1985). This is not to suggest that educational reform is only a recent phenomenon; indeed, such rhetoric and activity have a long, if not always remembered, history (Quick 1868; Simmons 1983; Cuban 1990). Nor is it to posit that what has been labelled as "educational reform" is always concerned with changing, let alone improving, education. Rather, as the quotations marks indicate, the practices, purposes, and consequences of "educational reform" must be treated as problematic, as something to be investigated, a text to be deconstructed (Cherryholmes 1988).

Thus, in this chapter, and in this book more generally, we seek to enhance our understanding of phenomena that have been

3

subsumed under the rubric of "educational reform." We hope to develop not only a clearer conceptualization of what is meant by "educational reform" but also a more comprehensive explanation of the timing and focus of associated rhetoric and activity.

In this chapter we critically review various theoretical approaches that have been employed to analyze "reform" talk and efforts. We examine both national level and world-system explanations and offer some suggestions for combining the contributions of both. With respect to both levels of explanation, we explore approaches developed within equilibrium and conflict paradigms and devote particular attention to the state and its relation to the economy. While we do not find the two paradigms equally compelling, we recognize the contributions of work done within both. At the same time we seek to avoid an overly deterministic account, one that explains "educational reform" without reference to the individual and collective actions of real people, that is sometimes represented by equilibrium and conflict structuralist perspectives.

Like others (Gumbert 1985; Paulston 1977; Simmons 1983a; Wirt and Harman 1986), we are attempting to develop our understanding of "educational reform" as a phenomenon occurring in economic, cultural, and political contexts. However, besides being oriented to theory building as a type of scholarly work and to comparative analysis as a basis for informing policy, our objective is to identify and clarify a number of issues to facilitate our reflection about and strategies for progressive action in relation to current and future "reform movements."

DEFINING EDUCATIONAL REFORM

Educational reforms, might be categorized in terms of the purposes for educational systems of the social transactions involved. For example, educational reforms have been described as focused on changes in the following aspects of education systems (Ginsburg, Wallace, and Miller 1988; Merritt and Coombs 1977; Sack 1981; Simmons 1983b):

a) size or number of students, teachers, administrators, and buildings;

b) goals and objectives;

c) policy-making and administrative/managerial system or power structure;

d) financing and budget making processes;

e) level of funding;

f) system organization: the types, statuses, and levels of as well as links and ages of transition between educational institutions;

g) curriculum: content and organization of what is taught;

h) pedagogy: social relations of teaching and learning;

i) selection, evaluation, and promotion criteria and procedures for students; and

j) selection, evaluation, and promotion criteria for educational workers (teachers, administrators, etc.).

However, not all educational reform activities can be understood as efforts designed with an intent to change some aspect(s) of an educational system. As Campbell (1982, 328) suggests about reform activity in general, educational reform may be seen as a "placebo," that is, "symbolic gestures designed to indicate governmental [etc.] awareness of problems and sympathetic intentions, rather than serious efforts to achieve social change." That is, the rhetoric and activity linked to "educational reform" may function to legitimate those with political power rather than to change education. And attention to education, whether serious and sustained or not, may, in fact, operate to deflect concern or conflict from economic, political and cultural problems (Mitchell 1987, 117-35; Cuban 1990).[2] Thus, we need to examine both the manifest and latent functions or consequences (Merton 1968) of "educational reform" movements for both education and society.

In defining educational reform in terms of its latent and manifest functions for education, culture, politics, and economy, we do not adopt the assumption imbedded in many equilibrium paradigm structural functionalist analyses that the intended or unintended changes (or lack thereof) are necessarily "for the better" as, for example, Merritt and Coombs (1977, 25) do. Thus, when some writers (Merritt and Coombs 1977; Simmons 1983b; Spaulding 1988) concerned with educational reform characterize the purposes of educational reform as *improving* the system's effectiveness, efficiency, and relevance or *increasing* equality, they are only focusing on certain possible outcomes viewed "positively" from one perspective.

One problem with viewing the consequences (or even the goals) of the rhetoric and activity of "educational reform" as improving education's effectiveness, efficiency, and relevance is that such goals may be contradictory or incompatible (Altbach 1974; Apple 1986; Carnoy 1976; Ginsburg, Wallace, and Miller 1988). Thus, from one perspective improving the effectiveness, efficiency, and relevance of the education system by improving its "articulation with the world of work," (Sack 1981, 43) may in fact, *increase* or at least reinforce inequalities in education and society.

A second problem with adopting the view of reform as improvement is that one must assume a consensual model of societal or global relations. In contrast, we think there are reality-based differences in perceptions of what the goals of education should be and in what ways education should prepare future generations for their participation in society. Thus, it is likely that many consequences will be viewed differently by different groups regarding whether effectiveness, efficiency, and relevance have been improved. As Altbach (1974) observes, what is constructive change to some people may be seen by others as either tokenism or destructive or regressive change to others. For instance, an educational system can be viewed to be as either more *or* less effective and relevant when it becomes more effective in preparing male and female students for "traditional," gender-differentiated roles that may characterize a particular society.

EXPLAINING THE TIMING AND FOCUS OF EDUCATIONAL REFORM

Over a decade ago Merritt and Coombs (1977, 249) commented that comparative educationists have tended to view "educational systems as largely autonomous, somewhat insulated, decision areas." For example, Beeby (1966, 69) adopting an evolutionary variant of equilibrium theory, stresses the autonomy of education systems when he claims that "there are certain stages of growth through which all school systems must pass . . . [and that] the stage of development is determined by . . . the level of education of the teachers, and the amount of training they have received." And, more recently, Green, Ericson, and Seidman (1980) suggest a high degree of autonomy for the education system, emphasizing that the education system of a particular society has a "life of its own." They argue that an educational system has a "logic" or "practical rationality" such that "the behavior of the system, its inherent processes, may become intelligible in a way that is independent of differences in political and economic ideology" (Green, Ericson, and Seidman 1980, xiii).

Merritt and Coombs (1977, 249) go on to say, nevertheless, that "the evidence is now incontrovertible that in most nations virtually all educational decisions, certainly including efforts at major reform, are highly interrelated with concurrent events in the cultural, social, economic, and political realms." Simmons (1983a, 72) proffers a similar claim, that "[p]olitical and economic factors are more important in shaping educational reforms than are factors internal to the educational system itself."[3] In agreeing with this, however, we do not adopt an overly-deterministic perspective in which education systems and the actors involved in them are completely structured by external systems or forces. As we will discuss further in the concluding section of this chapter education may be interrelated to broader societal dynamics but be relatively autonomous nonetheless.

Regardless of one's assumption about the degree of relative autonomy of the education system, one may incorporate cultural, economic, and political dynamics into one's model for explaining educational reform. In doing so, one's analysis can be based on assumptions of equilibrium theory and/or conflict theory, and one may conceptualize these relationships as occurring at the national and/or the world-system level. Therefore, we organize the discussion below around the following four general theoretical models defined by the cross-classification of the two above mentioned dichotomies: 1) national level equilibrium, 2) national level conflict, 3) world-system level equilibrium, and 4) world-system level conflict. While there is some important intra-model variation, each of the four approaches is built on a basic set of assumptions about the way education functions in political, economic, and cultural context. In discussing these four models we will identify the contributions and limitations of each. In addition, we will devote special attention to the "state," a concept we view to be central to understanding education and educational reform.

NATIONAL LEVEL EXPLANATIONS OF EDUCATIONAL REFORM

In his "review of major theoretical perspectives on educational change-cum-reform at the national level," Paulston (1977, 370) distinguishes between "equilibrium" and "conflict" paradigms (see also Paulston 1983; Simmons 1983b). Within the equilibrium paradigm change in education tends to be portrayed as natural movements toward ever-higher stages of societal development or adaptations required by system imbalances or societal needs. In equilibrium approaches it is assumed that society is fundamentally consensual and operates based on homeostatic principles. The "equilibrium paradigm . . . stresses the importance of functional integration, harmony, and stability [and] it assumes *a priori* that all members of society implicitly agree what the functional necessities are" (Simmons and Esping-Anderson 1983, 423-424). In contrast, the conflict paradigm emphasizes "the inherent instability of social systems and the conflicts over values, resources, and power that follow as a natural consequence"

(Paulston 1977, 376). From a conflict perspective educational change occurs through conflict and competition between social class, ethnic, national, religious, and gender groups, whose interests are incompatible or when structural contradictions (e.g., in the economy) are not being successfully mediated[4].

National Level Equilibrium Approaches

In national level equilibrium approaches the analysis of educational reforms is focused within the boundaries of nation-states, and functional, evolutionary, or system theory assumptions dominate. Paulston (1977, 28) illustrates the structural-functionalist variant of an equilibrium perspective when he says that education reform is:

> the result of interaction between society and the schools and follows five steps: (1) a need arises in society; (2) the school is assigned the task of meeting the need; (3) change in the educational structure takes place to accommodate the new function; (4) the new role is assumed by the schools; and (5) latent and manifest changes take place in society as a consequence of the new educational functions.

Merritt and Coombs (1977, 247) provide an example of this approach in explaining why "education in Europe and North America change[d] from a cottage industry into a gigantic, highly bureaucratized enterprise." They see the explanation of such changes in education to reside in changing societal *needs* for "workers with such basic skills as reading, writing and arithmetic, soldiers, who could handle the increasingly complicated technologies and tactics of warfare; and . . . an electorate that is literate and politically sophisticated." According to the assumptions of the equilibrium paradigm, education is changed because the needs of modern, industrialized, and urbanized society are not being fulfilled by the existing organization, content, and processes of education. The education system, as part of a larger homeostatic and consensual social system, is seen to evolve as society evolves or to adapt as functional incompatibilities or dysfunctions arise.[5] As societies become "modern" and "rational" their needs change, and educational systems must adjust to this change. The timing and focus of reform of the education subsystem are determined by the needs of the society to maintain an equilibrium in a homeostatic system undergoing change in other subsystems.

National Level Conflict Approaches

From a conflict perspective educational reform is not viewed as part of a homeostatic system's response to functional incompatibility that may arise from time to time. Rather educational reform is seen to be part of on-going struggles between groups, whose interests are fundamentally in conflict, and in the context of social relations that are inherently contradictory. Conflict approaches, especially those drawing on Marxist perspectives, explain the timing and focus of educational reform with reference to class relations under the capitalist mode of production (or sometimes to gender and racial groups involved in contradictory social relations). For example, Carnoy and Levin (1986, 37) explain that the "dynamic of education . . . can best be understood as a condensation of a much wider social conflict inherent in capitalist development."

From this perspective education, the state, and other superstructural institutions mediate (or, alternatively, exacerbate) contradictions in the economic base of society, and as a result of this education and the state in capitalist societies contain contradictions as well (Apple 1986; Baudelot and Establet 1971; Carnoy 1982; Dale 1989; Ginsburg 1988; Ginsburg, Wallace, and Miller 1988; Levin 1982). Dale (1982, 130-133) argues that the "dynamic for education systems" arises out of "three core problem areas confronting state education systems," which can only be solved by mutually contradictory strategies. These core problems are the 1) "support of the capital accumulation process," 2) "guarante-eing a context for its continued expansion," and 3) "the legitimation of the capitalist mode of production, including the state's own part in it."

It is important to clarify, though, that from this perspective reform in education is not some natural evolutionary development or functionally necessitated adaptive response to the "needs" of the capitalist political economy. Rather the contradictions within and between the economy and superstructural institutions, such as the state and education, constitute the terrain on which the bourgeoisie and the proletariat (and their allies within the middle class) struggle (Carnoy 1982, 84-85). And at times these struggles on the structural and ideological levels become labelled as "educational reform," whether or not they are associated with concerted efforts to change some or more aspects of education. Moreover, during periods of economic crisis in capitalist (racially stratified and patriarchal) societies, the tensions produced by these contradictions are heightened, thus shaking up the terrain of struggle. And when possible, capitalists and their allies within a national context are seen to shift the focus of the crisis away from the economy to the state and education (Carnoy and Levin 1976; Ginsburg, Wallace, and Miller 1988). According to Habermas (1979, 74):

> [T]he origins of the crisis still lie in the economic system in capitalism but . . . the Welfare State no longer allows the crisis to explode in an immediately economic form. Instead, . . . the symptoms are displaced into strains within the cultural and social order. . . . The result is a much bigger "ideological discharge" than in [less crisis-like] periods of capitalist development.

Thus, the timing of major educational reform activities can be explained by the occurrence of crises in the economy (as well as in contradictory gender and race relations) (Ginsburg 1988). The focus of the reform would, both in its rhetoric and activity, be shaped by struggles between classes and other groups, who are constrained and enabled by the contradictory dynamics within the economy, culture, households, education, and the state. Even if no concrete changes are attempted or implemented, an ideological struggle may occur. And while the focus of the crisis may be deflected from the economy, issues addressed in reform efforts may still implicitly or explicitly concern the relation between education, the state, and the economy, in terms of the cost and control of education, the kind of work force it is designed to produce, and the racial/ethnic and gender characteristics of those who are to be involved in such efforts in the home, school, work place, and community. Real changes may be attempted in how the work of educators is conceptualized, organized, and implemented as well as in the content and processes of education as individuals and groups struggle to serve what they perceive as their interests in the context of contradictory social relations.

WORLD SYSTEM LEVEL EXPLANATIONS OF EDUCATIONAL REFORM

In common with some of the national level explanations of change and reform in education, world system level analyses have focused on the state, specifically in terms of global trends of increasing state authority and power and of national government incorporation and control of education (Ramirez and Boli-Bennett 1982; Ramirez and Rubinson 1979; Ramirez and Weiss 1979). In analyzing states as well as culture, the economy, and educational systems, however, world system level approaches focus attention beyond the boundaries of the nation-state. As Ramirez and Boli-Bennett (1982, 15) articulate it: "educational systems . . . cannot be explained by standard comparative education discussions that treat national systems as essentially autonomous units developing in accordance with endogenous social and political forces" (see also Carney 1976; Coombs 1985; Ginsburg, Wallace, and Miller 1988).

While a number of scholars in education have adopted the term "world system" in their analyses, not all of them have followed a Marxist conflict theory approach that has been characteristic of the more general theoretical and empirical work under the label of world system analysis (Hopkins and Wallerstein 1982; Rymalov 1978; Wallerstein 1974, 1980, 1988).[6] Some have seemed to work within an equilibrium perspective although focused globally.

World System Level Equilibrium Perspectives

John Meyer and some of his colleagues have tended to emphasize cultural rather than economic factors and to treat the dynamics from an equilibrium perspective. Meyer and Hannan (1979, 298) refer to "a relatively unified cultural system,"[7] and Boli, Ramirez, and Meyer (1986, 107-112) analyze how education has been influenced by a world cultural system:

> The striking thing about modern mass education is that everywhere in the world the same interpretive scheme underlies observed reality. . . . [As] a secular procedure for constructing the individual . . . [schooling] helps meet the functional need for integration of the increasingly differentiated system.

Inkeles and Sirowy (1984, 139) claim similarly that there is a tendency for all national educational systems in the world to converge toward a common structure and set of practices. In the case of the more industrialized countries, change toward this common structure and practices is explained by the "'imperatives' built into the socio-technical systems . . . which drive them to similar responses to common problems."

For the less developed industrialized nations a somewhat different explanation is offered--one that while still within an equilibrium perspective is less explicitly structural functionalist. In the case of less industrialized societies change in education is explained to result from "borrowing" structures and practices from the more developed nations. Such "borrowing" occurs because of the less developed countries' "integration into the networks of influence through which ideas and social forms diffuse" (Inkeles and Sirowy 1984, 139). Thus, despite some national cultural, economic, and political dynamics tending toward divergence, there are greater global pressures toward convergence. These pressures, which at times get translated into "educational reform" movements, are diffused through a consensual world cultural system by representatives of international organizations and industrial nations' bilateral aid agencies who encourage all national educational systems to accept common international standards. In discussing this diffusion process Inkeles and Sirowy (1984, 159-60) stress the "moral force" and "persuasive efforts" of such representatives.

In explaining the convergence of different society's educational policies and practices, Guthrie (1990) also refers to a process of cultural diffusion facilitated by a growing network of international experts. However, he accords greater explanatory power to what he terms the "international economic imperative" or "human capital imperative," that is, the need of nations to develop their human knowledge and skill resources "as a strategic means . . . to gain or retain an economically competitive position in the global market place" (Guthrie 1990, 3; see also Guthrie and Kollich 1989).

Philip Coombs (1968; 1985) also provides an analysis based on an equilibrium perspective, and at the same time he may be considered a major actor contributing to the diffusion of ideas about needed educational reform in the world cultural system. It is interesting to speculate that *The World Educational Crisis*, published in 1968, which Coombs (1985, 7) describes as "widely read throughout the world" and having "helped to precipitate a widespread debate over and a reexamination of previously accepted educational orthodoxies," may have shaped the rhetoric and action related to educational reform in the 1970s and 1980s. Coombs (1968) suggested that the world educational crisis was created by a growing "disparity" between educational systems and their environment, especially the economy. He also lent his voice to concerns about the rising cost of schooling. Both of these problems as well as increasing unemployment among the educated populace were seen to require managerial solutions in which the education system was restructured to better fulfill its functions with respect to the economy.[8]

From this vantage point educational systems change in relation to changed ideas in and needs of an increasingly global cultural system, described by Ramirez and Boli-Bennett (1982, 18) as the "ideology of citizenship" linked with the "ideology of the state" and the "ideology of the individual." Schools take on the function of creating citizens in response to the world cultural system and to the increasing interconnections among states in what Meyer and Hannan (1979a, 218) call a "densely linked" world economy.

World-System Level Conflict Approaches

In contrast to equilibrium paradigm approaches, conflict paradigm approaches have given more attention to the economy, stressing that the world system is a capitalist system, incorporating capitalist *as well as* nominally "socialist" societies (Arnove 1982; Carnoy and Levin 1976; Chase-Dunn and Rubinson 1979; Ginsburg, Wallace, and Miller 1988),[9] both types of which are stratified into "core," "semi-peripheral," and "peripheral" countries (Altbach 1982, 469-84; Carnoy 1976; Zachariah 1986, 91-104). This does not entail ignoring cultural or political spheres, but seeing these in relation to the economic base of the world system.

In this context capital-labor relations are seen to take on a more complex form. In core societies there is "relatively 'free' wage labor," while in the periphery "labor is subject to a variety of forms of coercion," such that through multinational corporation capitalists in the core societies can "appropriate a portion of the surplus value produced in the peripheral areas" (Chase-Dunn and Rubinson 1979, 277-78). Thus, class struggle and conflict in the Third World or peripheral areas are:

> not simply between dominant and subordinate classes in a given country, but between subordinate classes (sometimes including fractions of the bourgeoisie and petty bourgeoisie whose interests are contrary to transnational development) and an alliance of local dominant groups with a transnational technocracy [or economic elite], whose power lies not only in its financial strength but also in the willingness of metropolitan governments to support its cause with military backing. (Carnoy 1986, 82)

Given these assumptions as a starting point, educational policy, financing, organization, content, and practice and efforts to reform these "are largely conditioned by the world system of capitalist production, by the way that the particular country's production has developed in the world economy, and by the way class conflict has developed in that context" (Carnoy and Levin

1976, 36). For societies in the periphery the construction and reform of education must be seen in relation to social relations of domination and subordination characteristic of the world capitalist system (Weiler 1988). Reforms that are implemented require at least the tacit support (or partial defeat) of local economic elites but also powerful groups outside the country (Carnoy 1976; Altbach 1982, 470). Educational reform in core nations also should be analyzed in relation to dynamics within the world economic system.

The world system, though, is not static. As Hopkins and Wallerstein (1979, 46) clarify, "core processes and peripheral processes are constantly relocated in the course of the world-system's development." That is, nation-states and regions do not necessarily have fixed positions in the world system. Moreover, world system dynamics occur through social struggles taking place on a terrain characterized by a set of fundamental contradictions. One of the important contradictions, termed the "economy-polity" contradiction, is that the "economy is primarily a 'world' structure, but political activity takes place primarily within and through state-structures" (Hopkins and Wallerstein 1979, 58).

We note, however, that the economy-polity contradiction is associated with more than just a "double level of competition among states and among capitalists" for accumulation or profits (Hopkins and Wallerstein 1979, 13). The social struggles, involving conflict and cooperation between nations, between capitalists, between capital and labor, between other social groups, should be seen as occurring in the context of efforts to legitimate both nation-states and capitalist relations of production as well as to foster accumulation at the local, national, and global levels.

Scholars in the world systems conflict perspective focus attention on the roles played in these processes by multinational corporations, corporate foundations, bilateral "aid" agencies, international organizations, and universities. Multinational corporations, whether involved in the industrial, agricultural, or financial arena, are seen to influence the timing and focus of educational reform, both in the center and periphery. Certainly, the practices and demands of large capitalist business and industrial firms have shaped the nature of the education system in England, France, and the United States (Archer 1979; Bowles and Gintis 1976; Katz 1975; Katz 1968). More recent educational reforms in England and the United States have also witnessed prominent involvement of corporate leaders. And multinational corporations have constituted a substantial, if not always visible, force in efforts to reform education in Third World societies. For example, Klees and Wells (1983, 339) discuss how a rise in industrial activity in El Salvador, stimulated by multinational corporations, was associated with an effort to revise the secondary school curriculum and introduce an educational television system. These reforms were designed to provide the types of skills and attitudes demanded by foreign capital. This in turn fostered a greater dependence on foreign investment to employ the new workers produced by the expanded school system. And with this economic dependence came substantial military aid to a series of Salvadoran governments, which have attempted to keep an impoverished, exploited, and oppressed worker and peasant population in that position.

Corporate foundations have also been analyzed by scholars in the world systems conflict tradition, with a focus on the ways these foundations operate not only to promote the interest of the multinational firms and other capitalist enterprises with which they are associated but also to serve the interests of elites in nations in which they are based and/or focus their efforts. For example, Berman (1983) analyzes the role of the Carnegie, Ford, and Rockefeller Foundations in shaping and reforming higher educational institutions and teacher education and public administration programs in the Third World as well as their related involvement in institutions in the United States. He argues that such activities must be seen as part of the foundations' "role in support of United States foreign policy objectives and . . . sustaining the world capitalist system" (Berman 1983, 3).

International organizations or what Kolko (1988) terms "supranational institutions" (such as the World Bank and the International Monetary Fund) and bilateral/multilateral agencies (including the British Ministry of Overseas Development, the Canadian International Development Research Centre, the Swedish International Development Authority, and the United States Agency for International Development) also receive attention. Unlike scholars adopting an equilibrium perspective (Inkeles and Sirowy 1984), who view these institutions as operating in a consensual environment and primarily through "persuasion" and "moral force," representatives of the conflict paradigm highlight economic, political, and military power (Hopkins and Wallerstein 1979, 52).

Moreover, the changes brought about are seen to serve primarily the interests of those who benefit by the existing unequal social relations in the world system (Foster 1989).

This is not to argue that all of these organizations serve the same interests all of the time. Given the competition among capitalists and among nation-states and because of the dilemmas associated with the accumulation-reproduction and economy-polity contradictions, this sort of perfect correspondence is unlikely. Rather this is to call attention to the way in which dynamics in the world economy impinge on different nation-states is affected, for example, by the research foundations, supranational organizations, and bilateral agencies sponsor and disseminate (Berman 1990). Moreover, through financial assistance or refusal of such aid as well as through specific "development" or "reform" projects, these organizations have affected in different ways reform efforts in education in core and peripheral societies. For instance, Altbach (1988, 139) discusses that:

> A large number of countries are dependent on external financing for increasing proportions of their investment . . . in education. . . . [T]he World Bank . . . is able to influence and orient investments made by other organizations because of its leadership position. World Bank financing is increasingly linked to policy adjustments deemed necessary for balanced and healthy development as defined by Bank experts.

Universities and academicians in the United States (and other nations) are also conceived to play a part in planning and implementing educational reform and not only on a domestic level (Powell 1980). For instance, Gonzalez (1982) discusses the involvement of the University of California at Berkeley in developing and attempting to implement *Plan Basico* in Colombia in the 1960s. This university reform project, coordinated by the U. S. Agency for International Development, was designed to reorganize and centralize campus administrative structures, thus reducing the power of faculty members; to depoliticize student culture; and to re-orient the curriculum toward technical training.

Gonzalez views these actions as an example of "imperial reform in the neo-colonies," in which "[c]orporate foundations, major universities, and multilateral international financial institutions combined to provide the funds, materials, research personnel, and political support to develop plans for the reform of Third World educational systems" (Gonzalez 1983, 332).[10] Universities may be seen, thus, not only as private corporations or government operations pursuing their own interests, but in the context of their "development" and "technical assistance" projects and other exchange programs as actively (if not always explicitly) involved in struggles on the terrain of contradictions of the world capitalist system.

Educational reform dynamics, however, should not be conceived of as some sort of functional response to the needs of economic elites or of the world capitalist system. From a Marxist conflict perspective change in education or other aspects of any state must be understood in a more complex and dialectical fashion. It may be true that peripheral states are more effective in controlling labor (including their wages, organizing efforts, political activity, and migration) than they are at regulating multinationals and the circulation of capital (Chase-Dunn and Rubinson 1979). And it may also be that "economic and political crises in the advanced capitalist societies . . . are out of control of the local dominant class" (Carnoy 1986, 83). Nevertheless, regardless of a society's location along the core-periphery dimension, it is still a part of the world system. And because of the contradictions in the world capitalist system and (as will be discussed more fully below) the contradictions within the state, the dynamics of the global economy do not determine in some simple direct correspondence fashion how education and the state in any society are structured or restructured.

Thus, national (and regional/local) cultural, political, and economic factors must be considered when explaining the timing and focus of educational reform. They should be examined not because they constitute the total source of explanation but because they interact with dynamics set in motion by contradictions and crises in the world capitalist economic system (Dale 1989; Ginsburg, Wallace, Miller 1988). For instance, nation-states in the core and the periphery may be seen as active in relation to the world economy in general and to multinational firms, corporate foundations, international organizations, bilateral agencies, and universities. They do not just respond to what is offered, nor do they merely accept what is given; economic and state elites (among other less powerful actors) can be seen to actively seek aid for their own purposes or attempt to redirect the uses of resources provided for other tasks.

We want to emphasize, moreover, that it is not just contradictions within the economic sphere that constitute the terrain on which these social struggles occur. Hence, we focus attention on the ways in which "educational reform" may be connected to struggles around contradictory race/ethnic relations (Hawkins and La Belle 1985) and gender relations (Mueller 1978).

NOTES ON THE CONCEPT OF THE STATE

From the above discussion we can see that the "state" is a key concept in both national level and world system level analyses, especially within Marxist conflict approaches. Thus, it is important to clarify how the state may be conceptualized. From one vantage point the state is treated as the government. But the state may also be conceptualized to include nongovernmental organizations which are financially supported through tax revenues (grants or tax breaks) and that perform functions of the state apparatus (Dale 1989). Some analyses of the state emphasize its political form--for example, representative democracy or totalitarian dictatorship, while other approaches highlight its economic functions--referring, for example, to feudal, capitalist, socialist, or communist states. Additionally, certain conceptualizations characterize the state as a mechanism through which popular opinions or dominant group interests are realized, while others treat the state as a site struggle or as a location for contradictory dynamics.

Here we will emphasize the state in relation to the economy, in particular economic dynamics within the world capitalist system. As Kolko (1988, 188) explains: "the state's primary function" in the contemporary era is "to renew the conditions for capital accumulation in a process of restructuring the world economy and the national segments of it." However, we want to clarify that "the state is not a monolith; there are differences within and between its various apparatuses in their prioritizing of demands made upon them and in their ability to meet those demands" (Dale 1982, 135). As Grace (1987, 196) observes, drawing on McLennan (1984, 3) "the State in education is understood not as a single and unified entity but as a set of agencies, departments, tiers and levels, each with their own rules and resources and often varying purposes." Because of this, the state, which we conceive of as encompassing more than the agencies of local and national governments, embodies contradictions and is a site of struggle, at least in capitalist economies where a structure of representative democracy exists.

We agree with Urry (1981, 102) that the "state . . . is never simply omnipotent, nor does it simply react to the demands and the needs of the economy. . . . Rather the state itself is to be seen as actively seeking to establish and sustain a particular constellation of social forces." This is not to argue that the state is such a heterogenous entity that it is irrelevant or operates neutrally in relation to the economy or with respect to educational reform. It is only to indicate, as Dale (1982)[11] notes, that "the functions of the State in capitalist societies are given not by the direct control of capitalists or capitalist sympathizers within the state apparatus, but are in fact objectively given by the imperatives of the maintenance and reproduction of the conditions of existence of the capitalist mode of production." That is, the state must ultimately reproduce a particular set of social relations, including relations of production, because the revenue which sustains its operation depends in part (via taxation) on the accumulation (of surplus value) process (Carnoy 1986; Dale 1989; Ginsburg, Wallace, and Miller 1988; Offe and Ronge 1981).[12]

Thus, although relatively autonomous from the global and national economic dynamics, the state is tied to the extant relations of production and infused, in different ways and to different extents in "capitalist" and "socialist" nations, with the contradictions of capitalism (Holloway and Picciotto 1978). These contradictory dynamics -- for example, accumulation and reproduction--create space for the state's relative autonomy. As noted above, the state needs for its own survival to foster the process of *accumulation*, that is, to maintain economic returns to capital in the context of declining rates of profit. At the same time, the state is involved in *reproduction*, that is, organizing and legitimating social relations appropriate to the means of production.

As part of the state an education system is an important site in which these contradictory dynamics are experienced and contested. It is within the space created by contradictions internal to and between the state, education, and the economy that such struggles and contestations take place. And it is within these processes that education is structured and restructured, often with implications for the professionalization or proletarianization of educational workers (Ginsburg, Wallace, and Miller 1988). Thus, educators must be part of the focus in analyses of educational reform, both because their labor process may be the target of reform efforts and also because educators can be seen to be key political actors in struggles in society (Ginsburg 1989). And because of the feminization of teachers and the way in which patriarchal relations characterize the work place of educators, these dynamics must be understood as involving struggles around gender as well as social class (Acker 1983; Apple 1988; 1989; Connell 1985; Dale 1989).

Nevertheless, in facilitating reproduction the state is not only promoting the "needs" of capital but also retarding the accumulation process of capital. As Dale (1982, 135) explains:

> The central contradiction is . . . that while the capitalist mode of production is driven by the creation (through the universalization of the commodity form) and the realization of surplus value, the conditions for its success and reproduction can only be guaranteed through the extraction of some part of that surplus value by the state.[13]

Additionally, state activity, such as reforming education, tends to embody contradictory movements, as Carnoy and Levin (1976, 38) comment, between efforts to "reproduce the educational inequalities required for capitalist efficiency and those which equalize opportunities on behalf of social mobility and democratic participation."

The state's involvement in promoting and undermining capital, particularly in times of economic crisis, is partly the reason why the state finds itself in a credibility or legitimation crisis (Habermas 1975). Thus, state dynamics, including efforts to propose and/or implement reforms in education, must be understood not just in relation to accumulation and reproduction processes of the economy but also in terms of attempts to maintain or re-establish its own legitimacy. As Weiler (1988, 265) explains:

> As the modern state . . . faces a chronic deficit of legitimacy, the recourse to the legitimating potential of symbolic action becomes an important strategy. . . . The idea, it seems, is to maximize the political gain to be derived from the design of educational reforms and to minimize the political cost of implementing them.

The contributions of the state (or its constituting institutions, such as education) to processes of accumulation and reproduction, however, are not always fully appreciated. The state, because of the ideological manner of in which it is characterized and because of its relative autonomy, is often perceived as completely autonomous and neutral (Carnoy 1986). Thus, as Young (1980) observes, the state can elicit social opinion (i.e., the residue of history, tradition, and established beliefs) or mold mass opinion (mediated by personal versus group interests) while seeming to mobilize public opinion (i.e., that which reflects genuine human interests and is derived from general population participative decision-making) (see also Ginsburg, Wallace, and Miller 1988). In Poulantzas' (1975, 173) words: "By means of a whole complex functioning of the ideological, the capitalist state systematically conceals its political class character. . . . This state presents itself as the incarnation of the popular will of the people/nation."

Therefore, analyzing educational reform rhetoric as ideological work can be a fruitful approach to understanding what is occurring. As noted above, "reform" rhetoric may not be concretely connected with efforts to change anything fundamentally about schools. In this case the object may be to define what the problems and possible solutions are even if no sustained change effort is launched. For instance, based on a study of the 1968 higher education reform in Sweden, Ruin and Lindenjo state that the "broad . . . political and interventionist objectives--growth, equality, reform capacity and freedom of choice . . . tended more and more to be reinterpreted towards narrower administrative goals of efficiency and [technocratic] rationality" (Ruin and Lindenjo 1982, 3). They also note that this "new view . . . help[ed] to create arguments and ideas . . . [making] it possible to interpret ongoing developments in the sector, motivate them and provide alibis for them" (Ruin and Lindenjo 1982, 10). Such ideological work can, of course, also be undertaken in the context of actions designed to restructure schooling internally and with respect to its external relations with the economy, the state, and families.

The struggle at the ideological level, like other forms of struggle, does not occur among individuals and groups with equal resources and power. Those with greater control over and access to the public and private modes of mass producing and mass distributing ideas tend to define the major issues in particular ways that shape the overall discourse. Voices expressing alternative frames for analyzing and addressing the problems may go unheard or be marginalized. The use of mass media and reports of government, corporate foundation, or international agency commissions must be understood as strategies for giving *and* denying voice.

CONCLUSION

In this chapter we have contrasted national and world system level explanations of educational reform. We argue that one cannot adequately understand dynamics in nation-states or localities without taking into consideration developments in the world system. This is true not only for Third World nations, which constitute the periphery in a stratified world system, but also for core societies whether labelled as "capitalist" or "socialist."[14] Therefore, when we examine educational reform efforts in any country or region, we need to investigate how the global structural and ideological contexts constrain and enable individual and group actors' transactions concerning education. This means attending to the workings of the world economy, to the content and the processes of production and distribution of ideas in the world cultural system, and to the involvement of multinational corporations, corporate foundations, international organizations, bilateral agencies, and universities.

Taking seriously the world system level in our analysis,

though, docs not require that we ignore national (regional and local) level cultural, economic, and political dynamics (Alger 1988, 321-340; Amin 1985; Gumbert 1988; Meyer and Hannan 1979b, 12; Therborn 1978). Thus, we agree with Simmons (1983a, 10) that "educational reform . . . is shaped by a complex interaction among local, national, and international factors." Or as Wirt and Harman (1986a, 4) explain, "national qualities operate like a prism, refracting and adapting [global] influences, without blocking all of them." And we should recall that processes are likely to be qualitatively and quantitatively different in core versus peripheral societies (Hopkins and Wallerstein 1979, 13).

In our discussion above we have given particular attention to the "state" and the way it functions in relation to other dynamics within the national context as well as in the world system. We also focus our gaze on negotiations among groups inside and outside the education system as Archer (1979) suggests in her discussion of political manipulation, external transaction, and internal initiation.[15] Educational workers and other groups (e.g., social class, racial/ethnic, and gender groups) in a given society should be seen as setting goals, developing strategies, and drawing on ideology, political power, and financial resources in their struggles to achieve these goals.[16] For instance, it has been suggested that even when educational reform is initiated by external forces, conceived as the demands of economic elites for greater correspondence between education and the economy, the "educational system . . . both resist[s] and accommodate[s] the reforms" (Levin 1982, 317). As Apple (1986, 70) articulates it, "the school is not a passive mirror but an active force." This is not to conceive of nation-states, education systems, or educators and the other individuals and groups, who constitute and are constituted by the cultural, economic, and political dynamics therein, as completely autonomous of world system dynamics, but to clarify their relative autonomy.

The point of including in our analysis the world system and national level structural and ideological contexts of education systems is not to identify how human activity involving educational reform rhetoric and action is determined. Rather, the point is to emphasize that dynamics in the world system constitute an important part of the terrain on which groups struggle over educational organization, goals, curriculum, pedagogy, financing, etc.

This point can be clarified by conceiving of the rhetoric and action of "educational reform" as text or discourse to be deconstructed. This is not to posit an idealist or voluntaristic notion of educational reform, such as Dunn's (1982, 293-326) discussion of "reform as argument" in which the focus is only on "purposive social processes" nor to render educational reform as determined by world or national level economic (cultural or political) dynamics or elites. Rather through a more dialectical approach, similar to that of Smith's (1988) analysis of the "discourse of femininity," we provide space for individuals and groups both verbally and through their practices "to express themselves . . . within discourse, to make choices" (Smith 1988, 55) while at the same time seeing the forms and content of discourse as constrained and enabled by local, national, and world system level structural and ideological dynamics.

Agreeing with Wirt and Harman (1986a) and others who work within an equilibrium paradigm about the importance of analyzing the interaction of world system and other levels does not require us to adopt other assumptions on which they base their work. We see advantages of conflict perspectives over equilibrium perspectives in accounting for the timing and focus of educational reform, although we find value in insights derived from work within the later tradition. In this sense we concur with Simmons (1983b, 13) that "the historical and statistical evidence appears to tip the balance in favor of the conflict theory." However, we reach our conclusion regarding the explanatory power of the conflict paradigm on somewhat different grounds than Simmons does.

Simmons' conclusion is based on a somewhat over-simplified conception of equilibrium (and conflict) paradigms. He seems to assume that the presence of overt conflict around reform efforts rules out an equilibrium approach. For instance, he concludes that "the experience of educational reform is impossible to analyze unless we systematically examine conditions of conflict and power" (Simmons and Esping-Anderson 1983, 425). Power is certainly not a concept alien to equilibrium tradition. And overt conflict can be understood within an equilibrium perspective as functional (or dysfunctional) in the same way that deviance is functional: it can clarify the boundaries of existing structures and values and precipitate change needed to reestablish equilibrium when other aspects of the system have changed (Coser 1962; Dentler and

Erikson 1959). The issue for the conflict perspective is not whether overt conflict occurs but whether the interests of different nations and social class, racial/ethnic, or gender groups are inherently and fundamentally in conflict.

The timing and focus of educational reform cannot be adequately understood by conceiving of society as a homeostatic system, characterized by consensual relations transacted through persuasion and led by those who possess a "moral force." Instead, we start with the assumption that at the world system and national levels the social formation is inherently conflict-laden and characterized by fundamental contradictions. Different nations, classes, ethnic/racial groups, and gender groups occupy different positions in extant relations of domination and subordination. Thus, because of this and because of the contradictory dynamics within the economy, the state, and education, there are always groups who would like to or are trying to restructure education to serve better their interests. At any time there are likely to be various groups (both inside and outside of education) expressing different criticism about education and articulating the "reforms" that should be implemented. Some, but by no means all, of these concerns and proposed solutions become a part of large scale educational reform efforts when broader economic, cultural, and political struggles reach a crisis point. Or at least they may be articulated as part of the ideological work that is undertaken in the contexts of debates about education, even if no concerted effort to change education occurs.

But we are not merely proposing a Weberian status group conflict model, because we conceptualize the terrain on which such struggles take place as containing fundamental structural contradictions. These contradictions constrain and enable the thoughts and actions of different groups of actors. They constitute the dynamics and tensions upon which people go about socially constructing their reality, including the way education is institutionalized, changed, and discussed.

Educational reform, therefore, would be more likely to occur during periods of economic crisis and restructuring in the world system and related to other economic, cultural and political crises in nation-states, when the contradictions (e.g., accumulation-reproduction and economy-polity) are not being successfully mediated by existing ideological and structural arrangements at national and world system levels. And it is in the space (or opportunities for movement) created by these contradictions that the struggles of social class, racial/ethnic, gender and other groups take place, not only in education but also in other segments of the state, in the cultural sphere, and in the economy.

Unless there is a relatively independent and well-organized mass movement (Carnoy and Levin 1976; Ginsburg 1987; Paulston 1980), economic elites, state elites (particularly in core regions) and their allies are likely to use their control over the means of production and distribution of knowledge, their greater power with respect to the national and international institution policy-making, their control over police and military force, and their dominant position in the economy to shape the focus of the rhetoric and action of educational reform. Nevertheless, because of the contradictions within and between the economy, education, and the state, and because of the contradictory dynamics of race and gender relations on which elites and other groups also try to navigate, this shaping will not always lead in the same direction nor even operate in the short run in all respects in the interest of economic and state elites. Because of the conflict between elites and because of the contradictory terrain on which these struggles occur, there are some opportunities for other groups, particularly if they form broad-based alliances amongst themselves, to shape the rhetoric and action to serve their interests. And economic and state elites, in pursuing both accumulation and reproduction as well confronting the economy-polity contradiction, find themselves working in ways that may favor other groups, although their efforts are designed to sustain or restructure social relations in their favor (see also Foster 1989).

We also adopt a conflict perspective rather than an equilibrium approach because we wish to avoid the problem identified by Paulston (1977, 51) that most of the studies of educational reform, which have been based on equilibrium assumptions, "present a narrow, unsophisticated, and largely technical assessment of why and how reforms take place" (see also Cuban 1990).

Developing a complex, theoretically and politically sophisticated understanding of various levels of dynamics associated with educational reform rhetoric and action is not just an academic exercise nor is it solely for guiding the policy-making and policy-implementing processes as undertaken by current or future government officials. Our comprehension of these phenomena must be profound as well to shape plans and actions for progressive action by groups (including educators) who seek to transform existing social relations (Ginsburg 1989).

This is not to argue that efforts to intervene in the rhetoric and actions concerned with "educational reform" can substitute for other kinds of struggle. By suggesting that we focus our attention and activity on the ideological and superstructural levels (e.g., institutions such as the education system and the state), we are not proposing that fundamental change can be brought about without struggling for change in the national or world-system economic base, as Epstein (1978, 255-276) suggests some radical educators do. What we are claiming, though, is that because of contradictions in the economy, culture, and the state, some interventions in educational reform rhetoric and activities may have progressive effects at least in the short term. Certainly, education and the state are sites for struggle, and an observer on the sidelines has a tendency to aid those who currently have the upper hand. Given that the debates and actions labelled as "educational reform" should be seen as dialectically linked to broader national and global contradictory dynamics, we must find ways to build and strengthen alliances--locally, nationally, and globally--with other groups and social movements in order to intervene successfully in "educational reform" movements. Certainly, dominant groups do not shy away from building such alliances. Working alone as individuals or in isolation as educators or "professionals" is unlikely to be productive, unless our goals or strategies happen to coincide with or be complementary to those of economic and state elites.

Moreover, the experience and solidarity with various groups that can be built in the context of such activity may be advantageous in building social and political movements focused on broader issues, including challenging unequal race, gender, and class relations and transforming the world economic system into one that is primarily structured around meeting human needs as opposed to producing profit (See also Alger 1988). Thus, while we do not want to celebrate educational reform as necessarily change for the better, as some equilibrium theorists do, we also do not fully agree with Frank's (1969, 408-409) conclusion that the "intellectual and Marxist will have to decide whether he [or she] will remain inside pursuing reformism or outside with the people making revolution." As we have discussed, given the contradictions within education, culture, the state, and national and world economic systems, it may be possible to be engaged in both reformist and revolutionary activity with an eye toward constructing fundamental change through both strategies.

NOTES

1. This chapter is a revision of an article published in the *Comparative Education Review* (Ginsburg et al. 1990), which was developed from a paper with the same title presented at the Comparative and International Education Society annual meeting, Harvard, 31 March - 2 April 1989. We would like to thank Shanon Gallagher for her assistance on this project.

2. As Lotta (1990, 8) states concerning political economic reform in Eastern Europe, such efforts may involve making "some changes in form and appearance, while leaving the essence unchanged."

3. Simmons (1983a, 74) treats politics and economics as variables rather than as processes, dynamics, or arenas of contradictions. Thus, he identifies political factors (type of regime, nature of leadership, its legitimacy, and kinds of coalitions) and economic factors (type of economy, labor-market needs, degree of economic inequality, and availability of financial resources). In this way historical process and struggle are conceptualized as causal relations between selected structural variables. The theoretical assumptions implied seem to fit most comfortably within a systems theory variant of the equilibrium perspective, although a figure presented in another chapter (Simmons 1983b, 11) in the same book appears to adopt a Weberian-type status or interest group conflict perspective. In this way his assumptions seem more similar to Archer's (1979), except that Simmons gives explicit mention to "international experiences and pressures."

4. Within conflict approaches one can contrast Weberian or status group conflict models (e.g., Archer 1979; Banks 1987; Collins 1979) that give primacy to cultural and political spheres and Marxist class/imperialist conflict models that emphasize economic relations. The Weberian

approaches tend to analyze educational reform in terms of struggles between ethnic/racial or economic status groups based on competition for scarce resources, e.g., educational credentials, but also jobs, income or wealth, status, and political power. Although Marxist approaches also attend to struggle, more emphasis is given to structural contradictions in the economy, ideology, and the state, and the focus is not so much on the distribution of resources as on exploitation, alienation, and control over the means of production. For Marxists struggle is linked to these contradictions and to efforts to mediate and thus reproduce or challenge the contradictions imbedded in extant unequal relations. Here we will draw primarily on Marxist perspectives within the conflict paradigm. Although not developed as fully here, it is possible to explain educational reform from liberal and radical feminist perspectives. Reform efforts would be perceived as the result of women and men struggling for credentials and other resources (liberal feminist perspective) or contradictory gender (as well as class and race) relations (radical feminist perspectives) (see Ginsburg 1988).

5.   Archer (1979) also emphasizes that change in education, including reforms, occurs as a result of functional incompatibilities. However, she argues that these dysfunctions or "obstructions" do not automatically lead to change due to some evolutionary process or homeostatic mechanism in society. Nor are changes "presumed to be more adaptive, efficient, stable or legitimate than preceding forms of education" (p. 143). Rather, from her Weberian conflict perspective, Archer views efforts to reform education as resulting from competing or conflicting groups' social interaction which is "conditioned" (not determined) by structural features of nations as perceived by the actors involved.

6.   Wallerstein does emphasize class structure and unequal economic relations between center and periphery but has been criticized for "explaining the fundamental economic dynamics of the [world] system in terms [e.g., markets] . . . usually stressed by liberal economists, while ignoring

the basic Marxist [concepts of] . . . social relations of production and surplus appropriation" (Skocpol 1977, 1079). For a similar critique see Brenner (1977). Wallerstein's world system theory has also be criticized as drawing on the same conservative intellectual traditions as the French *Annales* school of history and evidencing similarities to the structural functionalist work of Talcott Parsons, in that the system is "reified" and there is a "built-in assumption of equilibrium" (Pieterse 1988). Given these different readings of Wallerstein's work, it is not surprising that a world systems approach has been employed by scholars working within different paradigms.

7.   The focus on the unifying trend of culture globally should be seen in contrast to Wallerstein's work, which highlights a world economy, "that is, a single division of labor, but multiple polities and cultures" (quoted in Brenner 1977, 53).

8.   As Carnoy (1976, 249-51) comments in his review of Coombs' (1968) book, the solutions proposed included "the introduction of capital intensive methods like technology to replace teachers. . . . [Additionally], the economy and the schools must be aligned so there are more jobs available and more appropriate training in the schools to fill those jobs."

9.   According to E. Wallerstein (1984, 35): "There are today no socialist systems in the world-economy any more than there are feudal systems because there is only one world system. It is a world-economy and it is by definition capitalist in form." See Pieterse (1988, 256) for a critique of Wallerstein's conceptualization because "the parts are not granted autonomy and the whole . . . predominates as a totalizing principle." Here we retain the notion of capitalism as the dominant mode of production in the world system, although through the concepts of contradictions and the relative autonomy of states, culture, and national economic relations we seek to avoid postulating a totalizing principle.

10.   Silva (1980a, 1980b) also focuses attention on the role of universities in what he terms the centers of two major trading blocks: China and the Soviet Union in the "East" and the United States in the "West." The greater accumulation of wealth in the core countries of each trading block is used partly to develop more and more complex universities, which serve as a knowledge production apparatus. Knowledge moves from the center to the periphery of the trading blocs, with nations in the periphery accepting the transference of knowledge, even though it rarely addresses their needs. This paradox is due to the willingness of the "cultural elites" in the periphery to use "the standards of the center to guide their judgements about importing ideas" (1980b, 67). While this stratified system of knowledge production and consumption has a number of implications, it clearly bears on the circulation of ideas and practices for reforming education.

11.   Wallerstein's world system approach has been similarly criticized for its "reduction of state structure and policies to determination by dominant class interests" (Skocpol 1977, 1979).

12.   A caveat should be noted to this point. State revenue is extracted not only from surplus value accumulated by capitalists through exploitation of workers but also from worker's wages. This is part of the reason why struggles in the state are not just over the amount of taxes to be collected but the form of taxes, on corporation profits, investors' capital gains, property or wealth, or earned income.

13.   However, we must again clarify that the revenue acquired by the state through taxation can be drawn from capital's profits or from workers' income.

14.   In using "socialist" as a label, we purposefully avoid defining all or any of these countries as socialist in some more objective sense. How one views the nature of these societies obviously has implications for how one

understands and evaluates the recent changes in the Soviet bloc. Lotta (1990) categorizes the Soviet Union and Eastern Europe, at least since Khrushchev, as "state-capitalist" or "revisionist (phony socialist)" political economies occupying different positions in the "social-imperialist empire." In the current era due to crises of this empire, linked more directly since the mid-1970s to the world economic crisis as Eastern Europe began to borrow from Western banks and to come under austerity programs overseen by the International Monetary Fund, Gorbachev's "perestroika" and "glasnost" are part of a program to restructure these state-capitalist systems to increase profit (and exploitation), while at the same time to re-establish the legitimacy of the states.

15.   Archer (1979) focuses our attention on three types of "negotiation" among elites of conflicting groups or institutions:

    a)   "political manipulation" or working at the local or national level to influence government policy on education;

    b)   "external transaction" or efforts initiated by groups outside education or the state to obtain additional or better service by offering to provide resources directly to educators; and

    c)   "internal initiation" or efforts initiated by educators to supply expertise or other services for groups in return for additional resources.

In Archer's view political manipulation is the main or only avenue for negotiation in "centralized" education systems, while external transactions and internal initiation are also relevant in "decentralized" systems.

16.   In emphasizing the active role of individuals and groups, although seen as constrained and enabled by contradictory structural and ideological features of national and world systems that are not completely of their own making, we attempt to avoid the problems of reifying the system and

eliminating space for social struggle for which Wallerstein's work has been criticized (see Pieterse 1988). As has been indicated in this chapter and will be stressed more in the final chapter, social struggle is central to our analysis and our political project. However, we need to be clear on the ideological and structural constraints on ours and others' struggles.

REFERENCES

Alger, C. 1988. Perceiving, analyzing and coping with local-global nexus. *International Social Science Journal*, 117 (August): 321-340.

Altbach, P. 1974. Comparative university reform. In *University reform: Comparative perspectives for the seventies*, edited by P. Altbach, 1-14. Cambridge, MA: Schenkman.

Altbach, P. 1982. Servitude of the mind? Education, dependency, and neocolonialism. In *Comparative education*, edited by P. Altbach, R. Arnove, and G. Kelly, 469-84. New York: Macmillan.

Altbach, P. 1988. International organizations, educational policy, and research: A changing balance. *Comparative Education Review*, 32, 2: 137-42.

Amin, S. 1985. *Delinking: Towards a polycentric world*. London: Zed Books.

Apple, M. 1986. Ideology, reproduction and educational reform. In *New approaches to comparative education*, edited by P. Altbach and G. Kelly, 51-71. Chicago: University of Chicago Press.

Apple, M. 1989. Critical introduction: Ideology and the state in educational policy. In *The state and education policy*, edited by R. Dale 1-20. Milton Keynes: Open University.

Archer, M. 1979. *Social origins of educational systems*. London: Sage.

Archer, M. 1981. On predicting the behaviour of the educational system: An extended review. *British Journal of Sociology of Education*, 2, 2: 211-19.

Arnove, R. 1982. Comparative education and world systems analysis. In *Comparative education*, edited by P. Altbach, R. Arnove, and G. Kelly, 453-68. New York: Macmillan.

Banks, J. 1987. The social studies, ethnic diversity, and social change. *Elementary School Journal*, 87, 5: 531-43.

Baudelot, C., and Establet, R. 1971. *L'ecole capitaliste*. Paris: Maspero.

Beeby, C. 1966. *The quality of education in developing countries*. Cambridge: Harvard University Press.

Berman, E. 1983. *The influence of the Carnegie, Ford, and Rockefeller Foundations on American foreign policy: The ideology of philanthropy*. Albany: State University of New York Press.

Boli, J., Ramirez, F., and Meyer, J. 1986. Explaining the origins and expansion of mass education. In *New approaches to comparative education*, edited by P. Altbach and G. Kelly, 105-30. Chicago: University of Chicago Press.

Boli-Bennett, J. 1979. The ideology of expanding state authority in national constitutions, 1870-1970. In *National development and the world system: Educational, economic and political change 1950-70*, edited by J. Meyer and M. Hannan, 222-37. Chicago: University of Chicago Press.

Bowles, S., and Gintis, H. 1976. *Schooling in capitalist America*. Boston: Routledge and Kegan Paul.

Brenner, R. 1977. The origins of capitalist development: A critique of Neo-Smithian Marxism. *New Left Review*, 107: 25-92.

Campbell, D. 1982. Experiments as arguments. *Knowledge: Creation, Diffusion, Utilization*, 3, 3: 327-37.

Carnoy, M. 1976. International educational reform: The ideology of efficiency. In *The limits of educational reform*, edited by M. Carnoy and H. Levin, 245-68. New York: Longman.

Carnoy, M. 1982. Education, economy and the state. In *Cultural and economic reproduction in education: Essays on class, ideology and the state*, edited by M. Apple, 79-126. Boston: Routledge and Kegan Paul.

Carnoy, M. 1986. Education for alternative development. In *New approaches to comparative education*, edited by P. Altbach and G. Kelly, 73-90. Chicago: University of Chicago Press.

Carnoy, M., and Levin, H. 1986. Educational reform and class conflict. *Journal of Education*, 168, 1: 35-46.

Chase-Dunn, C., and Rubinson, R. 1979. Cycles, trends, and new departures in world-system development. In *National development and the world system: Educational, economic and political change 1950-70*, edited by J. Meyer and M. Hannan, 276-96. Chicago: University of Chicago Press.

Cherryholmes, C. 1988. Thinking about education poststructurally. In *Power and criticism* by C. Cherryholmes, 31-48. New York: Teachers College Press.

Collins, R. 1979. *The credential society: An historical sociology of education and stratification*. New York: Academic Press.

Coombs, P. 1968. *The world educational crisis: A systems analysis*. New York: Oxford University Press.

Coombs, P. 1985. *The world crisis in education: The view from the eighties*. New York: Oxford University Press.

Coser, L. 1962. Some functions of deviant behavior and normative flexibility. *American Journal of Sociology*, 68 (September): 172-81.

Cuban, L. 1990. Reforming again, again, and again. *Educational Researcher* 19: 31-13.

Dale, R. 1982. Education and the capitalist state: Contributions and contradictions. In *Cultural and economic reproduction in education: Essays on class, ideology and the state*, edited by M. Apple, 127-61. Boston: Routledge and Kegan Paul.

Dale, R. 1989. *The state and education policy*. Milton Keynes: Open University Press.

Dentler, R., and Erikson, K. 1959 The functions of deviance in groups. *Social Problems*, 7, (Fall): 98-107.

Dunn, W. 1982. Reform as Arguments. *Knowledge: Creation, Diffusion, Utilization*, 3, 3: 293-326.

Epstein, E. 1978. The social control thesis and educational reform in dependent nations. *Theory and Society*, 5: 255-76.

Fiszman, J. 1982. Educational and equality of opportunity in Eastern Europe. In *Comparative education*, edited by P. Altbach, R. Arnove, and G. Kelly, 381-410. New York: Macmillan.

Foster, J. 1989. Restructuring the world economy in a time of lasting crisis. *Monthly Review*, 41, 1: 46-55.

Frank, G. 1969. *Latin America: Underdevelopment of revolution?* New York: Monthly Review Press.

Giddens, A. 1979. *Central problems in social theory*. Berkeley: University of California Press.

Ginsburg, M. 1988. *Contradictions in teacher education and society: A critical analysis*. New York: Falmer Press.

Ginsburg, M. 1989. El process de trabajo y la accion politica de los educadores: Un analisis comparado (The labor process and political action of educators: A comparative analysis). *Revista de educacion* (August).

Ginsburg, M., Cooper, S., Raghu, R., and Zegarra, H. 1990. National and world system explanations of educational reform. *Comparative Education Review*, 34, 4: 474-499.

Ginsburg, M., Wallace, G., and Miller, H. 1988. Teachers, economy and the state: An English example. *Teaching and Teacher Education*, 4, 4: 317-37.

Gonzalez, G. 1982. Imperial reform in the neo-colonies: The University of California's basic plan for higher education in Colombia. *Journal of Education*, 164, 4: 330-50.

Grace, G. 1987. Teachers and the state in Britain: A changing relation. In *Teachers: The culture and politics of work*, edited by M. Lawn and G. Grace, 193-228. London: Falmer Press.

Green, T., Ericson, D., and Seidman, R. 1980. *Predicting the behavior of the educational system*. Syracuse: Syracuse University Press.

Gumbert, E. 1988. Introduction. In *Making the future: Politics and educational reform in the United States, England, the Soviet Union, China, and Cuba*, edited by E. Gumbert, 3-8. Atlanta: Center for Cross-cultural Education, Georgia State University.

Guthrie, J. 1990. The world's evolving political economy and the emerging globalization of education. Paper presented at the Comparative and International Education Society conference, Anaheim, California (March 22).

Guthrie, J., and Kollich, J. 1989. Ready, A.I.M., reform: Building a model of education reform and "high politics." Draft of a chapter in *Restructuring schools: An international perspective on the movement to transform the control and performance of schools*, edited by H. Beare and W. Boyd.

Habermas, J. 1979. Conservatism and capitalist crisis. *New Left Review*, 115 (May/June): 73-86.

Harbermas, J. 1975. *The legitimation crisis*. Translated by Thomas McCarthy. Boston: Beacon Press.

Hannan, M. 1979. The dynamics of ethnic boundaries in modern states. In *National development and the world system: Educational, economic and political change 1950-70*, edited by J. Meyer and M. Hannan, 253-75. Chicago: University of Chicago Press.

Hawkins, J., and La Belle, T. 1985. *Education and intergroup relations*. New York: Praeger.

Holloway, J., and Picciotto, S. 1978. *State and capital: A Marxist debate*. London: Edward and Arnold.

Hopkins, T., and Wallerstein, E. 1979. *World-systems analysis: Theory and methodology*. Volume 1. Beverly Hills: Sage.

Inkeles, A., and Sirowy L. 1984. Convergent and divergent trends in national educational systems. In *Current issues and research in macrosociology*, edited by G. Lenski, 137-165. Leiden: E. J. Brill.

Katz, M. 1975. *Class, bureaucracy, and schools: The illusion of educational change in America,* expanded edition. New York: Praeger.

Katz, M. 1968. *The irony of early school reform: Educational innovation in mid-nineteenth century Massachusetts*. Boston: Beacon Press.

Klees, S., and Wells, S. 1983. Economic evaluation of education: A critical analysis in the context of applications to educational reform in El Salvador. *Educational Evaluation and Policy Analysis*, 5, 3: 327-345.

Kolko, J. 1988. *Restructuring the world economy*. New York: Pantheon.

Levin, H. 1982. The dilemma of comprehensive secondary school reforms in Western Europe. In *Comparative education*, edited by P. Altbach, R. Arnove, and G. Kelly, 319-35. New York: Macmillan.

Lilge, F. 1977. Lenin and the politics of education. In *Power and ideology in education*, edited by J. Karabel and A. H. Halsey, 556-72. New York: Oxford University Press.

Lotta, R. 1990. Crisis in Eastern Europe and collapse of old-style revisionism. *Revolutionary Worker*, 11 (5 February): 73-138.

McLennan, G. 1984 *State and society in contemporary Britain*. Cambridge: Polity Press.

Merritt, R., and Coombs, F. 1977. Politics and educational reform. *Comparative Education Review*, 21 (2/3): 247-73.

Merton, R. 1968. Manifest and latent functions. In *Social theory and social structure*, enlarged edition, 73-138. New York: Free Press.

Meyer, J., and Hannan, M. 1979a. Issues for further comparative research. In *National development and the world system: Educational, economic and political change, 1950-70*, edited by J. Meyer and M. Hannan, 297-308. Chicago: University of Chicago Press.

Meyer, J., and Hannan, M. 1979b. National development in a changing world system: An overview. In *National development and the world system: Educational, economic and political change, 1950-70*, edited by J. Meyer and M. Hannan, 3-16. Chicago: University of Chicago Press.

Mitchell, B. 1987. Higher education reform and ad hoc committees: A question of legitmacy. *The Review of Higher Education*, 11 (Winter): 117-35.

Mueller, A. 1987. The "Discovery" of Women in Development: The Case of Peru. A paper presented at the annual meeting of the Comparative and International Education Society, Washington, DC (March): 13-15.

Offe, C., and Ronge, V. 1981. Theses on the theory of the state. In *Education and the state: Volume 1. Schooling and the national interest*, edited by R. Dale, G. Esland, R. Ferguson, and M. MacDonald, 77-86. Sussex: Open University Press.

Paulston, R. 1977. Social and educational change: conceptual frameworks. *Comparative Education Review*, 21, 2/3: 370-95.

Paulston, R. 1980. Education as anti-structure: Non-formal education in social and ethnic movements. *Comparative Education*, 16, 1: 55-66.

Paulston, R. 1983. Conflicting theories of educational reform. In *Better Schools: International Lessons for Reform*, edited by J. Simmons, 21-70. New York: Praeger.

Pieterse, J. 1988. A critique of worlds system theory. *International Sociology*, 3 (September): 251-166.

Poulantzas, N. 1975. *Classes in contemporary capitalism*. London: New Left Books.

Powel, A. 1980. *The uncertain profession: Harvard and the search for educational authority.* Cambridge, MA: Harvard University Press.

Quick, R. 1868. *Educational reformers.* London: Longmans Green.

Ramirez, F., and Boli-Bennett, J. 1982. Global patterns of educational institutionalization. In *Comparative education,* edited by P. Altbach, R. Arnove, and G. Kelly, 15-36. New York: Macmillan.

Ramirez, F., and Rubison, R. 1979. Creating members: The political incorporation and expansion of public education. In *National development and the world system: Educational, economic and political change, 1950-70,* edited by J. Meyer and M. Hannan, 72-84. Chicago: University of Chicago Press.

Ramirez, F., and Weiss, J. 1979. The political incorporation of women. In *National development and the world system: Educational, economic and political change, 1950-70,* edited by J. Meyer and M. Hannan, 238-52. Chicago: University of Chicago Press.

Ruin, O., and Lindenjo, B. 1982. U 68--A study of the origins of the reform of higher education. *R & D for Higher Education,* 4: 1-13.

Rymalov, V. 1978. *The world capitalist economy: Structural changes, trends and problems.* Moscow: Progress Publishers.

Sack, R. 1981. A typology of educational reforms. *Prospects,* 11, 1: 39-59.

Silva, E. 1980a. Cultural autonomy and ideas in transit: Notes from the Canadian case. *Comparative Education Review,* 24, 1: 63-72.

Silva, E. 1980b. Maple Leaf, British bough, American branch: Canadian higher education in developmental perspective. In *Universities and the international distribution of knowledge*, edited by I. Spitzberg, 63-92. New York: Praeger.

Simmons, J. 1983a. The approach of the study. In *Better Schools: International Lessons for Reform*, edited by J. Simmons, 71-85. New York: Praeger.

Simmons, J. 1983b. Reforming education and society: The enduring quest. In *Better Schools: International Lessons for Reform*, edited by J. Simmons, 3-19. New York: Praeger.

Simmons, J., and Esping-Anderson, G. 1983. Lessons from educational reform. In *Better Schools: International Lessons for Reform*, edited by J. Simmons, 400-32. New York: Praeger.

Skocpol, T. 1977. Wallerstein's world capitalist system: A theoretical and historical critique. *American Journal of Sociology*, 82: 1075-1090.

Smith, D. 1988. Femininity as discourse. In *Becoming feminine: The politics of popular culture*, edited by L. Roman, L. Christian-Smith, and E. Ellsworth, 37-59. New York: Falmer Press.

Spaulding, S. 1988. Prescriptions for educational reform: Dilemmas of the real world. *Comparative Education*, 24, 1: 5-17.

Therborn, G. 1978. *What does the ruling class do when it rules?* London: New Left Books.

Urry, J. 1981. *The anatomy of capitalist societies*. London: Macmillan.

Wallerstein, E. 1974, 1980, 1988. *The modern world system*, 3 volumes. New York: Academic Press.

Wallerstein, E. 1984. *The capitalist world-economy.* Cambridge, England: Cambridge University Press.

Weiler, H. 1988. The politics of reform and nonreform in French education. *Comparative Education Review*, 32, 3: 251-65.

Weiler, H. 1982. Educational planning and social change: A critical review of concepts and practices. In *Comparative education*, edited by P. Altbach, R. Arnove, and G. Kelly, 105-18. New York: Macmillan.

Wirt, F., and Harman, G. 1986a Introduction: Comparing educational policies and international currents. In *Education, recession and the world village: A comparative political economy of education*, edited by F. Wirt and G. Harman, 1-7. Philadelphia: Falmer Press.

Wirt, F., and Harman, G. 1986b. The editors: A view from across the board: The international recession and educational policy. In *Education, recession and the world village: A comparative political economy of education*, edited by F. Wirt and G. Harman, 163-80. Philadelphia: Falmer Press.

Young, T. 1980. The public sphere and the state in capitalist society. Paper presented at the American Sociololgical Association annual meeting. New York distributed by the Red Feather Institute (August).

Zachariah, M. 1986 Comparative educators and international development policy. In *New approaches to comparative education*, edited by P. Altbach and G. Kelly, 91-104. Chicago: University of Chicago Press.

RESTRUCTURING EDUCATION AND THE STATE IN ENGLAND[1]

Henry D.R. Miller and Mark B. Ginsburg

The 1970s and 1980s were decades of economic crisis in England, reflecting the crisis of the world capitalist system. This period also witnessed a severe fiscal crisis of the British state and a political crisis for a Labour government followed by the growing power of a Conservative government, which showed an increasing ideological virulence and political capacity to restructure the state and education in relation to the economy, families, and educational workers.

In the mid-1970s the Labour government led by James Callaghan launched a "Great Debate on Education," in which education and, more specifically, educators were criticized for not preparing a skilled work force with the needed motivation and discipline. The "debate" and subsequent period of "reforms" occurred in the context of continuing reductions in expenditure on education (and other social services), implemented at least partly because of conditions set by the International Monetary Fund for a loan sought by the Callaghan government to keep the British state fiscally solvent. The "reforms" proposed and implemented reflected a move away from the social democratic policies that had characterized the British state and politics since the mid-1940s.

Despite (or, perhaps, because of) this political manoeuvering by the Labour Party, the Conservatives under the leadership of Margaret Thatcher were victorious in the 1979 election. In some ways the Thatcher governments (the Conservatives also winning elections in 1983 and again in 1987) continued to pursue the policies of the Callaghan government, but clearly the Conservatives moved on a broader agenda attempting to profoundly redefine the state and its relation to education. This was reflected in the education sector in a series of Acts (1980, 1986, and 1988), the last one being the most far-reaching, in the changes proposed.

Meanwhile, participation of educators (and other workers) in the policy-making process, or even in the determination of their salaries and working conditions, has been reduced. The power of local educational authorities (LEAs) has also been diminished as the central government and, to some extent, parents and the "business community" have been reassigned authority and responsibilities once held by LEAs and organized teachers.

In this chapter we seek to address a number of the theoretical issues raised in the first chapter, drawing on dynamics in Britain. We first sketch historical developments to provide a context for comparing more recent events. We then examine the period of the 1970s and 1980s in more detail, and provide an analysis of the British case.

HISTORICAL CONTEXT

Britain's history as the first industrial power and the rise and subsequent decline of its colonial empire are reasonably well known (see Kennedy 1988). What may be less well understood is the impact that this history has on contemporary British economic and political life. Gamble (1985) argues that because of its history as the first industrial power Britain has remained, more than most centers, open to the forces of World economy. Moreover, Britain's economy's initial advantage, encouraging the development of finance commerce and empire, established an ideology among intellectuals and politicians which entrenched a view of Britain as a world power within a liberal world market economy. Gamble (1985, 35) comments further that internal challenges were accommodated in a series of compromises with organized labor which "preserved institutional continuity and the international orientation of the state and the openness of the economy. The political forces that might have implemented a successful programme of reconstruction were contained and diverted."

While the contemporary scene in Britain has been characterized by economic crisis, we should note that the problems of the British economy have a much longer history. As Perkins (1990, 36-37) describes:

> British capitalism reached its zenith in the late Victorian age . . . between the 1870s and the 1890s. The rate of economic growth began to slacken first in industrial production, then in national income, and Britain began to be overtaken in both by foreign competitors, notably the United States and Germany.

It is in this context that the state became a key actor in the sphere of education. Prior to 1870 education was not a state function in England; religious organizations and voluntary groups provided instruction for a small percentage of youth. The English Education Act of 1870 legislated for publicly supported elementary education, compulsory up to age eleven years, to be administered by local school boards. The same year the National Union of Elementary Teachers (later the NUT) was founded as an organized voice and collective body for teachers. The 1902 Education Act extended the state's involvement in education. A system of education was legislated, coordinated by a national level Board of Education (established in 1899), and local education authorities (replaced local school boards and) were given authority to offer post-elementary schooling.

The 1918 Education Act was described as a "children's charter," providing universal compulsory schooling to age fourteen, abolishing fees for state sector elementary schools, and legislating "physical training for all, improved standards for higher school classes, special provision for handicapped children, and nursery school places for who wanted them" (Perkins 1990, 239). The 1918 Act "together with the expansion of 11+ scholarships and 'free places' in grammar schools and from 1920 the few hundred state scholarships to the universities . . . breached the class barrier to more egalitarian education" (Perkins 1990, 239).

The discussion here applies essentially only to the state sector institutions. However, from the nineteenth century there has been a considerable independent, fee paying, "public school" sector, essentially elitist, to which the sons and some of the daughters of the upper classes and of the wealthier aspiring middle classes went. These schools supplied the oligarchy, controlling and administering most areas of British public life, the armed forces, civil service, judiciary, the established church, and the educational establishment, particularly Oxford and Cambridge. They also dominated the Conservative party in Parliament and provided an overwhelming proportion of Conservative Cabinets.[2]

The mid-nineteenth century through the mid-1920s was not a period of high levels of work or occupational autonomy for teachers, whether in relation to the (local) state or other groups (Grace 1978). This was a period in which payment-by-results--a system in which teachers' salaries were based on the pupils' achievement, as determined by inspectors' assessment--was imposed by the state and contested by teachers. During this same period, teachers "had an uphill struggle to gain any purchase on the administrative structures which were laid down to control education" because "teachers were not organized on a professional basis prior to the entry of the state in the educational field" (Parry and Parry 1974, 169). Teachers were less effective in this struggle because of internal divisions in the occupation attributable to school level, gender, social class, and religious differences, often reflected in multiple organizations. Nevertheless, teacher power was occasionally organized and effective. For example, in 1911 the NUT played a major role in a campaign that resulted in the resignation of Runciman from the presidency of the National Board of Education and Morant from the position of Permanent Secretary (Grace 1987, 202). And in 1921 a national salary scale for teachers was won through work on the Burnham Committee (established in 1919).

State-occupation relations were restructured significantly after 1926. The context for this period had some parallels with that of the more recent period which we will examine later. As Grace

(1987, 204) notes the "context of education was characterized by a sense of economic crisis." Thus, during the mid-1920s to mid-1930s educational expenditures were reduced, and teacher salaries were even cut in 1923 and 1932. However, unlike the more recent period, in 1926 educators' relations with the state were restructured to provide more curricular and pedagogical autonomy for head teachers and teachers at the school and classroom levels. This increase in autonomy was partly a result of the growing signs of teacher collective power, but more so because teachers generally were viewed by leaders of the ruling Conservative Party as a "safeguard" against the radicalization of schooling by "socialist" segments of the working class and their allies among educators (e.g., the Teachers Labour League). A centralized national state or even a strong local state was seen as too ripe an opportunity for the growing "socialist" movement in the Labour Party, which if it gained a parliamentary majority might impose (via schooling) its ideology on future generations (see also Grace 1978, 89-99).

It is certainly true that although educators, compared to other occupations during the 1940s and 1950s, did not experience dramatic improvements with respect to salary and working conditions, they did continue to exercise considerable workplace autonomy up until the mid 1970s (Baron and Tropp 1961). The one short but (as we can note in retrospect) critical deviation from this trend was during the Second World War. Between 1940 and 1945 teachers, mainly women, assumed new duties and experienced curricular directives emanating from the national government. Because of wartime demands, for the first time teachers agreed to "voluntarily" supervise meals and undertake other social service tasks as part of their job, and in other ways found their working hours extended beyond the normal school day and beyond the school week. Moreover, the "school curriculum was changed by the necessities of wartime . . . and through them tied to a national purpose" (Lawn 1987, 59).

Organized teachers, particularly the NUT, played a visible role in shaping the 1944 Education Act, known as the Butler Act, named after the Conservative Minister of Education responsible for its introduction by a coalition government that included Labour and Liberal members as well as a majority of Conservatives headed by Sir Winston Churchill. In striking contrast with the process associated with the 1988 Education Act (to be delineated later), the

1944 Act was the result of nearly three years of extensive discussion and consultation and emerged as a measure largely agreed upon by the major political parties, organized educators, and the churches.

The 1944 Act can be seen as one of the pillars of the welfare state, essentially extending secondary education along egalitarian lines advocated by Tawney (1922) and educational progressives. The Act abolished the category of elementary education, designed primarily for the working class, and created a staged system of primary and secondary education for all, compulsory up to age fourteen. The Act, though, allowed a stratified, "tripartite" organization of secondary education to continue and affirmed a national level of governance of schooling by creating a Ministry of Education (renamed the Department of Education and Science in 1964) out of the previous Board of Education (King 1979, 185).

From the early 1940s and into the 1960s, a degree of consensus in educational and economic thinking developed among the major political parties that alternated in their control of the national government. Their moves toward undermining the tripartite system and the associated 11+ exam and towards the development of comprehensive secondary education. The compulsory schooling age was raised to fifteen in 1958 and then sixteen in 1972. At the same time plans were made and were beginning to be implemented to expand and upgrade and extend the preservice training of teachers from two to three years.

We should emphasize again the high level of control teachers had over curricular, pedagogical, and evaluation aspects of their work especially during the 1960s. In 1964 a national body, the Schools Council for Curriculum and Exams, was established with a majority of the membership being teachers (especially NUT representatives). In 1965 the Certificate of Secondary Education was developed and provided more influence over the content and grading of exams by classroom teachers than the more university-influenced GCE "O" and "A" level exams that remained in existence. Furthermore, the celebrated Plowden Report on *Children and Their Primary Schools* of the Central Advisory Council for Education (1967) provided legitimacy for many of the progressive educational practices that some primary and secondary teachers had been developing and that some teacher training institutions were also promoting.

Even during this zenith of teacher power the long quest of educators to become a "self-governing profession" by establishing a Teachers General Council was not achieved. Both in 1959 and in 1965, despite a relatively rare united front organized across the various groups of teachers, the national government rejected the proposal (Archer 1979, 546). In the aftermath of these failures, in the context of growing student and worker (notably miners) militancy, and because of a continued lag in remuneration and other benefits, organized teachers also became militant during the 1968-74 period (Grace 1987). The NUT, after many years of debate, affiliated to the Trades Union Congress and a major victory on salary issues was achieved in 1974 in what is termed the Houghton Committee settlement.

In the higher education sector from the mid-1940s to the mid-1970s there was a period of expansion and relatively high levels of institutional and professorial autonomy. We should not forget, however, that with the notable exceptions of Oxford and Cambridge, the reality of university life was quite different in the nineteenth and first half of the twentieth century. Business interests were very influential in the founding and funding of the large provincial universities like Leeds, Manchester, and Birmingham (Smith 1988). It was only in the post World War Two period of expansion of higher education that central state funding became so predominant. So that in some ways one could see the proposals and practices of the 1980s as a return to the 1930s in terms of retrenchment or to the 1890s in terms of a celebration of the market and free enterprise (Walford 1988).

In the 1940s universities were essentially elitist institutions, involving in all only about 50,000 students, but this changed considerably during the next three decades. By 1960 there were 23 universities and the next decade saw a virtual doubling. In 1962 the then Conservative government made the provision of local education authority maintenance grants compulsory for all full-time students starting degree courses with a minimum requirement of two A levels. The Robbins Report on Higher Education (HMSO 1963) is a key educational document that proposed and legitimized a pattern of expansion founded on the double grounds of student demand and the needs of the economy. Eight new "greenfield" universities were being built by the time the Robbins Report was published in 1963.

The report legitimized these universities and called for the creation of more. Ten new technological universities were created based upon existing colleges of advanced technology. Harold Wilson's Labour government of 1964, proclaiming the spirit of the white hot technological revolution, established 29 polytechnics based on existing technical colleges with which, over time, many colleges of education merged to form the second half of a binary system.

The failure of British higher education in general and the universities in particular to maintain the rate of expansion of the 1950s and 1960s, and to keep pace with the growth of nearly all other industrialized countries from the early 1970s, reflects, Edwards (1982) asserts, " crisis of national confidence."Baron et al. (1981) conceptualizes the crisis in terms of the breakdown of credibility of Labour's reformist strategy, which placed too much faith on educational reform and expansion to develop economic growth as the basis for humanizing capitalism in an egalitarian direction.

CRISIS AND RESTRUCTURING AT THE NATIONAL LEVEL IN THE 1970s

Even before the end of the 1960s, and certainly following the upheavals of 1968, the consensus that had embraced both major parties and most educationists had begun to break down. Part of this consensus was based on an agreement that educational administration was best left to local education authorities, with advice and guidance from the central government and Her Majesty's Inspectors of Education. Curriculum, pedagogy, and much student evaluation were also seen to be most appropriately determined by "professionals"--teachers and head teachers.

The developing critique came from both right and left, attacking, on the one hand, the drive towards a more egalitarian society, and on the other, the failure of the drive to advance beyond a confused egalitarian rhetoric (Baron et al. 1981). In the wake of the crisis in the world economic system, exacerbated by the "oil crisis" of 1973, the prospects for any sustained economic "growth" had come to an abrupt end. The educational service, it was argued, had to take its share of "cuts"; demand management gave way to monetarism and the "failures" of centrist policies gave way to the right.

A conservative educational backlash (Cox and Dyson 1969) that had struggled for legitimacy developed in the later 1970s into a direct attack on comprehensive schooling on the grounds of falling standards and rising disorder (e.g., see Cox and Boyson 1975). The drive against progressive practices in schools strengthened, widened into a more general attack on teaching standards, exploded into the public arena and was amplified by the media. The then Labour Party Prime Minister, James Callaghan, launched the "Great Debate" on education at Ruskin College, Oxford, in October 1976. A series of staged and televised regional conferences followed that were organized around calls for teachers to prepare pupils better for work and to be more accountable for "standards." The major issues identified and then elaborated in a "Green Paper" published by the Department of Education and Science in the summer of 1977 were: standards, core curriculum, methods and aims of informal (read as progressive methods of) instruction, school and working life, and education and the training of teachers. Education was called upon to be the efficient servant of a corporately managed economy (DES 1977, paragraphs 1-16). Furthermore, the newly demanded improvement in "standards" had to be brought about without additional resources (Simon 1977).

Given the local government reorganization of 1974 and the subsequent implementation of corporate management techniques, there had already been a shift in the locus of power at County Hall that served to tighten the potential for control of policy through the allocation and distribution of funds tied directly to specific policies. The decline of the birth rate and the dramatic effect it was having on school rolls in some areas offered a readily available "problem" that could be "solved" by school closure and the employment of fewer teachers. The same can be said of many institutions specializing in preservice teacher education, which were closed down with many of the staff provided with early retirement or other forms of "redundancy."

Clearly, the government's orientation to schooling had been redefined (Donald 1979, Finn, Grant, and Johnson 1977; Ginsburg,

Meyenn, and Miller 1979). The redefinition signalled not merely a question of financial limitations on what may be spent on schooling but also a question of authority, hierarchy, and discipline: a question of cooling-out on a mass scale those "enhanced quality of life expectations" that were perceived as reaching crisis point in the schools (Taylor 1980, 3).

Part of the background to this process of redefinition was the developing crisis of British capitalism, increasingly apparent from the mid-1970s. Britain's economy has been in relative decline throughout the twentieth century. The start of the decline can be variously dated from the First World War, from the Great Depression of 1874-96, or even from the Great Exhibition of 1851. A relative decline reflecting the loss of a monopolistic position as merchant, banker, and insurer was perhaps inevitable, but when countries of the European Economic Community were overtaking the British standard of living in the 1960s, it looked as though the decline might become absolute. The oil crisis of 1973, a decline in exports, the balance of payments crisis in 1976, and the subsequent loan of 4 million pounds sterling from the International Monetary Fund all exacerbated the problem (Hargreaves 1986). The discovery of North Sea oil, having its effect on balance of payments figures by the late 1970s, tended to conceal the fundamental problems.

In hard figures Britain's economic growth in terms of Gross Domestic Product was actually negative in 1974 and 1975 for the first time since the depression of the 1930s. Inflation averaged 14.2 percent in the 1970s, and the value of one sterling pound in 1961 had dropped to 32 pence by 1972 (and 21 pence by 1985). Unemployment, always less than 3 percent between 1946 and 1971, rose in the late 70s to 7 percent (1.5 million) and doubled to 13 percent or 14 percent by the mid 1980s (3.5 million) (*Social Trends* 1987, 80).

RESTRUCTURING AT THE LOCAL LEVEL

It is important to note that although local authorities faced unprecedented cuts in expenditure following the 1973 oil crisis, money for capital projects has always been scarce. In particular, the space available for schooling had been declining throughout the 1960s (Wallace 1980a, 1980b). As the largest single item of expenditure of local government, state educational policies have always been tied to the level of generosity shown by the government in allocating funds, although the form of the allocation has changed over time. Since the Local Government Act of 1966, the necessary support has been incorporated into the process devised for allocating the Rate Support Grant (RSG).

Administrative changes under corporate management have had wide implications for negotiating procedures by fragmenting educational interests that were once under the direct control of the Local Education Committee and by significantly undermining informal interactions. This can be illustrated with reference to the dynamics in "Midlands County," where we were involved in a longitudinal ethnographic investigation focused on the experiences of middle school teachers (see Ginsburg, Meyenn, and Miller 1979, 1980; Ginsburg, Meyenn, Miller, and Ranceford-Hadley 1977; Ginsburg, Wallace, and Miller 1988; Wallace, Miller, and Ginsburg 1982). In "Midlands County," crucial economic decisions were vested in the powerful Policy, Resources and Finance (PRAF) Committee. Educational buildings became the concern of the Property Committee and teachers' shifts in the loci of the decision making tended to elevate financial considerations and to devalue the influence of social and educational criteria in policy deliberations about local schools (see also Cooke 1980).

There were also significant changes in the relation between the members of "Midlands County's" Education Committee and the elected representatives of teachers. Before local government reorganization of 1974, teacher representatives had held voting rights in one of the areas now amalgamated into one local education authority (LEA). Under amalgamation and with the reorganized system of local government, these rights were denied and the role was redefined as consultative only (see also Ozga 1987). The next major move occurred in the autumn of 1979, when representatives were informed that they should not imply that they represented anyone, as they were no more than individual teachers from whom the Committee might or might not wish to have an opinion.

A further area of change in relationships in "Midland's County" concerns the breakdown of the "informal networks" of communication that were once the means by which individuals responsible for educational interests, from the heads of schools through officials and County education officers and even up to the Minister of State, had been able to solve the day-to-day difficulties involved in making the education system work. Not only did the institution of corporate management procedures block direct informal communications between County education interests and the Department of State, but it also blocked many of the methods whereby schools had been able to get informal decisions make about their particular problems through the telephone calls from heads to County officials. Local Consultative Committees, made up of the Local District Inspectorate and Councillors, were set up to make decisions about local schools without necessarily consulting teachers at all, although a school's head and Chairperson of the Governors could be invited to attend specific meetings.

Alongside these new apparatuses of constraint there were developments at a rhetorical level, directed at defining the legitimate limits of democracy. A "Midland's County" Councillor stated that heads ought not to be using parents in a campaign against the legitimately decided policies of local government; this, when some heads sought to defend their own schools against particular decisions by rousing parental protest. Furthermore, the Conservative Party justified its over-weighting of committees (after its majority was reduced to a handful following the 1981 County Council elections) by claiming that as the party had been "elected to govern," it must be able to get its policies through.

RESTRUCTURING OF EDUCATION AND THE STATE, 1979-1986

The Conservatives defeated Labour in 1979 using an election slogan: "EDUCASHUN ISNT WURKING." Their campaign emphasized the fall in standards in reading and writing, which, although illusory, touched the popular consciousness. Right wing critics of education like Sir Keith Joseph and Rhodes Boyson, previously ridiculed by the progressive education establishment, became Ministers of Education. Teachers organizations found their influence diminished, for example, in terms of control of curricula, and central government control over local authorities increased.

The attacks on local government authority became the hallmark of Conservative ministers in the 1980s, particularly in the cities and industrial regions, where Labour controlled councils had established educational policies and practices that were an anathema to right-wingers in the areas of sex education, peace studies, racial awareness training or multi-cultural education. The abolition of the Greater London Council under the second conservative administration and the abolition of the Inner London Education Authority under the 1988 Act, despite popular support for both these councils and their policies, displays an emboldened centralizing pattern, based on a substantial parliamentary majority and three successive general election victories (1979, 1983, and 1987). It should be noted, however, that although these victories gave the Conservatives majorities in the House of Commons of 43, 144, and 102 members, respectively, they represented only 43.9 percent, 42.4 percent, and 42.3 percent of the votes cast in the respective elections.[3]

The Assisted Places Scheme was one of the first educational measures to be introduced by the Thatcher government of 1979. Rhodes Boyson, the Minister responsible, described the scheme as intended to give "able children from our poorest homes . . . the opportunity of attending academically excellent schools as excellence has been traditionally defined" (Boyson 1979). The scheme was part of the Education Act of 1980, which also required national secondary schools to publish examination results and strengthened parents' rights to challenge the allocation of secondary school places by the LEA. Those obtaining an assisted place at an independent school receive a means-tested government subsidy worth an average of about 2,000 pounds sterling in 1988-89. This is like a voucher system, except it is restricted quite tightly to parents of "academically able" children.

The scheme was attacked as a declaration of no confidence in the capacity of comprehensive schools to cater to able children, and as a deliberate enhancement of private education at the expense of the public sector (Edwards, Fitz, and Whitty 1989). The schools selected for involvement in the scheme had to be "academically competent" in a traditional sense, with a large sixth form, a wide range of "A" level subjects with good results and a high percentage of pupils going on to higher education. The scheme reinforced traditional notions of selecting academically able children into academic elite institutions, and those elite institutions, because of virtual demise of the LEA grammar school, were defined as private.

Generally and with increasing clarity and strength, the Conservative governments beginning in 1979 exhibited an attitude to public expenditure on social services inspired by a fairly crude monetarist economic philosophy following the U.S. economist, Milton Friedman. From this perspective these social service activities were seen as essentially parasitic or at least dependent on the wealth producing private sector. This was a part of a political ideology that celebrated the market, individual choice, and the maximization of profit as the key to efficiency and the good life. These attitudes and principles became increasingly applied beyond the production of goods and services by private corporations to the supply of social services in the public domain that were now seen as ripe for privatization.

The reworking and revitalization of this conservative political philosophy in a radical and populist mode with respect to both the economy and education was in the hands of Margaret Thatcher, a previous Minister of Education responsible for cutting the milk provision, and Sir Keith Joseph, an ideologue with intellectual pretensions. It seemed in the 1980s that both had vivid memories of the obloquy they had suffered from left academics, particularly social scientists, when proposing what in the 1970s seemed far-fetched theories about the free market or cycles of deprivation. From another perspective, the student agitation in British universities and colleges in 1968 had served to increase student participation in academic governance but also helped to foster the development of academic radical and Marxist critiques of higher education, especially in the social science fields, which they saw as having little to contribute to economic development.

Within this economic, political, and ideological context education, including higher education, would take its share of cuts in public expenditure, particularly, it would seem where it did not directly serve the "needs" of industry. Here contradictions emerged in practice as the general logic of monetarist cuts, initiated in 1981 but mediated by a conservative academic establishment, tended to protect the older universities and subjects through reliance on accepted and unexamined criteria of excellence. The cuts fell most heavily on the technological universities and hit the sciences as well as social sciences.

As the 1980s drew on, however, it became clear that the 1981 financial cuts were only the first stage of a larger plan to reduce universities' dependence on government funding. Universities were encouraged to build stronger links with industry and to seek alternative sources of financial support; they were to seek research contracts from industry and become more entrepreneurial. Further reductions in government funding occurred in 1985 and 1986, and from 1986 onwards funding was made on the basis of student numbers for teaching, while research monies were for the first time separated and funded on the basis of research reputations and the level of finance obtained from selected independent research grant awarding bodies.

So, at the tertiary level of the education system several interlinked processes were proceeding. Central government control of funding was increasing, but overall funding was being effectively reduced. At the same time universities and colleges were being encouraged to see themselves as market oriented with an increased responsiveness to the business interests. Britain's universities were less dependent on government grants than at any other time in the last 20 years. These changes have had an impact on academics in universities, colleges, and polytechnics. First, there has been a continuing relative worsening of salary and promotion prospects, which the 1987-88 and 1989-90 settlements have done little to improve. Second, there has been a growth in the number and proportion of staff employed on short-term, temporary contracts with no tenure provision.

In the field of teacher education the national government began intervening in a major way in 1984 with the establishment of the Council for the Accreditation of Teacher Education. Up to this point this sector had experienced central government-fostered tremendous expansion in the 1960s and early 1970s; then in the late-1970s central government sought to reorganize teacher education, closing and merging many institutions and programs. The content of teacher education curriculum, though, had not been the focus on national state action. Now, however, teacher educators, like their school teaching "colleagues" during the "Great Debate," were being seen as contributing to the "economic and moral decline of the nation" (Whitty, Barton, and Pollard 1987, 106). One major effect of this accreditation process was that programs that had developed a more "progressive" integrated curriculum found it difficult to satisfy the criteria applied in the accredition process that students must complete at least 2 years of course work in (separate) academic subjects.

In primary, middle,and secondary schools the developments paralleled those at the tertiary level. As is apparent from the title of Roy's (1983) book, *Teaching Under Attack,* school teachers continued to encounter challenges to their workplace autonomy from the state in the 1980s (Grace 1987). Head teachers' autonomy has also continued to be undermined as they have become a kind of "middle manager" (Lawn 1988), reinforcing the trend we observed in "Midlands County" (Ginsburg, Wallace, and Miller 1988) and rendering head teachers more like principals in the United States than had historically been the case (see Baron and Tropp 1961, 551). With respect to curricular and student evaluation matters the central government has been "concerned to increase their own control over education while weakening the power of LEAs, schools, and teachers" (Walsh 1987, 152). For example, the Schools Council was abolished and replaced with separate curriculum and examination committees, more subject to control by the Secretary of State for Education and on which teachers had a less prominent role. In 1983 the Manpower Services Commission, created in 1974 under a Labour Government to deal with the "skill deficiency problem" of unemployed young people outside of school, became a vehicle of Thatcher's Conservative government to direct funding for curriculum developments in schools, namely, the Technical and Vocational Education Initiative.

Nevertheless, the 1981-86 period cannot be adequately described with reference only to passive or compliant educators being the target of attack by a national state with an increasing Conservative Party majority in parliament. From 1984-86 England witnessed a period of heightened teacher militant action. National salary levels for teachers were initially the major issue, but as things developed the dispute had "as much to do about how the teaching force is managed as about levels of pay" (Walsh 1987, 147). Teachers unions used the kinds of strategies we witnessed in the late

1970s and early 1980s in "Midlands County": refusing to supervise meals and to cover for absent colleagues as well as mobilizing parents in support of their cause (Ginsburg, Wallace, and Miller 1988). As Pietrasik (1987) describes in detail, the dispute also was punctuated by a series of 3-day teacher strikes in different local educational authorities on a rotating basis and quite aggressive negotiating by teachers through the Burnham Committee and with the Arbitration, Conciliation, and Advisory Service. While annual pay rises were achieved during this period, these were less than teachers bargained for. Moreover, these rises were won only at the expense of worsened conditions of service and the linking of pay to performance. Thus, referring to national agreements at Coventry and Nottingham, respectively, Pietrasik (1987, 187) could conclude:

> Teachers [found] it difficult to understand how, after three years of a dispute which until the end of the Summer Term 1986 they had no doubt they [with strong parental support] were winning, they ended up with an unsatisfactory choice of a negotiated settlement or an imposed one, neither of which endorsed the principles for which they had fought the campaign.[4]

To make matters worse for teachers the High Court ruled earlier in 1986 that it was teachers' "professional obligation" to cover for absent colleagues and, by implication, to supervise during meals if asked to do so by school authorities. So what began during the Second World War as a voluntary action, motivated by a "professionalist" notion of an ideal of service, became teachers' professional obligation to the state. Moreover, the Education Act of 1986 not only abolished the Burnham Committee, the forum for teacher collective bargaining over issues of pay and conditions of service, but also instituted a national system of teacher-appraisal (see Walsh 1987). Clearly, relations between educators and the state had undergone significant restructuring, reversing the gains in teacher individual autonomy and collective power achieved or acquired since 1926. Even the notion of payment by results, which had been successfully contested earlier in the century, forcefully raised its head in the mid-1980s.

RESTRUCTURING UNDER VIRULENT THATCHERISM, 1986-90

If by 1986 the state and education had been substantially restructured, the best or the worst (depending on one's perspective) was still to come. Tomlinson (1989) and Scott (1989) distinguish two periods of change in Britain. The earlier period, roughly a decade from 1976 to 1986, spanned the Labour government of Callaghan to 1979 and nearly all of Thatcher's first two terms (1979-83 and 1983-87). During the first period the influence of monetarism, market ideas, and public expenditure cutbacks was profound. In this period there were a number of educational policy initiatives--the Assisted Places Scheme, the T.V.E.I., acts to strengthen the power of parent governors as well as considerable pressure to limit educational expenditure and to curb the power of teacher unions, but there was a degree of continuity with educational traditions and institutional forms. For example, the local educational authority remained a key power center. By 1986 and 1987 a new phase and radical political philosophy were becoming apparent of which the proposals for city technology colleges are a forerunner but which find their full expression in the 1988 Educational Reform Bill.

These radical moves can be partly understood as fueled by the third successive Conservative Party victory in 1987. The background to that of course is the program of successful privatization, the defeat of the miners in 1985 and teachers in 1986, a series of Acts (1980, 1982, 1984) limiting trade union power, a peak of over three and a half million unemployed in 1986, a growing polarization between rich and poor related to income tax and benefit cuts, and, perhaps more significantly, increased profitability and productivity, deregulation, and internationalization of corporate and financial enterprise (Britain 1989). Companies real rates of return rose from just over 6 percent in 1982 to just short of 12 percent in 1985 and 1987. Unemployment rates, even allowing for the manipulation of the figures, started to fall in late 1986, and the general population experienced real increases in living standards. Inflation rates were dropping, and it appeared to some as though the

Conservative economic program was having some success. It is perhaps this background and the political success of 1987 election that encouraged the Thatcher government to press on with the more radical measures of the 1988 Act.

The 1988 Education Reform Bill, known as the Baker Bill (named after Secretary of State for Education Kenneth Baker) was introduced in June 1988, just three weeks after the election. The proposals in the Baker Bill covered a wide range of educational provision, primary and secondary education as well as further and higher education, and relate to matters of curriculum, governance, and finance. The main provisions of the Act are as follows:

1. establish a national curriculum with specified core and foundation subjects for all pupils in maintained (i.e., state) schools;
2. institute a system of assessment including examination and testing at the ages of seven, eleven, fourteen, and sixteen;
3. change the arrangements for daily worship in schools, making a predominantly Christian act of worship mandatory;
4. require state schools to admit pupils up to the limit of their available capacity, initially defined by 1980 enrollments;
5. delegate to school governing bodies responsibility for the management of schools' budgets and the appointment and dismissal of staff;
6. enable a simple majority of the governing body or a number of parents equal to 20 percent of pupils at the school to call for a postal ballot, which with a simple majority of those voting can remove the school from the local education authority (opt out) and seek grant-maintained, i.e., central government funded, status.
7. establish independent city technology colleges in urban areas with funding from central government and business to provide free education for children of different abilities between the ages of eleven and nineteen with a broad curriculum but emphasizing science and technology;

8. abolish the Inner London Education Authority and transfer its powers to the London Boroughs;

9. redefine the size and membership of governing bodies of further education colleges so that 50 percent of the members are drawn from business, industry, and the professions or other fields of employment relevant to the activities of the institution, with no more than 20 percent appointed by the local education authority;

10. transfer colleges and polytechnics from local education authority auspices to governance by independent corporations funded by the Polytechnic and Colleges Funding Council from central government sources;

11. create a University Funding Council (UFC) and a Polytechnics and Colleges Funding Council (PCFC), replacing the University Grants Committee[5] and the National Advisory Board, respectively, with each body having 15 members appointed by the Minister of Education (between 6 and 9 having experience and capacity in higher education and the remainder with experience and capacity in industrial, commercial, or financial matters);

12. establish a Commission to determine new provisions relating to academic tenure in the universities, specifically appropriate provision for the dismissal of academic staff and for appeals against dismissal.

Criticism of many of the proposals contained in the Baker Bill were forthcoming from individuals and groups representing a range of ideological perspectives. For example, Professor Brian Simon (1988) and Ted Wragg (1988), on the left and in the center of the Labour Party, respectively, criticized the Baker Bill as representing an attempt to reinstate a selective system of schools. City technology colleges and opted-out schools would become a tier of pseudo-grammar schools in between the independent privately endowed public schools and comprehensive schools impoverished by financial restraint. Paddy Ashdown (*Guardian*, 2 March 1988, 6), the Liberal Party education spokesman and, subsequently, leader of the Liberal Democrats, roundly condemned the Education Act in similar terms:

> This Act is, without question the most dangerous single piece of legislation brought forward by any government since the war. Not just because of the damage it will do to the education service. It will create a divided education system to serve a divided nation. Instead of being broad-based we will have an education system which is cramped, narrow and utilitarian.

Ashdown went on to condemn the centralizing effects of the Act, seeing them as being a challenge to liberal values and the reality and concept of plural society. Similarly, Wragg (1988) critically analyzed the way in which the central government, particularly the Ministry of Education, would paradoxically extend its power in the process of implementing a reform to give more emphasis to market forces, competition, privatization, and the involvement of business interests in the control of secondary, further and higher education. A similar criticism was made by Sir Edward Heath, a former Conservative Prime Minister. During the second reading of the Bill, referring to Kenneth Baker, the Minister of Education, (Simon 1988, 167) reports that Heath said that "The Secretary of State had taken more powers under the Act than any other member of the Cabinet, more than my right honorable friends the Chancellor of the Exchequer, the Secretary of State for Defence and the Secretary of State for Social Services." As Professor Wragg (1988, 58) pointed out this "gives the lie to the claim that power is being devolved".

The arrogation of power by central government was further attacked by Stewart Sexton, Director of the Education Unit of the right wing Institute of Economic Affairs and a past advisor to former Conservative Secretary of State for Education, Sir Keith Joseph. On the proposed national school curriculum he criticized the "enormous power over what seven million children are to be taught . . . [being given] to one man" and on the changes in university statutes he complained that this was "central government control verging upon dictatorship (*Guardian*, 24 February, 6). And, finally, from a radically different ideological stance, Simon (1988) in his criticism of the Baker Bill drew parallels to the Tory reaction in 1902, when they abolished the school boards in an attack similar to the current one on Labour Party controlled local governments in the cities.

This range of opposition is not surprising in that the Bill challenged various established procedures and institutions--local authorities, universities, academic tenure--and it did so by a combination of what can be seen as mutually contradictory principles. On the one hand, central government control was to be increased and on the other, schools were to become independent vis-a-vis local authorities. The city technology colleges and polytechnics and other colleges providing higher education were to sever their links with and accountability to democratically elected local bodies.

The campaign against the Baker Bill, however, did not have the force, spontaneity, popular appeal, or public support that opposition to cuts in the Health Service generated during this period. Thus, despite a broad range of criticism, the Baker Bill was enacted as the 1988 Educational Reform Act. The success of the Conservative government in imposing the 1988 Education Reform Bill is indictive of the power of this ideological formation, but it also relates to the power of a British government that has a clear majority in the House of Commons. This, in turn, relates to the divisions and confusions within the opposition between Liberals, Social Democrats, Labourites, Socialists, Trade Unionists and educational workers, who during the 1980s were unable to unite in an effective campaign to mobilize public opinion in defense of a free and egalitarian education system. Similarly the various social movements--feminists, green, peace, disarmament, and ethnic minorities--found it difficult (or decided not) to articulate with a politics which could influence educational provision effectively.

But also significant was the rift between parents and teachers. The industrial action by teachers over the past years may have contributed, but more deep-seated is the failure by teachers to win parents to their view of what curricula, pedagogy, and school organization are appropriate for their children. There have been instances when parents were mobilized with and by teachers, for example, to resist attempts to demolish the comprehensive system as in Solihull near Birmingham in the early 1980s (see also Ginsburg, Wallace, and Miller 1988). Nevertheless, the right in the Conservative Party and the popular press have been able to exploit the fact that teachers and parent groups do not have a strong history of working together politically.

In August 1990 one can only begin to assess the overall impact of the 1988 Education Reform Act. The establishment of a national curriculum with all the associated working parties and the introduction of testing at seven, eleven, fourteen, and sixteen are just becoming realities. The two most significant provisions of the Act are open enrollment and local financial management, and they only go into operation in September 1990. These provisions will produce a situation where the management of schools will be placed on a more competitive and business-oriented position than it has been in the twentieth century. This is already leading to increased efforts to sell the school through the production of glossy publicity. Fluctuations in pupil roll and the devolution of teacher recruitment to the school level may make coherent planning and proper curricula provision increasingly difficult.

The provision to opt out and take on grant maintained status and the establishment of the city technology colleges have not been as significant as might have been expected. In the school year starting September 1989 only eight had been given grant-maintained status. Of the fifty-three schools that had balloted to opt out by April 1989, 39 had voted in favor. These included many schools scheduled for closure under LEA re-organization plans, and they were by no means all located in Labour controlled authorities (Walford 1990). The implementation of the city technology colleges has also been slower than originally planned. In 1986 Kenneth Baker, who traveled to the United States to visit the Bronx and Manhattan Science Schools as part of an effort to promote (and legitimate) the CTC concept, envisaged that there would be twenty CTC's by the beginning of 1990. In fact, only three had been opened by that date. The first in Solihull opened in September 1988, and two more began operations in Nottingham and Middlesborough in September 1989; five more were scheduled to open in September 1990. There have been two problems: most Labour local authorities, which mainly control inner city areas, have been reluctant to provide sites, and the scale of support from private business has not been as great as assumed. In November 1990 the original CTC plans were drastically revised with only fifteen CTC's to be established.

So compared to the total provision of secondary education in England and Wales (over 5,000 state schools), neither the opting-out grant-maintained schools nor the city technology colleges constitute a significant proportion. Nevertheless they are important symbolically. They have received much government and press publicity and represent a crystallization of an alternative to local education authority provision. Where they exist they have a considerable impact on the local authority provision, and the threat of schools opting for grant maintained status is ever present when a local authority (often under government pressure) attempts to rationalize its provision by closing a school. One can see the interaction effect of the different provisions of the 1988 Act in the area of North Solihull, East Birmingham, in the catchment area of the first city technology college. Here another secondary school was scheduled for closure, and the staff, head and parents saw this as precipitated by the establishment of the CTC. They applied for Grant Maintained Status, were refused, and the school was closed.

It is also difficult to predict the outcomes of the efforts to restructure education because of the contradictory ideological and structural basis from which the change efforts have been launched. As we observed in our field work in "Midlands County" during the 1976-81 period concerning issues of ability-grouping and subject specialist teaching, efforts to shift pedagogy and curricular arrangements to more appropriately reproduce the social relation of production stimulated a dynamic that was contradictory to efforts to make schooling more cost effective. That is, the push to have schools "produce" a more explicitly stratified population possessing various degrees of specialized knowledge came into conflict with a move to cut educational expenditure. We should also recall that in the 1920s these contradictory pressures were dealt with by enhancing the workplace autonomy of teachers rather than undermining it, as was the case in the second half of the 1970s (Ginsburg, Wallace, and Miller 1988).

Such contradictions and the fact that curricula reform may take many years to work through the system and find expression in examinations also help explain how the initial political impetus or educational ideology may be dissipated, absorbed, or re-formed to become part of the educational establishment. This has to some extent happened with the Technical and Vocational Education Initiative (T.V.E.I.), started in 1983 as a state-industry initiative under the aegis of the Manpower Services Commission and linked to the Department of Employment rather than the Department of Education. Its extra funding and need for the cooperation of teachers and local authorities have enabled those in schools who were already committed to progressive child-oriented educational practice to develop their curricula and pedagogy along liberal lines reminiscent of the 1960s rather than employing the more traditional forms valued by some of those who established and promoted the T.V.E.I.

At the tertiary level the Act established commissioners to ensure that university statutes make provision for the dismissal of academic staff because of "redundancy," that is, when an institution ceases to perform a specified teaching or research activity for which the person was appointed. This is in addition to the provision for dismissal for "good cause" (e.g., illegal or immoral action), which already applies to tenured and nontenured staff. The new provision only applies to staff appointed after 20 November 1988 or to staff who receive a promotion after that date. Thus, while the legislation is not retroactive it will introduce further divisions among academic staff over and above the existing differences in seniority or between those on continuing and short-term contracts. There is also the danger that dissenting or unpopular staff may be dismissed by simply defining their area of work as "redundant" within an academic plan. The possible effects of this measure are to reduce the capacity for free academic enquiry and teaching.

It is interesting to note that national salary negotiations for university teachers also now relate to local managerial control. The release of government money for the 1988-89 salary settlement was conditional on the acceptance of appraisal procedures for academic staff. Even more important it was conditional on an agreement that local university management should be able to determine professorial salaries without being bound by national averages and that merit awards and payments should take account of market conditions. This might not seem unusual to North American academics; indeed, the U.S. market model of professorial salaries is often cited by government. However, for British academics it is a significant breach of egalitarian collegial relations and national bargaining procedures. Similar moves are taking place in the polytechnic sector. Moreover, research focusing on Aston University in Birmingham, England, indicates that the universities may be increasingly targets of managerial prerogatives, which are associated with the strong state free-market political economy characteristic of the Thatcherite ideology dominant in the Britain of the 1980s (Miller and Walford 1985, Walford 1988, 90).

CONCLUSION

In the case of Britain we have clear evidence of educational reform (or the restructuring of state-education and state-educator relations) arising in the form of both rhetoric and action in the face of national and global economic crisis. The case also demonstrates, however, that educational reform is not merely some evolutionary or functionalist response to problems in the economy. Through our analysis of the longer-term historical developments and the more recent dynamics we have attempted to show that the structuring and restructuring of the state and education are the consequence of struggles between particular groups--political parties, educators' and other workers' unions, and business organizations--that seek to pursue the interests of particular social classes as well as racial/ethnic and gender groups.

At the time of our writing this chapter in the summer of 1990, Thatcher's Conservative government--and the dominant economic and cultural groups whose interest it seeks to serve-- appear to have the upper hand in the struggle. Workers, including those in education, have experienced a dramatic depowering (and, to some extent, deskilling). Opposition political parties found it difficult to challenge or even restrain the ideological and political agenda of Thatcherism. We should also note, however, that the outcome of the struggle is far from clear. We have indicated how contradictions within and between the economy, education, and the state have meant that even "victories" by those serving the interest of capital have not always resulted in policies and practices that promote accumulation and/or reproduction. One contradiction in recent years has been the strong state action through legislation such as the 1988 Education Act and the increase in centralized bureaucratic control of the curriculum, while at the same time introducing market principles and increasingly involving parents and other local community members in the governance of schools.

It is also apparent that although educators in schools and higher education institutions have been the target of proletarianizing attacks on the "professional" status and authority, they continue to be important actors in the struggle. There is evidence that they can exploit the space created by contradictory ideologies and structures to pursue an agenda at cross purposes to dominent groups and perhaps in the interests of subordinate groups in Britain and the world. The degree of success of such counter-hegemonic activity by educators, nevertheless, seems to depend on their inclination and ability to forge alliances with other groups, including parents and other workers.

How relations between education, economy and the state will be structured in the future in Britain will depend on how educators and other groups define their agendas, the strategies they pursue, and the alliances they form over the content, processes, and organization of education. These relations, though, will also be conditioned by dynamics within the world system, and thus educators and others in Britain will need to undertake a global analysis, pursue international strategies, and seek to establish alliances on a world system level. The challenge is here; the question only remains whether we can rise to meet it.

NOTES

1.   This chapter is a revised and updated version of an
        article, by Ginsburg, Wallace, and Miller (1988).

2.   This tradition, although somewhat attenuated by the
        emergence of new Conservatives with a grammar school
        background like Sir Edward Heath and Margaret Thatcher,
        is still powerful.   Only two members of the fifty (50)
        children of the 1988 Conservative Cabinet over eleven years
        of age attended state schools.   The Conservative Cabinet of
        1984, Thatcher's second administration included amongst its
        twenty-two members seventeen (77%) who were educated
        at Headmasters Conference public schools.   If we compare
        the percent of elite groups in a number of areas recruited
        from Headmasters Conference public schools between 1939
        and 1970-71, we find in the Civil Service (undersecretaries
        and above) a decline from 84.5% to 61.7%; in the Church
        of England (assistant bishops and above), slight decline
        from 70.8% to 67.4%; in the Judiciary (high court and
        above), no real change from 80.0% to 80.2%; among
        ambassadors (heads of embassies and consulates), an
        increase from 73.5% to 82.5%; and among directors of
        Clearing Banks an increase from 68.2% in 1939 to 79.9% in
        1970-71.

3.   Conservative Party political dominance is partly a product
        of the peculiarities of the British electoral system when a
        dominant party is faced by a split opposition.   It also can be
        seen to reflect the bankruptcy of the Labour Party social
        democratic policies, increasingly constrained by monetarist
        pressures in the 1970s and the failure to deliver a workable
        contract with the trade unions.   The split-off of the right
        wing of the Labour Party to form the Social Democratic
        Party in 1981 and that party's rise, alliance with the
        Liberals, and failure to redefine British politics are also
        relevant here.   Finally, we should note that the 1983
        election followed soon after Britain's military victory

against Argentina over control of the Falkland Islands or Malvinas, which strengthened the sagging support for the Conservative Party.

4.   The same fate was suffered by the mine workers during the same time period after a long bitter dispute with the Thatcher government on the issue of pit closures. It is interesting to speculate whether some alliance had been forged between teachers and miners (not to mention other workers), the outcome of their concurrent struggles with the government would have been different.

5.   It is worth noting that the UGC did not have any statutory existence. It originally arose as an advisory body to the Treasury and it was established by treasury minute in 1920. It was transferred to the D.E.S. in the mid-1960s but remained an advisory body, and, in the last instance, legal responsibility for funding lay with the Minister of Education.

REFERENCES

Archer, M. 1979. *Social origins of educational systems.* Beverly Hills: Sage.

Baron, G., and Tropp, A. 1961. Teachers in England and America. In *Education, economy and society*, edited by A. Halsey, J. Floud, and C.A. Anderson, 545-57. New York: The Free Press.

Baron, G., et al. 1981. *Unpopular education.* London: Hutchinson.

Bennett, N. 1976. *Teaching styles and pupil progress.* London: Open Books.

Bergen, B. 1988. Only a schoolmaster: Gender, class, and the effort to professionalize elementary teaching in England, 1870-1910. In *School Work: Approaches to the labour process of teaching,* edited by J. Ozga. Milton Keynes: Open University Press.

Boyson, R. 1979. Educational Concerns. *Daily Mail, (25 June).*

Britain, S. 1989. The Thatcher government economic policy. In *The Thatcher effect*, edited by D. Kavanagh and A. Seldon, 1-35. Oxford: Clarendon.

Carchedi, G. 1975. On the economic identification of the new middle class. *Economy and Society,* 41: 1-86.

Central Advisory Council for Education England. 1967. Plowden Report, *Children and their primary schools.* London: Her Majesty's Stationery Office.

Central Advisory Council for Education England. 1963. *The Robbin's report of higher education.* London: Her Majesty's Stationery Office.

Cooke, G. 1980. Too tough at the top. *Times Educational Supplement*, 4 (1 February).

Cox, C., and Boyson, R. Eds., 1975. *The fight for education: A black paper*. London: Dent.

Cox, C., and Dyson, A. Eds., 1969. *Right for education: A black paper*. London: Critical Quarterly Society.

Dale, R. 1983. Thatcherism and Education. In *Contemporary education policy*, edited by J. Ahier and M. Flude. London: Croom Helm.

Department of Education and Science. 1977. *Education in schools: A consultative document*. The Green Paper, Cmnd 6869, London: Her Majesty's Stationery Office.

Department of Education and Science. 1981. *Curriculum 11 to 16, a review of progress*. London: Her Majesty's Stationery Office.

Donald, J. 1979 Green paper: Noise of crisis. *Screen Education*, 30: 13-14.

Economic trends supplement, No. 12 1987 London: Her Majesty's Stationery Office.

Edwards, E.G. 1982. Higher Education for Everyone. *Nottingham spokesman*.

Edwards, T., Fitz, J., and Whitty, G. 1989. *The state and private education*. London: Falmer.

Edwards, T., Gerwitz, S., and Whitty, G. 1990. City technology colleges: A radical initiative? Paper presented at the Conference on 1988 Reform Bill, London, Institute of Education (April).

Finn, D., Grant, N., and Johnson, R. 1977. *Social democracy, education and the crisis.* Centre for Contemporary Cultural Studies, University of Birmingham. *Working Papers in Cultural Studies,* 10: 147-198.

Flude, M. and, Hammer, M. 1990. *The education reform act 1988.* London: Falmer.

Ginsburg, M., Meyenn, R., Miller, H., and Ranceford-Hadley, C. 1977. *The role of the middle school teacher,* Aston Educational Enquiry Monograph, 7. Birmingham, U.K.: University of Aston.

Ginsburg, M., Meyenn, R., and Miller, H. 1979. Teachers, the "great debate" and the education cuts. *Westminster Studies in Education,* 2: 5-33.

Ginsburg, M., Meyenn, R., and Miller, H. 1980. Professionalism and trades unionism: An ideological analysis. In *Teachers' strategies,* edited by A. Woods, 178-212. London: Croom Helm.

Ginsburg, M., Wallace, G., and Miller, H. 1988. Teachers, economy and the state. *Teaching and Teacher Education,* 44: 317-37.

Grace, G. 1978. *Teachers, ideology and control.* London: Routledge and Kegan Paul.

Grace, G. 1987. Teachers and the state in Britain: A changing relation. In *Teacher: The culture and politics of work,* edited by M. Lawn and G. Grace, 193-228. London: Falmer Press.

The Guardian. 1988. The Day in Politics. (February): 6.

Hargreaves, A. 1986. *Two cultures of schooling: The case of middle schools.* London: Falmer Press.

Hargreaves, A., and Tickle, L.,Eds. 1980 *Middle schools: Origins,ideology and practice.* London: Harper and Row.

Hobsbawm, J. 1987. *The age of empire*. London: Weidenfeld & Nicolson.

Holloway, J., and Picciotto, S. 1978. *State and capital: A marxist debate*. London: Edward and Arnold.

Jackson, M. 1989. C.B.I. struggles to save curriculum from Baker. *The Times Educational Supplement*, 5.

Kennedy, P. 1988. *The rise and fall of great powers*. London: Fontana.

King, E. 1979. *Other schools and ours*, 5th edition. San Francisco: Holt, Rinehart and Winston.

King, E. 1987. Feminists in teaching: The national union of women teachers, 1920-1940. In *Teachers: The culture and politics of work*, M. Lawn and G. Grace, 31-49. London: Falmer Press.

Lawn, M. 1987. What is the teacher's job? Work and welfare in elementary teaching, 1940-45. In *Teachers: The culture and politics of work*, M. Lawn and G. Grace, 50-66. New York: Falmer Press.

Lawn, M. 1988. Skill in school work: Work relations in the primary school. In *Schoolwork: Approaches to the labour process of teaching*, J. Ozga, Milton Keynes, U.K.: Open University Press, 161-176.

Marwich, A. 1965. *The deluge: British society and the first world war*. London: Bodley Head.

McLennan, G. 1984. *State and society in contemporary Britain*. Cambridge: Policy Press.

Miller, H., and Walford, G. 1985. University Cut and Thrust. In *Schooling in turmoil*, edited by G. Walford. London: Croom Helm.

National Commission on Excellence in Education 1983. *A nation at risk.* Washington, D.C.: U.S. Department of Education.

Ozga, J. 1987. Part of the union: School representatives and their work. In *Teachers: The culture and politics of work,* edited by M. Lawn and G. Grace, 113-46. London: Falmer Press.

Parry, N., and Parry J. 1974. The teachers and professionalism: The failure of an occupational strategy. In *Educability, schools, and ideology,* edited by M. Flude and J. Ahier, 160-85. New York: Wiley.

Perkins, H. 1990. *The rise of professional society.* London: Routledge.

Pietrasik, R. 1987. The teachers' action, 1984-86. In *Teachers: The culture and politics of work,* edited by M. Lawn and G. Grace, 168-92. London: Falmer Press.

Ransom, S. 1990. From 1944 to 1988: Education, Citizenship and Democracy. In *The education reform act 1988,* edited by M. Flude and M. Hammer, London: Falmer, 1-19.

Reid, M., Clunies-Ross, L., Goacher, B., and Vice, C. 1981. Mixed ability teaching, problems and possibilities. *Educational Research* 24, 1: 17-23.

Roy, W. 1983. *Teaching under attack.* London: Croom Helm.

Scott, P. 1989. Higher education. In *The Thatcher effect,* edited by D. Kavanaugh and A. Seldon, 198-212. Oxford: Clarendon.

Simon, B. 1977. Marx and the crisis in education. *Marxism today* (July): 195-205.

Simon, B. 1988. *Bending the rules.* Lawrence and Winhart.

Social Trends. 1979. London: Her Majesty's Stationery Office.

Social Trends. 1987. London: Her Majesty's Stationery Office.

Tawney, R. 1922. *Secondary education for all.* London: Allen and Unwin.

Taylor, W. 1980, September. Education: A redefinition. Talk given at a conference of local authorities and advisors, Mimeo, London Institute of Education.

Tomlinson, J. 1989. The schools. In *The Thatcher effect*, edited by D. Kavanaugh and A. Seldon, 181-95. Oxford: Clarendon.

Walford, G. 1986. *Life in public schools.* London: Methuen.

Walford, G. 1987. *Restructuring universities.* London: Croom Helm.

Walford, G. 1988. The privatization of British higher education. *European Journal of Education.* 23, 1/2: 47-64.

Walford, G. 1990. *Privatization and privilege in education.* London: Routledge.

Wallace, G. 1980a. Architectural constraints on educational aims and organizations: With particular reference to middle schools. *Journal of Educational Administration and History*, 12, 2: 47-57.

Wallace, G. 1980b. The constraints of architecture on the aims and organization of five middle schools. In *Middle schools: Origins, ideology and practice*, edited by A. Hargreaves and L. Tickle, 122-38. London: Harper and Row.

Wallace, G. 1983. Structural limits and teachers' perspectives on pedagogy. Ph.D. dissertation, University of Aston in Birmingham, England.

Wallace, G., Miller, H., & Ginsburg, M. 1982. Teachers' responses to the cuts. In *Contemporary educational policy*, edited by J. Ahier and M. Flude, 109-38. London: Croom Helm.

Walsh, K. 1987. The politics of teacher appraisal. In *Teachers: The culture and politics of work*, edited by M. Lawn and G. Grace, 147-67. London: Falmer Press.

Weiner, M. 1985. *English culture of the decline of the industrial spirit, 1850-1980*. London: Penguin.

Whitty, G. 1985. The great debate and its aftermath. In *Sociology and school knowledge: Curriculum theory, research and politics*, 101-19. London: Methuen.

Whitty, G. 1990. The new right and the national curriculum: State control or market forces? In *The education reform act 1988*, edited by M. Flude and M. Hammer, London: Falmer, 21-36.

Whitty, G., Barton, L., and Pollard, A. 1987. Ideology and control in teacher education: A review of recent experience in England. In *Critical studies in teacher education*, edited by T. Popkewitz, 161-84. New York: Falmer Press.

Williams, P. 1977. Too many teachers? *Comparative Education* 15, 30: 169-79.

Williams, R. 1961. *The long revolution*. London: Chatto & Windus.

Wragg, T. 1988. *Education and the market: The ideology behind the 1988 education bill*. London: National Union of Teachers.

THE POLITICAL ECONOMY
OF EDUCATIONAL
"REFORM" IN AUSTRALIA

Susan L. Robertson and Roger R. Woock

The past two decades in Australia have been remarkable for the movements and transformations taking place within the political and economic spheres. Yet, as Phillip Wexler (1987, 12) has remarked, "despite the salience of education to this linked series of these broad multi-form transformations the nexus has remained unconnected by many current observers." We would argue that few analyses have attempted to explore the dialectic between the nature of educational reform and its relationship to the state, the economy, ideology and human agency within the wider global context. While a constant unfolding of educational "reforms" have punctuated the education landscape in Australia since the collapse of the Keynesian settlement in the early 1970s, what is central to the changes in the 1980s is the depth of the restructuring and reorganization taking place.

It will be argued within this chapter that any critical analysis of educational reform must take into account major changes taking place both within the Australian and the global political economy and that the driving dynamic within current educational reforms in Australia is an attempt to meet the three core problems facing the capitalist state and state education systems: (1) support of the accumulation process, (2) guaranteeing a context for its continued expansion, and (3) the legitimation of the capitalist mode of production (Dale 1982, 132-33).

During the past decade domestic politics have been dominated by some form of crisis management by an increasingly interventionist state. Major administrative reforms within the state bureaucracy have been initiated in order to facilitate more flexible approaches to crisis management. More than ever the economic and political spheres have been fused in an effort to provide the conditions for accumulation. This fusion can best be described as *corporatism*. Corporatism can be defined as "a political structure within advanced capitalism which integrates advanced economic producer groups to assist them with representation and co-operative mutual interaction at the leadership level and the mobilization and social control at the mass level" (Panitch 1981, 24).

Organized labor, management, corporate ownership, and the federal Government in Australia have been formally intertwined since 1983. In public discussion in Australia, this agreement is referred to as the "Accord." While the Accord has the appearance of hegemony, the answers to such questions as who should hold power and what political and administrative strategy should pave the way toward creating optimum conditions for capitalist production and reproduction are not so clear. Struggle over these questions being waged within the wider social formation also exists within education, and it should come as no surprise that the struggle to develop a new dominant hegemony requires fundamental changes within the educational sector.

These changes are the focus of this chapter. We will look at the period of the Keynesian settlement, the political and economic crisis and the responses to it by the Whitlam and Fraser governments, and the Hawke ascendancy, followed by an analysis of recent changes in the educational bureaucracy, more general education reform, and finally the corporatization of higher education.

POLITICAL ECONOMY UNDER THE
KEYNESIAN SETTLEMENT

In the period following the Depression and the Second World War, Australia's prosperity was linked to vast natural resources and stability fostered by the emergence of United States hegemony and the establishment of a "Keynesian settlement." This settlement, as Freeland (1986, 215) observes, "promised the maintenance of aggregate demand at full employment levels through the operation of fiscal and monetary policies: the promise of full employment and security for labour and a promise of profitability for capital. To realize both these gains, both labour and capital had to make concessions." During this period the state played an increasingly significant role in the accumulation process, including guarantees to the productive sector for land, power, tariff protections, and negotiated export markets (Connell and Irving 1980, 277). Many of these developments, undertaken by large multi-national corporations, meant that by the late 1960s Australia was increasingly a developed, dependent economy caught in the vortex of three imperialisms: British, United States, and Japanese. By the 1960s, 40 percent of manufacturing and 50 percent of mining in Australia was foreign owned, with 60 percent of mining under foreign control (Krause 1984, 300).

Foreign ownership and control of Australia was paralleled by the concentration of capital in no more than two hundred monopoly enterprises, while corporate ownership in Australia shifted from the hands of individuals to corporations--primarily financial institutions (Karmel and Brunt 1962; Encel 1970). These large corporations subsequently played a major part in the emergence of a corporate settlement in Australia. The concentration in ownership, however, as O'Connor (1973) has pointed out, had clear industrial-relations implications. The largest two hundred enterprises employed about half of the labor force and accounted for 60 percent of fixed capital expenditure, resulting in increased homogenization of the labor force and the possibility for unions to increase their solidarity. However, popular discontent and political demands were defused by co-option and transformed into economic demands, although at the expense of other subordinate groups, including the reserve army of labour and unorganized migrant labor.

An important effect of the Keynesian settlement was, as Bowles and Gintis (1982) note, that the guarantee of a social wage through state programs made workers less dependent upon selling their labor for survival. This reduced the threat of unemployment, long used as a tool to control labor. At the same time the state, under the guidance of Keynesian policies, became even more protective of private business enterprises in order to engineer relative stability in the economy, and large private businesses became assured of continuous profitability. In other words, profits were made not through increased efficiency but by protection from competition. This led to the growth of an inward-looking, fragmented manufacturing base primarily concerned with supplying a restricted but heavily protected domestic market (Robinson 1978).

The post-war history of schooling in Australia reflected these broader political and economic changes, with power increasingly concentrated within the federal state. Australia has three tiers of government: local, state, and federal. While all of these levels operate within the broad parameters defined by the accumulation process, the interplay of levels has created tensions and opportunities for change. When the six states of Australia joined together as a nation in 1901, provision of education remained a state responsibility. Financial powers acquired by the state during the Second World War were used to consolidate state ideology "always within the framework of the economic and system stabilizing needs of capitalism" (White 1987, 5). Universities were increasingly relied upon to undertake research and development activities for industry. During this period important social divisions in Australia were maintained through the development of separate but "equal" dual systems of universities and colleges and private and public schools. Universities were to reproduce the dominant class and were fed by the private schools, while colleges were required to produce the technicians necessary for the development of Australia's manufacturing base.

School expansion was fostered by a variety of economic and social motives including, among others, the perception of schooling as being culturally "uplifting" (Connell et al. 1982, 18). By the late 1960s, however, the growing number of students in Australian schools placed considerable pressure upon the states. These tensions werc cxaccrbatcd by thc incrcasing mobilization by social movements over issues of class, gender, and ethnic inequality. Teachers increasingly joined a broader-based militancy within labor (Blackmore and Spaull 1987). Connell et al. (1982, 23) observes:

> So schooling became, for the first time since the late nineteenth century, a major source of difficulty for the state. Teachers' unions had become powerful and articulate. Parent organizations ceased to be content with running fetes and barbeques, linked up across the states, and demanded to be heard. Even students began to organize, in the wake of student mobilization in the universities. A flurry of agitation surrounded the schools in the late 1960s and the early 1970s.

EMERGENCE OF CRISIS IN THE POLITICAL ECONOMY

Freeland (1986, 216), Weisskopf (1981), Wright (1978), and Bowles and Gintis (1982) all point out that techniques of demand management and state intervention proved to be contradictory. The solutions to the earlier crises of the 1930s and 1940s contained fundamental contradictions and dislocations made visible in real and material ways by the early 1970s. Connell (1977, 113 14) notes that the industrial growth that had underwritten the long boom had left a series of intransigent political and economic problems. The class struggle had moved onto the political terrain, with the economism of the earlier years giving ground to political concerns. Industrial unrest increased among non-manual unions, including teachers. Strikes increased over issues such as the federal budget, relations with South Africa, aboriginal voting rights, and health services (Rawson 1978, 136-37). Heavy state protection of manufacturing industry against economic losses in Australia meant that the panacea of depression to improve competition and efficiency was ruled out.

The growth of the monopoly sector and the philosophy of entitlement fostered by the need for the state to legitimate the system, placed further pressure upon the state to expand its support for both legitimation and accumulation, ultimately creating, as O'Connor (1973) observes, further contradictions between legitimation and accumulation.

The Keynesian settlement was further undermined by developments within the domestic and international economies, underlining the relationship of dependence that comes from the globalization of production. With the emergence of an international division of labor, third-world countries offered a cheaper supply of labor and goods, attractive profits and a complacent labor market (Windshuttle 1980, 31-32). In order to compete, domestic markets turned to new technologies to reduce labor costs. This resulted in major structural changes in the domestic labor market, including further de-skilling, stratification, exploitation, and the creation of permanent part-time employment (Watkins 1985, 23-32). Key manufacturing companies, employing significant numbers, initiated a process of de-industrialization, moving "offshore" to countries such as the Philippines, Singapore, and Korea in search of cheaper labor (Windshuttle 1980, 31-32). Employment in manufacturing declined from 24 percent to 18 percent between 1973-83 (Bamber and Lansbury 1987, 99). This represented a major fall in profit and employment opportunities. Like the United States, Australia had developed into a predominantly service economy (66 percent of civilian employment).

The structural problems associated with being a developed but dependent economy came to the fore in Australia during the 1970s oil crisis. The newly deregulated financial market resulted in the equivalent of more than $3 billion in Australian currency entering the country during 1971-72 and contributed strongly to Australia's inflationary cycle (Catley 1978, 22). These problems were compounded by the emerging economic strength of Asian nations, such as Japan and Singapore and the severing of the umbilical relationship between Britain and Australia.

WHITLAM ADMINISTRATION
RESPONDS
TO THE CRISIS

It was against this backdrop of turbulence that the Whitlam Labour Government was elected in 1972. It appealed to a new set of interests broadly defined as socially progressive, including concerns for specific populations such as the poor, women, aboriginals, migrant groups, and concerns for other issues such as the equalization of the wage structure and increases in the social wage. Whitlam was temporarily able to develop a series of policies that addressed these concerns. His bid for power received considerable support from fractions within the corporate sector including notable developers (Connell and Irving 1980, 309-10) and media giants (Connell 1977, 103). There can be no doubt that Whitlam was also seen by particular fractions of capital as having the capacity to rein in the growing dissent among the union movement.

On assuming power the Whitlam administration initiated a generous Keynesian settlement. But the error of political judgement by the Labour Party was to assume the continuation of the long boom. The removal of the 25 percent tariff protection for industries in 1973 resulted in a flooding of the markets with foreign goods. In 1974 the Arbitration Commission, under pressure from elements within the Labour Government, increased the levels of parity between male and female wages along with a general increase in wages. Services in areas such as health, urban planning, and social security all received increased funding. Consequently, the state's social welfare expenditures rose dramatically. As Graycar (1983, 4) observes:

> Commonwealth Government social expenditures (social security, health, housing, urban and regional affairs, etc.) rose steadily in the decade to 1972 (from 11.8 percent of GDP in 1963/4 to 12.4 percent in 1969/70, to 14.3 percent in 1972/73) and then shot up to 20.6 percent by the time Labor lost office in 1975.

The promised educational reforms offered by Whitlam resulted in the removal of tertiary fees, increased funding to tertiary institutions, the establishment of the Commonwealth Schools Commission, and a massive injection of funding for primary and secondary education. The Schools' Commission funded a series of programs that would foster equality of opportunity and greater school-level development. This federalist approach cut across the traditional boundaries separating federal and state responsibilities for education and shaped in very direct ways the curriculum of the schools.

The international business communities' unease over the perceived threat to the status quo resulted in the sudden reduction of overseas investment in Australia and the flow of funds out of the country. Theophanous (1980, 305) observes:

> Investment by overseas companies dropped from an average of 40 percent in 1970-72 to 8 percent in 1973-74. At the same time there was a dramatic rise in company profits payable overseas, from an average of 28.3 percent in 1970-72 to 52.7 percent in 1974-75.

THE FRASER GOVERNMENT'S EDUCATIONAL REFORMS

During this time the Whitlam administration, discredited as economic managers amidst rapidly increasing unemployment and inflation rates, was skillfully manoeuvered out of office in a dramatic political coup by a conservative Liberal-Country coalition under Malcolm Fraser. The Liberal Party in Opposition orchestrated a constitutional crisis, refusing to pass the government's appropriations bills. This resulted in an unprecedented action: the dismissal of the Whitlam Government by the Governor General. Backed by multinational corporations, the technocracy, sections of the public service, and the media, a massive ideological shift to the right was effected in Australian politics, taking with it powerful factions from within the Labour Party (Jones 1982, 122). The new Liberal administration, however, could do little to solve the critical economic and political problems facing Australia. Structural changes were under way which dramatically increased the level of youth unemployment, the numbers of part-time as opposed to full-time jobs, and the average duration of unemployment.

Within this context education was increasingly under pressure. Harman et al. (1980, 7) notes that the end of the era of growth in funding came quite dramatically. This decline in level of funding, begun during the Whitlam Labour government and continued under Fraser's Liberal government, has continued until this day. Educational policy was increasingly being defined in terms of human capital, reflecting the ideology of the New Right conservative forces. Employers and the media engaged in a public witch-hunt, laying the blame for youth unemployment on the schooling system. Schools were accused of being responsible for students' inadequate literacy and numeracy, of fostering a poor work ethic, and of failing to provide adequate work skills for students entering the labor market. The Organization for Economic Co-operation and Development (OECD 1976) review of education published in 1976 entitled *Transition from School to Work or Further Study* provided considerable support for this critique of schooling, including the view that unemployment reflected a decline in the work ethic of young Australians.

This shift was also spelled out clearly in the report *Education, Training and Employment* (Committee of Inquiry into Education, Training and Employment 1979). Known as the "Williams Report," this policy document (commissioned by the Fraser administration in 1976 and presented in 1979) has been widely interpreted as an ideological attack upon the educational reforms promoted by the more progressive Whitlam administration and the post-war extension of educational provision in Australia. In its findings the Committee recommended the rationalization of the post-secondary sector and the re-focusing of education on a more vocationally-oriented curriculum. According to the Williams Committee, schools had failed to adapt to changes in the economy and society. The report explained youth unemployment in terms of shortcomings of the education system, thereby attempting to mediate the contradictions posed in the considerable restructuring already under way within the Australian economy. The Williams report promoted the view that education should be more closely linked to the "needs" of the labor market.

Pressure was increased on schools with the announcement of the Commonwealth School to Work Transition Program, which served ideologically to lay the blame for unprecedented levels of unemployment within Australia on personal failure rather than crisis tendencies within capitalism. Program funds were directed to the secondary and technical levels of education with those pupils identified as personally "at risk" defined as the central targets for funding. This resulted in a plethora of programs designed to provide courses and learning experiences to upgrade students' skills and change their attitudes. During this period increased emphasis was placed upon technical and vocational knowledge. Schools were encouraged by the state, corporations, and unions to promote limited periods of workplace-based experience as part of the students' educational program.

Such reforms were not without their contradictions. Many pupils contested the academic curriculum. They saw this curriculum as irrelevant, alienating and inappropriate, finding community-based work experience a welcome relief from the tedium of school life. Some teachers also actively resisted the state attack on schooling by developing critical courses, which incorporated living and social skills components, material on the nature of employment, trade unionism, and politics.

The first hint of rationalization at the tertiary level came with the restructuring and rationalization of resources in the college and university sectors in 1981. The Parliamentary Statement on the Review of Commonwealth Functions, commonly known as the "Razor Gang," began the process of reorganization within the existing tertiary structures, dramatically reducing the number of colleges of advanced education from sixty-eight to forty-five (Karmel 1984, 177). No additional resources were allocated to undertake these changes. Rationalization meant the amalgamation and incorporation of many colleges into multi-purpose institutions, the re-allocation of resources away from teacher education and liberal arts, and an emphasis upon technology and business studies (Karmel 1984, 180). The overriding concern continued to be defined in terms of the needs of the economy.

This period of rationalization was not accomplished without considerable resistance and the ensuing years created turmoil in many colleges, as they attempted to re-assert their own agendas and reject amalgamation or diversify their course offerings, reskill their academics, compete with larger more established institutions, and at the same time maintain their operations in the face of significant real reductions in funding. Academics in these institutions began to feel the consequences of larger classes, the development of new courses, the fatigue of teaching on a variety of campuses in the course of a day, and the turmoil created by the reality of changing political circumstances. Throughout this period federal expenditure on education was reduced from 9 percent of total federal outlays in 1976/77 to 8.1 percent in 1981/82.

Despite these educational reforms, by the early 1980s it was clear to policy analysts that the labor market had undergone permanent structural change and that educational policy would need to take account of these developments (Sweet 1987). Thus, the struggle for power waged within the state and the effort to re-establish the conditions for accumulation resulted in a new corporatist settlement, at the same time signifying fundamental changes in the form and content of education and in the legitimating ideology.

THE HAWKE ASCENDANCY AND THE CORPORATIST ACCORD

The political and economic crisis in Australia deepened in 1982 with unemployment, inflation, and wage demands at unprecedented levels. The sequence of historically significant Labour electorial victories at the state (in Victoria and Western Australia) and federal levels by 1983 laid the foundations for a corporate settlement to be forged, thereby establishing the conditions for renewed economic growth by the national and multi-national corporations in Australia. Under the Prime Ministership of the former President of the Australian Council of

Trade Unions (ACTU), Robert Hawke, the Labour Party assumed a pragmatic stance with the promise of an "Accord." The new distinctly corporatist nature of the state has meant that particular sections of the socio-cultural sphere and labor movement have been drawn into the administration of solutions within Australian life (such as the reduction in the social wage), while at the same time giving legitimacy to the re-assertion of power by corporate capital (Robertson 1990).

The Accord was initially struck between the Labour Party in opposition and the ACTU, promising the development of appropriate policies on prices, wages, non-wage incomes (capital gains), and taxation (Stilwell 1986, 11). The possibility of an accord was not a new one in labor circles. Labour parliamentarian Ralph Willis, a former ACTU advocate, is credited with the idea of a formal statement between the two wings of the labor movement after studying the British and European social contract experiments.

The Accord was a political coup for both the Labour Party and capitalists, earning the support of powerful individual corporate leaders, such as Rupert Murdoch (Carney 1988, 62). In the subsequent negotiation of the Accord to accommodate the corporations, significant differences developed between the original Accord and its implementation (Stilwell 1986, 11). This negotiation occurred at the National Economic Summit in 1983--a demonstration of the fusing of interests between the state, business and labor. This was formally acknowledged in the formation of the Economic Planning Advisory Council (EPAC) to advise the state on planning procedures, prospective economic developments, and government policy. Consensus was now the procedural norm that governed policy formation within the framework of functional representation, even though significant groups were excluded from the consensual processes and thereby marginalized. Those excluded were smaller labor unions as well as women's and aboriginal groups, which had to be represented by peak "legitimate" organizations. Clearly these groups experience major problems when their interests do not correspond. The Accord pre-supposes a commonality of social purpose and of certain shared assumptions concerning the future direction of Australian economic and political development (Triado 1984, 46). Indeed, in order for corporatism to be stable, it must not only generate but pre-suppose consensus.

The Accord has been an uneasy and unstable affair under

constant contestation, resistance, and negotiation. This instability is fostered by key departments within the state that have pursued free-market policies, including the de-regulation of the banking industry and the floating of the Australian dollar. The removal of almost all controls over the movement of money in and out of Australia resulted in investment funds flowing abroad at an unprecedented rate since the Accord (Bell 1987, 18), increasing Australia's foreign debt, and the failure of investment in Australia's manufacturing infrastructure.

The Accord has also served as a focus of attack for conservatives promoting a different hegemony: the "dry" or hard-line brand of political philosophy. These interests, identifiable as the New Right, have launched a forceful attack on state spending, state intervention, and union involvement in policy matters. This powerful but embryonic group has been outspoken on educational issues and pressed for the privatization of all education services.

Education is clearly implicated in this struggle for hegemony and the contradictions that have arisen because of the state's direct intervention in the economy to support the accumulation process. The state has deliberately fostered the development of a corporate ideology and administrative structures in public service and education.

CORPORATE MANAGERIALISM AND THE EDUCATIONAL BUREAUCRACY

Within the context of a corporatist settlement under the Hawke administration, there has been a series of far reaching changes within federal and state bureaucratic apparatuses in such a way that the limited autonomy of the educational system appears to be further constrained. The attempt to increase control over the bureaucratic apparatus is not surprising, but the transformation within the Australian public service during the current period may be the broadest and most profound in the history of the country (Considine 1988, 4).

The introduction of concepts of efficiency and effectiveness from the corporate management framework has been a political priority. This has had the effect of reducing the cost of state services, creating a new legitimating social discourse and practice shaped by the principles of the corporate sector, and reducing refraction through bureaucratic process. While these shifts are not uniform, most contain a core of concepts and values that sets them apart from competing management frameworks. This framework includes a commitment to program budgeting, complementary functional organizational structures, corporate planning, performance payment, systemwide forms of program evaluation, a senior executive service, and instruments to ensure greater accountability such as a revamped Auditor General's Department and efficiency scrutiny units (Considine 1988, 5).

According to Heydebrand (1983, 102) corporatism as a form of political representation is paralleled by the development of technocratic forms of administration. The state's effort to anticipate the crisis through developing strategies to reduce the complexity of the environment and control communication and feedback increases the state's capacity to internalize it in advance, thereby creating the possibility of ideologically concealing the character of the crisis.

During its first two years in office the Hawke administration mounted a major reform package of budget and financial reforms, which were gradually implemented during 1984-85 within a corporate management framework. This was paralleled by similar developments in the various states of Australia. These new arrangements were directed toward funding on the basis of outputs and were intended to inject a greater degree of "rationality" and "efficiency" into administrative processes through competition between departments. Considine (1988) identifies four guiding principles that have underpinned the process of bureaucratic restructuring: (1) the product format, (2) autocratic instrumentalism, (3) system integration, and (4) economic rationality.

First, within the *product format*, outputs are the achievements of organizations expressed in "commodity-like" fashion; they are given a cost value and placed within the marketplace. Costs are subsequently recovered by charging the consumer, in this instance the student. A student administration fee and the Higher Education Tax at the tertiary level are cases in point.

Within this context, equal opportunity programs are reframed in terms of what they can do for management improvement and therefore product value, rather than contributing to democratic outcomes (Yeatman 1987, 341). Thus, education is packaged and commodified to be bought and sold in the marketplace as a form of cultural capital. At the same time the corporate hegemony creates an image of the public service in the likeness of the corporation, including the reworking of administrative titles and language, such as "Chief Executive Officer" rather than "Director-General of the Department of Education." As Yeatman (1987, 339) observes:

> This change in nomenclature is not merely formal but indicates a change in the identity of public administrators and what should guide their practice. A managerialist orientation is built into current expectations of administrative practice . . . a results oriented management . . . a technical approach to public administration and public service couched within a broader policy framework dominated by economic considerations.

Second, through *autocratic instrumentalism*, power is redefined as being in the hands of the executive management and the Minister. This allows the Minister to more directly control the policy implementation process, thus increasing steering capacity. Goals are set at the top and converted into operation targets by departmental heads through programs. The flurry of papers from the Federal Minister's Office, including *Strengthening Australia's Schools and Higher Education* (Dawkins, J. 1988b), is an indication that educational policy and priorities have increasingly been centralized in the hands of the Minister. Struggle at the local level is thus over issues of resource allocation within a policy framework already set, thereby reducing conflict and the scope for decision-making. Adventurous educational programs with agendas outside of those centrally sanctioned or those which are difficult to quantify will be discouraged within the context of state and nationally determined performance indicators.

Thirdly, *system integration* is premised in the commitment to uniformity, consistency and the reduction of program duplication.

This can be seen embedded in a variety of educational reforms currently under way in Australia, including the attempt by the Federal Education Minister to promote a core curriculum in Australia (*Strengthening Australia's Schools*, Dawkins, J. 1988b), the further amalgamation of Colleges and Universities which fall outside of the Federal Minister's view on optimal size (*Higher Education Policy*, 1988), the demise of semi-autonomous administrative units such as the Commonwealth Tertiary Education Commission and the Schools Commission and their re-integration into a new mega-Department of Employment, Education and Training (DEET).

Finally, the corporate management framework holds up the concept of *economic rationality* (efficiency, effectiveness, and accountability) as the major organizing principle, thereby legitimizing the goals of more profitable accumulation in Australia within the context of substantial cuts to state spending embedded within the corporatist settlement. Economic rationality as the dominant logic can be seen in a variety of ways, including the fostering of business credentials among senior administrative officials within the various Ministries and Departments of Education. The creation of school principals as school site managers in the devolved structures further underlines the depth of change taking place in Australian education.

The overriding concern with efficiency can be seen embedded in all major proposed educational reforms at the federal and state level since 1983, including the *Participation and Equity Program* (1984), the *Report of the Quality in Education Review Committee*, the *Higher Education: A Policy Discussion Paper* (Dawkins, J. 1988a), *In the National Interest* (1987) and *Strengthening Australia's Schools* (Dawkins, J. 1988), and supported by papers from key advisory groups including a paper issued by EPAC *Human Capital and Productivity Growth* (1986).

In Western Australia efficiency and effectiveness in education is now a matter of government legislation, defined as greater output for reduced input (Treasury of Western Australia 1986, 903-4). Wise (1987, 48) argues that this form of legislated learning illustrates the "hyper-rationalism" of schools in an attempt to deal with problems emerging within the state; in other words, a range of economic, bureaucratic and scientific rationalities are used in the development of educational policy-making to increase the institution's legitimacy, although they represent unreasonable and irrational demands upon an essentially complex, people-centered institution.

The cornerstone of many of the efficiency and effectiveness initiatives in education throughout the various states of Australia has been to devolve responsibility (not power) to the local level. This process has been faciliated through appropriating the discourse of more authentic "grass-roots" educational reforms already under way, including notions such as "school development" and the "self-determining school." In commenting upon reforms in Victoria, Angus and Rizvi note (1986, 24):

> The current restructuring makes much of concepts that have been at the forefront of teacher activism for two decades (for example, access, participation, relevance, the rights of interest groups), and incorporates these into centrally mandated administrative practices. Similarly, teachers' unions, through direct representation at various levels, have become integrated into a centralized educational corporatism which involves the Ministry enhancing powers while simultaneously allowing participation in those powers by selected groups. In other words, participation is on terms already defined and not open for negotiation.

In operational terms schools in Victoria, South Australia, New South Wales, and Western Australia now receive school grants, must develop strategic plans based upon clearly stated performance objectives and measured output, and school-based decision-making groups or Councils are to advise on resource allocation and minor policy.

While these developments are premised on negotiation and consultation with major interests, it does not always occur. In Western Australia the traditional political representation for teachers, the State School Teachers' Union of Western Australia (SSTUWA), was completely bypassed in any consultation or negotiation with the Ministry of Education as to the form, content, or timing of major policy changes effected through the *Better Schools* report (Ministry of Education 1987). Instead, in classic corporatist style, the Union's power has been atomized and fragmented by the new structured participation of particular community representatives who now form the new functional interest groups defined by the state as the only legitimate voice.

ECONOMIC RATIONALISM AND EDUCATIONAL REFORMS

The low level of student *participation* and high levels of youth unemployment presented a major problem at the time of Hawke's accession to power in 1983. In 1982 approximately 64 percent of students left school without completing the final two years of high school (Smart 1987, 143). However, the high levels of unemployment rates throughout the 1970s and early 1980s appeared to have discouraged many young people from continuing their schooling, exacerbating the crisis of legitimacy and motivation. This decline was so alarming that a special investigation was instituted (Hunt 1986, 13).

In order to increase retention rates in school, the state replaced the Commonwealth School-to-Work Transition Program with the Participation and Equity Program (PEP). Equity within this context had taken on a much more pragmatic meaning, representing an amalgam of initiatives designed to reduce unemployment by keeping pupils in schools, develop specific vocational skills, foster positive attitudes to the world of work, all within the context of limited state funds. Like the tenets of the Accord, the PEP ideology was based upon the principles of negotiation and consensus (PEP Guide 1984, 3). The PEP policy is significant for its timing and ideological content--it drew into its realm of concern the lives of most ordinary Australians. PEP attempted to heal the divisions in Australia through the establishment of decision-making processes at the local level and by the articulation of a new "consensus" discourse. It is clear that equity within this context had taken on two specific meanings: (1) access to decision-making and consensus--regardless of the unequal relations among the participants (as in corporatist arrangements) and (2) equal opportunity to participate in unequal schooling and its unequal outcomes, while at the same time reducing unemployment. In short, PEP was instrumental in supporting the development of local-level decision-making structures, which would in reality endorse policy already decided in a different arena.

Improvement in retention rates for Year 12 (from 36 percent in 1982 to 57.6 percent in 1988) is cited as evidence of the success of PEP. At the same time unemployment figures fell for the fifteen to twenty-four age group. However, this was a result of the withdrawal of unemployment benefits for sixteen and seventeen year olds fostering a higher school participation rate rather than a consequence of improvements in the labor market (Smart 1987, 29; Sweet 1988, 332). During this period tertiary institutions were encouraged to enrol increased numbers of students, although this was not accompanied by an increase in operating funds (Karmel 1988, 123), resulting in a marked deterioration in the conditions of academic labor, which continues until today. The PEP policy illustrated the extent to which educational policy is used to mask fundamental structural changes occurring in the economy and the establishment of new institutional arrangements.

Throughout this period educational reforms have been directed toward fostering support for private education as well as the *privatization* of education. Drawing upon freemarket ideology, an EPAC-commissioned study from the New Right-affiliated Centre for Policy Studies at Monash University argued that the state should sell off its educational institutions and leave education to be determined by the logic of the marketplace view with which the Department of Treasury was known to sympathize (Stilwell 1986, 114-15). The fact that state support for private schools has increased over the past decade, because of pressure from fractions of the capitalist class, underlines the contradictions inherent in the conservative argument.

In his 1983 election campaign, Hawke promised to end funding to private schools by reducing funding to the wealthiest schools by some 25 percent. However, the wealthy private-school lobby and the Catholic Bishops were a formidable opposition (Smart

1987, 147). In the compromises that followed, a report was issued from the Schools Commissioners on funding policies, arguing that all schools should be eligible for funding to the community standard, including the funding of new places. This position was later ratified by a very generous government policy, leading observers to describe it as "a spectacular conservative coup" (Smart 1987, 154). In essence this state subsidy to private schools supports the reproduction of the upper-middle and upper classes and enables such groups to draw on state funds while continuing to directly control the schooling of their children. This facilitates the differential know-how embedded in public and private schooling cultures, essential to the long-term process of capital accumulation. Federal policy directed to the revamping of compulsory education, such as *Strengthening Australia's Schools* (Dawkins, J. 1988b), have not been directed toward private schools (Sedunary 1989).

The *marketization* of education has emerged as a dominant ideological theme in education reform since the corporatist settlement in Australia. The emphasis on selling a product has occurred on a large scale at all levels of education in Australia from small primary schools competing for a dwindling number of students to large tertiary institutions competing for both local and foreign fee-paying students, the latter with great enthusiasm. The Committee to Review the Australian Overseas Aid Program, known as the Jackson Committee, published its report in 1984. This pro-market report advocated that a key part of Australia's overseas student program should be to develop the Australian tertiary sector into an export industry (Lim 1989, 3-18). In the *Higher Education* policy document academics have been encouraged to market their consultancy and research services to the business community, and institutions are expected to come up with some of their lost income through commercial enterprise (Dawkins 1988a). These developments legitimize reduced expenditure on education, while at the same time giving greater control to the business groups to determine the output of the institution.

The shift toward a national curriculum for state schools has, however, continued to dominate the federal policy landscape in 1990. Of the 23 major reports and statements on education in the 1980s, all have highlighted the centrality of curriculum reforms. The Economic Planning Advisory Council in a document entitled *Human*

Capital and Productivity Growth has argued that for Australia to become competitive in international trade required upgrading the stock of human capital.

Strengthening Australia's Schools (Dawkins, J. 1988b) also advocated the reform of schools to accommodate a national perspective to be realized by a common curriculum framework, assessment, and teacher-standardized education. These proposals were designed to link primary and secondary education directly to the economy and to acknowledge Australia's increasing orientation to the Asia Pacific region. A common curriculum framework could, for example, emphasize the need for general levels of literacy, numeracy, and analytical skills across the nation. A major feature of a common curriculum framework would be criteria for determining content in major subject areas and criteria for methods of assessing achievement of curriculum objectives. However, the recent failure of the various State Ministers of Education to support a federally determined common curriculum, despite the previous affirmations embedded in the Hobert Declaration, suggest that these developments will face with some resistance from the states.

THE CORPORATIZATION OF HIGHER EDUCATION

Dramatic restructuring and reorganization have also taken place within higher education. In 1987 the Commonwealth Tertiary Education Commission (CTEC) was integrated into the new Department of Employment, Education and Training (DEET). According to Marshall (1988, 19), CTEC's independence from the Minister was seen to frustrate the government's policy initiatives in developing market modes of operation, privatization, and student fees. The Minister had invited the incorporation of the colleges and universities into a single Unified National System of higher education controlled by the Minister. This system will consist of "a range of higher education institutions with specific missions agreed upon and funded by the Commonwealth" (Dawkins 1988a, 27). In order to qualify for entry to the Unified National System, institutions must meet a minimum size (more than 2,000 equivalent full-time student units) or amalgamate as well as demonstrate a commitment to the state's equity goals, approved management procedures, credit transfers, staffing arrangements and a common academic year. Funding obligations also include details of the scope of the teaching program; how national, social, economic and industrial priorities would be met; research activities and a research management plan; and objectives for improving efficiency and effectiveness.

The details of the institutional profile and its funding implications are negotiated with the Chief Executive Officer of the institution. Funding is based upon institutional performance determined through the systematic use of performance indicators (completion rates, research, staffing levels, publication and consultancy rates). That these measures are fraught with problems regarding the quantification of educational experience is not acknowledged. Those institutions that fail to meet the requirements will not be funded, whilst those choosing to stay out of the system will be funded only for teaching on a contract basis. However, for almost all institutions, staying outside of the system is no option.

The new higher education policy has phased out the binary system of colleges and universities; emphasized science, technology, and business studies; and involved the corporate sector in course design and development. In political terms it represents the effective corporatization of the tertiary educational sector in order to establish the conditions for capital accumulation. According to Dawkins (1988a, 5) "education is one of the principal means for individuals to achieve independence, economic advancement and personal growth." By linking economic advancement to personal growth and independence, the nature of the "happy citizen" is re-cast into one who is economically productive. Individual economic advancement is then linked to the economic advancement of the nation. Any references to the arts and humanities are framed within a context that is primarily instrumental. To sell Australia's products abroad, tertiary institutions must develop a general education which fosters "well-developed conceptual, analytical and communication skills . . . essential to the building of a flexible, versatile workforce able to cope with rapidly changing technology" (Dawkins 1988a, 9).

A key forum for influence of higher education policy by

business will be exerted by the newly formed Council for Business/Higher Education. This group, with representatives from the Business Council of Australia (BCA), the Vice-Chancellors Committee, and the Australian Committee of Directors and Principals in Higher Education, has the potential for substantial influence in the area of education and industry links. According to McKinnon (1988, p.188), the Council has already recommended that a business liaison officer be appointed on governing bodies and that there should be more joint appointments. Not surprisingly, the BCA is a key player in the Accord. Many of the old established universities have publicly argued their opposition to these policies, declaring them to be interventionist, centralist, rigid, and fascist (Dawson 1988a, 7), but this has not slowed the momentum of the changes taking place.

The rationale for the new corporate approach to education assumes that a higher proportion of the population with secondary and tertiary education will cause a strong economic performance and, therefore, greater national productivity. Students are seen as resources to which education will add value, removing the political content in the category of student. Within the new public philosophy education is reified and commodified. As Huppauf (1989, 110) observes, "the apparent unreserved confidence in internal rationality of the process of scientific and technological advancement and its self-governing mechanics makes educational-philosophical and social-political definitions of students obsolete."

CONCLUSION

Philip Wexler has argued the current restructuring and re-organization of education in advanced capitalist societies reflects a shift toward a corporatist mode of social organization and a new set of social relationships. He argues that "the language of the market, the corporate language, presses toward total rationalization, toward the extension of the market to all social relations, a thorough triumph of the commodity form" (Wexler 1987, 62). Wexler suggests that corporatism as an advanced (and less democratic) form of capitalism works toward integration, thereby providing a more functional relation to the commodity. By dismantling the semblance of the old educational structures, attacking the school culture, reworking the curriculum, and reversing national educational equality, education is confronted with "a de-schooling from the right" (Wexler 1987, 69). Wexler further maintains that the commodification process re-defines broad areas of curriculum and it deskills teachers in the teaching-learning-evaluation process. These developments can be seen clearly in Australian society and education.

> Taken together, these processes of student and teacher deskilling and expansion of methods of measurable organization and administrative surveillance constitute the commodifying aspects of a large historic process of educational reorganization. . . . They empty the content of curriculum and teaching of any cultural history that is not reducible to narrowly defined technical skills. This routinized emptying is legitimated by appeals to the specific job requirements of high technology as well as by a more general appeal to an era of educational quality and intensified competition and sorting. (Wexler 1987, 70-71)

Australian education is undergoing a profound transformation concerning its nature and purposes. These changes are occurring in the context of fundamental struggles and transformations in the Australian and global political economy. We have also argued that in order to make sense of apparently contradictory educational policies, such as the support for private schools alongside the establishment of a Unified National System of Higher Education, it is important to understand that these policies are a result of ideological struggles within the state and the wider social formation concerning the appropriate strategies to foster the conditions for the production and reproduction of capitalist relations. The dilemma for the state appears to be whether to achieve its ends by direct intervention or market forces. Either way, life in educational institutions is being shaped by a new legitimating discourse--a discourse that needs to be challenged if the political response is to be an informed one.

REFERENCES

Angus, L., and Rizvi, F. 1986. Power and ideology in Victorian education. Draft of Paper presented to the 1986 Australian Administration and Research in Education Forum.

Bamber, G., and Lansbury, R. (Eds.) 1987. *International and comparative industrial relations.* Singapore: Allen and Unwin.

Bell, I. 1987. Australia's leaking economy: The new figures. *Australian Society* 6, 10: 18-19.

Blackmore, J., and Spaull, A. 1987. Australian teacher unionism. In *Educational policy in Australia and America: Comparative perspectives,* edited by W. Boyd and D. Smart. Basingstoke: The Falmer Press.

Bowles, S., and Gintis, H. 1982. The crisis of liberal democratic capitalism. The case of the United States. *Politics and society* 11, 4: 51-93.

Catley, B. 1978. Socialism and reform in contemporary Australia. In *Essays in the political economy of Australian capitalism,* edited by E.L. Wheelwright and K. Buckley, Vol. 2. Sydney: Australia and New Zealand Book Company.

Carney, S. 1988. *Australia in accord: Politics and industrial relations under the Hawke government.* Melbourne: Sun Books.

Committee of Inquiry into Education, Training and Employment. 1979. *Education, Training and Employment,* Vol. 1-4. Canberra: Australian Government Printing Service.

Connell, R. 1977. *Ruling class, ruling culture: Studies of conflict, power and hegemony in Australian life*. Cambridge: Cambridge University Press.

Connell, R., and Irving, T. 1980. *Class structure in Australian history: Documents, narrative and argument*. Melbourne: Longman Cheshire.

Connell, R., et al. 1982. *Making the difference: Schools, families and social division*. North Sydney: Geroge Allen and Unwin.

Considine, M. 1988. The corporate management framework as administrative science: A critique. *Australian Journal of Public Administration* 37, 1: 4-18.

Dale, R. 1982. Education and the capitalist state. Contributions and contradictions. In *Cultural and economic reproduction in education: Essays on class, ideology and the state*, edited by M. Apple. Boston: Routledge and Kegan Paul.

Dawkins, J. 1988a. *Higher education: A policy discussion paper*. Canberra: Australian Government Publishing Service.

Dawkins, J. 1988b. *Strengthening Australia's schools: Ministerial statement*. Canberra: Australian Government Publishing Service.

Dawson, C. 1988. Academics seek united stand against Dawkins. *Australian* (August 23), 7.

Economic Planning Advisory Council. 1986. *Human capital and productivity growth*, Council Paper no. 15. Canberra: FPAC.

Freeland, J. 1986. Australia: The search for a new educational settlement. In *Capitalist crisis and schooling: Comparative studies in the politics of education*, edited by R. Sharp. Hong Kong: The Macmillan Company.

Graycar, A. (Ed.) 1983. *Retreat from the welfare state: Australian social policy in the 1980s*. Hong Kong: George Allen and Unwin.

Harman, G.S., Miller, A.H. Bennett, D.J, and Anderson, B.I. 1980. *Academia becalmed: Australian tertiary education in the aftermath of expansion*. Canberra: ANU Press.

Heydebrand, W. 1983. Technocratic corporation: Toward a theory of occupational and organizational transformation. In *Organizational theory and public policy*, edited by R. Hall and R. Quinn. California: Sage Publications

Hunt, F. 1986. Australia. In *Education, recession and the world village*, edited by F. Wirt and G. Harmann. London: The Falmer Press.

Huppauf, R. 1989. The end of students by gradual dispersion. *Arena* 86: 109-121.

Jones, B. 1982. *Sleepers, wake: Technology and the future of work*. Melbourne: Oxford University Press.

Karmel, P., and Brunt, M. 1962. *The structure of the Australian economy*. Adelaide: W.F. Cheshire.

Karmel, P. 1984. The context of the reorganization of tertiary education in Australia: A national perspective. In *Melbourne Studies in Education 1984*, edited by I. Palmer. Melbourne: Melbourne University Press.

Karmel, P. 1983. The role of central government in higher education. *Higher Education Quarterly* 42, 2: 119-133.

Krause, L. 1984. Australia's comparative advantage in international trade. In *The Australian economy: A view from the north*, edited by R. Caves and L. Krause. Washington: The Brookings Institution.

Lim, D. 1989. Jackson and the overseas students. *Australian Journal of Education* 33, 1: 3-18.

Marshall, N. 1988. Bureaucratic politics and the demise of the Tertiary Education Commission. *Australian Journal of Public Administration* 37, 1: 19-34.

McKinnon, K. 1988. Higher education and industry. *Higher Education Quarterly*, 42, 2: 179-92.

Ministry of Education 1978. *Better schools: A programme for improvement*. Perth: Western Australian Ministry of Education.

O'Connor, J. 1973. *The fiscal crisis of the state*. New York: St. Martin's Press.

Panitch, L. 1981. Trade unions and the capitalist state. *New Left Review* 125: 21-43.

Quality of Education Review Committee (QERC) 1988. *Quality of Education in Australia*. Canberra: Government Publishing Service.

Rawson, D. 1978. *Unions and unionism in Australia*. Sydney: George, Allen and Unwin.

Robertson, S. 1990. The corporatist settlement in Australia and educational reform. Unpublished doctoral thesis. University of Calgary: Canada.

Robinson P. 1978. *The crisis in Australian capitalism*. Melbourne: VTCA Publishing Pty. Ltd.

Sedunary, E. 1989. The Minister's next domino: Towards a national curriculum. *Arena*, 86: 23-27.

Smart, D. 1987. The Hawke Labor Government and public-private policies in Australia 1983-86. In *Educational policy in Australia and America*, edited by W. Boyd and D. Smart. Basingstoke: The Falmer Press.

Stillwell, F. 1986. *The accord and beyond: The political economy of the Labor Government*. Sydney: Pluto Press.

Sweet, R. 1988. What do developments in the labor market imply for post-compulsory education in Australia? *Australian Journal of Education* 32, 3: 331-56.

Theophanous, A. 1980. *Australian democracy in crisis: A radical approach to Australian politics*. Melbourne: Oxford University press.

Treasury of Western Australia. 1986. *Financial Administration and Audit Act, regulations and treasurers instructions*. Perth: Treasury of Western Australia.

Triado, J. 1984. Corporatism, democracy and modernity. *Thesis Eleven*, 9: 35-51.

Watkins, P. 1985. *Technology, the economy and education*. Geelong: Deakin Press.

Weisskopf, T. 1981. The current economic crisis in historical perspective. *Socialist Review* 11, 3: 9-53.

Wexler, P. 1987. *Social analysis of education*. Cornwall: Routledge and Kegan Paul.

White, D. 1987. *Education and the state: Federal involvement in educational policy development*. Geelong: Deakin University Press.

Windshuttle, K. 1980. *Unemployment*. (2nd Ed). Melbourne: Penguin.

Wright, E. 1978. *Class, crisis and the state*. London: New Left
    Books.

Yeatman, A. 1987. The concept of public management and the
    Australian state in the 1980s. *Australian Journal of Public
    Administration* 36, 4: 339-53.

STATE CORPORATISM, EDUCATIONAL POLICIES, AND STUDENTS' AND TEACHERS' MOVEMENTS IN MEXICO[1]

Carlos Alberto Torres

The purpose of this chapter is to explain educational policies and practices in Mexico in the period 1970-1990, with a particular focus on students' and teachers' movements. The analysis centers on processes of negotiation, struggle, and compromise inside and outside the educational system. I employ a theoretical perspective emphasizing both a national level analysis, focusing on state interventionism linked to organized corporatist associations (Morales-Gómez and Torres 1990), and a world system analysis concerned with global economic and cultural dynamics.

One of the major preoccupations of cross-national researchers has been to understand national differences in the context of contradictory dynamics of the world system. I agree in part with Göran Therborn, who focuses on national specificities in examining the relationships between economic crisis and political processes. Considering Mexico's crisis, I share Therborn's assumption when he argues that:

> politics has a major impact upon economic performance and on unemployment. Differences in economic endowments, in exposure to exogenous shocks or other non-politically determined parameters of market behavior are not sufficient to explain national crisis trajectories. In other words, politics matters, a conclusion which not so long ago generated considerable controversy (Therborn 1987, 260).

These conceptual delimitations arise out of the specific history of the Mexican social formation and State. The Mexican State is a revolutionary state that has shown over the years a surprising reformist approach in education and in other social service areas. During the post-revolutionary period educational reforms have been undertaken by the Mexican State concurrently with the beginning of almost every new Institutional Revolutionary Party (PRI)-controlled government (Latapí 1976, 1980; Muñoz Izquierdo 1981, 389-445). The Mexican State also has a decisive and almost overwhelming control in educational matters, with minimal political participation and financial involvement from the private sector (Levy 1986; Pescador and Torres 1985). In addition, the Mexican State has shown in the past a tremendous degree of political autonomy, based on strong nationalist cultural policies, regarding the influence of international organizations (Pescador and Torres 1985, 85-117; Paz 1984). Since 1982, however, with the external debt and fiscal crisis and the launching of stabilization policies following International Monetary Fund prescriptions, this autonomy seems to be diminishing.

These features call for an emphasis on national level analysis of welfare and social policies. A world system approach, however, is not ignored in this analysis. It is kept in the background, fulfilling the role that lighting has in the performance of a play. The actors, the script, the choreography, are entirely independent from the lighting system. However, without lighting, or with poor lighting, the overall quality of the play, the shadows and colors in the scenery, the shape and intensity of actors' faces and gestures, or

even crucial signs and clues called for by the script, may not be
appreciated or even seen.

THE CORPORATIST STATE AND POLITICAL ECONOMY IN MEXICO

The study of education as public policy needs an explicit
theory of the state. In this analysis the state is conceptualized both
as a policy-making body, that is, a self-regulating administrative
system, and as a pact of domination. Hence, the state comprises the
institutional apparatus, bureaucratic organizations, and formal and
informal norms and codes that constitute and represent the "public"
and "private" spheres of social life (Torres 1989a, 86). The
peculiarity of the Mexican State is its corporatist structure (Pereyra
1979; 1981; Pescador and Torres 1985; Leal 1975a; 1975b; Kaufman
1977; Fuentes Molinar 1983; Córdova 1972a; 1972b). Due to the
early consolidation of revolutionary policies in Mexico and the early
dismissal of populist politics, the Mexican State is perhaps a state
that, although constrained by its associated dependent-development
model (see Cardoso 1973; Evans 1979; Morales-Gómez and Torres
1990; Stepan 1978), shares some traits with the welfare state as
developed in the advanced industrial societies in the first quarter of
this century (Therborn, 1984).

It has been argued that there is a basic contradiction in the
welfare state policies between accumulation-oriented and
legitimation-oriented policies. In other words, there seems to be a
continual antagonism between a state's need to "deliver the goods"
to the bulk of the population in order to maintain credibility with its
political bases and a state's need to maintain or enhance profitability
in order to foster accumulation and growth. In fact, Gough (1979)
forcefully argued that there is a recurring conflict between the
"social wage" and "social control" aspects of welfare policies. This
basic policy-tension has contributed to a "disorganized capitalism"
and the "fiscal crisis of the State."

Corporatism refers to a form of state that has a broad mass-base of popular support despite its capitalist character in the context of an uneven and dependent-developed national capitalist system. The concept of corporatism in Mexico is also used to refer to the incorporation of the socially subordinated sectors (peasants, workers, and middle class) into the political party apparatus and into the system of distribution of power and influence in the state. Following Lehmbruch and Schmitter (1982, 6), *corporatism* is conceived of as a system of interest group representation and industrial accord, having five main characteristics: (1) interest organizations are strongly co-opted into governmental decision--making as measured by representation in advisory committees or several forms of consultation; (2) large interest organizations, in particular labor unions, are strongly linked to political parties and take part in policy formulation in a sort of functional division of labor; (3) most interest organizations are hierarchically structured and membership tends to be compulsory; (4) occupational categories are represented by non-competitive organizations enjoying a monopoly situation; and (5) industrial relations are characterized by an accord between labor unions and employers' organizations and the government (which implies that unions would refrain from strongly employing the strike weapon or other militant tactics).

When emphasizing corporatist traits of state policies, some theoretical observations can be made. First, any form of corporatist policies (and policies advanced by welfare states) should be expected to reflect deals between the state and interest organizations (Therborn 1986, 141). Second, "the larger the welfare state, the bigger the power and the influence of these organizations. As a corollary, we should expect the political equality of citizens in large welfare states to be less than in less-developed welfare states" (Therborn 1986, 142). Finally, three aspects are commonly explored in understanding corporatist arrangements and their impact on public policy: the size of interest organizations (assuming that the larger they are, the more responsibly they will behave), the cultural homogeneity and sense of collective identity among organization members, and the capacity of the group's leadership to generate the compliance and discipline of its members (Offe 1984, 6-8).

These theoretical observations are very pertinent in studying public policy formation in Mexican education. The national teachers' union, Sindicato Nacional de Trabajadores de la Educación (SNTE), and the Secretariat of Public Education (SEP) are two of the most massive bureaucracies in Mexico. The SNTE has close to 1 million members, and the SEP is the marketplace for the vast majority of those teachers as well as a large number of experts, middle level functionaries and technicians, and high level bureaucrats and politicians working in the central unit and decentralized SEP's agencies. In addition, the SNTE is a fundamental institution in the Mexican political system and in the PRI control network, due to the fact that the SNTE's membership is the bulk of the rank-and-file membership in the Federation of State Employees (FSTSE), which is in turn linked to (and constituting a sizable part of) the National Confederation of Popular Organizations (CNOP), or the "popular sector" within the PRI. The popular sector jointly with the workers' sector and the peasants' sector constitute the three pillars of PRI hegemony in Mexico. Hence, educational policies play a central role in Mexico's corporatist arrangement. In addition, the indispensable role of the teachers in constituting modern and nationalist Mexico is celebrated as an essential part of teachers' symbolic folklore (Latapí 1976; 1980; Fuentes Molinar 1983; Torres 1989b).

The homogeneity and dominance of the leadership in the SNTE, referred to as the "Revolutionary Vanguard," has been recognized by many analysts (Campos et al. 1990; Fuentes Molinar 1983; Latapí 1980; Street forthcoming). Starting in 1979, however, growing opposition to the Revolutionary Vanguard formed a coalition of teachers' groups associated as the Coordinadora or National Coordination of Educational Workers (CNTE) that succeeded through its "democratization" efforts in partially overthrowing the old leadership of Revolutionary Vanguard in 1989. These events will be discussed later in this chapter. However, it must be stressed that the capacity of the teachers union leadership in demanding effective corporatist policies through negotiation with the state bureaucracy should be considered as the backdrop to understand educational policy making. In addition, the political crisis set off by the poor showing of the PRI in the elections of 1988 and the combined growing political pressure of a right wing party, Partido Acción Nacional (PAN), and left-wing coalition, Partido Revolucionario Democrático (PRD), headed by former Cuauhtemoc Cárdenas Solórzano, have affected state-teachers relationships in many ways. For instance, some segments of the teachers' movement may have supported Cárdenas' political campaign.

Educational polices are conceived of as powerful instruments of the state to achieve mass loyalty from the population in the context of the reproduction of social relations of production and labor force training (Carnoy 1984; Gramsci 1980). However, education is not a perfect instrument for reproduction, nor are educational sites under complete control of the state. Educational policies also appear as part of concrete welfare policies responding to citizens' pressure for higher standards of living and democratic practices. In so doing, education plays a mediating role in the conflicts and contradictions of the civil society. Educational institutions have become a terrain for political maneuvering of state bureaucracy; political cooptation of individuals, groups, and demands; political bargaining between corporatist interest groups; and even resistance of the socially subordinate classes and their organic intellectuals.

The legitimacy of the Mexican State can be linked to several sources, including first and foremost the Revolution of 1910, which gave the Mexican State the role of principal modernizer of the country. Other sources include the existence of a party in power for more than sixty years, a successful mechanism for leadership replacement and political administrative succession every six years based on the criterion of non-reelection of the president, and a sufficiently stable discipline of the working class, with the Chair of the National Confederation of Workers (CNT) holding office for almost forty years. The rate of sustained growth of the GNP (6.2 percent annually between 1940 and 1960--see Gill 1969, 9) and the success of the so-called "desarrollo estabilizador" (stabilizing development model) are uncommon features in dependent countries. Agrarian reform and solutions for industrial bottle necks also conferred legitimacy on the state, at least until the beginnings of the 1970s. The Mexican State's legitimacy and the stability of the Mexican political system have moreover depended on the capacity to provide the masses with the promise and sometimes the reality of social mobility and social benefits through skillful administration in agrarian, educational, labor, and electoral matters. Some analysts have particularly emphasized that educational policies are linked with the stability of the political system (Basañez 1981).

EDUCATIONAL POLICY IN THE LAST
TWO DECADES: PATTERNS

What are the particular features of education in Mexican society? Which are the determinants of the process of educational policy formation? I will argue that five main features have characterized the process of educational policy formation in Mexico in the past two decades: (1) the Federal Government has consistently increased the allocation of resources to public education; (2) the quantitative growth has not often been matched with improvements in quality or equality of opportunity; (3) educational policy has been deeply affected by alternative political and trade union projects; (4) although a technical rationale is operating in the process of educational policy formation, the underlying rationale is political-- to legitimize the state and its corporatist network of interest groups (e.g., SNTE, the national teachers union); and (5) educational policy formation not only reflects political crisis but also the fiscal crisis of the state and the more fundamental economic crisis of Mexico and the world system.

First, the Federal Government has followed a policy of consistent increases in the allocation of resources in public education until the disclosure of the external debt crisis. By 1970, 2.57 percent of the total GNP went to education; in 1975 3.9 percent of GNP; in 1982 5.2 percent of GNP; and in 1989 2.45 percent of GNP (Padua 1988, 172). In terms of total government expenditures, in 1970 6.58 percent was spent in education; in 1975 it was 7.20 percent, and in 1982 13.83 percent. Similarly, the spending on free textbooks for public education is impressive: between 1959-1964 the state produced and distributed free of charge 107 million books; in 1977 78 million books; and in 1983 93 million books (Morales-Gómez and Torres 1990, chapter 3; Guzmán Ortiz and Vela Glez 1989, 45). Federal participation in education had increased over time. The contributions of states and municipalities together during 1970-1984 did not account for more than 15 percent of the total expenditure in education and the investment from the private sector has diminished substantially over time. In fact, the private sector has dropped from 16 percent at the beginning of the

Echeverría administration (1970) to less than 6 percent at the end of the López Portillo administration (1982) (Morales-Gómez and Torres 1990, chapter 3).

Second, quantitative growth in education has not often been matched with qualitative improvements or greater equality of opportunity. Despite increased expenditures and educational expansion, dropout and attrition remain critical problems. By 1986 school efficiency had reached only 51.3 percent in elementary education and 74.4 percent at the junior high school level. Although school enrollments in the last three decades have grown by a factor of three, while the school age population only expanded by a factor of two, there are still serious problems of distribution of educational opportunities:

> Access to and persistence in the educational system has not been equitably nor randomly distributed. Those who have benefited from the educational expansion are the groups at the intermediate and higher levels of the social stratum, those that live in urban communities, and especially those who live in communities in the regions with higher relative development (Centro de Estudios Educativos 1979, 364--my translation).

Third, since public education is a contested terrain, educational policy-making has also been deeply affected by a conflict between alternative political and trade union projects (Padua 1988; Pescador and Torres 1988; Street 1989; Torres 1988). For instance, in analyzing the process of decentralization followed in Mexico since 1982, Street (forthcoming) emphasizes four lines of tensions or contradictions: (1) between the leadership of the Secretariat of Public Education (SEP) and the leadership of the national teachers union (SNTE), which was completely controlled until 1989 by a faction of the union identified as Revolutionary Vanguard;[2] (2) between university-trained bureaucrats and personnel of the SEP trained in teachers colleges (*normalistas*); (3) between educational policies built under assumptions of national unity and their application in the diversity and variety of regional peculiarities in Mexico; (4) between the political centralization and the administrative deconcentration of the SEP policies and administrative structures.

SNTE is the largest union in the country and one of the largest in Latin America. Since its inception in 1943, it has been a very powerful actor in the political arena in Mexico (Pescador and Torres 1985). In 1977-78 SNTE had 548,355 members, by 1985 it had almost 700,000 members, and by 1989 it had close to one million members. Politically it is the core of the State Workers' Federation and the central faction of the popular sector of the PRI. SNTE has controlled several senators and federal representatives and a few state governorships (e.g., San Luis Potosí). SNTE has organized systematic and nationwide boycotts of controversial decisions made by the Secretariat of Public Education, including plans and programs for teachers' colleges, the appointment of delegates to the General Delegations of the Secretariat in the States, the appointments of higher officials in the general administrative structure of the secretariat, and the process of administrative decentralization and other projects of educational reform attempted during 1982-1988 (Pescador and Torres 1988). However, despite their political clout, educators have not always benefitted financially (or otherwise) from the union's actions. For example, educational expansion has been possible by limiting teachers' real salaries. According to Aboites (1984; 1986), it took forty years for educators to reach, by 1960, the same level of real salaries that they had in 1921. In fact, considering the level that teachers' salaries could have reached if they have had a normal growth, the value of the salary of one teacher allowed the government to hire three teachers during 1950-1965.

Fourth, provision of mass, compulsory, and free education on a continuous and incremental basis has been primarily an expression of the legitimacy needs of the state. In Mexico education has become a compensatory instrument of political legitimation. The way in which educational planning has been applied in Mexico is a good example of a form of legitimation that sustains an existing structure of political authority and power both through normative principles related to the post-revolutionary state and through a set of procedural conventions, emerging from the dynamics of corporatism. The technical rationale expected to be found in policy decisions is thus easily subsumed under a political corporatist rationale of policy formation, and as McGinn and Street (1984) correctly claimed, the hidden curriculum of education has been not to produce human capital but to produce political capital for the state.

Educational policy and expenditures have been used to a large extent to counteract radical trends emerging from the political conflict in the society. A clear example is provided by the educational policies formulated during the Echeverría period (1970-1976) that attempted to counteract political unrest in the universities after the student movement of 1968[3] and the crisis and repression of 1971. The creation of the Autonomous Metropolitan University (UAM) and the drastic expansion of the National Autonomous University of Mexico (UNAM) in that decade are classic examples of this process of compensatory legitimation. The evolution of education in Mexico has been the result of a deliberate political project of the Mexican State. As part of the revolutionary image that the State and ruling party (PRI) attempt to maintain, public education has been a means to compensate for the lack of other benefits the majority of the population cannot, at least currently, enjoy.

However, it has already been noted that in recent years the corporatist arrangement has been deeply undermined by a number of factors, including: (1) growing political dissatisfaction in the capitol city and popular mobilizations after the earthquakes of 1985, the growth of urban popular movements, and the ineffective way in which the government handled the urban crisis (Eckstein 1988, 274-278), all of which resulted in a voting backlash for the PRI; (2) changing political coalitions in national politics, and more militant and effective opposition to PRI rule;[4] (3) the social repercussions of the economic austerity policies adopted by the government of de la Madrid[5] and followed during the current political regime of Salinas de Gortari; and (4) workers' unrest, including, foremost, the mobilization of "democratic" teachers fighting not only for increased salaries but also for the removal of the oligarchy (Revolutionary Vanguard) in power in the SNTE.

Fifth, dynamics within educational policy in Mexico are not only related to the crisis of the system of political domination but also to the fiscal crisis of the state. This fiscal crisis, arising from an economic crisis which Mexico and other nations in the world system have experienced since the 1970s, has a particular expression in the contradictions of educational policies. A principal challenge for the Mexican State, especially after 1982, has been how to maintain the level of educational investment of past decades. Despite that challenge, the Mexican State has attempted to cope with the social and fiscal crisis by cutting social expenditure, particularly in the public sector, and therefore affecting the employment opportunities of the middle classes. For instance, due to austerity policies negotiated with (or imposed by) foreign lenders, the participation of health, education, and housing in the GNP has fallen 24 percent between 1982-1988, and the rate of participation of salaries in the GNP diminished 35 percent between 1976 and 1987: salaries, participation rate in the GNP has fallen from 40.3 percent in 1976 to 25.9 percent in 1987 (Guzmán Ortiz and Vela Glez 1989, 44-45).

Mexican economic growth has not been evenly distributed. In 1980 5 percent of the population possessed 65.1 percent of the national wealth, and 1.3 percent of the top bracket of the population owned 40.6 percent of the total wealth. At the other extreme, worker's benefits from the national income diminished. In 1950 30 percent of the low-income families received 8 percent of the national income. In 1977 the same group got only 6.5 percent, and during 1977-1981 they received even less than 6 percent (Morales-Gómez and Torres 1990).

After 1970 the rate of GNP growth slowed down (about 4 percent per year), and the country started to borrow money. Since then there have been many devaluations of the currency, increases in inflation (that reached more than 100 percent in 1986-87), and all sorts of political turmoil, although controlled, in one of the most stable political systems of Latin America. Today, Mexico owes more than 100 billion dollars, and for the past five years its interest payments constitute approximately 70 percent of the total value of their exports (which had declined sharply due to the fall in oil prices until the Persian Gulf crisis of August 1990). By 1987 32 percent of the total GNP was devoted to the service of the external debt (Guzmán Ortiz and Vela Glez 1989, 45). Who in Mexico is paying for this crisis--a crisis not just of the Mexican economy and state but of the world economic system as well? Although the crisis has affected the Mexican social formation in total, the working class and *campesinos* or peasant groups have been the most affected. In 1970, for example, industrial workers' salaries constituted 35.7 percent of GNP, in 1985 it was 27.7 percent.

CONTRADICTIONS IN PUBLIC EDUCATION: CONFLICT AND COMPROMISE

To examine these five features of educational policy formation in more detail we will focus on dynamics associated with two examples: university students' unrest (1986-87) and the school teachers' struggle for democracy and increased salaries (1979-89).

University Student Unrest

University student unrest during the last quarter of 1986 and the beginning of 1987 at the National Autonomous University of Mexico (UNAM), the largest and most prestigious university in the nation, is related to the atmosphere of crisis described above[6]. UNAM has always been a sounding arena reflecting the contradictions of state policies. It was the student movement of 1968 (see note 3) and its "utopian democracy" that attacked the heart of state authoritarianism and prompted sweeping political reforms in the following years, including as a byproduct the expansion of occupational mobility for the educated middle classes (Zermeño 1978).

The student unrest of 1986-1987 is a good example also of the deterioration of the system in its capacity for political bargaining with key social actors. For instance, the constitutional premise to sustain a free, massive and public educational system is at odds not only with the lack of resources but also with the massification of the public institutions of higher education and the attendant low quality of instruction. Any attempt to modify the situation by increasing fees and creating admission quotas not only meets with resistance from students, parents, and some faculty members but also contradicts the Mexican Constitution, which calls for free public education and equality of opportunities for the lower classes.

Given the constitutional status of the university autonomy in Mexico and the role of universities in the overall political system, some analysts have argued that the university plays a very relevant role in the process of political legitimation of an authoritarian state (Levy 1979; 1986) and constitutes a key mechanism of the political socialization of Mexico's power elite (Camp 1986; Smith 1981, 95-102). This is so, in spite of the sporadic, although important, alterations of the national university-political regime relationships.

In this context of economic and fiscal crisis in Mexico the former President of the UNAM, Jorge Carpizo, produced in April 1986 a document suggestively entitled "Strengths and Weaknesses of the National University." In this document Carpizo outlined the problems to be tackled in 30 points and initiated a round of consultations in order to produce substantive reform. The first cluster of problems relates to students' low academic level, measured through (a) low grades students obtain in their admission exams to UNAM, (b) high student dropout exacebated by the fact that some students finish their coursework but do not graduate because they do not write their theses, (c) saturation of quota in some faculties due to amount of students entering with "automatic pass" (student coming from the UNAM-controlled high schools and constituting approximately 61 percent of the total of students admitted every year), and (d) the excessive number of "extraordinary" exams that students take to finish their course-work (i.e., remedial exams taken when the student fails to comply with evaluation requirements in a given course).

The second cluster of problems is related to the financing of education at UNAM. In spite of sky-rocketing costs of operating an institution of higher education in Mexico, the 300,000 undergraduate and graduate students at UNAM still only pay a nominal fee. The actual annual cost per student (in Mexican pesos) in 1986 at the *licenciatura* (B.A.) level was $327,428 and at graduate level was $311,986. On average, each student pays approximately 400 pesos per semester. This faction was considered too little in the context of shrinking university budgets; UNAM's budget declined from 0.33 percent of the GNP in 1978 to 0.18 percent of GNP in 1985.

The third cluster of problems relates to staff performance and distribution. Staff absenteeism is significant since many professors moonlight in other teaching or unrelated jobs, at least partly because of relatively low salaries. Some faculty appointments are made for "clientelist" or friendship reasons rather than university needs. Young professors without doctorates are the core of the faculty. In 1970 the University had 5,770 full-time professors; by 1980 there were slightly more than 30,000 full-time professors, representing a rate of increase well above the substantial increase in student enrollment during this period. While in 1982-1987 student enrollment remained constant, 6,236 new academic positions were created at UNAM. Some departments had 3:1 student-to-teacher ratios.

The fourth cluster of problems was seen to be political. On the one hand, University President Carpizo argued that there was too much bureaucracy within UNAM. Between 1972-1985, the student body grew 73.8 percent; the academic staff grew 95.5 percent, and the administrative staff (at all levels of the hierarchy) grew 159.1 percent. This administrative bureaucracy not only slows down university business but also hampers any attempts at university reform. On the other hand, Carpizo claimed that, given the political importance of UNAM in Mexico, many sectors and political parties consider it more a political arena than an academic institution. The notion of a "Popular University," Carpizo claimed, is not understood in its original meaning: an institution open to all social classes, promoting social mobility and social justice. Instead, it is considered as an arena for conflict around diverse issues and power struggles, some extraneous to university life.

To counteract this situation, several reforms were suggested, such as creating departmental exams, limiting the number of extraordinary exams a student can take, increasing user fees (and linking future fee increases to the rate of inflation), and increasing the control of academic and bureaucratic-administrative work.

When the reforms were approved by the University Council after a 16-hour session, September 11-12, 1986, they met with strong faculty and student opposition. There were a number of mass mobilizations, a major university strike, and an occupation of UNAM by the students. This constituted a setback for the President, who had to shelve the proposed reforms and to start a new round of negotiations in 1987. An agreement was reached that the reforms would be suspended and submitted for further consultation in June 1987 to the University Council with an enhanced representation of all the university sectors.

During 1988 there was a political "impasse" at UNAM. President Carpizo did not seek re-election, and by December 1988 a new President, José Sarukan, a noted scientist and member of the elite "National System of Researchers," was sworn in. He committed himself to convening the University Congress by the end of 1989 but stressed that the purposes, goals and content of the Congress should be eminently academic. At this point, the student movement had gone through a period of political and social hibernation, and the initiative was in the hands of the new University President and his staff.

On June 6, 1990, the University Congress convened by President Sarukan and attended by 848 delegates concluded its deliberations. Few changes were finally made to UNAM's structure and policies. The student movement lost in many of its demands, including the automatic pass for students coming from UNAM's high schools and keeping fees at their current low levels. There was agreement, however, to reduce the classroom size of undergraduate education and provide financial aid for needy students. Not a very flamboyant outcome for an university conflict and student movement of the magnitude outlined above.

Several key issues remain to be addressed by the new administration, including the quest for better salaries for university professors, the need to improve the quality of education in the context of massification, the pledge that higher education remains free of charge, and the fear of many professors that appointments would be terminated through a process of evaluating their academic performance. Indeed, the student unrest has been languishing, but if the economic crisis continues, and the students identify the figure of the new President of the University with the authoritarism of the government, there is a likelihood in the future that new demonstrations and strikes could occur. This, in turn, could paralyze academic activities and produce a stalemate like the one experienced by the previous university administration.

It is clear that the student unrest of 1986-1987 did not achieve the same national recognition and impact of its predecessor, the student movement of 1968. What happened is that in 1987 new channels of political participation and the expression of political opposition to the government were opened, and the students' action remained, by and large, an internal dynamic of the national universities, especially UNAM. The recent situation contrasts greatly with 1968 when students and workers engaged in struggle for a larger political agenda (see note 3).

Teachers' Movement

More than half a million primary and secondary school teachers went on strike on April 17, 1989, in Mexico City and in the states of Oaxaca, Chiapas, Zacatecas, Nuevo Leon, Guanajuato, Puebla and Michoacan. The strike was organized by the National Coordination of Educational Workers (CNTE) and challenged both the authority of the national teachers union (SNTE) and the authority of the Secretariat of Public Education (SEP). Their demands were twofold: a 100 percent increase in salaries (the government had offered 10 percent) and the democratization of the teachers union, which included the removal of the lifelong leader, moral guide and permanent counselor, Carlos Jonguitud Barrios, the head of the Revolutionary Vanguard. The teachers' strike was not an spontaneous act. Teachers' mobilizations against the lack of democracy in the teachers' union have a long history, but a turning point occurred in 1979 with the creation of CNTE. Ten years later demonstrations and teachers' strikes occurred, particularly in Mexico City, on February 15, and February 22-23, 1989.

On April 27, 1989, Jonguitud Barrios was obligated to resign all of the positions he held within the SNTE. A new General Secretary was appointed, but this change can be seen more as a reflection of the will of the government than as an expression of the will of the Revolutionary Vanguard or the CNTE.[7] That the new General Secretary, Elba Esther Gordillo Morales, is a woman is also important, at least symbolically, given the continued predominence of men in top leadership positions in the SNTE and the SEP, despite the fact that a large majority of educators in Mexico are women. Moreover, teachers obtained a salary increase of 25 percent, well above the ceiling imposed by the government's social pact between workers and business owners.

Due to federal labor law in Mexico, public employees are governed by labor legislation that severely restricts their right to association. Although many unions may exist, only one is recognized by the government. Therefore, in the 1970s and 1980s many independent unions started challenging the central corporatist unions by attempting to get their members elected to executive committees of locals or delegations of the corporatist unions. The CNTE, as a coordinating organization of many local groups, managed to mobilize close to 20 percent of the union membership by early 1980 (Pescador and Torres 1985). The CNTE strongholds were in the states of Chiapas (Street forthcoming) and Oaxaca (Cook 1989). One of the characteristics of this teachers' movement is that, as a coordination of regional movements or a set of alliances, CNTE has challenged the central power of institutions such as SNTE and the Secretariat of Public Education. In addition, CNTE has striven and achieved autonomy from political parties in spite of the fact that many leaders are affiliated to left wing parties. The key leaders are indeed closely related to the rank-and-file, sharing with them the suspicions that arise against any form of political organization.

The social class and gender of participants in this movement are important factors to consider. The active participation of women teachers (a majority, particularly in primary and preschool education) in the strikes and demonstrations and within the new leadership has been recognized by many commentators as a feature of the movement. The growing radicalization in salary demands from a working class perspective seems to be another feature (Street 1989; forthcoming; Hernández 1989a; 1989b). Finally, although using tactics of mobilization and confrontation with the officials of the union and the state bureaucracy, the movement has always attempted to win support inside the union and to dialogue with the government. These characteristics have challenged key elements of political domination in Mexico. As Street (1989) claims:

> [T]he struggles of the dissident teachers (between 1979-82) generated two processes within the bureaucratic apparatus of the state. One of these was undertaken by technocratic sectors that

re-elaborated the state discourse regarding the
rights of the teacher as a public employee. A
second one was realized by the dissident teachers
themselves who legally controlled Sections 22 and
7 of the SNTE and who, in taking decisions in their
capacity as workers, directly changed institutional
practices. The first result, fundamentally discursive,
strengthened the state apparatus as a system of
domination although allowing for small spaces for
opposition within it. The second one, fundamentally
based on practices, subverted the apparatus that the
teachers used for their own purposes as a system of
opposition. (p. 8--my translation)

Street has singled out three different competing projects in public
education in Mexico: "modernizing technocrats" (represented by the
Secretary of Public Education higher cadres), "controlling patrimonialists" (represented by the Revolutionary Vanguard of SNTE), and
"democrats" (represented by the CNTE) (Street forthcoming). Her
analysis has emphasized how the democrats have moved from being
merely a social force to become political actors in public education,
that is, decision-makers sharing responsibilities with the state.

Although Street presents a very valuable analytical model
that included social processes not subject to the institutionalized
rules of public policy, her interpretation of teachers' insurgency in
Mexico may be overly optimistic. In many respects, the democrats
have moved from a strategy (and theory) of resistance developed ten
years ago, to a strategy (and theory) of political struggle with
clearly conceived goals. Perhaps those goals are simply to initiate
political democracy rather than economic democracy in
Mexico--thus, bringing about a bourgeois revolution in public
education in Mexico. But indeed, the full implementation of the
premises of political democracy will imply the deterioration of
corporatist arrangements and could in fact produce a very significant
educational reform, revolving around the political control of the
school system. But, as Plank and Adams (1989, 2) have stated:
"Teachers and local educational administrators have far less power
in poor countries than they have in Japan or the United States, and
they seldom gain from educational reform."

The real gains of the democrats, beside having undermined the power of Revolutionary Vanguard, are still to be seen.[8] The new winds of "modernization" blowing in Mexico imply less relevant roles for working class organizations in the corporatist arrangement (Torres 1989b), and eventually, this may lead to the end of corporatism and profound political reaccommodations in the political system.

EDUCATIONAL REFORM, POLITICAL CONTROL, AND THE PROFESSIONALIZATION OR PROLETARIANIZATION OF TEACHERS

In this concluding section, two main issues will be addressed: (1) the connection between students' and teachers' movements and state modes of political control in Mexico and (2) the relationship between professionalization and proletarianization of teachers.

State Modes of Political Control

The crisis of the system of political domination in Mexico is also related to the fiscal crisis of the state and has its peculiar expression in the contradictions of policy formation in the educational arena. A principal challenge for the state, particularly after the heightened economic and fiscal crisis beginning in 1982, has been to keep the pace of educational investment at the high levels of the previous decade. In many ways, the fiscal, social, and political crisis in Mexico is also associated with the recent university student unrest and the school teachers' movement.

What can be learned from the students' unrest and the teachers' movement, and how are they related to changes in the patterns of institutionalization of corporatism in Mexico? The students' movement of 1986-87 was prompted by a proposal for university reforms. And although these reform proposals were stimulated by broader economic and political crises as they impinged on the university, the students' movement was not directed at these other phenomena nor even focused on matters such as state authoritarianism (as was the case with the student movement of 1968). Even though the traditional solution to corporatist crisis does not work in a period of financial austerity, most of the students' demands in 1986-87 were directed toward such solutions. Although the expansion of enrollment is no longer a guarantee for cooling off dissent and the cooptation of leadership, a basic thrust of the student movement was to stop the implementation of admission quotas and to obtain more resources for the university as well as more faculty positions. Furthermore, the demand for increasing participation in decision-making in the University contrasts with the overall modus operandi of a very centralized political system of control.

In the same vein, the teachers' movement showed that the confrontation between two corporatist actors (the SEP and the SNTE) gave room for the development of an independent teachers' coalition (CNTE), which has been characterized as democratic. However, there are serious contradictions within the new organization (CNTE), for example, between the old leadership that established its position during the initial teachers' movement of 1979 and a new, more radical leadership that emerged in the heat of the mobilizations of 1989 (Hernández 1989b, 57). If this new teachers' movement remains independent from the state, continues to gain ground at the regional and municipal levels, and remains politically united, it will challenge both the centralized mode of policy-making represented in the old corporatist negotiation between SEP and SNTE as well as state and corporate group authoritarianism (by demanding political democracy in union matters). In addition, if the radicalization in terms of gender and class demands of the movement is retained, all of this will have implications at the level of political and social control in Mexico.

The underlying theme of the contradictions in public education is found in the conflict between two modes of control in the public sector. The first one is based on the idea of *political control* as political agreements between meaningful social actors, at any cost within the corporatist network, and the second one is based on the idea of technical-*administrative control* and the administration of the crisis at a minimum cost. I would hypothesize that from the perspective of *political control*, the attempt is the *re-corporativization* of Mexico's politics following similar (although milder) nationalist principles than in the past. From the perspective of *technical-administrative* control the attempt is the *neo-corporativization* of Mexico's politics via a new neo-liberal market strategy, and perhaps a more plural political market.

The possibility of *re-corporativization* in Mexico (an adjustment of the rules with important balance of power held by the unions, perhaps less dependent on the state) or the *neo-corporativization* of Mexico's politics (i.e., a change in the rules of the game, incorporating the business community with a more preponderant role than labor) will have an impact in any policy domain, including education. However, the limits of the negotiation in state corporatism are apparent in the handling of conflicts with non-class organizations, including students and educated workers, such as teachers. The resolution of the demands resulting from the university student unrest of 1986-87 and the teachers' mobilization of 1989 offers some clues on the future of the logics of social control in Mexico and therefore on future educational policies of a corporatist state. It also offers some clues as to whether the very same model of corporatist negotiation will continue. It should be stressed, however, that although both social movements evidence dissatisfaction with the impact of the economic crisis, they seem to reflect less of a strong protest against the model of dependent-development than an attempt at re-accommodating forces in a very fluid political scenery.

If university reform reinvigorates the commitment toward equality of opportunity in undergraduate studies or if reforms of SEP and SNTE build new mechanisms of political participation in the relationships between the teachers union and state, then the political control project is prevailing. If any reform attempted in both domains is directed toward excellence, accountability and cost-effectiveness, hence admission quotas and significant increase in fees in the University or a thorough review of teachers' political representation and academic excellence, including their political rights and working conditions, then the technical-administrative project is dominant.

It has been argued that Mexican democracy is almost ungovernable (Whitehead 1979), and comparative political studies have demonstrated that corporativism has self-destructive tendencies that may lead to a crisis of legitimacy (Schmitter 1979, 4). The recent teachers' movement may justify these premises, particularly when the centrality of teachers' involvement in the system of political domination in Mexico needs no further justification (Pescador and Torres 1988; Raby 1989). Until now, a large corporatist teacher organization (SNTE) has behaved "responsibly" to the needs of the corporatist state. The fragmentation and regionalization of teachers' demands and the new "democratic" goals of the CNTE may prove damaging for the logics of social control of the state and political control of schooling (Sandoval Flores 1988).

There may be growing heterogeneity developing among teachers' rank-and-file, particularly in terms of political affiliation. Journalists have mentioned that many factions of the "democratic" teachers' movement may share the goals of the leftist Cardenista movement organized through the Partido Revolucionario Democrático (PRD), but the leadership presents a less monolithic ideological face when compared to the disciplined and PRI-oriented ideology of the leadership of Revolutionary Vanguard of SNTE. In addition, the lack of "self-esteem" stemming from a combination of poor working conditions and miserly salaries[9] may be undermining the identity of teachers as key actors in nation-building (Torres 1988). Moreover, with more political projects competing in public education (i.e., technocrats, patrimonialists, and democrats), the teachers' union leadership is less able to generate compliance and discipline the membership.

Professionalization and Proletarianization of Teachers

The policy tensions that may emerge between the alternative state modes of political control and the different political projects competing in public education will have important implications for Mexican teachers' work and class location. What are the relationships between professionalization and proletarianization?

From a Marxist theoretical perspective, Harris (1982, 70) argues that teachers can be identified with the proletariat:

> Teachers already resemble the proletariat in a large number of ways. Although salaried, they work for the wage form, and are contracted to perform agreed-on activities in return for agreed-on remuneration. They cannot select their clientele, and despite fairly intense struggle and some gains they have little occupational independence, little control over their labor process, and little access to the means of production--things which become clearly evident when teachers are compared with lawyers, doctors, or even university lecturers.

Although in comparative studies of sociology of professions, Harris' characterization may be challenged (e.g., Filson 1988; Ginsburg, Wallace and Miller 1988), his suggestion that teachers are similar to the proletariat but also differ in important ways with them (i.e., teachers are unproductive laborers and enjoy a marginal economic privilege because they possess some esoteric knowledge) could be useful as an starting point.

In Mexico, primary and secondary school teachers are not so distant, economically, from skilled unionized workers, and the wage differences seems to be narrowing. The social origins of teachers, however, are closer to peasants than workers; teaching has always been, particularly for men, a way out of rural Mexico and peasant life. The proletarianization of teachers is not new in Mexico, as measured by the vertical and horizontal corporativist controls of their actions, the increasing controls of the productive and pedagogical relationships in their marketplace (i.e., the Secretariat of Public Education), and their economic pauperization due to explicit policies of expanding education at the expense of teachers' real wages. Like most organized workers in the country, teachers have been very efficiently incorporated and controlled through corporatist mechanisms. In addition, there is enough evidence to argue that teachers lack autonomy, do not participate in the formulation or evaluation of educational policies, and are subject to more routine, segmented and, in some areas, more deskilled work than in the past (for instance, compared to the importance and autonomy of the rural teachers in the 1930s and 1940s).

The call for the professionalization of teachers has been justified as a means for upgrading teachers' qualification and enhancing self-esteem. In fact, any policy definition regarding teachers and teaching has, as its cornerstone, the notion of professionalization of the teachers, even if the consequences of the policies may have the opposite effect on at least some groups of teachers. In the last 10 years or so the debate about the origins, organization, role and function of the National Pedagogic University (UPN) has shown that whichever group prevails in imposing their own project of professionalization succeeds in the bureaucratic-political confrontation in public education (Pescador and Torres 1985). In short, there are as many projects of professionalization of the teaching profession as there are political-pedagogical projects represented by technocratic, patrimonialistic, and democratic teachers. While the "modernization" project proposed by technocrats or the clientelist policies promoted by patrimonialists have resulted in increasing the proletarianization and subordination of teachers, the model proposed by democratic teachers has still to show its main texture and dynamics.

The Mexican tradition of top-down approaches in educational reform may not be a feasible choice if teachers cannot be efficiently controlled in terms of labor discipline and salary demands in the short run. Similarly, the alternative of a bottom-up approach, through which teachers are striving to move from a strategy of resistance to a strategy of political participation in policy-making, may be considered a very risky undertaking by the state. There are still several possible scenarios for educational reform (Morales-Gómez and Torres 1990, chapter 6). However, the changes in the conditions of operation and patterns of corporativism or its eventual dismissal as a system of representation and control will continue to determine the scope, timing, rhetoric, and outcomes of educational reform in the near future.

NOTES

1. This chapter is related to my book with Daniel A. Morales-
    Gómez entitled *The State, Corporatist Politics and
    Educational Policy Making in Mexico* (New York: Praeger,
    1990). I would like to thank Iván Zavala and Mark Ginsburg
    for their comments on previous drafts of this chapter.

2. The National Union of Educational Workers (SNTE) was
    created by the government in 1943 with corporatist goals.
    The Revolutionary Vanguard was organized in 1972, during
    a period of conflicting relationships between the Mexican
    state and SNTE, and was sponsored by President Echeverria
    in an attempt to displace the previous leadership in the
    National Confederation of Workers (CNT). The leader of
    the Revolutionary Vanguard, Carlos Jonguitud Barrios,
    ruled through the Central Council of the SNTE, by
    controlling the appointments of the General Secretaries. He
    was a federal representative, senator and governor of the
    State of San Luis Pososi, and Director of the Social
    Insurance Institute of the Mexican government (ISSSTE)
    (Espinosa 1982). Until removed as a result of the teacher's
    movement in 1989, he had become the "lifelong leader,"
    "moral guide," and "permanent advisor" of SNTE.

3. The Student Movement, which developed between July and
    December 1968 in Mexico City, produced the most
    important social and political demonstrations since the
    Mexican Revolution. The origins of the movement were two
    independent, peaceful demonstrations, which ended up
    marching together toward the main government square on
    July 26, 1968. Before reaching their destination, they were
    attacked by police forces; the street battle left many people
    injured or dead. The following day students' strikes
    occurred in both the National Polytechnic Institute (IPN)
    and the National University (UNAM). On 30 July police
    occupied UNAM. The students' movement, born on August
    2nd with the leadership drawn from IPN and UNAM,

became a popular movement, with a leftist leadership not identifiable with any particular political party. At its peaks the movement counted on the growing participation of middle class "liberal" groups, independent trade unions, and workers and peasants groups. On October 2, 1968, a student demonstration was organized in Tlatelolco, the Square of Three Cultures, that mobilized 10,000 individuals. The army and the police charged and fired at the demonstrators, killing hundreds. Although the movement was dissolved by December 1968, it had important repercussions in Mexico's political life. In defying state authoritarianism, it activated the creation of independent unions, while showing the dissatisfaction of important segments of middle classes. Even the university unions are considered to be offspring of the movement of 1968. In addressing a larger agenda of political and economic democracy, the movement challenged PRI's supremacy and method of ruling, paving the way for the profound political reform of the Mexican system that took place a decade later. For further description and analysis, see Guevara Niebla (1978, 1983), Córdova (1979), and Zermeño (1978).

4.   The presidential elections of 1988 show the PRI achieving a meager 50.4 percent of the vote but more importantly ostensibly losing several regions in the center of the country, i.e., Mexico City and the states of Mexico, Michoacán, Morelos, and in Baja California Norte. In the elections of 1989, for the first time since 1929, the PRI conceded defeat, in 1989 to a right-wing party, PAN, in the elections for Governor in the state of Baja California Sur. Finally, the opposition created by the former Governor of Michoacán, Cuauhtemoc Cárdenas Solórzano has attracted to the Democratic Revolutionary Party (PRD) in 1988, and later on in a new coalition, the National Patriotic Front (FPN), many former PRI members, labor unions, popular organizations, and center-to-left oposition groups (Torres 1989b).

5.   The external debt has risen from 33.5 billion dollars in 1980
        to 108 billion in 1988 (Torres 1989b), and the politics of
        austerity of the government, besides the restriction in wage
        and salary increases through a process recently renewed in
        the "National Accord for Economic Recovery and Stability
        of Prices" in 1990, has produced a growing process of
        privatization of the public sector and has aimed at reducing
        union interference in economic planning. Perhaps the most
        illustrious example is the closing of the mining industry
        "Cananea" in August 1989, which in 1906 with its miners'
        strike and violent state repression that followed is said to
        have been the spark that initiated the Mexican Revolution.

6.   From a comparative perspective, it should be mentioned that
        there were simultaneously many student movements around
        the world during that time, for example, in France, Italy,
        China, North Korea, Argentina, Peru, Portugal, West
        Germany, Spain, Venezuela, and South Africa. In February
        1987 the Mexican student movement made contacts with the
        student movements of Italy, France, and Spain, but no
        coordination among them was established.

7.   Additional details can be found in Romero and Méndez
        (1989), Street (1989), Hernández (1989a, 1989b), and
        Campos et al. (1990).

8.   Regarding the political economy of teachers training in
        Mexico, many problems seem to remain. The President of
        the National University of Pedagogy, José Angel Pescador,
        has argued that: "There are four main problems regarding
        the teaching profession in Mexico. The first one is the
        conceptualization of teachers as subprofessionals. The
        second problem, resulting in part from the first one, is the
        lack of self-esteem among teachers. . . . A third problem is
        the salary conditions of the teachers, and the deterioration
        of their living standards, caused by inflation. A fourth
        problem has to do with teachers' training institutions. The
        National Pedagogic University, as the university of the
        teachers, has good facilities in its central campus in Ajusco,
        but does not necessarily have propitious conditions for

academic work in the other 74 campuses throughout
Mexico. And this is the situation at slightly more than 400
escuelas normales (teachers' training colleges) in Mexico,
including federal, state and privately controlled ones"
(Interviewed in Mexico City, August 27, 1989).

9.   In order for teachers' salaries (in real terms) to equal those
they received in 1976, it would have been necessary in 1989
for teachers to receive a salary increase of 300 percent
(Guzmán Ortiz and Vela Glez 1989, 49).

REFERENCES

Aboites, H. 1984. El salario del educador en México: 1925-1982. *Coyoacán. Revista Marxista Latinoamericana*, 8 (January--March): 63-110.

Aboites, H. 1986. Sesenta años del salario del educador (1925-1985). *Mexico. Los salarios de la crisis*. Cuadernos Obreros, 84-87. Mexico: CDESTAC.

Basañez, M. 1981. *La lucha por la hegemonía en México (1968-1980)*. Siglo XXI Editores. Mexico, DF: Siglo.

Bradenburg, H. 1964. *The making of modern Mexico*. Englewood Cliffs, NJ: Prentice-Hall.

Camp, R.A. 1980. *Mexico's leaders. Their education and recruitment*. Arizona: The University of Arizona Press.

Camp, R.A. (ed.). 1986. *Mexico's political stability: The next five years*. Boulder, CO: Westview Special Studies on Latin American and the Caribbean.

Campos, J.L. et al. 1990. *De las aulas a las calles*. Puebla: Informacion Obrera.

Cardoso, F.H. 1973. Associated dependent development: Theoretical and practical implications. In *Authoritarian Brazil: Origins, politics and future*, edited by Alfred Stepan, 142-78. New Haven: Yale University Press.

Carnoy, M. 1984. *The state and political theory*. Princeton, New Jersey: Princeton University Press.

Carnoy, M. & Levin, H. 1985. *Schooling and work in the democratic state*. Stanford: Stanford University Press.

Castañeda, M. 1987. *No somos minoría: La movilización estudiantil, 1986-1987*. Mexico: Editorial Extemporáneos.

Centro de Estudios Educativos. 1979. La educación y el cambio social: Resultados obtenidos, su explicación y posibles alternativas. In *La educación popular en América Latina: Avance o retroceso?*, 363-384. Mexico, D.F.: CEE.

Cook, M.L. 1989. Organizing opposition within official unions: The teachers movement in Oaxaca. Paper presented at a Research Workshop on Popular Movements and the Transformation of the Mexican Political System, Center for U.S.-Mexican Studies, University of California, San Diego, March 29-31.

Córdova, A. 1972a. *La formación del poder político en México*. Mexico: Ediciones ERA.

Córdova, A. 1972b. Las reformas sociales y la tecnocratización del estado Mexicano. *Revista Mexicana de Ciencias Políticas*, 17 (October-December): 61-92.

Córdova, A. 1979. *La política de masas y el futuro de la izquierda en México*. Mexico: ERA.

Eckstein, S. 1988. *The poverty of revolution. The state and the urban poor in Mexico*. Princeton, New Jersey: Princeton University Press.

Espinosa, J.A. 1982. Las dirigencias sindicales en la historia del SNTE. *Revista Historias*, (July-September): 67-105.

Evans, P. 1979. *Dependent development*. Princeton, New Jersey: Princeton University Press.

Filson, G. 1988. Ontario teachers' deprofessionalization and proletarianization. *Comparative Education Review*, 32, 3: 298-317.

Fuentes Molinar, O. 1983. *Política y educación en México*. Mexico: Nueva Imagen.

Gill, C.C. 1969. Education in changing Mexico. Washington, DC: Department of Health, Education and Welfare.

Ginsburg, M., Cooper, S., and Raghu, R. 1989. National and world-system explanations of educational reform. Paper presented at the Comparative and International Education Society Annual Meeting, Harvard University (31 March-April): 2.

Ginsburg, M., Wallace, G., and Miller, H. 1988. Teachers, economy and the state: An English example. *Teaching and Teacher Education*, 4, 4: 317-37.

Gough, I. 1979. *The political economy of the welfare state*. London: Macmillan.

Gramsci, A. 1980. *Selections from prison notebooks*. Edited and translated by Quintin Hoare and Geoffrey Nowell Smitt. New York: International Publishers.

Guevara Niebla, G. 1978. Antecedentes y desarrollo del movimiento de 1968. *Cuadernos Políticos*, 17 (Julio-Septicmbrc): 7-33.

Guevara Nicbla, G. 1983. *El saber y el poder*. Culiacán, Sinaloa: Universidad Autónoma de Sinaloa.

Guzmán Ortiz, E., and Vela Glez, J. 1989. Maestros 1989: Crisis, democracia y más Salario. *El Cotidiano* (July-August): 44-49.

Harris, K. 1982. *Teachers and classes. A Marxist analysis*. London: Routledge and Kegan Paul.

Hernández, L. 1989a. Maestros: Jaque al Rey. *El Cotidiano*, 28 (March-April): 30-35.

Hernández, L. 1989b. Maestros: Del gambito de dama al jaque mate. *El Cotidiano*, 30 (July-August): 55-58.

Huntington, S. 1968. *Political order in changing societies*. New Haven: Yale University Press.

Kaufman, R. 1977. Mexico and Latin America authoritarianism. In *Authoritarianism in Mexico*, edited by José Luis Reyna and Richard Weinert, 194-228. Philadelphia: ISHS.

Latapí, P. 1976. *Política educativa y valores nacionales*. Mexico: Editorial Nueva Imagen.

Latapí, P. 1980. *Análisis de un sexenio de educación en México, 1970-1976*. Mexico: Editorial Nueva Imagen.

Leal, J.F. 1975a. The Mexican state: 1915-1973. A historical interpretation. *Latin American Perspectives*, 5: 48-80.

Leal, J.F. 1975b. *Mexico: Estado, burocracia y sindicatos*. Mexico: Editorial El Caballito.

Lehmbruch, G., and Schmitter, P. (eds.) 1982. *Patterns of corporatist policy-making*. Beverly Hills: Sage.

Levy, D. 1979. *University and government in Mexico: Autonomy in an authoritarian system*. New York: Praeger.

Levy, D. 1986. *Higher education and the state in Latin America: Private challenges to public dominance*. Chicago: University of Chicago Press.

McGinn, N., and Street, S. 1984. Has Mexican education generated human or political capital? *Comparative Education*, 20, 3: 323-338.

Morales-Gómez, D.A. and Torres, C.A. 1990. *The state, corporatist politics and educational policy-making in Mexico 1970-1988*. New York: Praeger.

Muñoz Izquierdo, C. 1981. Análisis e interpretación de las políticas Educativas: El Caso de México 1930-1980). In *Sociologia de la educación: Corrientes contemporáneas*, edited by G. González and Carlos A. Torres, 389-445. Mexico, D.F.: Centro de Estudios Educativos.

Offe, C. 1984. Societal preconditions of corporatism and some current dilemmas of democratic theory. *Working Paper Nº 14*. South Bend, Indiana: The Helen Kellogg Institute for International Studies, University of Notre Dame.

Padua, J. 1988. Presiones y resistencias al cambio en la educación superior de México. *Estudios Sociológicos de El Colegio de Mexico*, 16: 129-178.

Paz, O. 1984. *El ogro filantrópico*. Mexico, D.F.: Cuadernos de Joaquín Mortíz.

Pereyra, C. 1979. Estado y sociedad. In *Mexico hoy*, edited by Pablo G. Casanova and Enrique Florescano, 289-305. XXI Editores. Mexico, DF: Siglo.

Pereyra, C. 1981. Estado y movimiento obrero. *Cuadernos Políticos*, (April-June): 35-42.

Pescador, J.A. 1989a. *El esfuerzo del sexenio 1976-1982 para mejorar la calidad de la educación básica*. Mexico: Ediciones de la Universidad Pedagógica Nacional.

Pescador, J.A. 1989b. *Aportaciones para la modernización educativa*. Mexico: Ediciones de la Universidad Pedagógica Nacional.

Pescador, J.A., and Torres, Carlos A. 1985. *Poder político y educación en México*. Mexico, DF: UTHEA.

Pescador, J.A. 1988. The educational role of the state in developing countries: The case of Mexico. In *Changing structures of political power, socialization and political education*, edited by Bernhard Claussen and Suna Kili, 67-87. Frankfurt am Main and New York: Peter Lang.

Plank, D., and Adams, D. 1989. Death, taxes, and school reform: Educational policy change in comparative perspective. *Administrator's Notebook*, 33, 1: 33.

Raby, D. 1989. Ideología y construcción del Estado: La función política de la educación moral en México, 1921-1935. *Revista Mexicana de Sociología*, 51, 220: 305-320.

Romero, M.A., and Méndez, L. 1989. SNTE, CNTE y modernización educativa. *El Cotidiano*, 28 (March-April): 40-43.

Sandoval Flores, E. 1988. La construcción cotidiana de la vida sindical de los maestros de primaria. *Revista Latinoamericana de Estudios Educativos*, 18, 1: 105-115.

Schmitter, P. 1974. Still the century of corporatism. In *The new corporatism: Social political structures in the Iberian world*, edited by F.B. Pike and T. Strich, 85-131. South Bend, Indiana: University of Notre Dame Press.

Schmitter, P. 1979. Speculations about the prospective demise of authoritarian regimes and its possible consequences. *The Wilson Center Working Papers*, No. 60. Washington, DC: Woodrow Wilson Center.

Smith, P.H. 1981. *Los Laberintos del Poder*. Mexico: Colegio de Mexico.

Stepan, A. 1978. *The state and society in Peru in comparative perspective*. Princeton, NJ: Princeton University Press.

Street, S. 1989. El magisterio democrático y el aparato burocráico del estado. *Foro Universitario*, 89 (January-April): 7-24.

Street, S. (In press). *Maestros en movimientos: Transformaciones de la burocracia estatal 1978-1982*. Mexico: Nueva Imagen.

The Wall Street Journal. 1986. Hard times hit Mexico's state university (31 October): 3.

Therborn, G. 1984. Classes and states. Welfare state developments, 1881-1891. *Studies in Political Economy*, 13: 7-41.

Therborn, G. 1986. Karl Marx returning: The welfare state and neo-Marxist, corporatist and statist theories. *International Political Science Review*, 7, 2: 131-164.

Therborn, G. 1987. Does corporatism really matter? The economic crisis and issues of political theory. *Journal of Public Policy*, 7, 3: 259-284.

Torres, C.A. 1987. Corporativism and higher education in Mexico: Recent developments. Paper delivered at the World Congress of Comparative Education, Rio de Janeiro, Brazil, July 6-10.

Torres, C.A. 1988. Political culture and state bureaucracy in Mexico: The case of adult education. *International Journal of Educational Development*, 9, 1: 53-68.

Torres, C.A. 1989a. The capitalist state and public policy formation. Framework for a political sociology of educational policy making. *British Journal of Sociology of Education*, 10, 1: 81-102.

Torres, C.A. 1989b. The Mexican state and democracy: The ambiguities of corporatism. *Politics, Culture and Society*, 2, 4: 563-586.

Weiler, H. 1983. Legalization, expertise and participation: strategies of compensatory legitimation in educational policy. *Comparative Education Review*, 27: 259-277.

Weiler, H. 1985. The political economy of educational planning. In *Educational planning in the context of the current development problems*, edited by H. Weiler. Paris: UNESCO-IIEP.

Whithead, L. 1979. Why Mexico is ungovernable--almost. *Working Papers 54*. Washington, DC: The Woodrow Wilson Center.

Zermeño, S. 1978. *México: Una democracia utópica; El Movimiento estudiantil de 1968*. Siglo XXI Editores. Mexico: Siglo.

THE SCENARIO OF THE SPANISH EDUCATIONAL REFORM

Sara Morgenstern de Finkel

At the present time the reform bill known as the LOGSE (General Organic Law for the Educational System) is under discussion in Parliament, having already won the assent of the Congress of Deputies though not as yet of the Senate. It is anticipated that its initial implementation will begin in the academic year 1991-1992. This bill is the product of a protracted process beginning in 1983 which, when completed, will put an end to a twenty-year period during which the Law of 1970, which reformed the educational system at the time, was in force.

In contrast to the 1970 Law the present reform is not concerned with the university, whose organization was modified by the University Reform Law of 1986. As we shall see later, in a country so deeply attached to bureaucratic legalism, the asynchrony between the University reform and the reform at the other educational levels creates a serious problem for the future viability of school reform, namely, the initial training of the teachers.

This educational reform is to be embodied, according to the manifest intentions of the Socialist government, into a consensual law. Almost the whole political spectrum, with the notable exception of the conservatives (Partido Popular), have agreed with the fundamental ideas of the project. In spite of their comfortable majority in Parliament, the Socialists reiterated on several occasions their commitment to generate broad support for the reform. The Minister of Education has been able to reach agreements with the seventeen autonomous governments, political parties, and the trade unions. Consensus has been achieved by an appeal to the modernization of the educational system as an implicit and explicit requirement for the final integration of Spain into Europe. For instance, in the preamble of the "White Book on the Educational Reform," the Minister of Education stressed that: "The culmination of the process of integration of our country into the institutions of the European Community have placed us within an environment wider than the national one, an environment which we share with other countries and within which the right of every citizen to a full mobility, reinforced by the perspective of the common market, as well as the consequences thereof, affect us all. Hence the requirement that our studies, training and degrees should increasingly conform to a quantitative and qualitative minimum" (Ministerio de Educación 1989, 4).

The perspectives being opened by the European Common Market constitute, no doubt, an important reason to reorganize the educational system. Spain's incorporation into the European Community, after arduous negotiations, is an indisputable accomplishment of the Socialist government. Whether the conditions and rhythms accepted by Spain will be favorable to the country is open to discussion, given the high social costs in terms of the industrial reconversion that had to be undertaken, the quotas on the agricultural and fishing products, not to mention the political cost of NATO membership. But it is undeniable that entrance into the European Community was an economic objective of a great magnitude, strongly supported by the financial and industrial capital, since otherwise their accumulation capacity would have been threatened.

At the same time, joining the European Community meant,

and still means, a challenge to leave behind the remains of Francoism that had kept Spain in isolation for so long. In this context only rarely has an appeal been made to the history of Spain, as if the parties' leaders fear bringing back to life the demons of the Civil War. This is regrettable in the case of the Socialist government and the left in general, since it was precisely the working class, both Anarchist and Socialist, that historically had created exemplary educational institutions, libraries, and publishing houses that were in the avant-garde of similar movements in Europe.

The presence of institutions such as the Council of Europe, the Organization of Economic Cooperation and Development, and the European Social Fund has had a perceptible influence on educational rhetoric, giving rise to new linguistic usages regarding the inevitability of technical solutions to problems, which in reality are open to different political options. It is likely that an in-depth analysis of the rhetoric contained in the discourse of the educational reform would evaporate the consensus. Subjects such as equal opportunities, comprehensiveness, relations with the world of work, have different meanings according to the class perspective adopted to analyze them. At what point the implementation of the future reform will break the consensus is difficult to predict.

SOME THEORETICAL CONSIDERATIONS ON THE EDUCATIONAL REFORM

An educational reform can be analyzed from different points of view, whether economic, curricular, or organizational. The sociological perspective excludes none of these dimensions, but requires a different approach, i.e., a reading of the relations of power. This means that a reform will become sociologically intelligible for us if we are able to understand which social forces are promoting it and whom it benefits. Any policy expresses class relationships, in other words, relations of power. Consequently, the dominant educational policy in a social formation is not just that which is planned by the dominant classes with the aim of maintaining and securing their power, but the one these classes are able to put into effect in the face of opposition by the subordinate classes. Although the vast majority of the existing literature, including Marxist literature, is mainly focused on the educational policies promoted by the dominant classes, it should not be inferred from this that the educational practices are only of their exclusive concern. Subordinate classes have their own educational policy proposals as well, although less likely to be explicit and structured and, under prevailing social relations, unlikely to have the backing of the state and the educational system.

Albeit class analysis constitutes the conceptual horizon for evaluating the meaning and orientation of a reform, some qualifications are called for. In the first place, if hegemony is rooted in the relations of production, it does not follow that it is their immediate expression. Following Gramsci (1971, 104) "politics in fact is at any given moment the reflection of the tendencies of development in the structure, but it is not necessarily the case that these tendencies must be realized." Hence, not all political activities, including education, can be considered as organic ones, i.e., linked to the interests of a fundamental class. The possibility of political mistakes or of lack of efficiency must not be discarded beforehand. Class power is not expressed, nor can it be expressed, directly through an educational policy. The state is not an instrument in the hands of the dominant classes, but since it exists in a class-divided society to be sustained it must preserve (or be seen to preserve) the unity and cohesion of the society, while also guaranteeing the conditions of capital accumulation.

In addition, not all social agents involved in an educational reform have a clear-cut class situation. Teachers' class position, for instance, has been hotly debated, and it is often said they and other intellectuals occupy an ambiguous or contradictory location within the class structure. Moreover, educational reform entails ideological aspects, such as religious instruction, national identification or sexist content, which are not reducible to class interests.

Two additional points should be briefly mentioned. First, attention must be given to the problem of efficiency, which is seldom taken into consideration, since it is attributed with functionalist and Taylorist connotations. It is a mistake, both politically and conceptually, to underestimate the sociological analysis of the technical problems involved in education or other social changes. Financing, regionalization, cost-effectiveness of the various programs, scientific content of instruction, are problems that should not be trivialized. Second, the political efficiency of education is usually analyzed around two polarized situations: consent and resistance. But between them, there is an often neglected third possibility, that of apathy, which shows traits of both but does not generate an alternative of its own (Finkel 1988).

THE CONFIGURATION OF THE EDUCATIONAL SYSTEM SINCE 1970

The reform proposed by the present Spanish government will substitute for the General Education Law (GEL) of 1970, which, although minimally modified to make it compatible with post-dictatorship legislation, is essentially still in force. The GEL, passed under the decisive influence of the Opus Dei, has thus been in operation for almost two decades, fourteen years of which have been under democratically elected governments.

The political influence of the Opus Dei became apparent in the late 1950s, once the Franco regime decided to alter the economic policy of autarchy that had kept the country in a state of permanent stagnation. It was during this period that U.S. economic aid began in exchange for military bases. This agreement helped weaken the position of Falange in Franco's government, since in addition to the low technical qualifications of this group, its overtly fascist nature was seen as a political embarrassment for the U.S. Although the Falangists were not totally excluded from power, they were replaced in the major Ministries by young religious technocrats, many of whom were members of the Opus Dei.

The ideology of the Opus Dei--an anticipation of that of the New Right--was a combination of Catholic traditionalism, political authoritarianism, and instrumental rationality, a synthesis that provided a modernizing appearance to the dictatorship. The educational ideology of the Opus Dei was expressed in a total rejection of nineteenth century Spanish Liberalism, associated with its three main enemies: Freemasonry, Socialism and the ILE (Institución Libre de Enseñanza).[1] But the Opus Dei viewed itself not as a mere response to these heresies; it had the mission of coping with modernity as well by offering a new outlet to the tension between religion and the world.

When finally the Opus Dei gained control of the Ministry of Education in 1968, the Spanish economic context had undergone a significant change. The stabilization and liberalization plan of 1959 was a turning point in the development of the economy. It was successful in dealing with chronic monetary and fiscal problems, in reducing internal and external government controls and in paving the way for a considerable influx of foreign capital. Foreign currency earnings from tourism and the repatriation of savings by emigrant workers in the countries of the EEC also aided economic expansion. During the years 1962-1970 Spain experienced one of the highest rates of growth among the OECD countries. Industrial development accelerated under the impulse of low wages, a growing domestic market, and the integration into the international capitalist economy. The result was a transformation of the work force, which took three main forms: (1) massive migration to the urban centers, (2) rapid industrialization, and (3) growth of a service sector no longer linked to an inflated bureaucracy but to tourism and urban life (Soler 1969, 12; Tamames 1977, 382).

The educational system was not able to cope with the new demands resulting from the changing social structure nor able to satisfy the requirements for a qualified labor force envisaged in the First Development Plan (1963-67). In this context the reform of education began to take shape in 1970 when the General Education Law was passed. It was preceded by a Ministerial report under the title of "El Libro Blanco" (The White Paper) (Ministerio de Educación 1969), which was widely publicized in the media at the time, although its discussion was restricted to the corporate organs of the Franco regime. The report proposed the framework that was the basis for the 1970 law. Whatever the shortcomings and limitations of the Law, what cannot be denied is that it represented a major effort to modernize the obsolete structures of Spanish education.

The 1970 law was conceived as a global and integrated plan, embracing the different educational levels. It established free education for all up to the age of fourteen. It replaced the previous dual track system by which students at the age of ten either remained in primary education or went to the secondary school. It emphasized improving the qualitative aspects of teaching, including teachers' training. It helped to overcome the prevailing schoolish view of education by connecting it to the broader issues posed by the general evolution of labor and society. The 1970 law thus contained contradictory aspects. The law embodied, on the one hand, a modernizing and, to a certain extent, a democratizing effort, and, on the other hand, the law signaled a move to a new authoritarian ethos based on bureaucratic expertise.

The more traditional Francoist sectors opposed the reform plans from the beginning, partly because the reforms were aimed at, at least rhetorically, guaranteeing equal opportunities for everybody. To implement these policies a deep transformation of the educational system would have been necessary, affecting in particular the privileges enjoyed by private schools. If the White Paper is compared with the final text of the Law, the conflicts among the different political groups within the regime can be easily inferred (Cuadrado 1970). The White Paper proposed that state support should be limited to those private institutions that exercised a social function. The Bill included as well fiscal reform designed to make education really free. The Organic Cortes, however, did not pass this decisive aspect of the Bill, thus limiting the scope of the reform even before it was put into practice (Puelles 1980, 417-422).

It is generally accepted that the reform introduced by the Law of 1970 was the educational counterpart of the Development Plan in the sense that it was aimed at the modernization and extension of educational services. This was explicitly emphasized in all official statements of the time, but we may well consider it to be only a half-truth. The other half resides in the fact that, whatever its technical improvements, the reform was at the same time an important part of a political project to ensure the perpetuation after the dictatorship of the same structure of class power. In this sense, we miss, within the copious extant literature on the reform, an analysis taking into account the socio-political unrest prevalent in Spain during the 1960s, thus transcending the strictly economic or educational explanatory framework. Even those authors critical of the reform tend to view it in terms of a mechanical correspondence between needs of accumulation and needs of human resources

(Bozal and Paramio 1974/75; 1977; Fernández de Castro 1963).

Indeed, between the years 1962 and 1966, the country witnessed a succession of mass strikes, carried out by a new working class that had found new forms of consciousness and organization. By 1966 the Workers' Commissions ("Comisiones Obreras") were so well organized that the regime proved totally unable, even through severe repressive means, to prevent the growth of the movement. In those same years, a few timid actions of a limited scope, organized by the teachers, occurred outside the framework of the official trade unions under the control of Falange. The universities were also during the 1960s focal points of political unrest, with persistent student protests on the streets. The conflicts reached their climax in 1968, parallelling those in France, Mexico, and the United States. The Spanish movement shared with them an anti-authoritarian and anti-capitalist ethos, but it had an additional and more concrete aim: overthrowing the dictatorship of Franco. The students' protests led in the end to the resignation of the Minister of Education, who was replaced by Villar Palasí, the architect of the 1970 educational reform.

Under those circumstances it was necessary for the dominant class to map out a political strategy for the future, not just based on mere repression but on a new form of social equilibrium grounded on an enlarged consensus. The new strategy could work if two conditions were fulfilled: (1) isolating the workers' movement, and (2) providing the middle classes, and particularly their more educated sectors, with new political outlets.

The educational reform of 1970 was an important part of this strategy. Its proponents did not hesitate in identifying it as a "passive revolution," designed to prevent conflicts that loomed dangerously ahead. That legitimation was the number one priority, more important than modernization or adjusting to the economic demands, is evidenced by the fact that neither a policy for expanding technical careers nor a reorientation of the university enrollment was implemented. Briefly, the main target of the reform was a political one, namely, the attempt to neutralize social mobilization by means of three interrelated policies: (1) expansion of access to all levels of education; (2) development of a meritocratic system, where selection would be rooted in the educational credentials; and (3) as a consequence of the needs posed by (1) and (2), an increase in the size of both the teaching force and a more highly trained educational bureaucracy.

Obviously, the main beneficiaries of these policies were bound to be the middle classes, who were in a position to press for greater demands in terms of more jobs and more educational opportunities for their offspring. It is not by chance that university education experienced a remarkable quantitative growth, the number of students tripling within a period of fifteen years (1970-84). The new strategy would only make sense if the threatening political radicalization of large sections of the middle classes could be made to give way to a technocratic reformism. This shift, however, did not become visible until several years after Franco's death, when democratic processes were established in Spain.

During the last years of the dictatorship political mobilizations increased in number and strength. Teachers particularly confronted the regime but more from a political rather than a professional perspective. One should not forget that many participants were among the most active elements in the semi-legal opposition, many of them were associated with the Communist and Socialist parties. However, we must not lose sight of the fact that corporate self-interest counted as well, since the bulk of the activists were the worst paid, i.e., those working in the private schools, as well as the PNN ("Profesores no munerarios" or temporary, non tenured staff) at the secondary level in state education (Robinson 1983, 330-331).

Starting in 1971 a teachers' movement began slowly to consolidate and finally crystallized into the "Alternative for Teaching." Among the main proposals of the Alternative were: (1) compulsory schooling between the ages of four and sixteen; (2) defining education as state-provided public service and gradually phasing out subsidies for private schooling; (3) tuition-free education at all levels; (4) curricular changes aimed at a rational and scientific education; (5) academic freedom; (6) bilingual education in Galicia, Catalonia, and the Basque country and a greater recognition of the values of the various regional cultures; (7) a single unified school system replacing the dual track systems; (8) democratic management of schooling with the participation of teachers, pupils, and parents; and (9) non selectivity in access to a university education (Seminano de Pedagogía de Valencia 1975; Universidad de Madrid 1974-76; Bozal 1977).

In education, as in other spheres of social life, the transition from the Franco dictatorship to democratic politics was characterized by a policy of moderation and compromise. A consensus was reached on certain historically conflictive issues such as the relationship between the State and the Catholic Church, the control of the regional educational systems by the autonomous governments, and bilingual education in both Castilian and either Catalan, Basque or Galician. However, other contemporary problems, including the education of teachers, which could have become sources of political dispute, were overlooked. It is symptomatic that in spite of the frequent appeals for a democratization of the school, no government since Franco's death has dared to tackle the problem of renewing teacher education. For primary teachers the 1971 teacher education syllabus is still in force. For the secondary and technical teachers practically no pedagogical training exists and the same can be said for teachers of infant, adult, and special education. From a political and practical point of view it is imperative that reforms of the school system be linked to changes in the content and form of teacher preparation. Teachers' skills and attitudes are central to the implementation or nonimplementation of any school reform.

THE SOCIALIST GOVERNMENT

At the beginning of the democratic transition many people were afraid that if the Socialist Party acceded to the government, there would be continuous conflict with the old Francoist forces who held positions in the various state apparatuses. In 1982 the Socialists won the parliamentary elections with an absolute majority. They repeated in 1986 with a slightly reduced, but still an absolute, majority but a much less ambitious program. In 1982 there were great expectations "for a change" ("por el cambio"), which was the main slogan for the electoral campaign. This referred to what was thought of as realistic, social-democratic goals, i.e. reforms of the state administration, social services, health and education, similar to the partial successes achieved by many local governments, where the socialists had been in office since 1980.

During the eight years of Socialist administration the Spanish economy grew appreciably, with an annual rate as high as 5 percent. This situation, together with the prevailing political stability, attracted an inflow of foreign investment, greater (in terms of percentage increase) than in any other European country. The road was not an easy one, since it was necessary to convert unprofitable industries, almost all of them state owned and with a great number of workers. This added appreciably to unemployment, reaching a high of 20 percent; even today the registered unemployed number is 15.31 percent of the labor force (INEM 1990).

Up to 1988 the growth of the economy took place within a context of a relative stability although with serious localized social conflicts. However, starting in that year, the class-conscious trade unions, especially the Union General de Trabajadores (UGT or General Workers' Union) and the Comisiones Obreras (CCOO or Worker's Commission) objected to bearing most of the weight of the conversion process. They demanded a greater share in the distribution of the economic surplus, whose main beneficiary in the present model of accumulation is financial capital. In fact, according to the latest official statistics, the growth in the GNP did not result in an improvement in the lot of the workers; indeed, the salary component of the GNP diminished slightly during 1985-89 from 46.2 percent to 45.8 percent (*Instituto Nacional de Estadística* 1989, 353). Moreover, the official opinion surveys show that 86 percent of the respondents consider wealth to be unjustly distributed in Spain, although nearly 30 percent declare the economic situation of their household to have perceptibly improved during the past three years (*Revista Española de Investigaciones Sociológicas* 1989, 227-231).

In terms of macro-structural orthodox indicators, the Spanish economy shows signs of health. However, the political costs might eventually become too high for the Socialist Party, although the situation is very fluid. By the end of 1989, for example, a virtual rupture with UGT, intimately linked with the party since its inception, seemed inevitable. In a report on social policy the UGT did not find a single positive achievement in the last legislature in terms of improvement in the quality of the public services, housing, or social welfare. The UGT criticized the persistent high levels of unemployment and the fact that 26 percent of the new jobs were temporary, viewing these problems as a consequence of the Socialist government's policy, which was described as "developmentalist, technocratic and dogmatic in its defense of the values of the market, de-regulatory in its labor policy and the cradle of a new Eldorado for foreign capital" (UGT 1989, 8). By the middle of 1990, however, the relations between the government and the trade unions improved as manifested in the resumption of a dialogue on social matters. Future relations are difficult to predict, since in the next two years it is likely that they will be affected by the completion of the process of access to the European Common Market.

In spite of the conflicts, the electoral majority of the Socialist Party has not substantially decreased. Neither the political forces on the right nor those on left have been able to seriously challenge the Socialists, although in the last general elections, the United Left coalition increased their share to around 9 percent of the total vote. The more visible consequence is an increase in the electoral abstention, which is the correlate of demobilization and political apathy, a subject of crucial importance in understanding the context of future educational reform.

EDUCATIONAL PROPOSALS OF THE SOCIALIST PARTY

The Socialist Party's electoral program on education included the development of the public sector (held back under Francoism); the promotion of the teaching profession, equating their salaries with those of the rest of the state officials of comparable qualifications; the reform of all levels of schooling in order to ensure equal opportunities; and democratic participation at all levels of the system from the Ministry itself down to the schools and faculties.

In order to implement a program of this magnitude it was obviously necessary both to have access to considerable economic resources and to be able to count on the support of social agents, those technically qualified as well as those politically identified with the project. Neither of the requisites seemed to be in place. On the one hand, the educational proposals, formulated in terms of a Welfare State approach, were in open contradiction with the general economic policy, defined in terms of a rigorous neo-liberal scheme. On the other, it was unthinkable that the very same officials of the dictatorship, particularly those belonging to the higher corps, would be willing to dismantle the authoritarian structure of the educational system.

With respect to the latter, three alternative possibilities were open: (a) leave everything as it was; (b) remove a few technical officials from key posts to avoid their interference with the political decisions; and (c) convert state functionaries to real civil servants, making professional competence the prime consideration in appointment, retention, and promotion rather than granting life tenure in the post. The Socialist Ministry adopted a hybrid, compromising stance, retaining most of the distinctive features of the Francoist bureaucracy: corporativism, life posts, slightly modified "oposiciones" for access to teaching jobs, bureaucratization of merit, etc. More than 4,000 new positions were added to the old and new technocracy formed by the Opus Dei. Most of these were not new technical positions, but were temporary transfers to tenured teachers, because strangely enough the Administration only recruits non-functionary personnel under exceptional circumstances, no matter how bright they might be. The new positions were assigned the responsibility for planning, managing, and developing the reforms under way. Many of these recent recruits were active in the opposition groups of the 1970s, for example, in the pedagogical renewal movements and in the Socialist trade union. It is still to be seen whether they will be coopted or whether they will manage to stay loyal to the old struggles.

The university was the first objective of the projected reforms. Supposedly, one of the main aims was to guarantee full autonomy with respect to teaching and research for each of the universities in order to overcome the almost Orwellian uniformity among them and to allow a creative development of alternatives. In practice, however, the legal bases for this reform stipulated almost everything from the organs of government and representation to the procedure for selecting teaching staff.

The complexity of bureaucracy is also likely to be a major obstacle for the success of the reforms at the primary and secondary levels. In 1985 an experimental reform plan of secondary education was launched in a few selected schools whose teaching staff volunteered to participate. However, this project was later substantially modified, without any explanation, let alone justification of the changes, when a new staff assumed responsibility for the plan.

In 1987 a new project for educational reform was disclosed by Minister José Maria Maravall, which contained the following aspects: (a) development of infant education from age four; (b) extension of compulsory schooling age from the present fourteen to sixteen; (c) restructuring of secondary education to eliminate the present social class-linked streaming represented by the two unique options of either a general "Bachillerato" or "Formación Profesional" (Vocational Education); (d) expansion of the range of curricular options and addition of new contents related to personal and social development (Ministerio de Educación y Ciencia 1987, 1988). The project involved a reorganization of the educational system, implying the creation of a compulsory secondary cycle for twelve to sixteen year olds and a post-compulsory two-year cycle, with three main modalities of "Bachillerato": (a) Human and Social Sciences, (b) Natural and Health Sciences, and (c) Technical. The Technical Bachillerato was to consist of two varieties, Technical-Industrial and Administration and Management; Technical-Professional training outside the "Bachillerato" was also foreseen.

CONFLICT BETWEEN TEACHERS AND THE GOVERNMENT

As the reform proposals were being developed Minister Maravall was replaced in July 1988 by Javier Solana, who hastened to declare that he was going to maintain the reform project. This shift in leadership occurred because Maravall's authority had been seriously eroded during the teachers' strike of 1988 and the secondary school student conflicts of 1987. The 1988 teachers' strike is significant both as an indicator of consent towards future reforms and in terms of the state's role in the professionalization or proletarianization of teachers. All teachers unions, from left to right, jointly called a strike with two basic demands: (a) increased salary and (b) improved working conditions (length of the working day, responsibility in case of accident, transfers, etc.). The second part of the platform was easily accepted by the Ministry and did not give rise to conflicts. The salary demands, on the contrary, revealed many contradictions, both from the left-wing trade unions and from the government.

Three months before the beginning of the strike, in December 1987, the first elections took place for the teachers to choose their union representatives. Ten years had elapsed since the massive strike of 1977, when an agreement to hold elections had first been reached. In the 1987 elections at least eight different trade unions took part, and the results varied somewhat by teaching level and/or region. With these and other qualifications, the global results allow us to infer that little more than half the Spanish teachers of primary and secondary schools opted for trade unions, which define themselves as classist and progressive, in contrast with those propounding a "politically independent" corporativism. In the university the tendency was quite the contrary but with a much higher level of abstention; the UGT, the trade union related to the Socialist Party, was defeated.

At the beginning, in March 1988, the strike was adhered to by more than 90 percent of the staff at the primary and secondary levels (235,000 teachers) and, as mentioned before, summoned by all trade unions, including the UGT. From the perspective of the various unions their salary demands merely called for the Socialist Party to honor one of the electoral promises, that teachers' salaries should match those of other state officials of comparable qualifications. The negotiations were hard and were marked aggressiveness on both sides; at one point the Minister stubbornly refused to meet the teachers' representatives. In the midst of protests and street demonstrations the leadership of all of the teachers' unions (with the exception of Comisiones Obreras [Workers' Commissions], the organization connected with the Communist Party) accepted a pre-agreement on salary increases to be distributed over two years. A few days later the pre-agreement was massively rejected in a country-wide referendum with 90 percent of the teachers participating, 78 percent of whom voted negative. At the beginning of the summer holidays, however, counting on the seasonal demobilization of the teachers, the government decided to approve by Royal decree the basis of the pre-agreement.

We should note first that the Socialist Party's relationship with teachers was not strong enough to secure their consent to the "new educational order" presumably implied by the reforms. In fact, one of the points more widely discussed by the national press in this period was the inviability of the reforms without the support of the teachers. Second, most of the teachers' union leaders were shown to be out of step with their membership as evidenced by the results of the referendum. Third, the success of the mobilizations under the banner of an equalization of salaries with the rest of the state officials hides, at the same time, a political defeat for the left-wing class-conscious alternatives. Equalization, entails an acceptance of functionarism as an articulating principle and, therefore, an admission of different incomes for different corps. This situation no matter how conjucturally it may be raised as a trade union objective, means a rejection of the idea of a single corps, an issue which represented the clearest point of division between these teachers unions and with Francoist bureaucratism.

THE NEW EDUCATIONAL ORDER

The conflict with the teachers diminished considerably after July 1989. This provided a respite for the new Minister of Education and created a more favorable climate for a resuming "dialogue." Voluminous documents of the reform were disseminated by the Ministry and were publicly presented in a massive campaign. Besides the "White Book" of the Reform, a Teachers' Training and Research Plan and the Basic Curricular Design for all areas and cycles of compulsory education were disseminated.

The official discourse, as evidenced both in the published documents and in Minister Solana's statements before Parliament, insists that the future LOGSE should be the result of the consensus among all social and political forces defending modernization and a redistributive justice. The new policy would also need to support an educational system at the level of the European Community standards as well as taking into account the various regional, cultural and personal specificities. A clear indication of the search for consensus is given by the sympathetic evaluation of the 1970 law and the deferential treatment accorded to its main proponent, Diez Hochleitner. Moreover, the new organizational principles of the educational system gave rise to no new conflicts.

The more notable aspects of the change are the following:

(a)   A definition of the importance of child education, from zero to six years old. Though only voluntary, the administration shall promote an increase in the number of available vacancies to satisfy the demand, especially in the period zero to three years.

(b)   An extension of free and compulsory schooling from fourteen to sixteen years of age. The cycle twelve to sixteen years constitutes the stage of compulsory secondary schooling, which is terminal in itself and at the same time preparatory or propaedeutic for those who will continue their education, both through the various modalities of "Bachillerato" or through Middle Level Technico-professional Teaching, all with a duration of two years.

(c)   Compulsory secondary schooling is presented as a basic education, with a common curriculum tending to comprehensivity and at the same time guaranteeing the possibility of choosing among optional subjects, especially during its latter part.

(d)   Bachillerato will comprise common and optional subjects as well, according to the orientation of the four different modalities, namely, Arts, Natural and Health Sciences, Humanities and Social Sciences, and Technology. The common subjects will be Physical Education, Philosophy, History, Castilian Language and Literature, eventually the local languages of the autonomous communities and a foreign language. The particular subjects in each modality are not specified, since they will be established by the Government according to "the needs of society and the educational system."

(e)   Professional training as a part of the educational system aims at preparing students for a future activity in a professional field through a diversified instruction allowing them to adapt to eventual occupational changes. It is organized in two levels, middle and higher, and will include both basic and more specialized professional training. The latter will be subdivided into theoretico-practical modules corresponding to the various professional fields and the possibility will be open for them to be carried on in the enterprises.

(f)   For the first time the regulation is undertaken of special, artistic, foreign languages and adult education, whose teachers have been until now in a precarious situation of juridical indefiniteness.

(g) The administration is going to pay special attention to all those factors favoring an increase in the quality of instruction, namely, initial qualification and in-service training of the teachers, curriculum development, educational research and innovation, educational and professional guidance, and supervision and evaluation of the educational system.

(h) A special emphasis is laid on the development of compensatory education, by means of preventive actions, scholarships, specific programs of the Autonomous Communities, etc.

Most of the other parties accepted the Socialist government's general proposals, except some Conservatives. The basic agreement on the main lines of the Reform Bill did not prevent the introduction of many modifications in the parliamentary debate, especially concerning financing, which the Ministry was open to accept. The main point of contention, as is usual in Latin countries, centered around the question of religious education and the financing of private schools, most of them Catholic in the case of Spain.

The government considered these subjects separately and decided not to innovate the present arrangement of subsidies to private schools. This avoided a confrontation with a section of private school owners, those grouped in the Spanish Confederation of Teaching Centers. The more recalcitrant Catholic Education Council declared itself against the LOGSE and convened a public demonstration in which they managed to gather no more than 8,000 persons, the majority of whom were priests and older people (*El País* 10 June 1990, 21).

The other question, teaching of religion as a school subject, raised considerable opposition. Teaching of the Catholic religion would continue to be voluntary, but--this being a politically charged innovation--the alternative subject of Ethics would not be compulsory for those not opting for religion. If religion loses its scholarly status, one may foresee that many of those currently choosing religion as a subject to study may in the future opt out. Conscious of the importance of counting on Ethics as an alternative compulsory subject, the curious situation arose of the Episcopal Council becoming its main proponent and not hesitating to attack the Socialist government, saying that they "should abandon their radical laicism, as they did with marxism" (*El País* 19 May 1990, 27).

However, it would be too rash to conclude that these superstructural agreements, involving most of the political parties and the various state apparatuses, mean that there is a broad consensus regarding the philosophy behind the reform proposals. It is important to note that many have abstained from participation in the debates, reflected in part by the political demobilization of the last decade in Spain. For example, teachers, whose qualifications and commitment are determining conditions for the success of the reform, have not shown interest in becoming involved in the policy discussions, in spite (or because) of the broad campaign of diffusion and consultation organized by the Ministry. The reactions towards the project were frequently of a corporative nature, such as opposing primary school teachers working in the twelve to sixteen year old cycle, the suppression of the corps of "catedraticos de Bachillerato," or the reduction in the number of hours of instruction for certain subjects. At best, only general questions affecting the teaching profession were posed, such as salary increases, in-service training within the school timetable, or the requirement of a "Licenciatura" for all teachers, irrespective of the teaching level. Only occasionally did the teachers react towards the reform project as a whole, which would have implied the transformation of a mere corporative conscience into a political conscience.

The intellectual sectors have also not taken the reform as an important issue. In journals in the fields of sociology and education, for example, papers discussing the reform are scarce, and in no case have they given rise to a debate. In general, the predominant analysis is evasive and lacking in commitment, referring to non-controversial issues and aiming more at an academic legitimation based on citations from different authors, mainly British and North American, than at a rigorous analysis of the real problems of education in Spain.

CONJECTURES ON THE VIABILITY OF THE REFORM

In spite of the agreement on the main aspects of the reform many critical and potentially contentious points remain, especially as the proposals get translated into practice. The first and decisive question is: which social classes or groups will reap the highest benefits from the reform's future implementation? It cannot be denied that the broadening of compulsory schooling will extend the educational opportunities to many young people. The school enrollment estimates for 1987-88, the academic year marking the end of the transition period, are 100 percent of the population between three and fifteen years old and 80 percent of the young people between sixteen and seventeen years old will be attending Bachillerato (Ministerio de Educación y Ciencia 1989, 288). These estimates should be treated with caution, given the high rate of dropouts in the Spanish educational system, around 60 percent in the present professional training and 50 percent at Bachillerato levels (Idigoras 1987, 303). The problem is much more acute for the former, where about a third of the first-year students drop out, being left with no better future than a degraded job in the hidden economy, when not an outright descent into social marginality (Méndez 1989, 379).

The attention accorded to technical-professional education is perhaps the clearest indicator for a sociological analysis of an educational reform, since after all its main beneficiaries are still mostly students of working class or peasant origin. The official discourse extols the social value of a technical culture and the social promotion implicit in the new structure of these studies,

euphemistically called "professions," following the linguistic uses
of the European Community. The integration into the Common
Market has also influenced the system of professional training in
that qualifications are being readjusted to the potential demands of
technological development and the labor market (Ministerio de
Educación y Ciencia 1989, 149).

Although both technological development and the labor
market are portrayed as natural bases for professional training, we
should harbor serious doubts about whether this alleged
modernization actually constitutes a stimulus for social promotion.
It is true that the often celebrated comprehensive nature of
compulsory education legally eliminates the dual track, since there
will no longer exist two different degrees. But the question remains:
what will happen to those dropping out of the system? It is difficult
to believe that this problem will be solved merely on the basis of a
legal disposition and, indeed, the Ministry itself does not appear
very optimistic when it foresees organizing specific programs for
those failing to obtain the compulsory education certificate, hence
providing them with an opportunity to become incorporated into
active working life.

Neither is it very clear what the educational responsibilities
are expected to be of the social agents implied in the planning of the
future professional training system, particularly with reference to
the business community. We should also remember that the
detonating factor in the 1988 general strike was the frustrated Youth
Employment Plan, which, under the guise of "work training,"
actually hid a scheme for exploiting young people, making them
compete with adult workers for scarce jobs. It is actually rather
difficult to characterize the general philosophy behind the proposed
changes in professional training, because social-democratic
ideological conceptions postulating comprehensivity, polyvalence,
etc., are mixed together with viewpoints which are very near to what
has been described as New Vocationalism. In concrete terms, the
question is whether the Spanish educational system will function in
the future on the basis of the Neo-liberal scheme of the two-thirds
society, or whether it will take care as well of the other third,
silently expelled until now from school. To take this problem
seriously requires something more than compensatory policies and
scholarships, especially since the latter cover only small expenses
for fees and not the so-called opportunity cost.

The Socialist government as yet has not clarified the priorities of the reform nor how it will be financed. The general impression is that the proposal is not being followed up by a serious planning effort. The failure of the 1970 reform should serve as a warning in the sense that there is no viability without resources. And even counting on adequate resources, the priorities adopted establish a hierarchy of political objectives and put into sharp relief the nature and extent of the sectors that will benefit from the reform. For example, what relative importance will the different branches of Bachillerato have in the future? How will the educational expenditures be apportioned among the various levels of the system? Will general education be given priority or rather employment-related instruction? One may also ask about the Socialist government's plans to continue to finance private education, which represents an annual expense of U.S. $2 billion at present, with the added prospect of a 50 percent increase if the subsidies to the new three to six and fourteen to sixteen year old cycles are implemented. In some respects, the concerted private schools receive greater support than the public schools, even though in most cases they count on a better infrastructure.

Public outlays in education have increased during the Socialist governments from 2.7 percent of GDP in 1982 to 3.2 percent in 1987 and are foreseen to reach 4.8 percent in 1997 but are still insufficient and comparatively low in relation to the European Community average, which is around 6 percent. Once the reforms are put in motion, there is no doubt that great economic efforts will be necessary to face the needs in infrastructure and personnel that have been postponed up to the present.

There is also a lack of school buildings in the periphery of the great cities, while many others are old, in need of repair, or without workshops and laboratories.

Up to what point the government will prove capable of putting into practice this ambitious project with all its consequences is hard to predict. The educational reform, with its limitations and improvations, represents an attempt at legitimation within the framework of a distribution model characteristic of the welfare state but in open contradiction to the Neo-liberal accumulation model of the government's economic team.

A class analysis of the content of the reform must also consider the role of teachers. We have seen that most of them were and still are trained and socialized under a scheme of study designed by the Francoist technocracy. All the documents available put a special emphasis on the autonomy of the teacher to organize the curricula, which are defined as open. It is not likely for teachers, having been socialized into authoritarian and bureaucratic practices, to be able to structure teaching on different bases, unless they are made to feel a part of a momentous collective effort.

NOTES

1.   Institución Libre de Enseñanza (ILE) was created in 1875 as a teaching institution, free and independent from both Church and Government control. Its founder, Francisco Giner de los Rios, who was largely inspired by the idealist philosophy of Krausse, soon developed a modernizing and (at the same time) progressive theory of education. Although it was quite selective and elitist, its educational proposals were integrated into the platform of the Spanish Socialist Party, and later on they had a strong influence on the intellectuals of the Second Republic.

REFERENCES

Apretar pero sin ahogar. Los directivos españoles se sitúan entre los más favorecidos por el fisco en Europa. *El País*, Negocios (10 June 1990): 31.

Bozal, V., and Paramio L. 1974/75. Sistema Educativo - Sistema de Clase. *Zona Abierta*: 2.

Bozal, V. 1977. *Una alternativa para la Enseñanza*. Madrid: Centro Press.

Comisiones Obreras. 1989. *Trabajadores de la Enseñanza*, T.E. Newsletter. (November).

Cuadrado, M. (Ed.) 1970. *Cambio social y modernización política*, Chapter V. Madrid: Cuadernos para el diálogo.

Datos de opinión. 1989. *Revista española de investigaciones sociológicas*, 46 (April-June): 227-231.

8000 personas asisten en Madrid a una manifestación católica contra la LOGSE. 1990. *El País* (10 June): 21.

Finkel, S.M. de 1988. La socialización en la apatía. Cómo se gesta un pasota In *El proceso de socialización*, edited by M. Peralbo, J. Torres, and J.M. Sánchez. Santiago de Compostela, España: Universidad de Santiago de Compostela Press.

Fernández de Castro, I. 1963. *Reforma Educativa y Desarrollo Capitalista*. Madrid: Edicusa.

Garzón, B. 1990. Escuela pública en la encrucijada. *Trabajadores de la Enseñanza*, (June): 114.

Gramsci, A. 1971. *El materialismo histórico y la filosofía*, de B. Croce. Buenos Aires: Nueva Visión.

Idigoras, B. 1989. Consideraciones previas a la reforma de la Formación profesional. *Revista de Educación* (May-August): 289.

Ilustre Colegio de Doctores y Licenciados en Filosofía y Letras del Distrito Universitario de Madrid. *Bulletins*. 1974-76.

INEM (National Employment Institute) Information as of 30 June 1990.

Instituto Nacional de Estadística 1984. *Anuarios Estadíscticos*. Madrid: Instituto Nacional de Estadística.

Instituto Nacional de Estadística. 1989. *Avance del anuario estadístico de España 1989*. Madrid: Instituto Nacional de Estadística.

Los obispos españoles afirman que no encabezarán manifestaciónes contra la LOGSE. 1990. *El País* (19 May): 27.

Méndez, X. and Macia, D. 1989. Programa para la prevención del abandono escolar en la formación profesional. *Revista de Educación* (May-August): 289.

Ministerio de Educación y Ciencia. 1987. *Proyecto para la reforma de la enseñanza. Educación infantil, primaria, secundaria y profesional. Propuesta para Debate*. Madrid: Ministerio de Educación y Ciencia.

Ministerio de Educación y Ciencia. 1988. *Proyecto para la reforma de la Educación técnico-profesional*. Propuesta para debate. Madrid: Ministerio de Educación y Ciencia.

Ministerio de Educación y Ciencia. 1989. *Libro Blanco para la reforma del sistema educativo*. Madrid: Ministerio de Educación y Ciencia.

Ministerio de Educación y Ciencia 1969. *La educación en España. Bases para una política educativa.* Madrid: Ministerio de Educación y Ciencia.

Puelles Benitez, M. 1977. *Educación e ideología en la España contemporánea.* Editorial Labor. Madrid: Centro Press.

Robinson, J.G. 1983. The authoritarian state and the new middle class. Ph.D. Dissertation. University of California, San Diego University.

Seminario de Pedagogía de Valencia 1975. *Por una reforma democrática de la enseñanza.* Barcelona: Avance.

Soler, R. 1969. Spain - A weak link? *New Left Review*, 58: 3-27.

Tamames, R. 1977. *La repúblic. La era de Franco. Historia de España*, Volume VI. Madrid: Alianza-Alfaguara. *Entrevista de Campo Vidal*, TV1 (7 June 1990).

Unión General de Trabajadores, Instituto Sindical de Estudios 1989. *Informa Anual.* Madrid: Unión General de Trabajadores.

Unión General de Trabajadores. 1989. *Propuesta Sindical Prioritaria.* Madrid: Unión General de Trabajadores. (November).

IDEOLOGICAL PLURALISM IN NICARAGUAN UNIVERSITY REFORM

Rolland G. Paulston and Susan Rippberger

> "I will not abandon my struggle while my people have one right yet to win. My cause is the cause of my people, the cause of America, the cause of all oppressed people."
>
> Augusto Cesar Sandino

This study examines a case in Nicaragua in which an educational reform effort, involving the practical use of the natural sciences at the undergraduate college level, attempted to promote broad social and economic change. The educational reform followed as a key element in the major political transformation put in motion by the Sandinista-led revolution of 1979. This radical break was brought about by an ongoing desire for a more equitable society and division of resources and an end to the United States' chronic military and political presence (LaFaber 1984; Marcus 1985).

RESEARCH FRAMEWORK

Both world and national systems perspectives as Ginsburg et al. (1990) argues may be valuable for contextualizing reform in geographical and historical space and time. However, they may need to be supplemented with a focus on reform practice, as in this study seeking to "explain" university reform in the specific context of Nicaraguan revolutionary transformation. A dependent system had been intact for decades prior to the 1979 revolution. The power shift that took place then presented the possibility for breaking Nicaragua's long economic dependency on the United States and for creating a place for applied science within the educational curriculum. Here a world system explanation is compelling.

In contrast, our analysis of reform in higher education is based on a radical humanist and critical pragmatic framework. The "radical humanist paradigm," exemplified by Sandino's opening quote, has more recently been defined by Burrell and Morgan (1979, 32) as a:

> frame of reference [which] is committed to a view of society which emphasizes the importance of overthrowing or transcending the limitations of existing social arrangements . . . [T]he radical humanist places most emphasis upon radical change, modes of domination, emancipation, deprivation and potentiality.

Our perspective is critically pragmatic in the sense that meaning is seen to be constructed within the practice of reform and in the context of crisis (Paulston 1990). We do not dismiss Marxist grand theory seeking to frame and drive explanation--or any other metatheoretical myth divorced from reform practice for that matter. We would argue, however, that a critical pragmatic perspective, because it accepts and assesses all arguments in light of what works in practice and what crisis requires, provides for more contextualized explanations and, accordingly, has greater utility for practical action.

While this approach may furnish a basis for comparison and

reflection it does not provide a universal explanation for all cases involving the United States and Latin America. The present study must be viewed as an event within a specific setting. Different governments, time frames, and world views will engender their own specific issues and meanings (Paulston and Tidwell 1991). The degree of lasting change in the structure and values of this attempted reorientation to applied science also remains to be seen. Short-term beneficial effects of the Science reform project in Nicaraguan higher education were evident, even amidst the destruction waged by U.S.-funded counter-revolutionary forces. Whether the modified curriculum remains in place with continued maintenance of the laboratories and equipment and whether university students are willing to choose applied science careers instead of more traditional studies in law and philosophy also remains to be seen (Aiges 1986c).

In this paper our objectives are to identify the major stakeholders in the science reform efforts and their diverse ideological orientations; to describe in detail the planning, implementation, and evaluation of the reform; and to draw some implications for development theory and practice. Our notion of ideology is broad, consisting of ideas and theories that reflect the social needs and aspirations of individuals, groups, and classes.

HISTORICAL AND ECONOMIC BACKGROUND

Since the 1850s, economic exploitation by U.S. business interests in Nicaragua helped to establish and maintain a dependent economic system. Later, in the 1920s and 1930s, the U.S. government used problems of "political and economic instability" as a rationale to send military forces to Nicaragua.

Nicaragua's dependent relation with the United States reached an apex during the subsequent Somoza family reign from 1934 to 1979. During this time the poorest 50 percent of the nation's workers received 15 percent of the nation's total income, while the wealthiest 20 percent received 60 percent. The Somoza family alone owned approximately 20 percent of the nation's land and industrial wealth (Arnove 1986). Neither the Samoza government nor the national and international business interests they usually represented expressed the slightest concern to raise living standards for the masses through education (De Castilla 1972). According to Black and Bevan (1980, 6) the 1979 revolution put an end to an oppressive government "installed and supported by the USA for half a century; a government which served foreign interests, and those of the Somoza family, rather than those of the Nicaraguan people."

EDUCATION IN NICARAGUA BEFORE AND AFTER THE 1979 REVOLUTION

Before 1979 the educational system clearly mirrored Nicaragua's dependent status. While the constitution guaranteed free and compulsory primary education for all children, educational facilities remained class linked, urban, and largely underdeveloped (Consejo Superior 1965). As in many Latin American countries, the Nicaraguan government provided extensive education at public expense to children of the urban elites but very little primary education or even basic literacy to the majority of children, who lived in poverty in both urban and rural settings (Carnoy and Torres 1990, 321). Illiteracy ran approximately 50 percent in urban areas and 75 percent in rural areas. Only 65 percent of the school-aged children actually enrolled and attended school. Of those children entering school, about 20 percent completed sixth grade. The fact that only about 15 percent of the high school-aged population attended school gives an indication of the small number prepared academically for higher education (Arnove 1986).

Traditionally, Latin American higher education has offered professional studies in the humanities, philosophy, and law, relying primarily on lecture and rote learning. The strong emphasis on theoretical and philosophical studies has been largely unrelated to positions required for economic and technological development (De Castilla 1972). Since applied sciences found few supporters, laboratories, and opportunities for practical experience and extension within the academic setting rarely existed (Castrejon et al. 1975). Even at the Universidad de Centroamerica (UCA), located in Managua and established in 1960 to develop personnel needed to facilitate industrialization, more students enrolled in business administration and economics than in engineering, technology, or agriculture programs (Tunnerman 1976; UNAN 1977).

The Sandinista National Liberation Front (FSLN), which came to power in 1979, dedicated education to shape a "new person" or selfless Sandinista revolutionary. Guidelines for the new educational policy called for (1) participatory education for the masses; (2) adult education; (3) the elimination of illiteracy; (4) educational innovation for scientific and technical fields, linking education to productive work; and (5) the transformation of education to support the new economic and social model (Borge 1983; Cardenal 1980; Fonseca 1980). Higher education would help the country emerge from the dependent capitalistic system of the old regime and address three new priority areas of the revolution: medical science, formal education, and land reform (Consejo Nacional de la Educacion Superior 1980; Tunnerman 1980a).

Initial efforts by the Ministry of Education to make education correspond to ideals of the revolution included a literacy campaign, that reduced illiteracy from 50 percent to approximately 15 percent; the establishment of ongoing adult basic education; a 100 percent increase in school enrollment; teacher salary increases of 50 percent to 100 percent; the establishment of a national textbook industry; the revision of curricula; and the use of more participatory instructional methods (Borge 1980; Cardenal and Miller 1981; Ministerio 1980).

Higher education under the Sandinista-led government became critically involved in meeting the resource needs of the country. Enrollments in agricultural science, medical science, educational science, and technology increased by as much as 18 percent, while enrollments in humanities declined by almost 35 percent. The Universidad Nacional Autonoma de Nicaragua (UNAN), located in Leon, became a center for natural and physical sciences, while the private Catholic institution, Universidad de

Centroamerica (UCA) in Managua specialized in the humanities, law, and public and business administration (Dettmer 1983).

The shift from elite domination of a powerless majority to their empowerment with guns and ballots also presented the possibility for developing greater economic independence. This was facilitated by applied science programs at the university level. In developing applied research programs, the Nicaraguan government had little if any experience and sought the help of knowledgeable but non paternalistic collaborators with resources and technical skills (Aiges 1986a).

THE CREATION OF THE LASPAU/USAID PROJECT

Since 1966 the Latin American Scholarship Program for American Universities (LASPAU), with funding from the United States Agency for International Development (USAID), had been providing scholarships to Nicaraguan and other Latin American university faculty for training at university graduate programs in the United States. Over the years LASPAU had built a successful program and strong rapport with the Nicaraguan university staff. LASPAU/USAID scholarships had been granted to 79 UNAN and UCA faculty and administrators (Paulston and Henderson 1984). At the request of the U.S. Embassy in Nicaragua, LASPAU reestablished their relationship with Nicaraguan universities after the victory of the Sandinista-led revolution in 1979. LASPAU staff met with USAID officials and the rector of UNAN to discuss possibilities for contributing to university reforms still in the planning stage.

Sending Nicaraguan faculty to the United States was not practical for a number of reasons. As a result of a new open enrollment policy the university's student population doubled, forcing faculty to shoulder excessive teaching loads. The Nicaraguan government had funded 300 scholarships to send students abroad to study fields that corresponded to production needs (i.e., forestry, farming, mechanical engineering, textiles, electricity, chemistry, hydraulics, geology and mines, marine biology, and fishing (Consejo Nacional de la Educacion Superior 1980) but this did little to reduce enrollment pressure.

Consequences of rapid enrollment expansion in higher education were also exacerbated by the fact that approximately one third of the most highly qualified full-time university professors had either resigned to work in the revolutionary government or had fled the country with the fall of the Somoza regime. The hiring of thirty-seven professors from Mexico, Cuba, and Venezuela helped to fill some positions but, given explosive enrollment growth, faculty shortages persisted (Rojas 1982). As staff shortages made it difficult for the administration to grant sabbatical leaves for professors to study in the United States, the rector of UNAN suggested that a few professors might be granted scholarships for study in the United States, if they could be replaced by professors from U.S. universities chosen by Nicaraguan university authorities.

As a result of discussions beginning in 1979 the Nicaraguan government and the Carter administration in the United States agreed to collaborate. LASPAU, with funding from USAID, would create a reform project in applied science at two of Nicaragua's universities (UCA and UNAN). The project would be implemented from 1981 to 1983, a period that would involve a new United States Administration, headed by Ronald Reagan, with different political, economic, and military objectives in Nicaragua. Visiting U.S. professors would teach science and conduct applied research in nutrition, aquaculture, forestry, and medical and ecological biochemistry -- areas identified by Nicaraguan university authorities as critical for national development and human welfare.

The LASPAU/USAID project in Nicaragua is also noteworthy as a planned, systematic break with the weak science tradition in Latin American higher education (Palmer 1984; Segal 1987). It provided a small scale, practical, participatory activity with immediate application. The attempt at change was not only structural, i.e., concerned with restructuring departments, curriculum, laboratories, and the like but it was also value oriented. Project goals sought a widespread application of science and technology as a necessary condition for success in achieving revolutionary goals for liberation and structural transformation (Paulston and Henderson 1983).

The LASPAU project also offered the possibility for the

governments of the United States and Nicaragua to work together in a way agreeable and beneficial to both parties. Immediately following the revolution, United States policy toward Nicaragua sought to limit Marxist influence and strengthen centrist political elements in the ruling revolutionary alliance (Leogrande 1985). Willing to compete with many varieties of Marxist thought in Nicaragua, the Carter administration sought out opportunities to advance democratic ideals as well as technological development. While concerned with a growing Cuban presence, United States Ambassador to Nicaragua Pezzullo commented that Nicaragua and the Sandinistas presented "an acceptable model" of revolution (Leogrande 1985, 427). For the Nicaraguans the project, under full LASPAU administration, would bring technical assistance without domination. The program offered greater health and production to the nation through improved science education linked with practical application largely in rural areas (Tunnerman 1980b).

The project also addressed the expectations of other major stakeholder groups. For LASPAU the project offered an opportunity to reconfirm a trusted relationship and respond to the faculty development needs of Nicaraguan universities with an on-site reform. The two university campuses eagerly accepted the opportunity to build stronger science programs in coordination with the revolutionary government's agenda for human and national development. And United States professors would have rich opportunities to develop and apply their specialized skills and advance their careers while initiating new and useful programs.

By early 1980, after several months of negotiation and planning, USAID officials, administration and faculty from the universities, and LASPAU staff had hammered out mutually acceptable goals and objectives. The request for proposals distributed by USAID, framed in a modernization theory perspective, also addressed the human resources goals of the new Nicaraguan government, i.e., "to improve the quality of education in Nicaragua . . . by expanding the pool of skilled technical expertise available for national development needs through training of university students" and to "assist the Nicaraguan universities to develop more highly trained manpower in priority fields for national development" (Paulston and Henderson 1983, 45).

LASPAU, a non-governmental organization had complete operational control of the project, was trusted by Nicaraguan government officials, and drew upon an extensive network of United States and Latin American academic contacts. After a lengthy screening and selection process, LASPAU recruited 10 professors who were then successfully vetted by the Nicaraguan project directors. The recruits were young professors actively engaged in science teaching, research, and development in United States universities. The professors needed to be open minded and collaborative but not highly politicized. As direct hire Nicaraguan university employees, they were to see themselves as colleagues and equals of Nicaraguan professors rather than USAID employees or privileged outsiders. Of these ten, eight stayed the full length of the project: one returned to the United States early, and the other died in an automobile accident at Leon and was buried as a "hero of the revolution" by Sandinista students.

Tasks for the visiting United States professors included curriculum and faculty development, inservice courses, laboratory construction, classroom teaching, course development, research supervision, applied research, project development, and mass media presentations on project achievements. Their mission would be to make operative a new strategy for higher education through which science would be translated into development activities that could be disseminated throughout the country via governmental ministries and grassroots organizations (Aiges 1986b; Hector 1985).

IMPLEMENTATION OF THE LASPAU/USAID PROJECT

In many ways the project serves as a model for the establishment and support of applied science in third world higher education. In two years, at a cost of less than one-half million dollars, the reform project produced a significant impact on the UCA and UNAN science departments. It added valuable new science courses, led to improvement in existing courses, and enhanced teacher inservice training. Outstanding collaborative research and development projects took place involving United States and

Nicaraguan professors, advanced students, and government agencies and ministries. For the first time, Nicaragua's university faculty and students helped to translate science into applied research and community projects.

LASPAU's strategy in delegating responsibility to the visiting professors played an important part in securing project goal attainment. They hired the best candidates available and allowed them freedom and flexibility to achieve project goals of innovation and reform in context. The program's flexible organization and the high quality of its personnel, the mid-term evaluation and resulting remedial actions, and LASPAU's intelligent and timely logistical support all worked to create a successful program.

The experiences of the United States visiting professors and their Nicaraguan colleagues at each of the campuses are summarized in FIGURE 1. Specific reform achievements may be seen in an expanded and more development-oriented science curriculum. United States professors carried out over ten research projects, taught university extension classes, reported project activities in the mass media and on national television, and formed links with communities and government offices. In this way the project's impact on the universities gained widespread recognition and respect across Nicaragua. On both campuses over 2,000 students received instruction through semester-long classes, laboratory experience, seminars and workshops. In addition, visiting professors guided and advised students in their departments on theses and monographs, and presented numerous refresher courses for their Nicaraguan faculty colleagues.

At UCA the visiting professors in Aquaculture and Fisheries worked with colleagues to create a new practical specialization and helped the nation to link aquaculture with community development in rural areas. The faculty of Forestry created the means for more efficient natural resource management and fuel policies. Nutritional Science professors improved teacher education and formal school instruction on eating habits and child health.

At the UNAN campus, achievements related to national development included the addition of an ecological impact/appraisal study in governmental planning, improved health knowledge and a greater availability of health services. The biology unit is credited with the creation of alternatives to imported pesticides. The zoology

FIGURE 1: APPLIED SCIENCE PROJECTS, LINKAGES,
AND OUTCOMES IN NICARAGUAN UNIVERSITIES

UCA CAMPUS

	AQUACULTURE/ FISHERIES	FORESTRY & FOREST ECOLOGY	NUTRITIONAL SCIENCES
SPECIAL RESEARCH AND DEVELOPMENT PROJECTS:	O FISHPOND CONSTRUCTION O FISHFARMING IN RURAL DEVELOPMENT O FISHMEAL PROJECT	O CARTOGRAPHY & PHOTO-INTERPRETA-TION LAB O FORESTRY INVENTORY O FORESTRY MAPPING PROJECTS	O NUTRITIONAL LABORATORY O CHILD FEEDING PROJECT O TEACHER EDUCATION PROJECT O SOLAR FOOD DEHYDRATION O EAT FISH, TV PROMOTION
LINKS TO NATIONAL AND INTERNATIONAL ORGANIZATIONS:	O MINISTRY OF EDUCATION O NATIONAL WOMEN'S ASSOCIATION O RURAL DEVEL-OPMENT AGENCIES O COOPERATIVES	O MINISTRY OF NATURAL RESOURCES O NATIONAL FIREWOOD PROJECT	O MINISTRY OF NATURAL RESOURCES O FOOD AND AGRICULTURE ORGANIZATION (FAO) O MINISTRY OF AGRICULTURE
OUTCOMES:	O PIONEERING IN APPLIED SCIENCE AT UNIVERSITY O NATIONWIDE AQUACULTURE CAPABILITY	O MORE EFFI-CIENT NATURAL RESOURCE MANAGEMENT AND FUEL POLICIES	O IMPROVED INSTRUCTION O IMPROVED EATING HABITS O IMPROVED CHILD HEALTH

FIGURE 1: APPLIED SCIENCE PROJECTS, LINKAGES,
AND OUTCOMES IN NICARAGUAN UNIVERSITIES (CONT'D)

UNAN CAMPUS

	BIO-CHEMISTRY, ECOLOGICAL	BIO-CHEMISTRY, MEDICAL	BIOLOGY & ZOOLOGY
SPECIAL RESEARCH AND DEVELOPMENT PROJECTS:	0 DEVELOP ECOLOGY LAB 0 ECOLOGICAL SURVEY & TRAINING	0 NICARAGUAN HEREDITARY DISEASE SURVEY 0 MEDICAL SURVEY 0 MEDICAL SERVICES DELIVERY	0 PEST CONTROL PROJECT 0 INVENTORY OF NATIVE BIRDS
LINKS TO NATIONAL AND INTERNA-TIONAL ORGANIZA-TIONS:	0 VARIOUS NATIONAL PLANNING AGENCIES	0 MINISTRY OF HEALTH	0 MINISTRY OF AGRI-CULTURE
OUTCOMES:	0 ECOLOGICAL INPUT IN GOVERNMENT DEVELOP-MENT PLANNING	0 IMPROVED HEALTH KNOWLEDGE 0 IMPROVED HEALTH SERVICES AVAILA-BILITY	0 ALTERNA-TIVES TO IMPORTED PESTICIDES 0 EXPANDED KNOWLEDGE 0 IMPROVED WILDLIFE MANAGEMENT

SOURCE: PAULSTON & HENDERSON (1983)

unit provided expanded knowledge at the university level as well as an improved system of wild life management.

LASPAU carried out two assessments: a preliminary evaluation provided the opportunity for in-progress alterations, and a final evaluation measured program outcomes. Nicaraguan administrators, faculty, and students and the United States agencies and professors all responded favorably to both evaluations (Paulston and Henderson 1983). The preliminary evaluation focused on three areas: the professors' adjustment to their new setting and the progress of their academic work; suggestions for project modifications; and feedback from the professors and the Nicaraguan Universities on LASPAU's administration of the program. Despite the intensifying "Contra war," initiated and funded by the Reagan administration, LASPAU found that both United States and Nicaraguan professors saw their collaboration in science reform as productive and congenial.

The final evaluation team also found persuasive evidence of a very successful program. Project goals were met and university administrators and faculty expressed strong interest in continuing the project but only under LASPAU's auspices. The Nicaraguan rectors and department heads at UNAN and UCA showed consistent support and overall satisfaction with the project. While not criticizing LASPAU's efforts, they regretted that the project had failed to recruit professors in physics, mathematics, and computer science. University administrators and faculty saw the visiting professors' leadership and systematic, scientific approach to research as highly appropriate role behavior for UNAN professors and students in their task of revolutionary reconstruction.

The visiting United States professors evaluated the project favorably, though they differed in their appraisal of their experience depending on which campus they were involved. The three professors placed at the UCA campus, a Jesuit institution and a stronghold of liberation theology, expressed enthusiasm about their opportunity to do pioneering work in applied science. With involvement in important decisions in their departments and close proximity to the government ministries in the capital, they felt they could easily collaborate with ministry officials in planning and implementing joint projects.

The seven professors at UNAN, a center of Sandinista activism and thought, experienced less control over their activities and felt somewhat less effective. Working in the provincial city, Leon, they experienced isolation and little flexibility in their assignments, which were not always congruent with their specializations. Rather than creating new programs as originally envisioned, they revised traditional theoretical courses in basic sciences, seeking to increase their relevance to development needs in ecological and medical biology and zoology.

LASPAU also rated the reform program a successful and productive professor exchange. It enabled them to reaffirm academic ties with Nicaragua after the 1979 revolution, to initiate an innovative scholarship program of teacher exchange, and to make a direct contribution to reform within a Latin American educational system.

USAID mission personnel representing the Reagan administration provided a more guarded and confrontational assessment. While they acknowledged the projects' practical contributions, they dismissed them as just a small part of the Carter administration's misguided strategy to compete with massive technical assistance to the revolution from communist states (Grigulevich 1981; Schwab and Sims 1985).

The program ended, in fact, because political relations between the two governments had deteriorated to such a point that the Reagan administration just after the start of the program refused additional funding for the LASPAU controlled project. Where the United States chose to work with the Sandinistas in 1979, in 1983 the new United States administration sought to topple the Sandinistas through an economic embargo and a "Contra war." In this context the United States decided to further punish the Sandinistas by denying them a highly successful project that they had hoped to continue and even expand.

IMPLICATIONS FOR DEVELOPMENT
THEORY AND PRACTICE

How do we explain the success of this reform given the simultaneous United States military intervention in Nicaragua? We would note again the limitations of a solely external explanation via metatheoretical analysis and suggest that internal factors must also be included in the explanation. In the Nicaraguan case, for example, we would highlight Sandino's practice of ideological pluralism as adopted and practiced by the Sandinista leaders (Hodges 1986). As indicated in FIGURE 2, the Sandinistas saw the reform largely from the global change ideological perspectives of revolutionary socialism and liberation theology (Cardenal 1983; Noland 1984). This provided the political will necessary to break with traditional practice and stress applied science for economic development. Recognizing their lack of experience and technical skills, the Sandinistas sought and engaged United States participants operating from modernization and grassroots development orientations to advance practice. This critical pragmatic approach worked reasonably well as long as major participants concentrated on practice and recognized the legitimate requirements of revolutionary reconstruction. When the United States under the Reagan administration shifted its priority from practice to ideological, economic, and military warfare, i.e., seeking to dominate Nicaragua and to eliminate the Sandinista's global change orientations, the collaboration ended (Fuentes 1988).

Cooperative assistance and mutual tolerance--between revolutionaries and United States academics, and indeed among all the stakeholders--were key elements of the successful science program. Now that the Sandinista government has been replaced by what appears to be a more compliant government, the opportunity for programs such as the one elaborated by LASPAU may become possible again (Rippberger, Ginsburg, and Paulston 1991). Current United States technical assistance policy remains wedded to modernization ideology that supports applied research and national development through higher education (Bujazan 1987). But for a project such as LASPAU's to be successful it must also be a priority

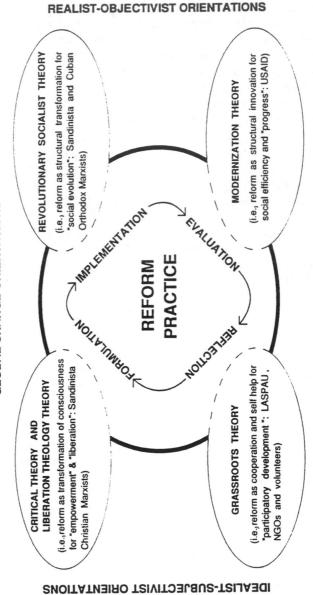

FIGURE 2 : EDUCATIONAL AND SOCIAL CHANGE THEORIES
IN NICARAGUAN HIGHER EDUCATION REFORM PRACTICE

REALIST-OBJECTIVIST ORIENTATIONS

GLOBAL CHANGE ORIENTATIONS

INCREMENTAL CHANGE ORIENTATIONS

IDEALIST-SUBJECTIVIST ORIENTATIONS

REVOLUTIONARY SOCIALIST THEORY
(i.e., reform as structural transformation for "social evolution": Sandinista and Cuban Orthodox Marxists)

MODERNIZATION THEORY
(i.e., reform as structural innovation for social efficiency and "progress": USAID)

CRITICAL THEORY AND LIBERATION THEOLOGY THEORY
(i.e., reform as transformation of consciousness for "empowerment" & "liberation": Sandinista Christian Marxists)

GRASSROOTS THEORY
(i.e., reform as cooperation and self help for "participatory development": LASPAU, NGOs and volunteers)

REFORM PRACTICE

IMPLEMENTATION

EVALUATION

REFLECTION

FORMULATION

of the new Nicaraguan government led by Violeta Chamorro and the National Opposition Union (UNO). With the return of traditional economic elites and growing political strife, prospects here are less than promising (Jimnez 1990; Uhlig 1990).

The collaborative project described above demonstrates that much can be done at reasonable cost to link applied science training, development, and extension courses to rural communities. The essential conditions call for a context where political will for greater equity and applied science for enhanced productivity can be merged in a critical pragmatic orientation to educational reform; one which evaluates ideas and theories against the dual standards of what crisis requires and what works in practice.

REFERENCES

Aiges, S. 1986a. Foreign educators aid Sandinistas. *The Chronicle of Higher Education* (Dec. 10): 42.

Aiges, S. 1986b. Nicaragua's universities, once for the elite, now struggle to train skilled professionals. *The Chronicle of Higher Education* (Dec. 10): 38-39.

Aiges, S. 1986c. Under Sandinistas, Nicaragua's universities become instruments. *The Chronicle of Higher Education* (Sept. 3): 118-123.

Arnove, R. 1986. *Education and revolution in Nicaragua.* New York: Praeger.

Black, G., and Bevan, J. 1980. *The loss of fear: Education in Nicaragua before and after the revolution.* London: Morning Litho Ltd.

Borge, T. 1980. Hay que aprender de las masas para educar a las masas! *Patria Libre* (March): 26-30.

Borge, T. 1983. La educación nueva en la Nicaragua nueva. *Barricada* (March 14): 1-3.

Bujazan, M., Hare, S., La Belle, T., Stafford, L. 1987. International agency assistance to education in Latin America and the Caribbean, 1970-1984: Technical and political decision making. *Comparative Education*, 23, 2: 161-71.

Burrell, G., and Morgan, G. 1979. *Sociological paradigms and organizational analysis.* New Hampshire: Heinemann.

Cardenal, E. 1980. Cultura revolucionaria, popular, nacional, antimperialista. *Nicarauac*, 1: 163-168.

Cardenal, E. 1983. Toward a new democracy of culture. In P. Rosset and J. Vandermeer (Eds.) *The Nicaraguan Reader: Documents of a revolution under fire* (346-356). New York: Grove Press.

Cardenal, F. and Miller, V. 1981. Nicaragua 1980: The battle of the ABCs. *Harvard Educational Review*, 51, 1: 1-26.

Carnoy, M. and Torres, C. 1990. Education and social transformation in Nicaragua. In M. Carnoy and J. Samoff (Eds.) *Education and social transition in the third world* (313-357). Princeton: Princeton University Press.

Castrejon D., et al. 1979. La educación superior en ocho paises de América Latina y el Caribe. In *Educación y Realidad Socio-económica* (39-51). México: Centro de Estudios Educativos.

Consejo Nacional de la Educación Superior. 1980. *Resumen del plan de desarrollo para la educación superior* (1980-1981). Managua: Consejo Nacional de la Educación Superior.

Consejo Superior Universitario Centroamericano. 1965. *El Sistema Educativa en Nicaragua*. Costa Rica: CSUCA.

De Castilla, M. 1972. *Educación para la modernización en Nicaragua*. Buenos Aires: Ed. Paidos.

Dettmer, J. 1983. Nicaragua: La revolución superior en la educación. *Revista Latinoamericana de Estudios Educativos*, 13, 1: 103-130.

Fonseca, C. et al. 1980. *Qué es un Sandinista?* Managua: Secretaria Nacional de Propaganda y Educación Politica del FSLN.

Fuentes, C. 1988. Prologue in D. Ortega *Combatiendo por la Paz*. México: Siglo Veintiuno Editores.

Ginsburg, M., Cooper, S., Raghu, R., and Zegarra, H. 1990. National and world systems explanations of educational reform. *Comparative Education Review*, 34, 4: 474-499.

Grigulevich, J. (Ed.) 1981. *Nicaragua: Glorioso camino a la victoria*. Moscow: USSR Academy of Sciences.

Hector, S. 1985. The grass-roots organizations. In T. Walker (Ed.) *Nicaragua: The first five years* (65-89). New York: Praeger.

Hodges, D. 1986. *Intellectual foundations of the Nicaraguan revolution*. Austin: University of Texas Press.

Jimenez, M. 1990. Neoliberalism in the classroom. *Barricada internacional*, (June 16): 3.

LaFaber, W. 1984. *Inevitable revolutions*. New York: W.W. Norton.

Leogrande, W. 1985. The United States and Nicaragua. In T. Walker (Ed.) *Nicaragua: The first five years* (425-446). New York: Praeger.

Marcus, B. (Ed.) *Nicaragua: The Sandinista people's revolution*. New York: Pathfinder Press.

Ministerio de Educación. 1980. *La Educación en el primer Año de la revolución popular Sandinista*. Managua: Ministerio de Educación.

Noland, D. 1984. *The ideology of the Sandinistas and Nicaraguan revolution*. Coral Gables, FL: Institute for Interamerican Studies, University of Miami.

Palmer, R. 1984. *Problems of development in small, beautiful countries*. Lanham: North South Press.

Paulston, R. 1990. Towards a reflective comparative education? *Comparative Education Review*, 34, 2: 248-255.

Paulston, R., and Henderson, F. 1983. *U.S. professors in Nicaraguan universities: The LASPAU/AID Nicaragua Project*, ED 252 101.

Paulston, R., and Tidwell, M. 1991. Education in Latin America-- comparative. In M. Alkin (Ed.), *Encyclopedia of educational research* (6th Ed.). New York: Macmillan.

Rippberger, S., Ginsburg, M., and Paulston, R. 1991. Educational reform in Nicaragua. In P. Cookson, A. Sedovnick, and S. Semel (Eds.), *International handbook of educational reform*. Westport: Greenwood Press.

Rojas, M. 1982. *El Aula Verde*. Habana: Union de Escritores y Artistas de Cuba.

Schwab, T., and Sims, H. 1985. Relations with the communist states. In T. Walker (Ed.) *Nicaragua: The first five years* (447-466). New York: Praeger.

Segal, A. 1987. Latin America: Development with Siesta. In A. Segal (Ed.) *Learning by doing: Science and technology in the developing world* (33-54). Boulder, CO: Westview Press.

Torres, C. 1989. Education under fire: Nicaragua 1979-1984. *Compare*, 19, 2: 127-135.

Tunnerman, C. 1976. La investigación en la universidad latino-americana. *Colección Deslinde de la UNAM*, No. 75, Mexico.

Tunnerman, C. 1980a. El nuevo concepto de extensión universitaria y difusión cultural. *Colección Pensamiento Universitario de la UNAM*, Mexico.

Tunnerman, C. 1980b. La nueva filosofia educativa del Gobierno de Reconstuccion Nacional. Revolucion Sandinista y educación. Special issue of *Encuentro*, 15 September, 99-111.

Tunnerman, C. 1980c. *Pensamiento Pedagogico de Sandino*. Managua: Ministerio de Educación.

Tunnermann, C. 1980. *Hacia Una Nueva Educación En Nicaragua*. Managua: Ministerio de Educación.

Uhlig, M. 1990. Man the monuments! A new war has started. *New York Times International* (3 August): 2.

Universidad Nacional Autonoma de Nicaragua (UNAN) 1977. *La UNAN en Cifras*. Leon, Nicaragua: The University.

SHIFTS IN SOCIOECONOMIC AND EDUCATIONAL POLICY IN TANZANIA: EXTERNAL AND INTERNAL FORCES

George E. Urch

Education on the African continent faces major problems as the world enters the last decade of the century. In spite of nations allocating substantial amounts of their budget for education and in spite of the dramatic increase in the number of students enrolled in formal education during the past three decades, persistent and debilitating problems remain. An entrenched colonial heritage, overcrowded classrooms, a scarcity of teaching material, and inadequately prepared teachers are just a few of the most pressing problems. Added to this is a rapid growth in the number of children seeking schooling during a period of scarce financial resources (World Bank 1988, 1-2).

However, the most persistent problem concerns the relationship between education and national development. At one time there appeared to be a formula that predicted socioeconomic development based on educational growth. That formula is now under serious question. While the number of students attending educational institutions on the continent has quintupled in the past thirty years, the relationship of this accomplishment to national development is still not clear. In other words, the return on the investment in education, in terms of sustainable economic growth and the improvement in the quality of life, is still under study.

Nowhere on the continent is the relationship between education and national development more perplexing than in the East African country of Tanzania. Since independence in 1961, this nation of 22 million people has attempted to pursue a twin policy of African socialism and economic self-reliance. The government policy was designed to link education to the full participation of the people in the nation's social and economic life and to reduce Tanzania's economic dependency on dominant societies in the world system. During the first two decades after political independence these goals were not achieved to the satisfaction of the majority of Tanzanians, despite a number of government efforts in developing and implementing socioeconomic and educational policies. The 1980s, particularly since 1985, have witnessed a dramatic redirection in the policies pursued by the Tanzanian state. Tanzania seems to have retreated from what it had earlier proudly held up as an alternative model for other newly independent, developing nations--a model that neither required becoming integrated in a dependent position in the world system nor necessitated fostering capitalist social relations. Education, which had been seen as a key institution in both periods, has also been the target of restructuring in recent years.

This chapter will describe the efforts to develop and implement socioeconomic and educational policy in Tanzania during these two periods. It also will examine dynamics that help explain why certain goals were not achieved and why the direction or priority of goals seems to have shifted. Attention will be given both to internal (local and national level) forces and to external forces--those associated with the world political economy and with international organizations and bilateral agencies.

TANZANIA AND EXTERNAL FORCES--
THE WORLD SCENE

As the Third World enters the fourth U.N. development decade, there is an increasing awareness of the disparities in economic performance among the developing countries. While some nations have shown a pattern of steady economic growth, others have seen their performance decline and their economies stagnate. There is little doubt that many nations on the African continent now have economies that face difficulties in competing in a capital-driven world economy. Among the most noticeable reasons for those difficulties are the continuing economic dependency begun under colonialism, the penetration of multinational corporations, and a shifting world economy brought on by the dramatic increase in the price of oil during the 1970s.

The colonial period saw the Western nations lay the foundation for an economic division. Most often the colonies were viewed as the suppliers of raw materials and natural resources to the dominant industrialized capitalist western nations. As competition increased among Western nations their colonies were asked to supply specialized and valuable export products. The development and export of such products often stayed in the hands of a few European traders, who were not necessarily interested in the overall development of the colony but only in the profit brought about through the quantity of exports. Over time there developed a dependent situation in which the underdeveloped colonies became economic appendages to the developed metropolitan power (Frank 1979, 104).

When political independence came to the continent, the economic dependency remained. However, the processing of exports was now transferred to a small indigenous elite group, whose political projects shaped the policies and actions of the newly independent states. The export trade did not necessarily become part of the internal economic structure of the newly independent countries but rather continued as an extension of Western economies. The result was viewed as underdevelopment and economic dependence.

Enhancing the dependency of many African countries were the fast growing multinational corporations with parent headquarters located in one country, usually a former colonizer, and subsidiary operations in several other countries. A major characteristic of such a corporation was its efforts to maximize the profits of the parent company. Some global economists saw multinational corporations bringing to the continent needed technology, financial resources, and employment opportunities. Others saw the continuation of the colonial model of exploitating labor and raw materials and transferring out financial resources. The new political leaders recognized that they had little control over the corporations, which safeguarded their monopolistic positions and moved capital and companies about at their discretion, but the political leaders also perceived their economic options to be limited.

Compounding the economic problems found on the continent was the quadrupling of oil prices in 1974, followed by further price increases by the end of the decade. Hard-earned international currency now had to go toward a dramatically increased oil import bill. Added to this during the 1980s was the World Bank estimate that commodity prices fell from one quarter to one third of what they had been in the 1970s (Harden 1987). As a result of all the above-noted factors the steady economic development seen in some countries during the 1960s was reversed in the mid-1970s and 1980s as many nations experienced severe economic decline (Hoogvelt 1986, 3).

SOCIOECONOMIC POLICY IN THE 1960s AND 1970s

After independence in December 1961, the government of Tanzania committed itself to building a socialist society that would reduce Tanzania's economic dependence on foreign capital. The early commitment became evident in a pamphlet published in 1962 by the ruling party, Tanganyika African National Union (TANU), written by the new Prime Minister, Julius K. Nyerere, and entitled "Ujamaa: The Basis of African Socialism." Nyerere wished to see his country become a socialist state based on the social values of traditional Africa. For Nyerere this meant an attitude of mind that embodied the African traditions of equality, cooperation, and freedom. The movement was encapsulated in the Swahili word "Ujamaa," meaning familyhood. Tanzanian socialism was opposed to both capitalism, which attempted to exploit people, and doctrinaire socialism, which spoke of the inevitable conflict between people. Nyerere saw Tanzanian socialism based on human brotherhood and the unity of Africa (Nyerere 1968, 12).

The commitment of the new government and the ruling political party to pursuing a socialist policy soon became evident. By the end of 1962, Nyerere was elected President of the Republic, and he took his philosophy to the countryside where he launched a vigorous campaign in support of self-help schemes. Simultaneously, his government began to convert freehold land to leasehold ownership on the grounds that land belonged to all the people. In addition, market cooperatives were encouraged as was public ownership of economic activities. This was highlighted by the government takeover of the country's private electric company (Nyerere 1968, 1).

In spite of these early measures, it became clear to the government that the people, especially in the rural areas, did not fully understand what Ujamaa meant and what socialism could do for them. Nyerere's original essay was not a call to action but rather a statement of humanistic ideals. It did not define what needed to be done. There still appeared to be confusion over the specific direction that development should take. To clarify the situation several clear articulations of policy were issued in 1967 that committed the country to a socialist path. In February 1967, TANU adopted the Arusha Declaration, a proclamation on building an Ujamaa society. The Declaration was followed by two subsequent policy statements from the President. In March 1967, the government released "Education for Self-Reliance" and in September they published "Socialism and Rural Development."

The Arusha Declaration has provided the foundation for Tanzania's development policies since 1967. The document was based on the principles of equality, dignity, and a fair return for labor. It shifted thinking away from industrial expansion toward a renewed emphasis on rural development with a focus on self-reliance and a commitment to hard work on the part of all members of society. Development was to be brought about by people not by money from outside the country (Nyerere 1968, 28-29).

Following the Declaration, steps were taken immediately to nationalize industry and commerce. Commercial banks were taken over by the National Bank of Commerce. Import and export firms were taken over by the State Trading Corporation. The government also acquired 60 percent of the shares of the seven largest industries and nationalized 60 percent of the sisal industry. By 1970, wholesale trade was nationalized and large rent-earning buildings were requisitioned by the government in 1971 (Kahama 1986, 33). The final feature of nationalization called for the grouping of small, autonomous companies and enterprises into large parastatal companies that were placed under the supervision of government ministries. Examples of the new parastatals included the Tanzanian Tourist Corporation, The National Agricultural and Food Corporation, and the State Mining Corporation. The government provided compensation to the individuals involved, and attempts were made to retain foreign management. Partnerships between government parastatals and foreign firms also were encouraged. Yet it was clear to local and foreign investors that the road to socialism had a definitive direction.

The Arusha Declaration called for a complementary shift in education. The policy statement, "Education for Self-Reliance," called for the development of self-contained schools that would teach the cooperative values necessary for socialism. The new education system was to prepare students to work productively in rural areas and better integrate educational values with work experience (Nyerere 1968, 72-73).

The final policy document of 1967 was Nyerere's, "Socialism and Rural Development." The document recognized the value of the traditional extended family with its emphasis on personal respect, common ownership, the sharing of basic goods, and the obligation to work. The policy called for the establishment of larger communities where people would live and work together for the common good. The communities would be organized around the principles of equality and cooperation, established on the basis of local conditions, and operate for the good of the country. Tanzania was to move from being a nation of individual peasant producers to a nation of Ujamaa villages where the people would cooperate directly (Nyerere 1968, 143). The old system of scattered huts and villages with small plots tilled to produce enough food for the family was now to be replaced by cooperative villages. These large villages were to produce a surplus which could be used to purchase consumer goods and to build schools, health clinics, and better roads. TANU, the only political party, was charged with the implementation of the new policy.

During the first year, education and "friendly persuasion" primarily were used to encourage the voluntary formation of cooperative villages, with each region setting its own pace. At year's end there were 180 Ujamaa villages with a total population of 58,000. In 1969 there was a shift toward guided and induced implementation with a concomitant discouragement of private individual farming. The villages were identified as the main source of economic growth in rural areas, and government officials were urged to increase the villages' productivity. The new thrust was further clarified in the nation's Second Five-Year Plan (1969-74). The plan gave priority to Ujamaa villages for the location of new schools and dispensaries as well as the allocation of money through the Regional Development Plan (Tanzania 1969). The plan called for government officials and party leaders to work together to initiate the change. The new policy helped to increase the number of villages to 2,668 and their population to 840,000 by 1971. During that year even stronger measures were introduced, and by the middle of 1973 the government counted 2,028,164 people living in Ujamaa villages (Kahama 1986, 36). However, in the minds of some government officials there still existed the problem of a scattered population working without coordination and obstructing the drive toward rural socialism. In November 1973, President Nyerere ordered that the entire population was to be in Ujamaa villages by 1976. Toward that end a new administrative structure was established through the Villages and Ujamaa Villages Act of 1975. By 1980, the overall strategy led to the movement of fourteen million people or 91 percent of the rural population (Kahama 1986, 42). The challenge now was to provide the farmers with the skills and incentive to adjust their farming to a cooperative style of socialism.

INITIATIVES IN EDUCATION IN THE
1960s AND 1970s

The role education was to foster in the new society had been outlined in 1967 in Nyerere's "Education for Self-Reliance." Nyerere stated that the educational system must prepare young people for the work they will be called upon to do in the society that exists -- a rural society where improvement would depend upon the efforts of the people in agriculture and in village development. The schools had to foster the social goals of living and working together for the common good. This meant that schools must emphasize cooperative endeavors and not individual advancement. They also must stress concepts of equality and service-oriented responsibility -- and in particular the schools must counteract the temptation of intellectual arrogance (Nyerere 1968, 51).

Nyerere said that the existing system was elitist, divorcing the youth from the society in which they lived and engendering the belief that all worthwhile knowledge was acquired from books and "educated people." The primary school of that time was oriented toward the preparation of pupils for the secondary schools. Yet only about 13 percent of primary school children would get into secondary schools. The remaining 87 percent were referred to as those who failed to enter secondary school rather than those who had finished primary education. This type of education was considered detrimental to the attitudes required for an egalitarian society (Nyerere 1968, 55).

Under "Education for Self-Reliance" major changes were to take place. These changes were further clarified in 1974 with the publication of the "Musoma Resolutions" (TANU National Executive Committee 1974). The schools were called upon not only to explain socialism but to practice it by becoming working communities in miniature and integrating themselves more completely into the communities. All schools, both primary and secondary, were to move toward becoming economically self-supporting. Every school community would have teachers, pupils, and farmers.

At the primary level, schools were to be made available for everyone through the introduction of "Universal Primary Education."

Primary education was to be seven years in length and terminal. Only four out of every one hundred students were to gain admission to secondary schools. The primary school entrance age was to be raised to at least seven so that children would learn more quickly and be ready to become productive members of their community when they graduated. School farms were to be introduced along with the teaching of practical skills needed to develop rural areas. Swahili was to be the language of instruction.

Secondary education also was expected to be terminal with only one student out of every one hundred, who began primary school, gaining admission to higher education. The schools were expected to diversify and vocationalize. Instruction was to be in English. Each secondary school was to introduce at least one of four practical and work-oriented subjects--agricultural science, domestic science, a commercial course, or a technical (trade) course. School farms were to be prototype socialist communities with the students responsible for planning and running each farm. Students were to be graded for these practical subjects. The Cambridge Overseas Examination, a post-secondary school selection mechanism, based in England and used since the colonial period, was to be replaced with an East African modification. The reality of the situation was that most secondary students would return to the village and the land.

Those fortunate enough to receive higher education were seen to owe a huge debt to the society that provided their education. It was estimated that it took the per capita income of fifty people to support one university student. Before admission to higher education, students would spend one year in a productive capacity and at least part of every holiday working on a community service project.

To bring about the revolutionary goals of socialism and self-reliance, Nyerere turned to the teachers. Nyerere frequently stated that it was the teacher, rather than the legislator, who would shape what Tanzania would become. He called teachers "apostles of the idea," and they were exhorted to live according to the Ujamaa ideology. Teachers were asked to join their students in work and study, both in the classroom and the field. They were to help develop proper attitudes toward socialism and to blur the distinction between manual and mental labor. As the models of socialist behavior, teachers were to be the implementors, interpreters, and conveyers of the concept of Ujamaa (Psychas 1982, 185). At the primary level, this meant that they were expected to be directors of community education and teachers of a political ideology. At the secondary level, teachers were expected to teach one of the four practical subjects and to join in the work on the farm. Toward this end, political commitment was taken into account in the selection of those who planned to teach, and special courses were provided in political education and civics in all teacher training colleges (Tanzania 1984a).

Not to be neglected in this overall educational effort were the adults. The formal system of education was to be merged with a wide variety of nonformal educational opportunities for all members of a community. Such a nation-wide learning system was designed to develop understanding and enthusiasm for community participation in building a socialist society that followed the principles of Ujamaa. It was expected to provide the knowledge and skills necessary to improve the productivity of the people. In addition to consciousness raising and imparting productive knowledge and skills, adult education was given the responsibility for eradicating illiteracy, providing follow-up education for school leavers to help them settle into Ujamaa villages and providing leadership training for various aspects of rural life (Institute of Adult Education 1971).

To accomplish these goals, the primary school was seen as the focal point and the primary school teacher the main instrument for adult education in every village. In addition, teachers and students from secondary and higher education were to teach specific crafts and skills, while rural district and national training centers were to provide courses for leadership training. Additional classes could take place anywhere a group of people could be brought together. These were intended to be self-directed with the members deciding what they wanted to learn (Thompson 1981).

Clearly "Education for Self-Reliance" was seen as more than just a slogan in Tanzania. An evolving definitive plan was designed to move from a philosophical stance, through policy formation, to the implementation stage. All members of society were to be engaged in bringing about revolutionary change, and the principal instrument to produce this change was education. Still, in spite of careful planning, education for self-reliance in the 1980s often remained more of a slogan than a reality. Despite all efforts and exhortations, there appeared to be a widening gap between Nyerere's philosophical position and the perceived role of education by the people. The vision of a model socialist society in which education helped the rural populace work cooperatively toward accepted goals was countered by the reality of young people pursuing education in order to remove themselves from the Ujamaa villages and seek life in the cities. These shortcomings of education in preparing people for their place in rural socialist society were compounded by the limited success in developing the nation's agricultural, commercial, and industrial economic base.

CONTEMPORARY SCENE: AN ECONOMIC CRISIS

As Tanzania prepared for the decade of the 1990s, it was faced with an economy in deep trouble. This gloomy picture was in sharp contrast with the economic situation during Tanzania's first decade of independence where the growth rate of the gross domestic product was a steady 5 percent per year. During the 1980s Tanzania saw its national debt rise to over 3.4 billion U.S. dollars, its credit exhausted with the world's oil-producing nations, and its reliance on foreign aid sharply increased. Import income declined by 50 percent between 1977 and 1982. By 1985 Tanzania was the third largest recipient in sub-Saharan Africa of bilateral aid from Western countries; and close to 15 percent of its Gross National Product was supported by outside funding (Country Profile 1987, 27). During the 1980s Tanzania's manufacturing output declined by 50 percent from what it was in 1978. The lack of foreign exchange needed to import spare parts and raw materials caused the nation to produce at only one-quarter of its capacity (Powers 1985, 10).

The country's agricultural production also was in trouble. The lack of transport equipment, fuel, and spare parts contributed to difficulties in distributing essential fertilizers and farming implements as well as in the collection of crops grown (Country Profile 1986, 9). In 1984, after several dry years, the crops failed and agricultural exports dropped precipitously. This was compounded by rapidly declining prices for agricultural products on the international market. The new farm collectives were in a state of disarray. Farmers were being paid in Party IOU's and the rural banking system was in trouble. There was little opportunity or incentive for farmers to grow more than what their family could eat. Food was in short supply in urban areas. The state corporations, established to buy, sell, and export agricultural products, were facing insurmountable problems. In 1986 the largest state marketing organization, the Agricultural Products Export Corporation, was dissolved by the government (*The Economist* August 23, 1986).

The government's two Five-Year Development Plans consistently called for an emphasis on rural development and the collective establishment of Ujamaa villages. The formation of these villages helped bring basic health care and clean drinking water to rural areas and helped produce one of the highest literacy rates on the African Continent. However, villagization did not bring economic prosperity. Most Tanzanians strongly resisted attempts to collectivize production and to take away their land. Many had not declared themselves socialists and their tradition of mutual cooperation tended to be family based and did not extend to communal ownership of land (Fagerlind 1983, 224). Besides, villagization violated a fundamental principle that had long been recognized in government policy statements: participation of the people in the important decisions that affected their lives (Kahama 1986, 314). One consequence of this unilateral decision was that villagers did not see the need to work very hard on communal land. As a result there was a dramatic drop in the production of Tanzania's export crops.

The inability of the industrial and agricultural sectors to support an export base sufficient to generate foreign exchange, the increased costs of needed imports, and the growing national debt (associated with increased borrowing and sky-rocketing interest rates) are the primary reasons for the present economic crisis. A vicious circle can be seen in an export base economy that was highly dependent on imports of oil and raw material without which there was low productivity and an inadequate generation of foreign exchange (Country Profile 1986, 9). Two regional political developments also clearly exacerbated the conditions discussed above. The first was the breakup of the East African Community composed of Kenya, Tanzania, and Uganda. Its demise in 1977 broke up opportunities for regional economic cooperation. Ideological differences between those promoting socialist versus capitalist roads to national development helped to bring about the split. The second development was the military operation against Uganda. The war eventually led to the overthrow of Uganda's self-declared head of state, Idi Amin, but the cost was exceedingly high, both in terms of financing the war effort and loss of productivity from Tanzanians involved in the military operation.

In addition, problems were encountered in implementing the educational programs developed designed to move the society on a socialist and self-reliant road to national development. These problems along with many Tanzanians' perception of continuing and even increasing inequalities (between rural and urban dwellers as well as between those with and those without education and political connections in both settings) have underminded the legitimacy of the education system and the state. The rural people were especially affected by these problems and dissatisfaction with the state system became stronger. In response the government attempted to take firmer control by passing two acts. The Economic Sabotage Act, which sentenced people up to fifteen years in labor camps for evading the government's economic controls, and the Human Resources Development Act, which empowered urban authorities to return the urban unemployed to their villages. As the state began to rely on legal and forceful means to mobilize the population for certain ends its legitimacy was further undermined.

A LEGITIMATION CRISIS IN EDUCATION AND THE STATE

There were clear indications that the policy of education for self-reliance had not progressed as far and as fast as it should have. While the ideology behind it was clearly stated, the practice required a value orientation that was slow to develop. The values center around the creation of a "new" socialist person who would place collective interests ahead of personal ones. This means the eradication of capitalistic modes of thought left over from colonial days. The objectives of socialist development were in direct conflict with the aspirations and expectations for educational and occupational achievement found in the colonial situation (Fagerlind, 1983, p. 229).

However, the colonial heritage alone could not be blamed. The difficulties encountered in motivating people to enhance the principles of Ujamaa have much to do with widespread frustration over little personal gain and aspirations not being met. If government policy were to be implemented, it was essential for the schools to address this frustration and to adjust to their new role in preparing people for their place in a socialist society.

Yet, like all societies, Tanzania needed technical and administrative skills of the highest order to improve the economy and manage the government. The Third Five Year Development Plan emphasized the need for highly educated personnel and called for all middle- and high-level positions to be Tanzanianized. This policy required an increased number of competent primary school leavers to be selected for further education. The dilemma was how to balance a dual system of education, which economically rewards those with advanced educational certificates, while asking the rural population to view primary education as terminal.

Unfortunately the dual system of education, designed to cater to different sectors of society, increased and institutionalized the inequalities found in society. As long as the systematic inequalities were evident in the educational system and elsewhere in society, youthful aspirations would be toward the favored urban sector. The results were evident--rural-urban migration, low response to education for villagization, and growing frustration and hostility due to perceived blocked opportunities.

Many students believed that formal education should be regarded as a passport to a paid job away from the rural village. While the government expected students who received a primary education to assist in rural development, young people viewed returning to the land as a sign of their failure to gain admission to secondary education. Their reluctant return to the village was not likely to encourage them to become the model farmers necessary to show others the way (Kim 1979). The views held by students were reinforced by their parents. Contrary to government policy, parents did not expect primary education to be terminal for their children, and they were not particularly keen for their children to return to the farm after schooling. The farm was not seen as a place for an educated person. Parents still expected their children to acquire paid employment in order to support them in their old age. Money and time invested in education would be considered lost if this were not the case (Psychas 1982, 177).

The reluctance of primary school leavers to return to the farm also was fueled by the observable inequalities all around them. The economic rewards and opportunities for advancement went to the educated elite. For the majority the one apparent avenue to upward mobility was through education. The educated could call for an egalitarian society, but their life style said otherwise. The hope that the educated youth would emerge with egalitarian values, obtained by an education which emphasized cooperative rather than individual accomplishment, was not being realized. The contradiction was that the group that had to lead the transformation toward socialism was the educated political elite, who benefitted materially from their leadership positions.

Some of the more affluent regions began to subvert government policy and develop private secondary schools. These schools began to emerge in fairly large numbers by the mid-1970s and were usually assisted by a coalition of local church personnel, politicians, and government officials. Often the local leadership was responding to the pressure of the community that saw in a secondary school future power and influence (Samoff 1987, 347). Initially, the Ministry of Education opposed this development. It meant the unequal distribution of educational opportunities in the country and was in contradiction to a centrally managed and socialist-oriented educational system. When opposition failed to slow down the development, the Ministry established regulations and standards that the schools were expected to follow. However, with the rapid increase in numbers and the implication that this was a form of self-reliance, it was difficult to control the expansion.

The adaptation of an education for self-reliance program also was hindered by the teachers. Clearly, much depended upon the capacity of teachers to communicate appropriate policies, foster socialist attitudes, and organize village development. Yet there was some question as to whether teachers had the attitude or the inclination to do so considering their own previous experience in education. Most teachers in Tanzania earned academic credentials through a process that rewarded individual initiative and competitive behavior. Often these teachers saw themselves as a disadvantaged educated elite group. For many, their privileged position was challenged by asking them to engage in agricultural work and requiring them to involve community leaders who were considered uneducated. Whether teachers were viewed as seekers of wealth and status or as overworked, unappreciated civil servants, what they were expected to do was not happening. Perhaps the role the teachers and their schools had been allocated was beyond their capacity, their apparent failure may have been due to unrealistic expectations rather than the schools themselves (Thompson 1981).

There was growing doubt that the schools alone could transform society. Even under ideal conditions it would be difficult for the schools to inculcate a set of values that ran counter to social and political forces. Schools did not operate in a vacuum; societal and global attitudes had to be considered. The people possessed a shrewd understanding of where their own interests were and they learned to evaluate statements made by those who had won their place in the sun. It was reasonable to assume that as long as those in the rural agricultural sector had a lower standard of living than those employed in the lowest positions of the urban economy, it was highly unlikely that the attitudes of parents and students would dramatically change. The legitimacy of the policy of education for self-reliance, and indeed the legitimacy of the state and the one political party, was being questioned.

PROBLEMS OF MANAGEMENT AT NATIONAL AND LOCAL LEVEL

There are certain problems inherent in any attempt to centrally administer a nation, especially when the administration must be balanced between central authority and local responsibility. Government officials learned early that neither platform policy-making nor shouting slogans provided the answer. Tanzania needed leadership from central ministries, which would produce a local response through regional, district, and village organizations. Part of the explanation for Tanzania's not achieving its stated national economic and political goals must be associated with flaws in the systems of management. Most observers saw the management system as having difficulty in moving the nation toward accepted goals.

No one doubted that one important reason for managerial difficulties was the limited number of people with managerial skills. Well-educated people in such fields as education, health, and banking were not necessarily prepared to manage others. To compensate for the lack of trained and experienced administrators, the central government kept a tight rein on financial resources and had a tendency to increase the number of people and steps to approve a decision. Without proper finances it was difficult for a manager to allocate resources to key areas and to move people in responsible directions. By creating layers of people to compensate for a lack of individual management capabilities or at least for a lack of trust in those exercising such functions, large bureaucracies were formed.

One clear indication of a burgeoning bureaucracy was the development of parastatals. To obtain more direct control and assure responsible action, the central government established approximately four hundred state corporations or parastatals. Many of them were involved in the agricultural and industrial sectors of the economy. They were designed to bring the government closer to the people for better accountability. However, each new parastatal developed a new hierarchial structure of bureaucratic management that increased the number of government employees and duplicated ancillary services such as transportation and dispensaries (Kahama 1986, 316).

At various stages the bureaucracy was accused of being too conservative, elitist, neo-colonial in attitude, and a major detriment to achieving socialist goals. At times it was castigated by the political party and top government officials and the general public. One result of this criticism was that key administrators were reluctant to take responsibility for failures or shortcomings. Instead of becoming problem solvers, they became problem dodgers who either found someone else to blame or saw circumstances as beyond their control or responsibility. Policy implementation became less important than having a political base and social contacts to help protect their position (Kim 1979). Independent and innovative thinking also appeared to be discouraged. Changing existing practices could be seen as a potential threat to administrators who had little experience in coping with managerial change.

Not all accountability for mismanagement could be passed on to the central bureaucracy. A close look at district and local administration showed several clear problems. Many local communities did not see why they should assume financial and administrative responsibility over areas that should be central government responsibilities. This was frequently the case when initial attempts were made to decentralize the administration of the schools, particularly in rural areas. Local citizenry had to assume leadership in areas where they had little training. It was one thing to manage local problems but quite another to assume responsibility to prepare youth through the schools for a productive and positive role in the local community. In some areas there appeared to be a genuine state of crisis, and village administration of education became totally broken down.

However, even strong management did not necessarily mean "enlightened" management. Strong management might not necessarily imply support for such practices as preparing the youth for work on farms. Given freedom of action, local managers could follow a course that would subvert national policy. In those communities that had the wealth and initiative to provide what they deemed a good education, this could lead to academically oriented primary schools, the support of private secondary schools, and more students seeking higher education. When this occurred, it created regional inequalities.

MOVEMENT AWAY FROM SOCIALISM AND SELF-RELIANCE

Political officials in Tanzania were well aware of the external pressures and internal criticisms levied at the government. The economic problems were real, whether caused by the world economic crisis and/or internal problems. Education had not responded in the manner anticipated by the nation's leaders, and the requisite forms of management at national and local levels had not been achieved. In this context and given that social inequalities remained a visible feature of Tanzanian society, the state and the one political party experienced a crisis of legitimacy. The high level of confidence that people in rural and urban areas had for the nation's leaders immediately after independence had all but evaporated. Clearly change was necessary. Most governments in power shift direction slowly and often with reluctance. In Tanzania the rapidity of the change surprised people, both inside and outside of the country.

Nyerere and other government officials were aware of the political and economic difficulties of socialism. Some within the party were closely linked with the state bureaucracy and benefitted from state control of the economy. Other reformers wanted to see a greater reliance on market forces and an economy that was much freer from government intervention. Nyerere was aware of these competing forces and had usually been able to effectively balance them. At a public meeting in May 1985, he admitted making a mistake in nationalizing the sisal estates. The result was the debilitation of one of the major cash crop industries for foreign exchange. Nyerere directed the state-owned Tanzania Sisal Authority to hand over all improperly managed estates to private ownership (*Daily Nation* May 5, 1985, 1), relaxed the law, which had been used to nationalize any home that was rented for profit, and permitted the import of goods for anyone who could afford it. Simultaneously, he endeavored to reduce government expenditures by cutting the number of civil servants.

In October 1985, the nation elected Ali Hassan Mwinyi as its second President. Mr. Mwinyi, President of Zanzibar since 1984 and a former Prime Minister, was selected by Nyerere as his successor. The smooth transition was a tribute to the leadership of Nyerere and the strength of Chana Cha Madinduzi (CCM), which had became the only political party in 1977 after a merger of the Tanganyika African National Union (TANU) and Zanzibar's Afro Shirazi Party. When Mwinyi was elected President, Nyerere still retained the position as Chair of CCM with Mwinyi becoming Vice-Chair. There was some speculation that Nyerere would step down as head of the party and give full rein to Mwinyi. However, at the Third National Party Conference held in October, 1987, Nyerere maintained the position as Chair of the Party for the next five years (*Tanzania Sunday News* November 1, 1987, 1).

The reason Nyerere maintained the leadership of the party was clear. He wanted to ensure that his special brand of socialism continued to guide the country. When Nyerere stepped down from the presidency, he acknowledged that some of his socialist policies had led to an economic decline by nationalizing too many industries and centralizing too much power in the government. Still, Nyerere was leery about moving away from the chosen path of African socialism, which in the short time since independence, had had considerable success in providing basic social services to the population. In rural areas, 41 percent of the people now have access to safe water, and 95 percent access to a dispensary within three miles. In addition, the adult male literacy rate was over 60 percent, and 73 percent of the eligible youth were enrolled in primary schools (Country Profile 1986, 7). Moreover, despite the difficulties encountered in achieving self-reliance, Nyerere remained committed to that goal for Tanzania. Financial assistance from the West in the form of loans and grants did not distract his vision. He saw such organizations as the World Bank and the International Monetary Fund as tools of capitalist powers and instruments of destabilization in the Third World that took advantage of weak developing countries (Harman 1987).

However, others in the newly formed government under President Mwinyi disagreed. Soon after President Mwinyi took office, Tanzania approached the International Monetary Fund and secured a loan of $78 million. The World Bank followed with a commitment of $100 million. However, there were conditions for these loans. Tanzania was expected to move closer to a "free market" and "free enterprise" system. This meant dismantling some state corporations, releasing expropriated property to private owners, lifting some restrictions on overseas transactions, and devaluating the official exchange rate of the Tanzania shilling. The new government established a farm price policy that gave incentives to individual farmers, loosened the government's hold on the grain marketing system, and eased foreign exchange restrictions (Harden 1987a). However, when the shilling was devalued, consumer prices

soared and urban dwellers directly tied to fixed incomes began to
suffer. By 1987 Tanzanian's foreign debt was moving beyond $3.4
billion. Servicing the debt with hard-earned foreign currency made
it impossible to make new investments for growth. To compound the
problem, the price of coffee, which made up 40 percent of
Tanzania's exports, was at a five-year low in 1987. In the same year
the World Bank declared Tanzania as one of the twelve
"debt-distressed" African countries and called for additional funds
to relieve the burden (Harden 1987a).

EDUCATIONAL REFORM: A NEW DIRECTION

The dilemma in education, as in other areas of economic
and social policy, was whether to continue down the path of
self-reliance and socialism or to become more fully integrated into
the world system and establish within the society inegalitarian,
capitalist social relations. The development of expertise in
technological and commercial fields needed to compete with the
Western world was seen as incompatible with the goal of equality
through schooling for all. Tanzania's growing economic problems
and the legitimation crisis encouraged state elites to act. President
Nyerere in 1980 appointed a thirteen member Commission to review
the entire educational system and make recommendations for its
consolidation or reform. The Commission collected the suggestions
and views of a wide range of people and deliberated for over a year.
In 1981 the Commission submitted its report to the President, who
turned it over to the political party and to various government
agencies for further deliberation. In 1984 the recommendations of
the Presidential Commission on Education, approved by the party
and the Government, were published and the Ministry of Education
had a new blueprint for education (Tanzania 1984). To implement
the new plan the Chair of the Commission was appointed as
Minister of Education.

The Commissions' Report noted that at the secondary level
education had not been able to satisfy national requirements for

skilled workers. As a consequence, the "Manpower Needs Approach" would be used in preference to the "Social Demands Approach" and attempts would be made to expand secondary education so that not less than 15 percent of children completing primary education would enter government secondary schools by the year 2000 (Tanzania 1984, 10-11). The Report also called for a clearly defined government action plan to promote scientific and technological growth. Provisions were to be made for graduates from vocational centers and technical colleges to transfer directly to places of higher education. The University of Dar es Salaam was to be expanded specifically to satisfy national work force needs and the directive that required secondary school graduates to work for two years before entering the University was relaxed (Tanzania 1984). The President's Commission also singled out the teaching of English as an area to be strengthened and charged the Ministry of Education with the responsibility to develop and implement an action plan to improve the teaching and use of English at all levels of education (Tanzania 1984, 21). This was based on the recognition that the English language was a window on the world--in business, commerce and trade. They also recognized that all textbooks, library books, and reference materials were in English at the secondary level and in higher education.

With the new educational plan in place and the movement away from socioeconomic policies of socialism and self-reliance, particularly after the election of Mwinyi as President, new initiatives in education began to emerge. The United States Peace Corps was invited back to Tanzania in order to help supply science, math, and English teachers for the secondary schools. Selected ex-patriots were hired from East Germany and Western countries to fill specific science and math positions in higher education; and the British Council began to take a more active role in working with teacher training colleges and secondary schools to upgrade English teaching.

Perhaps the most notable initiative was a three-year project funded by the United States Information Agency with ample assistance from the Tanzanian Government. Known as the Teacher/Text/Technology Program, its primary purpose was to strengthen secondary and teacher education in the areas of science, math, and English. To implement the Program, a grant was awarded to the University of Massachusetts Center for International

Education. The University established a collaborative relationship with the Ministry of Education and Dar es Salaam College of Education, a key organization for preparing secondary school teachers for the nation. During the period 1985-88 a series of projects were undertaken. Math and science tutors from the Dar es Salaam College of Education enrolled in specially designed master's degree programs at the University of Massachusetts, while personnel from the United States were in residence at the Dar es Salaam College. A series of short-term intensive programs on curriculum development, educational management, evaluation, and English writing took place at the University of Massachusetts for selected Tanzanian administrators, teacher-training tutors, and secondary school teachers. In addition, University staff, with the assistance of Tanzanian educators, conducted a series of intensive summer workshops in Tanzania for secondary school teachers of science, math and English. While conducting the workshops, University staff helped to train Tanzanian educators to initiate similar workshops. The project was designed to develop a cadre of skilled educators who could continue the work initiated during the first three years.

CONCLUSION

In the context of a growing economic crisis, efforts organized under the rhetoric of socialism and self-reliance have only slightly altered the nation's economy and have done too little to create the "new" socialist person. Teachers, their students, and parents do not yet possess the attitudes necessary to promote cooperation and service and must still attain the knowledge and skills necessary for an economy to prosper. Not only must the focus remain on rural development, but experience with a world economy has shown the need to expand scientific and technological education for industrial and commercial activity.

Plans to restructure education along these lines have been made, in part as a result of internal pressures and in part as a consequence of external conditions. The degree to which it is possible to implement the plans is still not clear. Much will depend on the new leadership in the country under the direction of President Mwinyi as well as those external and internal political and economic forces that are not always recognized by educators in most nations. The direction is clear, but resources are limited. To retain legitimacy the new leadership must enhance the nation's economic productivity without resorting to force and coercion and without creating too much social inequality. Education is clearly implicated, but it remains to be seen whether these leaders will have the luxury of time to carry out this process.

REFERENCES

Bauer, P. 1971. *Dissent on development: Studies and debates in development economics.* London: Weidenfeld and Nicolson.

Bienen, H. 1967. *Tanzania: Party transformation and economic development.* Princeton: Princeton University Press.

Country Profile. 1986. *Tanzania, 1986-87.* London: The Economist Publications.

Country Profile. 1987. *Tanzania, 1987-88.* London: The Economist Publications.

Fagerlind, I., and Saha, L. 1983. *Education and national development: A comparative perspective.* Oxford: Pergamon Press.

Frank, A. 1979. The development of underdevelopment. In C. Wilber (Ed.) *The political economy of development and underdevelopment.* New York: Random House.

Harden, B. 1987. Africa's poor on brink. *Washington Post* (7 June): A1.

Harden, B. 1987. Two years after retirement Nyerere sparks new debate. *Washington Post*, (11 July): A15.

Harden, B. 1987. Nyerere reconsiders retirement. *Washington Post*, (1 November): A43.

Harman, N. 1987. East Africa: Turning the corner. *The Economist*, 303, 7503 (20 June): 56:3-18.

Harris, N. 1983. *Of bread and guns: The world economy in crisis.* Harmondsworth, Middlesex, England: Penguin Books.

Hoogvelt, Ankie, M.M. 1986. *The Third World in global development*. London: Macmillan Education.

Ingle, C.R. 1972. *From village to state in Tanzania*. Ithaca: Cornell University Press.

Institute of Adult Education 1971. *Adult education now (Elimuya Watu Wazina)*. Dar es Salaam: University of Dar es Salaam.

Kahama, C., Maliyamkond, T., and Wells, S. 1986. *The challenge to Tanzania's economy*. London: James Curry.

Kim, K., Mabele, R., and Schultheis, M. (Eds.). 1979. *Papers on the political economy of Tanzania*. Nairobi: Heinemann Educational Books.

Kurtz, L. 1972. *An African education: The social revolution in Tanzania*. Brooklyn: Pageant-Poseidon.

Legum, C. 1984. Socialist Tanzania may be climbing out of its economic hole. *Christian Science Monitor* (4 December): 10.

Nyerere, J. 1967. *The Arusha Declaration and TANU's policy on socialism and self-reliance*. Dar es Salaam: Publicity Section, TANU.

Nyerere, J. 1968. *Ujamaa: Essays on socialism*. London: Oxford University Press.

Nyerere regrets nationalizing sisal estates. *Daily Nation* (Nairobi), 1985 (May 5): 1.

Powers, C. 1985. Tanzania: A vision worn thin. *Los Angeles Times* (26 December): 10.

Psychas, G. 1982. *Schools for self-reliance: Two Tanzanian secondary models*. Ed.D. Dissertation, University of Massachusetts.

Samoff, J. 1987. School expansion in Tanzania: Private initiatives and public policy. *Comparative Education Review*, 31, 3: 333-360.

Socialism wins landslide victory. *Tanzania Sunday News* (Dar es Salaam) Nov. 1, 1987.

TANU National Executive Committee. 1974. Directive on the implementation of education for self-reliance. *The Musoma Resolution*, Dar es Salaam: TANU.

Tanzania: The end of Ujamaa. *The Economist* (London) August 23, 1986.

Tanzania, The United Republic of. 1969. *Tanzania's second five-year plan for economic and social development: 1 July 1969 to 30 June 1974*. Dar es Salaam: Government Printer.

Tanzania, The United Republic of. 1979. *Third five-year plan for economic and social development*: 1 July 1976-30 June 1981. Dar es Salaam: Government Printer.

Tanzania, The United Republic of. 1984a. *Basic facts about education in Tanzania*. Dar es Salaam: Printpak.

Tanzania, The United Republic of. 1984b. *Educational system in Tanzania: Toward the year 2000*. Dar es Salaam: Government Printer.

Tanzania, The United Republic of. 1986. *Basic education statistics in Tanzania, 1981-1985*. Dar es Salaam: Ministry of Education.

Thompson, A. 1981. *Education and development in Africa*. New York: St. Martin's Press.

World Bank. 1988. *Education in sub-Saharan Africa*. Washington, DC: World Bank.

World Bank. 1985. *World development report 1985.* New York:
    Oxford University Press.

PERSPECTIVES OF EDUCATIONAL REFORM IN HUNGARY

Peter Darvas

Hungary lives in a period of reevaluation. There is a massive willingness to push for institutional reform in the midst of a deep economic and political crisis--a crisis brought on by dynamics in Hungary and in the world system. All the participants in and outside the formerly exclusive central policy-making institutions are involved in a transformation of their social and political relations. New strategies are introduced into old political and governmental institutions.

The Hungarian Socialist Workers Party (HSWP) first gave up its monopoly of power, then destroyed its own mass-party character, changed its name to Hungarian Socialist Party (HSP), disbanded party cells in workplaces and armed partymilitia, and relinquished privileges, such as the exclusive use of state-properties and the control of information channels. In other words, it limited itself to being one of the contenders in a multiparty system. The parliament, even before those elections, tried to engage in effective legislative activities, giving voice to critical and sometimes even radical political ideas. Since the election the new government seeks an effective political strategy not determined by a conservative party, the Hungarian Democratic Forum (HDF).[1] This strategy contains elements of market-oriented reform proposals,which are seen to be the way out of the economic crisis.

Meanwhile new pressures are placed on old institutions from outside the ruling authorities. Since the second half of 1988, the political arena has taken on a more complex character; new parties, associations, popular demonstrations, and other initiatives of a reinvigorated civil society are reshaping policy-making processes. The reform proposals and political actions show that practically none of the institutions can avoid radical transformation. Not only are their function and their content subject to sometimes unpredictable changes, but there has also been a shift in the way people think and communicate about them.

The educational system has not been an exception; indeed, it is in the center of current dynamics. Its situation within the broader social, political, and economic environment and its internal political, administrative, and organizational structure are the subjects of heated debates and conflicting actions. This chapter will also focus on the historical and institutional context that offers us a perspective on these contemporary developments.

HISTORICAL TRADITIONS FROM 1777 UNTIL 1945

Before becoming part of the "Eastern block" Hungary belonged to the Austro-German cultural, economic, and political interest zone for 250 years. Education shows the strong effect of these long traditions. In 1777, Empress Maria Theresa issued the zone's first educational decree, "Ratio Educationis," aimed at organizing elementary education. The 1806 education act made school attendance compulsory, although this was not achieved for quite some time (Hanák 1988). The first comprehensive Public Education Act was issued in 1868 by Baron József Eötvös, approximately a year after the Compromise between Austria and Hungary, that created the Austro-Hungarian Monarchy. The law made elementary schooling compulsory and placed it under state supervision. It is noteworthy that the Act elevated elementary school teacher training to a secondary education level. Before that time the standard required of teachers was two years of training in a model elementary school after the completion of their own studies.

We should note that the secondary schooling system operated under Austrian administrative and cultural dominance, and the elementary and secondary levels remained socially and academically separate. The training of teachers for the middle schools and beyond was independent of the training of the elementary school teachers, and the former even gained the level of higher education in the 1910s, providing high social prestige for those who graduated (Kozma 1984).

This split was clearly expressed by the structure. Elementary education was obligatory for children until age twelve, after which the majority of the graduates who did not enter secondary school either chose an apprenticeship or entered the labor market. At age ten, however, children could transfer to the "citizens' school," which offered preparation for middle-level technical fields or upper secondary commercial or trade schools.

The elementary and citizens' schools together represented the "practical" pattern of schooling for youth destined for unskilled work in the rural areas, skilled labor in small industries, and careers in middle-level technical fields. At the core of this pattern were the "volkschool educators," who were the leading intellectuals in the rural areas and small towns. They also served as leaders of populist movements, which from the 1920s promoted a nationalist road for social and economic development.

The third choice, the gymnasium, similar to its Prussian origin, provided ten- to 18-year-olds with 8 years of academic (versus practically oriented) knowledge of science, math, classics, and literature. After completing their study in the gymnasium, students could take the prestigious Maturity Exam, which led to higher education. The gymnasium teachers identified themselves with their academic field, designed their own curriculum, organized local workshops, wrote and published their textbooks.

All levels of schooling were administered by the state, and most of them were free, except some church-owned gymnasia, which charged tuition.

POLITICAL CONDITIONS AFTER
WORLD WAR II

After the end of the Second World War Hungary belonged
to the "Soviet" or "Eastern" Block, with which was associated a
specific type of modernization process. Hungary and other Eastern-
Central European countries experienced a longstanding effort of a
particular pattern of modernization with revolutionary political and
economic transformations in societies where traditional cultural
features remained.

Hungarian socialism basically promoted the Soviet system
with a nationalized, centrally-planned economy and a monolithic
political structure. The outside threat of the Cold War oriented the
state towards the radical mobilization of social forces and
accumulation of capital. This strategy was administered from the
center of the party-state system by militant and repressive means.
Through the conjunction of the state and the Communist Party (from
1949 the Hungarian Socialist Workers Party, HSWP) the entire
social system was restructured in a monolithic and hierarchical way
to achieve centrally issued political goals. Even family life, leisure,
or migration within the borders became subject to regulation by the
central political and administrative machinery. Every social
institution, including the educational system, had to be organized
and subordinated to the centrally determined economic and political
aims.

Education became one of the most important battle fields
in the "class-struggle." In 1948 the schools were nationalized,
including those run by the Church. The system had three primary
tasks: (a) to correct the former cultural monopoly of the
"bourgeoisie" (although in reality primarily undermining the status
of the middle stratas, including those who earlier filled professional
and administrative positions); (b) to promote upward social mobility
of manual workers (based on a notion of historical justice, though
statistics show that as soon as the key positions of the polity,
economy, and administration were controlled by the party, the
workers' participation began to decrease); and (c) to serve the

heavy-industry-oriented economic development, the new industrialization (Lukacs 1989).

For these aims the structure and the content of education was radically changed. A unified eight-grade general school was created by merging the elementary, citizens' schools, and the lower level of gymnasia, and a common curriculum was put in place in an attempt to eliminate regional and social inequalities. Schooling was made compulsory until age sixteen, though selection for different types of secondary schooling occurred at age fourteen.

The polytechnic character of secondary schooling became dominant for political and economic reasons. This strengthened a tradition of public vocational education, which first appeared on a large scale in 1938, when the economic expansion (and an act forbidding Jews to fill certain middle-rank professions) created labor shortages. After the Communists took state power only the four-year grammar school retained an academic curriculum profile. Its graduates (preferably those with manual worker family origin) were supposed to go on to higher education and replace the administrative and intellectual strata that were socialized before the war and, therefore, could not be trusted. The majority of secondary schools were vocational and offered a maximum of two to three years of practical training. Most secondary schools did not prepare for the Maturity Exam and, thus, did not lead to higher education. A new type of school, the vocational secondary school, was supposed to connect the two functions by giving both vocational training and academic preparation for further studies. This institution generally failed both purposes by not giving sufficient training in either vocational or general knowledge for those attending.

In practice the social and cultural tasks of the education system received less and less attention; its primary purpose was vocational and technical to meet the increased demands for skilled labor. The National Planning Bureau and the National Labor Planning Office (later the Office of Labor Reserves) had a special place in the structure of the central administration rather than the Ministry of Public Education and Religion (Darvas 1984).

The lack of independent or at least separate educational policy implied the lack of separate teacher policy. The fate of the teachers was determined by the fact that while education was thought to be important, the teachers and their professional problems were not. The dominance of macro-political factors hindered the representation of the professional interests of educators. At the same time the roles of teachers had to be homogenized for the general pattern of schooling and reoriented to achieve the main role of socialist re-education. The central political control of educators was even tighter than on other groups in the society.

The ideal role of the teacher was derived from the former model of volkschool teacher (Nagy 1988). The division between elementary and secondary school teachers was to be eliminated, and this purpose was illustrated by the new name given to the members of the homogenized teaching force: pedagogues. The ideal image of the pedagogues was identified with their ideological function even to the point of subordinating their vocational-technical training role. The ideological function involved socializing students to adopt the value system and thinking determined by the party and state as consistent with the broader political circumstances.

Teacher training programs as well as schooling were the target of control. The relative independence of teachers' organizations from the state was also challenged by the Communist Party. Initially, it made considerable efforts to dominate the existing unions and then created a single union, the Hungarian Teachers Free Union, to which all teachers had to belong, that was totally controlled by the Party. The Union was to assure that teachers would carry out the Party's resolutions and governmental decisions.

Besides seeking to control the union-movement, the Party began to attack teachers' subject matter pedagogy-oriented associations. In 1948 a State Council for Textbooks was created in order to place the curriculum policy in central hands. In 1949 the Advisory Body of the Educational Governance was suspended, and the Scientific Institute, which had been designated to replace it, was abolished a year later. The local organizations of parents were also brought under control of a central body. In 1951 the Hungarian Pedagogic Society was abolished. Except for a short period of liberalization after the death of Stalin, the only organization with a pedagogical profile that functioned publicly was the Pedagogical Branch of the Association of Hungarian-Soviet Friendship (Halasz 1988).

In 1954 the Scientific Institute of Pedagogy was founded in order to create a legitimate relationship between the political system and the educational community. The Institute throughout the following decade attempted to implement the official Marxist educational theory distilled from the works of the Russian educator, Makarenko. His basic model was that of "community-education," where the relations between teachers and students are family-like. The main purpose of education is the "upbringing" of youth through both the school and the youth movement. A major problem with the model was that its implementation was difficult with large classes of students.[2]

The quantitative development of education was indeed substantial. The number of secondary school pupils rose from 52,000 in 1939 to 330,000 by the 1980s. Along with student attendance, the number of teachers (i.e., pedagogues) increased by roughly 100,000, becoming three times larger by the 1980s than it was in the late 1940s (Kozma 1984). The quantitative growth, however, left qualitative problems and structural imbalances. The quality of education and its social and cultural aims became subordinated to its economic and political functions. For example, hundreds of thousands of people were provided with special maturation certificates after a few months of part-time studies, without having aquired the adequate level of knowledge. These adults, mostly industrial workers, could then "continue" their studies in higher education without really going through the secondary level. The emphasis on vocational training undermined the quality of general education, and the central planners determined the nature and quantity of graduates according to the workforce demands.

EDUCATIONAL REFORMS SINCE THE 1960S

After the death of Stalin there was increasing dissatisfaction with and resistance towards the oppressive politics, the plan-command type economy, and the ideologizing of society and culture. These dynamics, along with the uncertainty caused by Khruschev's Secret Speech, led to the revolution of 1956. This was the most radical form of popular uprising against a Stalinist regime in the Eastern block until 1989. The leadership of the Party recognized that the entire society had to be reformed if they were to retain their legitimacy and power. The efforts to reform the social system, including education, have been part of the Hungarian politics ever since.

From the early 1960s a series of reforms were introduced to deal with the tensions among the social, political, and economic functions of the educational system. Neither professionals, parents, nor other lay interest groups participated openly in these decision-making processes, because the reforms were designed in relation to hidden agreements. These strategic decisions came once in every four or five years and often moved the system in opposite directions.

The 1961 Education Act structured the basic conditions of the educational system up to 1985. The Act aimed at ensuring secondary schooling for everyone until the age of 18. It was based on the general assumption, shared by all governments in the Soviet bloc, that rapid development of society and economy would need a rapid expansion of education (Halasz 1986). It also opened the door the Makarenkoist pedagogy. However, the lack of funds for the central development of a comprehensive secondary school, together with a dramatic increase in the number of children reaching the age of entry into secondary school in the mid 1960s, made central planners modify the Act (Halasz 1987). The amendment aimed to orient the post-WWII baby-boom cohorts to the previously expanded programs of vocational training. This increased the vocational character of the educational system.

Toward the end of the 1960s educational policy became linked to the new economic system introduced in 1968. The political elite proposed a "New Economic Mechanism," promising uncontrolled private lives, the possibility of personal wealth, and a relatively developed consumer market. Since that time educational reforms have been implemented in the shadow of economic reform. They either functioned to strengthen or to counterbalance the changes in the sphere of economy. The introduction of limited "market-oriented" measures, however, resulted in tensions and public discussions about whether and how to extend the market orientation and the principle of decentralization to other spheres of the society (Darvas 1989). Market regulation and decentralization were contradictory to central planning, and groups such as those running heavy industries tried to mobilize their political influence to turn back the marketization and decentralization tendencies. In addition, the limited and often contradictory reform measures raised the question of how far the economic reform could go without a parallel process of political reform. Marketization, decentralization, and democratization were the most frequent issues of public and informal debates, including the debates in the arena of educational policy.

In 1972 the Central Committee of the Hungarian Socialist Workers' Party (HSWP) passed a resolution for a comprehensive reform of curricula (HSWP 1972). The aim was to reduce the rigor of the central curricula, so that it would be easier for all students in general schools to reach the official standard (Bathory 1972). The policy, therefore, stressed "equality" over "excellence." The lowering requirements signalled the dominance of the position that the "too high academic standards" were biased against students of working-class origin and increased unnecessarily the social selectivity of the system. The implementation of the curriculum reform was initiated in 1978, when the economic situation began to worsen, and financial and organizational problems appeared in most of the social institutions. This situation was exacerbated as the second post-WWII baby boom, children of the first one, reached school age.

Another tendency of the second half of the 1970s was the increasing involvement of academic "experts" in the school policy making process. This entailed greater attention by social scientists to analyzing the educational system. Educational research was initiated in the fields of sociology, economics, organizational analysis, system analysis, and (later) policy analysis. Natural scientists and other academics also became more actively involved in the development of school curricula related to their own fields. By 1979 these social science-based educational researchers and subject matter specialists created a detailed program for education, which in 1981 led to a Party resolution on schooling and higher education. The main purpose of the resolution was to establish a long-term plan to aid in the bargaining processes for governmental funding and possibly lead towards a new Educational Act to replace the outdated 1961 Act

Additionally, in 1981 a new institution, the Institute for Educational Research, was created, bringing together groups formerly affiliated with the Academy of Sciences, Ministry of Culture, and other agencies. The Institute focused on using social science theory and methods in the field of education, counter balancing the previously dominant pedagogical approach. The influence of the Institute grew considerably when its director, Ferenc Gazso, a sociologist, was nominated as Deputy Minister of Education in 1983. Gazso's main task was to prepare a new Education Act, which was introduced in 1985. The 1985 Act acknowledged the necessity of a legal framework for the decision-making process in which professional and lay interests could be represented independently of the administrative bodies of the state. This conception of policy making was clearly different from the previously dominated one, in which the Party and state apparatus established the direction to be followed by the educational system (Howell 1988).

ECONOMIC CRISIS AND POLITICAL DYNAMICS: 1970s AND 1980s

By the second half of the 1970s the economic problems began to increase. The second wave of the oil crisis reached Hungary, and the world market prices for Hungarian products became more and more unfavorable. The latter development was significant because Hungary, like other East European nations, had been counting on export income to generate the capital needed to repay Western banks for the loans obtained earlier in the 1970s. Because of its movement toward a market-oriented economy, Hungary was given access to loans and credits from Western banks and nations. These loans and credits allowed the Hungarian State to maintain a relatively high level of funding for social services and continue an industrial policy of additional investment without any significant restructuring of the centrally planned economy (Tardos 1988). The Hungarian State, thus, was able to avoid fiscal insolvency and retain some level of legitimacy. However, when in 1978 the West abruptly reduced the loans and credits at a time of sky-rocketing interest rates, Hungary's economic crisis became more severe and more apparent for all to see.

In 1979 the regime acknowledged publicly the financial crisis and called for a "new path of development," although the leaders of the Politburo and the Government seemed uncertain about what road to follow. At the beginning of the 1980s Party and State authorities tried to calm public concern by saying that the end of the tunnel is visible, but their predictions were sharply contradicted by worsening economic indicators. In 1985, for the first time since World War II, the level of production as well as the living standard began to decline. Trade and financial deficits increased, and the government introduced new income and value added taxes. This undermined the motivation of people who since the mid-1970s had worked extra hours in the second economy.[3] To most people it was clear that radical restructuring was needed, but those in power were afraid of the political consequences.

One could distinguish two possible directions of change. The first was the road towards marketization and privatization of the economic system. The supporters of this direction were the "reformers," while the elderly conservative elite, which been in power since 1956, viewed it as dangerous politically. The other possibility was a thorough reconstruction of the institutional and organizational order, necessitating the introduction of disciplined forms of rationalization and centralized control of the economy and politics in order to get rid of ineffectiveness and corruption. The supporters of this direction were the "partisans of order." Neither the ruling elite had the strength nor the people the patience to implement this policy.

The first half of the decade passed without resolution, but by 1985, when the acuteness of the crisis became manifest, even conservative factions of the party began to call for reform, although this reform rhetoric was not matched by energetic and consistent action to bring about change. By 1988 the two factions within the party, the "reformers" and the "partisans of order," reached a compromise and removed Janos Kadar, the First Secretary of the Party since 1956 and the conservative leader of the Party. They agreed upon a stabilization program and shared control of the government and party to implement it. The following two years showed that the program designed by the new First Secretary of the HSWP, Grosz, was too late and too moderate to control the erosion of Party's and State's legitimacy. The reform process was overtaken by outside political forces, and politics was no more the private business of the Party elites.

The party and the State had pursued contradictory policies and partial reforms in the Hungarian political economy of the 1970s and the 1980s. The situation was exacerbated by the fact that the conditions set by the IMF and the World Bank, which since 1982 oversaw the relations between Hungary and Western banks, were focused more on "exchange rates, interest rates, tax reform, and subsidy cuts" rather than on denationalization and privatization (Tardos 1989, 13). These national and international actions fed Hungary's growing debt burden. As Greenhouse (1990: C-5) reports, "Hungary's debt service will total about $3.2 billion this year, including $1.4 billion in interest payments and $1.8 billion in principal." This circumstance led the IMF to seek an agreement, signed on 14 March 1990, in which Hungary "pledged to hold this year's deficit to $550 million, instead of the more than $1 billion that had been planned" and "to slash exports to the countries of the COMECON, the Soviet trade group, to which Hungary had a huge surplus last year" (Greenhouse 1990: C-5).

SEARCH FOR A NEW IDENTITY OF EDUCATIONAL REFORM

Education was highly dominated by a conservative ideology in the early 1950s and early 1970s, and was slow in following the currents of reform in the late 1960s, and--as we will see--mid-1980s. Centralization of decision making in education has even exceeded that of the economy or other parts of public administration. This type of decision-making system limits the political participation of teachers, parents, and lay interest groups, while also restricting the autonomy of individual school administrators and teachers.

The role of teachers has traditionally been subordinated to politics mainly through their ideology function. They had specific instructions about the manner and timing of influencing the political consciousness of the students as well as obligations to limit their religious practices. Since the 1960s public values had been in flux, and accordingly teachers had to respond to the changing everyday problems of their students. Meanwhile, what and how they taught remained subordinated to national educational plans (until the 1970s) and to central curricula (until the mid-1980s). While students, reflecting shifts in popularly expressed values, became less interested in the values related to communities and social sensitivity and more attuned to the values of consumption, the centrally determined educational plans remained conservative by requiring socialization to the values of the socialist ideology. Teachers were also overwhelmed by their responsibilities of teaching the academic subjects under not quite "academic conditions." They had shortages of equipment and space and "surpluses" of administrative requirements and student discipline problems. These conditions were at the root of the conflict during the discussion of the 1985 Education Act, when teachers criticized the bill because it did not provide them with any solution to the problems of everyday teaching activity (Nagy 1985).

During the first steps of decentralization in 1984 the Ministry of Education introduced a policy workload statement, which listed those tasks that were and that were not compulsory for teachers. This considerably decreased their regulatory burdens. Later, further steps were taken towards deregulation and towards increasing teachers' autonomy in choosing alternative curricula, using their own innovations, and even electing the superintendent of schools.

These measures to increase teachers' autonomy, however, did not have that effect immediately, and there is some question whether they could achieve this result. Teachers often did not believe they had enough power or enough energy to innovate, and many feared that autonomy would result in their isolation, especially since their professional associations did not have any legitimacy. The "command for autonomy" was not popular in a system where it was seen to increase responsibility but not authority (Nagy 1985). Educators did not trust the policy and expected that they would be subjected to new types of regulations without the protection of the old routines.

Although decentralization of educational administration started in the 1970s and continued in the 1980s, several obstacles limited this process. The educational system, particularly the vocational and higher education segments, sat comfortably with the central planning system. This was despite the fact that since the mid-1970s the central planning system was seen to have failed (in education and other sectors) to develop and mobilize workers' and managers' capacity to keep the economy growing (Kozma 1985).

During the 1980s the increasingly restrictive budgeting policy of the government left education and its central administration in crisis and caused legitimacy problems. Educators criticized not only the administration but also their union officials, who were not seen to be providing enough protection against the worsening economic conditions. Those outside of education also criticized the conditions that resulted in a process of counterselection: namely, fewer candidates entered teachers colleges and, even among them, fewer would teach after graduation.

Second, the centralized policy-making mechanism in education is no longer synchronized with other policy arenas, which had moved toward more decentralized and participatary forms of decision-making. The Ministry of Education, which in the centralized system had the right to initiate or abort "reforms," found limited room to maneuver as the government's tight budget restricted any attempts at radical restructuring. At the same time the move toward decentralization, which began in the 1970s and was strengthened by the Educational Act of 1985, diminished the Ministry's administrative function and reduced its power. With the diversification of the political arena new, alternative unions and parties began to seek influence policy in education and attracted considerable legitimacy from teachers, parents, and other groups.

The Ministry experienced a crisis in its own leadership throughout the decade, which became acute in 1989 with the resignation of Bela Kopeczi, the Minister during most of the 1980s, and Ferenc Gazso, the Deputy Minister whose main role had been the implementation of the Education Act of 1985. In an interview after his resignation, the Deputy Minister commented quite skeptically on the prospects of carrying out the reforms of the Education Act in 1985, which according to him were limited by the Ministry itself. He "had to acknowledge that a bumptious dilettantism was the order of the day in the Ministry, and the wheels of reform were no longer driven there by the adherents of culture and education" (*Magyar Hirlap* 1989, 3). A major problem that the Deputy Minister recognized was that while the Educational Act was aimed at decentralizing the educational system, he was trying to carry out the reform by the Ministry, which itself is part of the central administration. Consequently, Ministry personnel were reluctant to implement the reform measures by which they would lose their authority.

The efforts of the Deputy Minister were not welcomed by some of the educational experts, for whom real reform meant the centralized restructuring of the ideological content of education. They urged the Ministry officials to mandate nationally the new teaching methods and curricula that had been developed on an experimental basis in a few local education authorities. This contradicted the direction of the 1985 Act, which had its main purpose "not to bring contents created above into education." This was considered by the critics (mentioned above) as "failing to react to the requests and suggestions of educators." This, the critics argued, was the reason "that countless efforts oriented towards the real reform of schools fell apart" (*Magyar Hirlap* 1989, 20).

The position of the Party in the matter of education was not much different from that of the government. After transforming itself into Hungarian Socialist Party (HSP) from the Hungarian Socialist Workers Party, it gave up its monopoly in the political arena and designed a new political program with social democratic values. Interestingly, the designers of this policial program devoted only one paragraph with three short statements to education. In this brief statement, however, the HSP called for major changes in the educational system: eliminating the state's monopoly of education, giving more autonomy to the schools, guaranteeing freedom of learning, and restricting central administration to the necessary technical regulation of the system (*HSWP* 1989).

NEW PARTICIPANTS IN THE POLITICAL ARENA

The political transformation of the country promotes "new" participants in the arena of educational politics. Although these participants had been involved previously, they are "new" in the sense that they have became more prominent actors in the process of educational policy. We can distinguish three main types of participants: academic experts, new associations of educators, and new political parties.

Academic Experts

Earlier I mentioned two basic approaches of academic experts. The first approach is based on the science of pedagogy and on analysis of the internal processes of teaching. The second was developed during the 1970s, borrowing methods from the social sciences, and is concentrating on the broader, systemic character of education.

For the pedagogy experts political reform necessitates restructuring the national curricula in accord with the new societal values: democratic politics, entrepreneurship in the economy, and nationalism. Moreover, pedagogically oriented experts see the need of centrally initiated reform to assure authentic changes.

In contrast, the social science experts are critical of centrally initiated educational reform. They published a book that expressed their views on educational change (Lukas-Varhegyi 1989). In this volume they claim that reforms are "par excellence" decisions initiated at the top. Based on a critique of the past and on an analysis of the current situation, they objected to this centralized process. Instead, they offered a view of how to open the educational system and to adopt democratic procedures (Lukas-Varhegyi 1989).

Educators

Until recently teachers did not have an independent professional association through which they could affect educational policy. Although the Hungarian Pedagogic Society was re-founded in 1967, its primary activity was to call public attention to teachers' inadequate pay and working conditions. The only official educators' trade union was the Union of Pedagogues (UP). Similar to other branches of the National Council of Unions, the UP served to communicate decisions downward to its members rather than acting as a forum for policy formulation or as a proponent of teachers' interests.

In the context of movements toward political democratization educators created new associations to pursue their group interests. Some efforts have been made to create associations organized according to subject matter specializations (e.g., Association of History Teachers), institutional types (e.g., Union of Special Educators), or educational levels (e.g., Union of Workers in Higher Education). Another initiative involved the creation of a new general trade union, the Democratic Union of Pedagogues (DUP), which is neither controlled by the government nor linked to political parties. The DUP was created on November 22, 1988, and was focused on enhancing educators' participation in the educational policy formation process rather than on representing the employee interests of teachers. The DUP, thus, assumed a clearly political character rather than a classical trade unionist one. Soon after its creation the DUP published its reform plan, "The Program of the Democratic Union of Educators," which, as we will see, challenges the whole system of public education (PDSZ 1989).

Political Parties

The parliament officially legalized a multi-party system in October 1989. However, political organizations independent of the former monopolistic party, HSP, had been operating openly since the end of 1987. These parties first focused on promoting further political democratization and developing their own structure and ideology. Therefore, very limited attention was paid to articulating policy proposals for education, the economy, or other areas of social policy.

The Hungarian Democratic Forum (HDF) was the first alternative party created and functioned initially as a coalition of diverse political orientations, only sharing a demand for political reform. Subsequently, the HDF developed a more concrete political ideology, representing a populist approach with a strong nationalistic value system. Nevertheless, the HDF intends to keep the character of a social movement, which is flexible enough to incorporate various political currents. The HDF's political strategy is reflected in their educational program, which is a list of value positions rather than concrete reform proposals or policy measures. They generally claim, that "education is a strategic branch" and it should be considered so in budgetary matters. Their "basic principles are freedom, autonomy, democracy and colorfulness" (HDF 1989).

The program of the Alliance of Free Democrats (AFD) was originally created by the democratic opposition, which from the 1970s until 1988 worked as an underground political movement. At the point of their legalization, they joined with other groups, mostly urban intellectuals, certain professional groups (such as economists, legal experts, and social scientists) committed to radical restructuring of the whole social system. Accordingly, their "Program for Changing the System" contains a detailed strategy concerning a multi party system, democratically elected and functioning parliament and other political institutions, a non aligned status in terms of foreign policy, an orientation towards economic and cultural ties to the European Community, a modern market economy with mixed ownership and limits of monopolization, and a social policy that really aims to help the poor and disadvantaged (SZDSZ 1989). The AFD's proposals on education include eliminating the state monopoly in education and strengthening lay local control of the system.

The programs of the AFD, the HDF, and the HSP are similar in their values and goals, but their tone and terminology are distinguished, reflecting differences in the social groups they aim to reach. While the HDF targets the support of the middle class, which is afraid of the shock therapy of marketization, the AFD's radical political image is oriented to the intellectual "class," who have traditionally occupied an exclusive position in the social hierarchy (Szelenyi and Konrad 1970). The HSP developed out of the HSWP and, thus, embraces the groups who have held positions in the state apparatus.

COMPARING THE PROPOSALS FOR EDUCATIONAL REFORM

In this section we will compare the different groups' proposals in two general areas to indicate how the general similarities in programs are articulated somewhat differently: (1) democratizing the policy area and (2) regulating the system.

Democratizing the Policy Arena

While the proposals vary in terms of proposed social functions of education, one aim is shared by the different groups: a public and democratically regulated political arena for participants, who have more or less articulated interests in education. This means open access for lay interest groups, including those organized through various political parties, and the opportunity for educators to form various types of associations to pursue their interests. This also entails, at least for some of the groups, the possibility for individuals, families, and communities to choose among types of educational provision. The Alliance of Free Democrats (AFD) seeks the "liberation of education from the power of the monopolistic ideology" to clear the system from its role as a "direct legitimating institution of the party-state" (SZDSZ 1989). Second, their program aims to free education "from the power of scientific and pedagogic interest groups" (SZDSZ 1989, 5). According to the AFD, "the pressure of these groups resulted in oversized, sometimes unteachable curricula" (SZDSZ 1989, 3). At the central level decisions should be assigned to the parliament, and there policy-making should be limited to the financial matters. Most policy decisions (e.g., about curriculum, organizational structures, and personnel) would be made at the local level by regional school councils and school boards. The basic concepts of the program are the rights for individuals to choose, for citizens to found schools, for professional groups to make changes in structure, and for schools to act autonomously (SZDSZ 1989).

The Hungarian Democratic Forum (HDF) is more careful about calling for further decentralization because its members fear that limiting the role of the national government in educational policy-making might lower education as a funding priority and because they believe that the best way to strengthen the national identity of the society is through a nationally functioning curriculum.

The Democratic Union of Pedagogues (DUP) aims to increase the power of teachers and the independence of schools. This is expressed in the demand for the democratic election of school principals by teachers, the vesting of school-level policy decisions in committees of teachers, and the possibility of controlling the central government's decisions by a "Chamber of Schools." Their program also proposes financial independence for schools, the individual rights of schools to select students, and the intellectual independence of teachers (PDSZ 1989). The DUP also sketched an institutional framework of the local self-regulating bodies. They urge the creation of a school board with representatives and a corporate body. Half of the members would be elected among the inhabitants, and the other half would be appointed from institutions with interests in the system: local councils, schools, political organizations (PDSZ 1989).

The social science academic experts propose in their program the creation of a "National Coordination Council," which would stand above the level of Ministries in order to coordinate decisions. The national government control should be based on continuous evaluation of effectiveness rather than on direct regulation and on balanced power relations between national and local institutions. The program also emphasizes that the state monopoly of schooling should be eliminated, central government's role should be restricted to financing the system, and central administrative control of pedagogic activities should be limited (Lukas 1989).

Means of Regulation

Drawing on teachers' daily encountered problems with central and regional administrative authorities, the DUP's proposals identify specific corrections. They want the government to limit the mandatory working time[4], introduce new alternative curricula, particularly in the social sciences, and allow local curricular initiatives and alternative organizations (political organizations for the youth and unions for teachers) (SZDSZ 1989).

The AFD separates two basic principles on how to regulate the system. One is to regulate the process of selection by a public system of exams independent of the schools. The program states that this would eliminate those hidden processes of selection that may reinforce social inequalities. In other words, it would make the process more visible and accessible to public control but would keep the necessary structure of selection (SZDSZ 1989, 10). According to the AFD proposal an inevitable problem of the selection process is linking the educational system and the labor market in terms of both job level and type of industry. The strategy served earlier as a means to supply the preferred economic sectors with trained workers in the situation of shortage. The program urges the "break with the dominance of central apparatus of labor force distribution" and promotes the use of market-forces and business-interests in designing vocational educational programs (*Program of HSWP* 1989, 2). The marketization of the economic system on the other hand, requires multiple points to enter or exit the educational system, and new institutions for further education, retraining, and special care of the young unemployed.

The other commonly discussed principle is the need to limit the state regulation of schools to the financial area. This aim is commonly shared by the DUP, AFD, HDF and the academic experts. Deregulation would significantly decrease the power of the central bureaucracy. The proposals of AFD and DUP suggest that the distribution of resources for the maintenance and development of institutions would be organized on a per capita basis instead of the previous functioning hierarchical distribution through the Council system. The proposal of the HDF would eliminate the Council system and create a independent regional institution for education. The AFD's proposal also calls for the introduction voucher system as a radical break with the former administrative traditions. Vouchers, however, are usually mentioned only as a vague idea rather than representing concrete reform plans (Darvas 1989).

CONCLUSION

The transformation of the political arena implies radical changes in the orientation of the whole educational system. This has meant that the Soviet-type model has lost its dominance, and Western European educational policies are beginning to be influential, especially in relation to new retraining systems to help solve problems caused by increasing unemployment, etc.

The last government, elected under the one-party system, already established a policy urging closer ties to Europe. This orientation was expressed by the Minister of Culture when he identified the new governmental priorities: (a) changing the foreign language requirement from Russian to other languages; (b) introducing a "new moral basis for learning" aiming at higher academic standards, and competition; (c) strengthening local control of education; (d) providing schools with modern equipment (quality rather than quantity); (e) providing higher wages and further education for teachers; and (f) encouraging and supporting religious institutions (Glatz 1989).

Besides such political declarations some concrete steps were taken by the government towards establishing agreements with international organizations. These included: (a) a new equivalence conference was organized aiming at harmonizing the structure of credentials of the educational system with the Geneva convention and (b) the government began consultations with the World Bank to initiate and support programs aiming to improve the system of vocational education and to finance agricultural training programs (Glatz 1989).

The reform process of the Hungarian educational system in the 1980s is not primarily an educational phenomenon. The introduction of a market system, the steps towards a decentralized administration, the quest for a democratic political arena, the reconstruction of the financial system, and the search for national cultural traditions are all the part of a "big picture."

The centralized system, introduced 40 years ago, attempted to insure that sub systems adapted to the dominant tendencies. In the early 1950s this meant that education had to function like a big factory as part of the economic plan and was supposed to produce a specific quantity and quality of trained people. Typically the introduction of changes in macro-level policies is easier in the centralized decision-making system than the reconstruction of local independent policy-making arenas. This sort of reform results in a situation in which the educational sphere is subordinated to one set of values, principles, or priorities, and the "reformers" try to force the adoption of the appropriate curricula, structure, or credential system. This strategy of reform is still typical in the centralized Hungarian educational political arena.

In the long term, however, the emergence of relatively autonomous teacher organizations, the rationalization of administrative procedures, and the creation of local, lay interest groups should result in a different type of reform, one which allows all participants to identify their interests and to influence the policy making process through their position. The fact that this type of reform gets increasing attention makes clear that at least the rhetoric, if not the practice, of educational reform is undergoing a dramatic change.

NOTES

1.   This analysis was written in April 1990, at the time of parliamentary elections.

2.   It was partly over the question of class size and adequate resources for education that the defenders of "authentic pedagogy" came in conflict with the Party and the State. By their commitment to a pedagogy oriented to working in small groups for classroom communities, the defenders of "authentic pedagogy" were in effect challenging the legitmacy of the ambitious graduate numbers of the Central Plan and were seen to endanger the central political and economic aims. Consequently, the Party and the State challenged those who wanted to implement an authentic pedagogy and education. For an example, the well-known Marxist psychologist, Ferenc Merey, who was considered a major proponent of an authentic pedagogy, was banished from the field (Halasz 1988).

3.   The "second economy" represents the private sector and the black market, which functioned to supply goods and services that the planned and state-dominated "first economy" was unable to provide.

4.   A limit in mandatory classes and administrative requirements.

REFERENCES

Archer, M. 1979. *Social origins of educational systems.* London: Sage.

Bathory, Z. 1986. Decentralization issue in the introduction of the new curriculum: The case of Hungary. *Prospects*, 16, 1: 33-50.

Darvas, P. 1984. *Labor force policy and the system of education in Hungary at the beginning of planned economy (1949-1956).* Budapest: Institute for Educational Research.

Darvas, P. 1989. Reform policy and changes in the educational system. *Higher Educational Policy*, 1, 3: 38-43.

Ferenc, L. 1989. Equal chances and elite education. *Magyar Hirlap* (10 March): 5.

Glatz, F. 1989. Az oktatasra forditott penz, a kulturaval valo torodes nemzeti erdek (The money spent on education, the care about culture belong to the national interests). *Kozneveles* (22 September): 3-6.

Greenhouse, S. 1990. Hungary sees no need to reschedule its debt. *New York Times* (6 March): C-5.

Halász, G. 1988. *Az ifjusag nevelese es az oktataspolitika Magyarorszagon a hatvanas evek elejen: torteneti-politikai elemzes.* (Bringing up the youth and the educational policy in Hungary at the beginning of the sixties: Historical-political analysis). Budapest: Institute for Educational Research.

Halász, G. 1986. The structure of educational policy-making in Hungary in the 1960s and 1970s. *Comparative Education*, 22, 2: 125-136.

Halász, G. 1987. A new education act. *New Hungarian Quarterly*, 27, 106: 108.

Hanák, P. (ed.) 1988. *One thousand years. A concise history of Hungary.* Budapest: Corvina.

Howell, D.A. 1988. The Hungarian education act of 1985: A study in decentralization. *Comparative Education*, 24, 1: 125-136.

HSWP 1989. *The program of the Hungarian socialist workers' party.* Hungary: HSWP (September).

Kozma, T. 1985. Conflict of interests in educational planning. *Prospects*, 15, 3: 347-360.

Kozma, T. 1989. Equal chances or elite-education? *Magyar Hirlap* (4 February): 5.

Kozma, T. 1984. Teacher education in Hungary: System, process, perspectives. *European Journal of Teacher Education*, 7, 3: 255-265.

Lukacs, P. 1989. Changes in the selection policy in Hungary: The case of the admission system in higher education. *Comparative Education*, 25, 2: 219-228.

Lukacs-Varhegyi, G. (ed.) 1989. *Csak reformot ne. Szakertok az iskola vilaganak megujitasarol* (Anything but reform. . . . Experts on the renewal of the world of schools). Budapest: Edukacio.

A Magyar Demokrata Forum oktatasuugyi programja (The Educational Program of the Hungarian Democratic Forum). 1989. Hitel (Credit) No. 13.

Nagy, M. 1988. Teachers, as a professional group in the Hungarian education system. Paper presented for the Comparative Seminar of American-Hungarian Policy-Researchers on Education, Esztergom, Hungary. 23-29 May 1988.

Nagy, M. 1985. Utasitas onallosagra (Command for Autonomy). Manuscript, Institute for Educational Research.

PDSZ. 1989. *Oktataspolitikai koncepcio* (Educational policy conception). Hungary: PDSZ.

PDSZ. 1989. *A pedagogusok demokratikus szakszervezetenek programtervezete* (The program of the democratic union of educators). Hirek, Hungary (February): PDSZ.

The prosecution of reform depends on openness. Last interview with Deputy-Minister, Ferenc Gazso. 1989. *Magyar Hirlap* (3 March): 6.

Szekely, T. 1989. Comment on an interview. *Magyar Hirlap* (20 March): 8.

Szelenyi, I., and Konrad, G. 1970. *The road of intellectuals towards class power*. New York: Harcourt Brace Jovanovich.

SZDSZ. 1989. *A rendszervaltas programja* (The Program of Changing the System). Budapest: SZDSZ.

Tardos, M. 1989. Reforms or transforming the system. Unpublished manuscript, Institute of Financial Research, Budapest.

THE STATE, ECONOMIC CRISIS, AND EDUCATIONAL REFORM IN CÔTE D'IVOIRE

N'Dri T. Assié-Lumumba
and
Tukumbi Lumumba-Kasongo

The main thrust of this study is to analyze the formation, functions, and structures of a modern African state, its relationship to the world economy, and its domestic policies. Of particular interest are policies to reform the educational system of Côte d'Ivoire in order to achieve certain intended objectives officially defined as national ones, although they may tend to reflect some specific domestic or global class interests. The state is dealt with as problematic and educational policy, and reforms are analyzed as a reflection of this problematic within the framework of the world system and its economic crisis.

In this chapter we use a political economy approach derived from concepts articulated by dependency theorists and complemented by Third World forum advocates. That is to say that the analysis will be framed within the general intellectual

parameters and logic of historical structuralism. One of the aims of
the chapter is to look at the sets of relations between state apparata,
those who control them, and the economy and society at large. The
general approach is summarized by Immanuel Wallerstein (1973,
377):

> In peripheral areas of the world economy . . . the
> primary contradiction is not between two groups
> within a state, each trying to gain control of that
> state-structure, or to bend it. The primary
> contradiction is between the interests organized and
> located in the core countries and their local allies,
> on the one hand, and the majority of the population,
> on the other. In point of fact, then, an "imperialist"
> national struggle is in fact a mode of expression of
> class interests.

Dependency theorists (Frank 1984; Cardoso and Faletto
1978) tend to deal with political economy (for instance, issues
related to production, accumulation and consumption, labor,
markets, wages and their politics) with more emphasis on the
dynamics of imperialism. Scholars such as Samir Amin (1985; 1989)
and Claude Ake (1985), who represent the Third World forum
approach,[1] have offered complementary arguments within a
tradition of the historical structuralism. Though they do not reject
the dependency theory, its paradigms and assumptions, they tend to
put more emphasis on the dynamics of the world system in local
social conditions and their peculiarities. This helps define peripheral
formation as dynamic and "semi-autonomous" to a certain extent.
From this perspective, national culture, productive forces, the
character of the ruling class, and the nature of state formation must
be taken seriously.

Questions such as the following will be raised in this
inquiry: What are the objectives of state policy? What are its
ideological, material and human resources available to actualize
those objectives? How does the state produce and reproduce itself
within the context of the world economy? What role, if any, did
educators play as employees of a one party-state (until April 1990)
in the formulation and implementation of the educational reform?

These questions, among others, are relevant for understanding Ivorian educational reforms.

This chapter first deals with the formation of the Ivorian state and political economy. The development of the educational system of Côte d'Ivoire is presented. Next, the educational reform proposed in the 1970s is discussed in terms of its rationale and objectives. The nonimplementation of the reforms is analyzed in relation to global and national economic crises. The chapter next focuses on the role of teachers in the process of educational reform and the subsequent period of political liberalization. A concluding section summarizes the main arguments and indicates other directions for further investigation.

STATE FORMATION IN CÔTE d'IVOIRE

The state can be viewed as a creation of the rich or property owners to maintain their position as a dominant class and to preserve inequality (Carnoy 1984, 19-21). In terms of its operation, the state creates and uses various forms of domination, some of which seem to be "differentiated and disassociated from the ruling class, . . . and [thus] appears as an objective force standing alongside society" (Ake 1985, 1). Therefore, state policy is, in principle, the combination of vision, ideals, wishes, and beliefs of the ruling class in a pragmatic form to either legitimate its own power and economic benefits or create some form of solidarity with other segments of the society.

Especially in the context of dependent, peripheral societies such as Côte d'Ivoire, however, we must analyze the functioning of the state from an international perspective. The main goals of the state, hence, also include controlling local resources (people, their culture, their labor, and raw materials) and serving militarily and ideologically as a *gendarme* of the metropolis (Nkrumah 1966; Leys 1974). Côte d'Ivoire reflects many of the characteristics of dependent, peripheral, capitalist states, which according to Amin (1967) are constituted by: (1) a national economy dominated by merchant bourgeoisie in the wake of dominant capitalists; (3) tendency toward a peculiar bureaucratic development, specific to the contemporary periphery; and (4) the incomplete, specific character of the phenomena of proletarianization. The Ivorian state's policies and actions, therefore, must be understood in relation to the interests of dominant classes in both Côte d'Ivoire and France.

To adequately understand the workings of the Ivorian state in educational policy and educational reform, we must go beyond these generalities to a consideration of specific groups, organizations, struggles and events. The process of state formation in Côte d'Ivoire was different from countries that were involved in national or popular revolutions such as Algeria, Angola, Guinea-Bissau, Mozambique and Namibia. Ivorian nationalism, led by the emerging modern African elite of the 1930s and the 1940s, contributed to the formation of a larger French African community strongly attached to France, especially after 1950. Many state reforms formulated and implemented in the 1940s and the 1950s were the outcomes of the work of both the emerging Ivorian bourgeoisie and progressive forces in the metropolis. As part of these reforms in the 1940s and 1950s, when France agreed that Africans could participate in the French national assembly, the goal was not one of transforming colonial political and economic relations but rather one of trying to maintain the *status quo*.

State formation in Côte d'Ivoire must be viewed as a legalistic and deliberate political effort of France to minimize any potential for revolution. The actual and potential progressive forces in Côte d'Ivoire were systematically crushed through the use of military force in the early 1950s, while a rapproachement was being undertaken by the Ivorian elite who survived. State building in Côte d'Ivoire was part of the general reforms undertaken in the French colonies in Africa and Asia. After World War II, new forces started to articulate the issues related to political independence. At the Brazzaville conference of 1944, where only representatives of the metropolitan French state and the colonialist French administrators met, a new constitution was proposed that provided a certain level of autonomy for the colonies within a *Union Française*. This conference recommended representation of Africans in French political assemblies, access to all occupations by Africans, abolishing forced labor, developing education, and providing

Africans with the means for enhanced agricultural production (Chaffard 1965, 33-34). In general, the reform agenda was not locally determined, though later the new emerging African bourgeoisie became involved in order to advance its own interests and those of the French capitalists.

Taking advantage of opportunities proposed by the policy makers at the Brazzaville conference and the support of a communist governor, who had been sent to Côte d'Ivoire when leftist political parties participated in the coalition government in France in 1944, seven Ivorian plantation owners founded the *Syndicat Agricole Africain* (SAA). At the time of its formation, the intention of its members was not to challenge the existing power structures of the colonial administration nor to struggle for power sharing. Their goal was mainly economic; the SAA members wanted to sell their cocoa and other agricultural commodities at the same price granted to French farmers.

Gradually, this economic organization, having attracted unexpected popular support, was transformed into a political formation: *Rassemblement Démocratique Africain* (RDA), with the *Parti Démocratique de Côte d'Ivoire* (PDCI-RDA) as its subsection in Côte d'Ivoire. RDA with its local sub-section became more radical as they attracted support from Leftist parties in the metropolis, especially the French Communist Party. Thus, equality between French colonists, colonialists, and Africans, especially the emerging African bourgeoisie, became a key issue on PDCI-RDA's agenda. This party transcended, in terms of claims and organization, the colonial geographical boundaries of Côte d'Ivoire; it was represented and widely supported in other colonies of the *Afrique Occidentale Française* (AOF) and *Afrique Equatoriale Française* (AEF).

An important element that must be mentioned in an analysis of state formation in Côte d'Ivoire is the impact of "*Loi Cadre.*" Proposed by the ruling class in France and Houphouët-Boigny (the first chair of both SAA and RDA), the *Loi Cadre* was adopted in 1956. It authorized the 1958 constitutional referendum, in which Côte d'Ivoire and other French colonies (except Guinea-Conakry) voted in favor of the *Communauté Française*, thus, attaining a limited degree of independence from France. This community, despite French claims of equality between Africans and metropolitan

French citizens, meant basically the continuation of the French domination--culturally, politically, and economically--in Africa.

Côte d'Ivoire's external relations have involved economic, military, and technological cooperation with France in exchange for financial assistance. Thus, a dependent state was created. In general, Côte d'Ivoire has not been very influential in determining and controlling the production and the price of its major agricultural products. It is only recently and especially within the framework of multipartism that the Ivorian economic and political elites began disagreeing openly with Western nations over the selling price of raw materials. But they have little or no power to intervene in the world economic system.

After the *Loi Cadre* was adopted, Ivorian independence was negotiated by the plantation owners who founded the SAA, and they have maintained power since then. For instance, Houphouët-Boigny, the first president of SAA, was also elected president of RDA in 1946. He has been the president of Côte d'Ivoire since the country was granted its nominal political independence in 1960. This African elite group played a role in promoting both the metropolitan and its own local class interests in all areas, including economy and education. They articulated these interests by drawing on a combination of modern and traditional political ideologies, including Marxism and nationalism/pan-Africanism.

While Côte d'Ivoire opted for a liberal economy, this principle did not have its political equivalence. For instance, a multiparty system or some forms of popular participation did not exist before April/May 1990. But neither did the system produce a Bonapartist regime like that of Mobutu in Zaire or a militarist regime like that of Eyadema in Togo. As compared to Zaire or Togo, there is a relatively stable ruling class (a patrician class) in Côte d'Ivoire. Though the Ivorian state is strongly linked to the Ivorian (and French) ruling classes, it has created political and social alliances with various social classes. That is to say that this state has also a cultural and social base in the country; its legitimacy does not come only from its relations with the metropolitan France and the capitalist world. The education system has been one of the major institutions through which elites have sought to legitimate economic relations and the state.

HISTORICAL BACKGROUND OF THE EDUCATION SYSTEM

The structure and function of the system of education of Côte d'Ivoire at the time of its political independence, like those of other French colonies in Africa, were modeled on the religious, selective, and elitist traditions of medieval France. However, the French colonial administration did not implement the assimilation policy in the domain of education until emerging African elites demanded it in the 1940s.

By the time Côte d'Ivoire formally became a French colony in 1893, there were in fact two separate systems of education in France,[2] designed for different social classes: one for the dominant class or *le Secondaire/Ecole des Notables* and the other for the masses or *le Primaire* (Chevalier 1968; Prost 1968). The system established for the dominant class was created first and was shaped by religious congregations such the Jesuits and Oratorians. It included pre-school, elementary, secondary and university levels, which were integrated and articulated as one system. Its curriculum was classical and academic, aimed at providing humanist and universal knowledge[3] (*éducation de l'honnête homme*), in the sense that it included ancient and contemporary societies and civilizations. By contrast, the system for the masses was composed of elementary education and two to four years of post-elementary education for those who did not leave school at the end of their elementary education. This post-elementary education for the masses was provided in three types of institutions: *Ecole Primaire Supérieure*, *Cours Complémentaire*, and *Ecole Pratique*. This elementary school system was mainly to train young men and women of the Third Estate (*Tiers-Etat*) for local technical and clerical jobs. Thus, the curriculum was vocational and varied from one region to another according to the region's economic activities.

In accordance with its ideology of colonization, the French colonial administration transferred to its colonies in Africa the elementary system designed for the masses (Assié) system was established in 1911. Even when in France the former two separate systems merged to become the *Ecole Unique* (a single educational system), the colonial administration continued to provide the elementary system for its colonies. Indeed, the main objective of education[4] in the colonies was to train a few Africans to perform subordinate roles. Even the schools for the chiefs' sons were geared to socialize future local leaders who would unlike those chiefs who were fighting the colonial establishment, seriously challenge the French domination.

In Côte d'Ivoire as well as in other colonies, formal education introduced by the French was rejected by the Africans, who considered that type of education irrelevant, since it provided the training for jobs they thought unimportant. The French education system in Côte d'Ivoire was also viewed as alienating and an integral part of colonial exploitation. Thus, in the early years of colonial education Africans who attended schools did so by force. "Tribal" chiefs were required by the colonial administration to provide specific numbers of children, with specific social background, to be enrolled in the colonial schools.

However, soon Africans realized that literacy in French and indirect exposure to post-revolutionary French political culture and ideas could serve as a powerful basis for questioning the foundation of the colonial situation and for organizing nationalist movements to achieve equality in the colonies and independence (Ki-Zerbo 1972; Assié 1982). Thus, after World War II and the Brazzaville Conference, as part of the broad quest for equality, Africans demanded that the technical/short stream system (*Système Primaire*) of education in the colonies be replaced by the *Ecole Unique* system, which had been adopted for the entire metropolitan population and the citizens of the communes in Senegal. They were demanding the implementation of France's proclaimed policy of assimilation, which, in the specific case of education meant a transfer of the French system to the colonies. This demand was satisfied, and in 1960, when Côte d'Ivoire was granted its nominal political independence, its system of education replicated the system of metropolitan France.

THE EDUCATION SYSTEM SINCE 1960

Since political independence in 1960 the system of education in Côte d'Ivoire has remained tied to the contemporary French system. The structure, the curriculum, the administration, etc., especially at the secondary and university levels, have paralleled the French ones, and changes introduced in France have been also adopted and applied to the Ivorian system. However, unlike the situation in France, education in Côte d'Ivoire is neither compulsory nor *de facto* universal even at the primary level. For years, especially in the 1960s, the demand for education exceeded the number of places available. Thus, the elitist and selective nature of the inherited system has been exacerbated.

The system is divided into primary, secondary, and tertiary levels. Primary education lasts six years and the official admission age is six. Admission to secondary education is competitive and based on a number of criteria, the most important being achievement and age. Progress through secondary schools, admission to post-secondary education, and promotion within each cycle are based mainly (at least officially) on achievement.

Côte d'Ivoire was one of the African countries which, at the May 1961 Addis Ababa conference sponsored by UNESCO, resolved to achieve by the 1980s universal primary school attendance and increased participation at the secondary and tertiary levels. In as much as formal education was declared "priority of the priorities," it has been the social program that has benefited most from state revenues. Until the early 1980s Côte d'Ivoire, compared to other nations, devoted a high proportion of its revenues to formal education: 7.4 percent of the GNP and 31.7 percent of public expenditures in 1973 (Tuinder, 1978) and 10.0 percent and 45.0 percent in 1981 (World Bank, 1983).

In the late 1960s and early 1970s at the peak of Ivorian economic growth, up to four ministries dealt directly with formal education (Ministry of National Education, Ministry of Primary and Television Education, Ministry of Technical Education and Professional Training, and Ministry of Scientific Research). Several institutions in charge of training teachers for the different types of schools were created and/or expanded. Private demand was so high that in relatively rich rural areas such as the Cocoa Belt (*Boucle du Cacao*), parents built many schools with their own resources. In cases where the central government did not provide teachers for these schools, local residents hired their own teachers.

The 1960s were years of great expectation and hope in terms of the ability of formal education to help achieve socio-economic development. These optimistic views were supported by the renewed popularity of human capital and modernization theories in Western industrial countries. The heavy investment in education during the first decade after political independence of Côte d'Ivoire was done without questioning the nature of the system of education. In contrast to other former French colonies, such as Guinea and Mali, which carried out some educational reforms immediately after political independence, Côte d'Ivoire kept the inherited system without making major changes. In fact, it has been a "normal" policy to adopt and implement in Côte d'Ivoire the educational laws and decisions of the French National Assembly or Ministry of National Education (Assié 1982; Assié-Lumumba 1983b).

The euphoria of the 1960s was followed by growing scepticism about the ability of formal education to lead to socio-economic development by training the needed work force. Universal primary education had not been achieved, and the "fortunate few," who graduated from secondary schools or even obtained university degrees, started having increasing difficulties in finding jobs appropriate to their credentials. Furthermore, while in the 1960s Côte d'Ivoire was presented as the successful case of economic attainment in Africa (Assié, 1975), by the early 1970s the indicators of economic performance started to show signs of malaise.

What went wrong? What were the causes of educated unemployment and the economic problems? In their search for a precise diagnosis and thus an effective and efficient treatment, Ivorian leaders initiated a systematic study of the educational system.

EDUCATIONAL REFORM PROPOSALS IN THE 1970s

On August 29, 1972, a National Commission for the Reform of Education was created as an institution of the political party (PDCI-RDA). The head of the state, as head of the party, appointed the members of the Commission to include representation from "all the social strata of the nation" (Commission 1972, 1). Although there are good reasons to speculate on the representativeness of the Commission's membership, it is fair to say that the government wanted an objective assessment of the system. This is why some strong and outspoken members of the higher education teachers union were appointed as members of the Commission.

The mandate of the Commission was defined in several documents, including a declaration of the Political Bureau of the PDCI-RDA at a seminar organized on June 12-16, 1972; the speech of the Chairman of the National Assembly and Secretary General of the party to the members of the National Assembly and the members of the Commission on August 28, 1972; and a letter from the President of the Republic to the Chair of the Commission dated December 21, 1972. An *Inspecteur Général de l'Enseignement* and member of the Commission whom we interviewed in 1979 said that the mandate of the President was clearly stated: "make sure that all Ivorian children who enter the school system find jobs when they complete their education." It is important to recall that this was a time of high economic growth which, despite the growing unemployment problem, contributed to Ivorian leaders' confidence that, with more adequate human resource planning, the educational system would have a higher external efficiency, thus reducing the unemployment problem.

The Commission sought initially to understand the education system, to "identify its weaknesses, the problems of adaptation and their consequences, and to find new objectives and solutions" (Commission 1972, 1). Despite the proclaimed diversity of social groups on the Commission, however, the method of data gathering adopted can be characterized as managerial in that an emphasis was put on gathering the opinions of those in high-ranking positions as opposed to seeking input from the masses. Thus, the Commission organized several meetings with and presentations by the heads of ministries concerned with formal education and/or employment, namely the ministries of National Education; Technical Education and Professional Training; Youth, Popular Education and Sport; Armed Forces and Civil Service; Agriculture; Labor and Social Affairs; and Planning; and State Secretariat in Charge of Primary and Television Education.

After the preliminary work of fact finding, the Commission came out with a critical assessment of the system of education in Côte d'Ivoire. In terms of the curriculum and the organization the Commission reported that the educational system was still a copy of the French system, with a few notable exceptions. By copying the French system, despite differences in the economy and human resource needs of the two countries, Côte d'Ivoire had a system of education that did not match local labor force needs. The Commission, for instance, cited a lack of technical and professional programs at the secondary level because of an emphasis on academic preparation for university-level liberal arts studies. As a result, the majority of secondary school leavers did not have any professional/technical skills. According to the Commission, the curriculum was essentially alienating, because it did not take into account Ivorian culture, economic needs, and society in general. Such a system, the Commission argued, was not likely to lead to socio-economic development of the nation.

It is important to point out that the Commission did not deal openly and specifically with the point that Ivorian society is not homogenous, and, therefore, although the system of education is alienating for a majority, it was working efficiently for many of those in power. Furthermore, the key issue of the structure of the economy was not addressed by the Commission. The assumption underlying the Commission's assessment was that if the educational system is reformed, there would be jobs waiting for the graduates and other school leavers, simply because they would have the appropriate training.

After its assessment, the Commission concluded that it was necessary to restructure the entire system of education. The new system had to be organized to satisfy the educational and the human resource needs of the country. Instead of organizing the entire education system as if every child will graduate from university, each cycle would be considered terminal and geared to developing students with the knowledge and skills required by the economy. The curriculum, moreover, was to have a clear purpose of "asserting the cultural identity of the nation" (Commission 1972, 12) rather than reflecting France's social reality.

A draft of the reform text was submitted for consideration to the government. On August 18, 1977, the National Assembly voted in favor of the 1972 Commission's proposed reform, and the new system, *Ecole Nouvelle Ivoirienne*, was to be implemented as soon as application decrees were promulgated. The goals of the *Ecole Nouvelle Ivoirienne* are defined in its articles 2-5 as follows:

> The goals of institutions (public and officially recognized private schools) are to develop a mind that takes initiatives and likes actions, to provide an education, learning and training in accordance with the objectives of national development, to achieve social and cultural integration of Ivorian citizens within the national community as well as in the main streams of universal civilization. They must give equal chances to all the children to be admitted in upper grades without any differences between classical and technical education, by allowing them to discover their vocations and abilities and to be cultivated, while they are being trained for jobs that they will perform in society. They must contribute to the nation-building through the assertion of the Ivorian identity, Ivorianization and Africanization of the curriculum. (*Loi de la Réforme* 1977, 1-2).

This new concept of education, which included attention to schooling and life-long learning, was to contribute to the development of village communities and regions. It was to train children, youth, and adult learners in "civic virtues," providing them with sense of responsibility and giving them the opportunity to put this in practice through their active participation in the organization of schools. An emphasis was to be put on science and technology as well as on manual labor. Scientific and technological education was to develop and encourage an understanding, appreciation, and commitment to improve rural and urban life.

One of the important missions of the proposed educational reform was to build a national culture by blending the subcultures of the different ethnic groups in the country. This was to deemphasize French culture, which had been imposed during the colonial era but had continued to dominate the society and the educational system. The proposed reform recommended the use of a few selected local languages as media of instruction at least in the lower grades.

The elitist nature of the old system was to be replaced by a popular, democratic one. Unlike the old system where the management of education was in the hands of administrators and technocrats, the new one was to involve different social groups in the decision-making process. For instance, the National Commission of Selection and Placement, which decides the academic career and professional orientation of individual students, would not be composed only of school administrators as in the past; it would also include representatives of the relevant Ministries, the National Assembly, the Parents Association, teacher unions, various professional groups, and students of each level (*Loi de la Réforme* 1977, Article 41).

THE NONIMPLEMENTATION OF THE REFORM

This major reform of the Ivorian education system, though proposed by the 1972 Commission and enacted into law by the National Assembly in 1977, has yet to be implemented. A number of explanations for this can be offered, including the lack of political commitment by the Ivorian dominant class to implement the reform. For this group the education system, created under French colonialism and refined under neo-colonial relations with France, functioned well to perpetuate its claimed cultural superiority and legitimate its political and economic power (Assié-Lumumba

1987). While economic stagnation hurt the dominant class, they were still able to enjoy a lifestyle well above the average Ivorian. Furthermore, the populist orientation of the Commission's report and the *Loi de la Réforme* may have served rhetorically to reduce the Ivorian state's legitimation crisis, but implementing the reform would have been working against the interests of the dominant class, Ivorians, and French living in Côte d'Ivoire.

A fiscal crisis of the Ivorian state, at least partly derived from Côte d'Ivoire's experience with the world economic crisis, also restricted the implementation of the reform. The report of the Commission specified that the implementation of the proposed fundamental changes in the educational system requires that "very large amounts of money be available" (Commission 1972, 72-73), but by the late 1970s such a requirement seemed less and less achievable as the economic crisis drained revenue from the government's treasury.

The cost of public education in Côte d'Ivoire is basically borne by the government. As Bourgoin and Guilhaume (1979) explain, there are three sources of the government's revenue: (1) income and other taxes collected, constituting a relatively small proportion of revenues; (2) external aid and loans, which are almost always assigned to specific projects; and (3) endowments of *Caisse de Stabilisation et de Soutien des prix des Productions Agricoles* (CSSPPA). Revenue is generated for CSSPPA through the following profit-oriented mechanism:

> under the Ministry of Agriculture, [CSSPPA] stabilizes prices paid to producers of agricultural export products. Cocoa, coffee, cotton, and vegetable oils are the most important ones. Profits are made when the difference between the export prices and export costs is positive. (Tuinder 1978, 66)

Although there has been some effort to diversify the cash crops since the 1960s, cocoa and coffee still constitute the backbone of the economy. Thus, a crisis in agriculture has a much more profound impact on the fiscal condition of the Ivorian state and political economy than a crisis in manufacturing or any other sectors. Indeed, the euphoria of the 1960s and 1970s corresponded to the period when agricultural commodities were sold internationally at a relatively high price, creating a relatively large amount of financial resources through CSSPPA for education. The 1980s, however, presented a radically different global economic context for Côte d'Ivoire. CSSPPA's revenue from the export of cocoa and coffee had fallen to (U.S.) $1.5 billion by 1985 and dropped further to (U.S.) $776 million by 1988. While there were record crop productions, especially cocoa, in 1987-88 and 1988-89, Côte d'Ivoire's gross domestic product (GDP) continued to decline. The public sector deficit rose sharply in 1988, and another austerity budget was adopted for 1989. Interest rates have been raised to underpin the currency.

In the 1960s and 1970s, external aid for education was minimal, since the country was considered to be relatively strong economically. For example, from 1960 to 1979, only about 3 percent of what Côte d'Ivoire spent for the construction and equipment of academic secondary schools was provided by external sources (Assié 1982). This situation changed during the 1980s as revenue generated by the CSSPPA from exporting agricultural commodities has declined. The relative contribution of external funding agencies to the Ivorian state revenues has thus been growing with an attendant increase in external influence on state policy and practice.

THE ROLE OF TEACHERS AS A PROFESSIONAL INTEREST GROUP IN THE REFORM

Côte d'Ivoire has basically been a one-party state from its political independence in 1960 until April/May 1990. Yet, multipartism flourished in the 1950s, although PDCI-RDA was the most popular. Parties such as *Parti Progressiste* operated during the elections and referenda. Although, according to the Article 7 of the Constitution, different political parties can be legally formed, several means were used by the ruling party to prevent the development of any opposition parties. In absence of other means of expression of opposition, teachers' unions have sometimes functioned as proxies for political parties or at least provided a forum for expressing views critical of the government. This has been the case more so for secondary school and higher education unions than for the primary school union.

The ruling political party has different organizations through which the party and the state incorporate and seek to control different groups: students (*Mouvement des Elèves et Etudiants de Côte d'Ivoire*, MEECI), women (*Association des Femmes Ivoiriennes*, AFI), and workers (*Union Générale des Travailleurs de Côte d'Ivoire*, UGTCI). UGTCI was supposed to be, at least officially and theoretically, the sole organisation of workers; thus, any other workers' union had to be integrated into UGTCI. However, teachers are an exception in that they are organized into three major unions: *Syndicat National de l'Enseignement Primaire de Côte d'Ivoire* (SYNEPCI) for primary education, *Syndicat National de l'Enseignement Secondaire de Côte d'Ivoire* (SYNESCI) for secondary education, and *Syndicat National de la Recherche et des Enseignements du Supérieur* (SYNARES) for higher education. Among the three unions, only the one at the primary education level is affiliated to the UGTCI as required by law. The two others were formed as independent unions and they have remained so. Given the structure of political power as conceived by PDCI-RDA, the strength and independence of these two unions are significant.

The dilemma faced by the political elites was that these unions have been perceived as too strong and operating almost totally beyond the Party's control. Yet an attempt to incorporate them in the UGTCI may present even more of a danger as strong members of SYNESCI and SYNARES would be likely to try to control UGTCI from the inside, undermining the Party's control over one of its vital sections. This would constitute a major threat to the Party's power. The PDCI-RDA's leaders opted to let SYNESCI and SYNARES remain independent of UGTCI so that they could at least ensure their control over other workers. Over the years, several attempts have been made by the party, mostly through the actions of the Ministry of National Education, to decrease the strength of the secondary and higher education teachers' unions and to control them even though they remained outside UGTCI. For example, in the 1988-89 elections clashes occurred between the Ministry of Education and the anti-PDCI-RDA wing of the union over which candidates should be elected to leadership positions in SYNARES. As a result of these clashes, the incumbent General Secretary of the union was tried and served a jail sentence for alleged mismanagement of SYNARES' funds, and a professor in linguistics at the Université d'Abidjan who used an excerpt of the transcript of this trial in a class was dismissed.

As noted above, various groups, including members of the primary school teachers' union (SYNEPCI), the two independent unions, SYNESCI and SYNARES, were invited to participate in the National Commission for the Educational Reform. Many teachers who participated in the Commission represented the hard-liners of their unions as opposed to other members who shared the views of the government and party. Especially the secondary and higher education teachers' unions' representatives were influential in shaping the reform document adopted by the government in 1977. They made both a critical assessment of the current system and recommendations for a new system that would be oriented towards the local reality and needs instead of the continued application of the French system. For example, the recommendation regarding the use of selected national languages (such as Dioula and Baoulé) as media of instruction rather than French was expressed by teachers as were proposals for disassociation from the French system of education, a change in the philosophy of education, a more egalitarian-oriented education system and society.

In post-independence Côte d'Ivoire, there is a long-standing tradition, initiated by the head of state, of giving the entire population the opportunity to express views on specified issues during *les journées du dialogue*. Giving citizens an opportunity to express their views and to publicly criticize the party, government, policies, and specific leaders has proven to be a very efficient means of avoiding a build-up of discontent and, thus, preventing any real threat to the *status quo*. The party and the government have rarely responded to the criticisms and proposals, but they have provided a forum for the population to express its views. In this context, it is not surprising that the reform that appeared impressive on paper has not been followed by application decrees since 1977.

As recently as during the September 1989 *journées du*

dialogue, teachers have demanded that the reform be implemented. Some of the most critical interventions during these *journées du dialogue* were made by the current Secretary General of SYNARES, Marcel Etté, a Professor of Medicine, and Gbagbo Laurent (chercheur en histoire) both members of SYNARES. The latter had been in self-exile for several years and had created a political party that the government considered illegal until the April/May 1990 changes. As a result, new discussions have been initiated concerning the implementation of the reform program that was proposed by the Commission in 1972 and adopted as government policy in 1977. The government officials continue to argue that the economic and fiscal crisis prevents much progress being made.

Furthermore, like in many other areas of the world in recent months, events have moved at a speed that is now difficult to control. The attempt by the government to implement in July 1989 an austerity program triggered social unrest that crippled the government for months. On February 19, 1990, after many parts of the country, including students' residences, were affected by a total blackout,[5] students protested because of the potential negative impact on their mid-term examinations. The initial action of the students, which was centered on specific student concerns, broadened as the government retaliated and kept many of them in custody. The students were soon joined by other groups, including workers. The students demanded that the government pay the farmers whose agricultural products had been taken in exchange for vouchers instead of money, dismantle MEECI, build a new university to accommodate more students, and dismiss the unpopular Minister of Education. On February 22, after the intervention of security forces, the Secretary General of SYNARES issued a strong statement in support of students and their broadening list of demands. The students also demanded political freedom and immediate implementation of Article 7 of the Constitution so that other political parties could be formed. Despite desperate efforts by the government to contain the situation by closing all schools from primary to university levels, the pressure became so great that in April the government announced that it would allow other political parties besides the PCDI-RDA to operate legally. As of August 1990, 26 political parties have been formed and more are expected to be organized before the December 1990 elections.

What is remarkable is the predominance of teachers as founders of most of the new political parties. For example, le *Front Populaire Ivoirien* is led by Gbagbo Laurent; *Le Parti Ivoirien des Travailleurs* is led by Professor Francis Wodié; and *l'Union des Sociaux-Démocrates* is led by Bernard Zadi Zaourou. And in the 1990 elections 42 of the 175 members of the national legislative body elected were teachers.

CONCLUSION

The processes of both state formation and educational policy development in the post-colonial era in Côte d'Ivoire have been consolidated by strong cooperation between the Ivorian leaders and the French ruling class and institutions. Thus, the post-colonial state formation can be characterized by the continuation and reproduction of the metropolitan structures and objectives in the local African conditions. This continuity and the stability of the Ivorian state have created the conditions of dependency par excellence. Côte d'Ivoire finds itself trapped by the conflict among interests of the dominant class in imperialist France, Ivorian political and economic elites, the socio-political objectives of the developing countries, and the dynamics of the world capitalist system.

Côte d'Ivoire's politics and its policy options have produced a highly stable state organized and dominated by a ruling class and its allies. This class, which was once the commercial social stratum that challenged the interests of the European farmers and the colonial administration, succeeded to transform itself by means of negotiation after several years of open conflict and bloodshed into a national elite.

Educational reform is partly a product of this elites nationalist political agenda, which questioned the whole nature of the Ivorian education system that was modelled after that in France. However, if the proposals by the 1972 Commissioners are taken seriously, education for all, based on the local values and requirements, means moving toward a new model of society, one which is not likely to be sanctioned by the elite. The reform has also not been implemented yet because of the crisis of the national and world economy[6] and the attendant fiscal crisis of the Ivorian state. In addition to these two factors, the austerity measures associated with the Structural Adjustment Program (SAP) of the International Monetary Fund (IMF) and the World Bank's recovery program have not permitted the political elite to implement some aspects of the educational reform with whatever limited resources are available even if they had the political will to do so.

The educational crisis in Côte d'Ivoire is also derived from the rigidity of the state and politics that has, up to recently at least, prevented genuine dialogue from occurring between various teachers' unions, the party, and the state. In the one-party state (until April 1990) all the teachers' claims were in principle expected to be channelled through the ruling party. The party and the state are managed and controlled by the same forces that seem to have resisted the idea implementing the reform.

But the implementation of the educational reform is first of all a political problem rather than a technical one (as viewed by the World Bank and the IMF). The educational system inherited from France is unlikely to be transformed into a dialogical, national, and liberatory education system, embodied to a certain extent in some aspects of the proposed reform unless power relations change at the national level and between Côte d'Ivoire and both France and the international organizations. The emerging political pluralism dominated by teachers' activism is likely to challenge the traditional nature of the Ivorian state. And the question of the stability of the state after the impending death of President Houphouët-Boigny is an important factor toward the implementation of reform.

It is likely that political vitality, contained since the 1950s after the PDCI-RDA leaders reached a comprise with France, will be renewed. The formation of more than ten new political parties, from the Left (the dominant trend) to the Right, and an independent labor union, less than a month after the April 25 speech is a good indication of such a renewed vitality. But in the 1990s, unlike the 1940s, the scene will be dominated by the teaching force. The Ivoirian leaders, who declared education the "priority of priorities," have helped to create the foundation for questioning the existing political system. We should note the parallel between this situation and the way those who attended colonial schools, often against their will, learned not only technical skills and obedience to the colonial administration as planned but also the ability to question the colonial situation.

In the current context the issue of education is a major one. The assessment of the current system, which was proposed by the Commission in 1972, is recalled, and there is a strong pressure from teachers' unions (viz., SYNESCI and SYNARES) to make the recommended fundamental changes. The question of both what kind of education and education for whom must be in the center of this process of change. Côte d'Ivoire is socially and politically in transition. The success of the new articulated society will depend on a combination of factors among which the quality of political discourse, the dynamism of the emerging nationalism, and the performance of the national economy are vital.

NOTES

1. The Third World forum has developed out of the research centers in Africa, especially UNITAR in Dakar, to contribute to the understanding of social phenomena from a Third World perspective. This perspective is represented by organic intellectuals such as Samir Amin, Claude Ake, Mahmood Mamdani, who are arguing that though dependency theory can provide a universal explanation of the causes and structures of underdevelopment in Africa, the dynamics of the local conditions such as culture and class must be taken seriously as part of the objective conditions. There is an intellectual tendency here to go beyond the metropolis/satellite relations and see the objective conditions as essentially dynamic.

2. As indicated previously, these two systems were designed and worked for centuries (except for some ephemeral changes during and after the revolution) and were still prevalent in France at the time of its colonial adventure in Africa. It was only after World War I that, under the pressure of many individuals, institutions, interest groups, unions, and Leftist political parties that participated in the 1936 coalition government, a major reform was adopted in France: the two systems were merged into a single school system. In reality, the elementary system was absorbed by the other one. That is to say that basically, the reformed French system kept its traditional elitist, selective, academic and humanist nature. Even today, after several other reforms, the French system still offers unequal chances to youth from different socio-economic background to succeed.

3. This knowledge was considered important and even necessary for the future leaders of the country (Isambert-Jamati 1970).

4.   Education in the colonies was organized on a pyramidal basis. From the local to the central level, there were four types of schools: village schools, regional schools, urban schools, and federal schools.

5.   According to the government's explanation, this blackout was caused by an explosion at a generating station, but rumors (*"Radio Treichville"*) were that electricity workers had literally pulled the plug as part of a strike protesting the government's plans to implement the austerity program, which recommended the reduction of salary and fringe benefits.

6.   The effects of the crisis and the contradictions of the world capitalism are deepening in Côte d'Ivoire, and France's economic interests, especially her foreign investments, are declining (total French investments in Africa as of 1989 were 26 percent compared to more than 40 percent in the late 1970s).

REFERENCES

Ake, C. (Ed.) 1985. *Political economy of Nigeria.* London and Lagos: Longman.

Amin, S. 1989. *Eurocentrism.* New York: Monthly Review Press.

Amin S. 1985. *Delinking: Towards a polycentric world, an essay on social formations of peripheral.* New Jersey and London: Zed Books.

Amin S. 1976. *Capitalism: Un-equal development.* New York: Monthly Review Press.

Amin S. 1973. *Neo-colonialism in West Africa.* New York: Monthly Review.

Amin S. 1967. *Le Développement du capitalisme en Côte d'Ivoire.* Paris: Minuit.

Assié, N.T. Juin 1975. Economie de plantation et changements socio-economiquee en Pays Baoulé (Côte d'Ivoire). Mémoire de Maitrise. Lyon, France: Université Lyon II.

Assié, N.T. 1982. Educational selection and social inequality in Africa: The case of the Ivory Coast. Unpublished Ph.D. Dissertation, University of Chicago, Chicago.

Assié-Lumumba, N.T. 1983a. Social inequality and access to schooling in the Third World: An African case. Institute For Higher Education Law and Governance, University of Houston, Monograph 83-4.

Assié-Lumumba, N.T. 1983b. Equality and public school finance: Policy of resource allocation in the Ivory Coast. Institute For Higher Education Law Governance, University of Houston, Monograph 83-5.

Assié-Lumumba, N.T. 1983c. Determinants of educational success and of attrition in Africa. Institute for Higher Education Law and Governance, University of Houston, Monograph 83-9.

Assié-Lumumba, N.T. 1984. Social class and attitude towards schooling: cross-national comparison. Paper Presented at the 28th Annual Conference of Comparative and International Educational Society, Houston (March).

Assié-Lumumba, N.T. 1985. The fallacy of quota-like solutions to unequal educational opportunity: The case of female education in the Ivory Coast. Paper presented at the 29th Annual Comparative and International Education Society Conference, Stanford, California (March).

Assié-Lumumba, N.T. 1987. Educational reforms and the difficulties of their implementation in Africa: The case of Côte d'Ivoire. Paper prepared and that was read by Professor Tukumbi Lumumba-Kasongo at the 31st Annual Comparative and International Education Society Conference, Washington, D.C., U.S.A (March).

Bourgoin, H., and G. 1979. *La Côte d'Ivoire: Economie et société*. Paris: Stock.

Cardoso, F.H., and Faletto, E. 1978. *Dependency and underdevelopment*. Berkeley: University of California Press.

Carnoy, M. 1984. *The state and political theory*. Princeton, NJ: Princeton University Press.

Chaffard, G. 1965. *Les carnets secrets de la décolonisation*. Paris: Calmann-Levy.

Chevalier, P. et al. 1968. *L'enseignement français de la révolution à nos jours*. Paris: Mouton.

Cliffe, L. 1985. Rural political economy of Africa. In *Political economy of contemporary Africa*, edited by Gutkind and I. Wallerstein (117-143). Beverly Hills, California: Sage.

Cockroft, J.D., Frank, A.G., and Johnson, D. L. 1979. *Dependence and underdevelopment*. New York: Monthly Review Press.

Commission Nationale de Réforme de l'Enseignement. (Undated). *Rapport de la Commission Nationale de la Réforme de l'enseignement*. Abidjan, Côte d'Ivoire [compilation of all the reform documents].

Coquery-Vidrovitch, C. 1985. The political economy of the peasantry and modes of production. In *Political economy of contemporary Africa*, edited by Gutkind and I. Wallerstein (pp. 94-116). Beverly Hills, California: Sage.

The Economist Intellegence Unit, No.1 (1989).

Frank, G. 1984. *Critique and anti-critique: Essays on dependence and reformism*. New York: Praeger.

Isambert-Jamati, V. 1970. *Crises de la société, crises de l'enseignement*. Paris: Presses Universitaires de France.

Journal Officiel de la République de Côte d'Ivoire (Texte paru dans le Loi No. 77-584 du 18 Août 1977 portant Réforme de l'enseignement). No. 50 du 21 Novembre 1977.

Ki-Zerbo, J. 1972. *Histoire de l'Afrique: d'hier à demain*. Paris: Hatier.

Leys, C. 1974. *Underdevelopment in Kenya: The political economy of neo-colonialism*. Berkeley and Los Angeles: University of California Press.

Lumumba-Kasongo, T. 1985. An agricultural policy in Tanzania: 1967-77 submitted to *The University of Liberia Journal*.

Lumumba-Kasongo, T. 1984. An agricultural policy as blockade of development: The case of Congo. Unpublished manuscript.

Nkrumah, K. 1966. *Neo-colonialism: The last stage of imperialism.* New York: International Publishers.

Prost, A. 1968. *Histoire de l'enseignement en France: 1800-1967.* Paris: Armand Colin.

Tuinder, D.A. 1978. *Ivory Coast: The challenge of success.* Baltimore: Johns Hopkins University Press.

Wallerstein, I. 1973. Class and class conflict in contemporary Africa. *Canadian Journal of African Studies,* 7, 3: 375-80.

Wallerstein, I. 1985. The three stages of African involvement in the world economy. In *Political economy of contemporary Africa,* edited by Gutkind and I. Wallerstein (35-63). Beverly Hills, California: Sage.

World Bank 1983. *Comparative education indicators.* Washington, DC: The World Bank (5 June).

EDUCATIONAL REFORM IN NEW ZEALAND

John Barrington

Between 1988 and 1990 the most radical and wide-sweeping administrative changes in the history of public education in New Zealand were made to the country's entire national educational system. All levels, from early childhood to tertiary, were affected. This particular chapter focuses on the changes as they affected primary and secondary schools. Two reports, *Administering for Excellence: Report of the Taskforce to Review Education Administration* (1988) and *Tomorrow's Schools: The Reform of Education Administration in New Zealand* (New Zealand Government 1988), "ushered in a period of educational upheaval unique in New Zealand's history" (McLaren 1989, 1).

Aspects of the New Zealand reforms undoubtedly link to wider school reforms in an international context. Indeed, features such as decentralization of greater responsibility to the governing bodies of individual schools in areas such as priority setting and financial management, greater parental involvement in school governance, and measures to increase the accountability of schools to parents and local communities are remarkably similar to changes in England, the United States, Australia, and Canada. But other aspects make the New Zealand reforms radical and probably unique. This partly stems from the way in which the entire national system was restructured simultaneously, partly from the integrated rather than "clip on" nature of the restructuring, and partly from the sheer speed of implementation. One overseas observer has described the New Zealand approach as the "earthquake method" of change when compared with reform efforts in England, New South Wales and Hawaii, with virtually all new structures and procedures being implemented within one year (Holdaway 1989). Another feature of particular note was the removal of intermediate units between the central Ministry of Education and the new Board of Trustees of each individual school; most of the international literature on decentralization of national systems discusses decentralization to a regional or local unit such as a state board of education. Also significant was the emphasis given to linking structural changes of the administrative system to equity issues, particularly efforts to provide increased support for pupils from low-income families or families in which adults were unemployed and to promote greater gender and racial equity in schooling.

New Zealand's educational reforms need to be viewed against significant political and economic changes in the 1980s and struggles between competing groups. These struggles extended to educational groups and produced sometimes bitter conflict, particularly between the secondary teachers' union and the government. However, before turning to a more detailed examination of these aspects, it is important to briefly outline relevant aspects of New Zealand's political, economic, and educational history.

HISTORICAL, POLITICAL, AND ECONOMIC CONTEXTS

New Zealand has a comparatively small population of 3.3 million people. Its two main islands (the North and South) are relatively isolated in the South Pacific Ocean, some 1,200 miles from Australia. Its land area of about 103,00 square miles is approximately the size of Italy. Its first settlers, the Maoris, suffered population decline as the result of wars defending their tribal land against European encroachment and introduced diseases, but by the end of the nineteenth century the population had begun to recover and subsequently increased rapidly. Today, Maoris comprise 9 percent of the total population. Over 80 percent of this population is European, primarily from the British Isles but with some migrants from countries like Holland and Yugoslavia. Since the 1960s Pacific Islanders (particularly Western Samoans) have migrated in increasing numbers and today make up nearly 4 percent of the total population (Royal Commission on Social Policy 1988).

New Zealand's provincial form of government was abolished in 1876, and central government soon became dominant. The country has never developed either a written constitution guarded by the courts, a federal system, a second legislative chamber, or strong local authorities like other western democracies. The political party in power consequently becomes constitutionally all powerful. The central government has always had a significant influence on the economy, and since from the 1890s a free market economy was viewed as likely to produce unacceptable price instability for the country's major exports of primary products and an unfair distribution of resources (Blyth 1987). Central government monetary and regulatory instruments were therefore used to moderate or alter the workings of the free market in all areas of the economy, including banks and other financial institutions, industrial protection, the development and operation of transport including railways and airlines, forests, communication and energy resources, marketing of farm products, the development of state housing, industrial relations, wages, prices, education, health, and so on.

The first Labour government, elected in 1936, created the welfare state. A famous statement by the Minister of Education, Peter Fraser, in 1939 expressed the basic tenet of government policy as being that "all people whatever [their] level of academic ability, whether [they] be rich or poor, whether [they] live in town or country, have a right, as citizens, to a free education of the kind for which [they are] best fitted and to the fullest extent of [their] powers" (Dakin 1973, 32). Welfare Labourism portrayed education as a public good that the central state had a responsibility to provide, expand, improve in quality, and make freely available (Grace 1990). Labour continued the tradition of a protected and regulated economy, viewed as necessary to provide stability in pastoral exports, allowing the development of manufacturing and ensuring the economic stability necessary for maintaining the welfare state. Central government has usually been viewed as:

> A progressive force in New Zealand, protecting unions, workers, the sick and the aged, and opening up the land for small farmers. Indirectly, the state has subsidized the national wage bill, by paying for the health, education and retirement costs of workers. More directly, the state has fostered and subsidized the business community. Virtually every sector of business has benefitted from state support: cheap loans for farmers, import controls and high tariffs for manufacturers, cheap timber for pulp and paper companies, and cheap power for industry in general (Jesson 1989, 32).

Britain's entry into the European Common Market ended New Zealand's traditional reliance on her as the major assured export market. This development, combined with changes in the global economy and oil price rises, produced a sense of structural crisis in the New Zealand economy. However, the National Party in government from 1975-1984 maintained and even extended the very protected and highly regulated economy and the welfare state while following conservative policies (in a New Zealand context) in the areas of foreign policy and social issues. However, beneath the surface "free-market" ideas were circulating and increasingly gaining influence within the important central government department of the Treasury. Ideas and policies originating in Europe and the United States often follow a kind of "drip-down" process with regard to New Zealand, and this applied to the international revival of right wing politics and economic policies in the 1970s. According to Jesson (1988, 40): "Chicago was the main intellectual influence on our economic policy makers by the mid-80s, and the market approach was also favored by several influential members of the Labour opposition, particularly the shadow finance spokesperson, Roger Douglas."

Labour was elected in July 1984 in an atmosphere amounting to a crisis of legitimation in terms of the central government's ability to cope with the prevailing economic situation and implement policies to maintain economic growth and manage the economy. Prime Minister Robert Muldoon had "come to be perceived by many as epitomizing some of the worst authoritarian features of a welfare capitalist state in which highly centralized forms of public administration had been blatantly and intolerably undemocratic" (Codd 1989, 192). Douglas and his supporters in the new Labour cabinet, aided by fervent monetarists within Treasury, utilized the sense of a crisis to gain control of economic policy and claimed that monetarist solutions were the only realistic way to solve the economic problems the new government had inherited.

The speed and scope of subsequent financial and economic changes under Labour after 1984 have not been equalled in either western European countries or the Pacific region over the past two decades (Harper and Karacaoglis 1987). A veritable revolution in economic policy, described variously as "liberalization," "deregulation," "more market," or "Rogernomics" (after the Minister of Finance), saw a dramatic change from a strong government preference for regulated markets to an equally strong distaste for them (Blyth 1987, 5). Neo-liberal economic policies have been adapted in a number of countries irrespective of "political color" (i.e., Labour in Australia and New Zealand, Conservative in Britain, and Republican in the United States) focused on achieving certain common ideological purposes: reducing the size of the central state, deregulating markets, exercising greater control over public expenditure, a heavy emphasis on the need to reduce inflation and letting "the national forces of enterprise, work and thrift bring about prosperity" (Blyth 1987, 4).

After 1984 the New Zealand government created a "New Right Revolution aimed to foster a Thatcherite enterprise culture . . . [T]he prime agency for the promotion of these policies has been the Treasury which . . . advocated some of the most pristine New Right policies to be seen anywhere in the Western world" (Lauder 1990, 1). The Treasury was undoubtedly influential and its advice to the incoming Labour government in 1984 was set out in *Government Management* (1984). Jesson (1989, 54) identified a "libertarian bias" in this report that "builds up a theory of government from a discussion of individual rights: the result is an unstated bias for the minimal state." The thinkers the report draws on "are in the individualist tradition, ranging from Ayn Rand to

classical liberals like [John] Locke, to modern liberals like John
Rawls and the libertarian minimal state theorist Robert Nozick"
(Jesson 1989, 54).

The Labour government privatized substantial sections of
the public services. These included the postal services, forestry, and
broadcasting. Government subsidies were removed from the farming
sector. Treasury viewed the size of public expenditures in health,
education, and social welfare as a problem and recommended
increased privatization. One significant outcome of government
economic restructuring and policies after 1984 was a rapid rise in
unemployment. In 1961 only 6,900 people were unemployed; by
1989 that figure had risen to 165,000 with Maoris, the young, and
those in rural areas particularly negatively affected. Government
officials informed the public that while the effects of these policies
were painful in the short term, the benefits would be felt when the
government turned its attention to social policy if reelected for a
second term.

However, many members of the Labour Party had by this
time become increasingly apprehensive about the form the
government's "free-market" and "user-pays" approach might take if
applied to areas like health and education. The government's brand
of "market socialism" had confused and divided the Labour Party
and alienated much traditional Labour support within trade unions.
Some suspicion of the government bureaucracy had been traditional
amongst many Labour people. It was viewed as a conservative
move, more oriented to preserving the Party's position in the
government than in advancing the interests of the kind of
progressive and reforming government Labour had been in the past.
Many Labour Party members still rejected outright the notion that
a totally free market could achieve the principle of economic and
social justice. The Party's President, Margaret Wilson, expressed
this view:

> We were concerned that if the state sector withdrew
> from the responsibilities of delivering essential
> social services such as health, education,
> communication network, energy and so on, it would
> be impossible to have a just distribution of wealth
> in accordance with the principles of the party. Our
> main fear was not the reform of the public sector to

provide more efficient services but privatization of
those services. (Wilson 1987, 80)

After Labour's re-election in 1987 a power struggle
developed within the Government between those led by Roger
Douglas, who advocated a "more-market" approach, and those
represented by Prime Minister David Lange, who favored a more
traditional Labour approach in the area of social policy. According
to Grace (1990, 33), Lange recognized that "the market culture
would triumph in the education sector, unless the settlements over
welfare policy Labour had achieved in the 1930s could be given a
new form, direction and vitalization." To achieve this, Labour
would somehow need to incorporate the current concern for
"efficiency" and "excellence" as well as its traditional concern for
equity. This struggle eventually led to the resignation of both men
and the promotion of Geoffrey Palmer as Prime Minister, an
outcome many viewed as reducing the possibility of a more extreme
free-market or privatizing approach extending into areas like health
and education.

THE EDUCATION SYSTEM: PRE-REFORM

Education became a central government responsibility in
1876 and the 1877 Education Act created a national system of "free,
secular, and compulsory" primary education and a central
government Department of Education. All educational funding,
policy making, and administrative authority increasingly became the
responsibility of a strong central government acting through the
Minister of Education and the Department of Education. The central
structure also became associated with the notion that equal
educational provision should be guaranteed for all New Zealand
children of school-age irrespective of their geographical location.
Ten regional education boards were established to administer
primary schools and acted chiefly as the administrative agents of the

central Department of Education.

A primary teachers' union, the New Zealand Educational Institute (NZEI), formed in 1883, aimed from the outset to provide an effective lobby group for teachers by influencing national level decision making on pay, conditions of service, and educational policy. Indeed, the Institute contributed to the growth of a strong, centralized Education Department by successfully seeking national government protection for its members in the late nineteenth century against what it viewed as capricious appointment and termination decisions by lay members of local education boards and school committees (McLaren 1974). Over time, consultation procedures developed whereby most new national educational proposals and regulations were submitted to the union for comments before implementation. The secondary teachers' union, the Post Primary Teachers' Association (PPTA), was formed much later (in 1952) and also became involved in the central consultative process on such matters as curriculum and assessment. However, its relationship with the central government and the Department of Education was conflict laden as union officials fought hard to protect wages and working conditions. Unlike the NZEI, which adopted a more conciliatory approach by attempting to influence policy centered around improving the "professionalism" of teachers by non-militant tactics whenever possible, the PPTA frequently encouraged its members to organize strikes and other militant actions (Gordon 1988, 197). The PPTA's reputation for "militancy" over the years endeared it neither to politicians nor the bureaucracy.

The New Zealand system came to epitomize the model of a very highly centralized system, funding guaranteeing the Department's central role and justifying McLaren's (1974, 3) description of it as a "triton amongst the minnows." The whole system was carefully controlled by a maze of centrally determined regulations and the powers of local bodies inevitably remained either weak or virtually nonexistent in such a structure. Each primary school was administered by a committee of elected parents, but its duties were primarily confined to fund-raising through activities such as school fairs to provide "extras" and keeping the grounds in good order. The board of governors of each secondary school could appoint the principal and staff but its other powers were limited. The regional education boards "had little connection with local control. They neither control nor can they be considered local. They are regional and administrative. . . . The New Zealand education system is characterized by lay boards which put in a great amount of work for education but have no or little control over it" (Ingle 1967, 352).

The Labour government in power from 1972-1975 attempted to stimulate greater public participation in education at the local level as part of its interest in reforming and strengthening local government generally. Public forums to discuss educational issues were convened throughout the country, and a strong desire for greater local autonomy emerged. Typical statements from reports included the view that "local schools should be run by local people . . . so that instead of uniformity there may be an appropriate diversity, reflecting variations in local needs and circumstances" (Nordmeyer 1974, 162). There should be "devolution of authority to regional organizations and to the schools as far as practical" and there was a "need for greater responsibility in other areas such as finance" (Holmes 1974, 14-16). Student representation on secondary school boards was recommended as was the need to ensure that more Maori and Pacific Island parents were represented on school governing bodies (Holmes 1974, 115 and 133).

Despite strong parental involvement and interest nothing resulted from these various recommendations. Nevertheless, proposals for reform continued. The McCombs Report on Secondary Education, *Towards Partnership* (1976), identified serious flaws in and dissatisfaction with the existing structural arrangements for education including the concentration of educational decision-making in the Department of Education, the relative isolation of school boards from the constituents they served, and the confinement of most parents' responsibility for the school to relatively inconsequential matters. The McCombs Report urged that the majority of members of secondary school boards of governors should be the parents of pupils attending the schools, and boards needed better reporting procedures to the local community if they were really to look after its interests. The Report was also assertive in its view that "too many boards take a narrow view of the idea that the principal is responsible for the professional side of the school. The Board should express community views about curriculum" (McCombs 1976, 79).

Research I carried out on secondary school governors in the

early 1980s (Barrington 1985) confirmed the sense of powerlessness amongst elected parent governors. Boards were seen as approving decisions made elsewhere either by the national Department of Education or the principal. The term "rubber stamp" was mentioned frequently: "We never get to grips with education matters--the staff, education department, architects decide everything, we rubber stamp"; "schools are run by teachers for teachers"; "important thinking and policy formation regarding education takes place in the Minister-Department-Principal-Staff line. School Boards are to all intents and purposes outside like a small child playing with a ball on the sidelines at a rugby match--it makes no difference whether she/he is there or not" (Barrington 1985, 26). The word "trivia" was repeatedly used to refer to various aspects of board business. The problem was often seen as "the Department" or "the bureaucracy." Boards were "up against" the Department, which could "stymie good proposals," they were "bogged down by red tape," confronted a "maze of regulations" and an "absence of full financial control" (Barrington 1985, 28). These characteristics produced one major effect above all others in the eyes of many elected parent members: inordinately long delays in implementing local developments they considered vitally important.

These problems were compounded by equity issues with regard to representation. In 1976 only approximately 10 percent of all members of secondary school boards of governors were women, while representation by Maoris and other Polynesians was negligible (NZSSBA 1976).

MORE RECENT INFLUENCES ON REFORM

Dissatisfactions with aspects of the education system were paralleled by greater awareness of other issues. During the 1970s racial inequality not only became more obvious (Maoris students are more than twice as likely as non-Maoris to leave school with no formal qualifications) but also more politicized (Thompson 1990).

Concerns also surfaced about New Zealand's ability to compete economically in the world economy and the adequacy of standards of education and training in relation to other countries. Serious crime increased and during the 1980s there was a rapid rise in unemployment. While it is quite unrealistic to "blame" the education system for these problems, their very existence did make education seem more vulnerable to attack by critics.

Other influences had come from overseas research, particularly conflict theories of education, which demonstrated that rather than reducing social inequalities, schooling was reproducing a socially stratified society. According to McCulloch (1990, 60), these ideas "posed a formidable challenge to the liberal assumptions about schooling that had previously seemed so convincing" and had produced by the 1980s "a well-developed left-wing critique of New Zealand education," which had "done much to undermine earlier confidence in the education system."

Paralleling this development was a growing attack from the opposite direction as New Right advocates also interpreted international trends in education for a New Zealand context. In the United States a conservative renaissance emphasized "quality," "excellence," "choice," and "accountability," and these ideas were prominent in the influential *A Nation At Risk* published in 1983. The New Right agenda followed by Margaret Thatcher's Conservative government in Britain had also been observed. These significant overseas precedents, combined with the growing feeling of many parents and politicians that education was not living up to its promises, had "begun to shape a potential New Right critique in New Zealand also" (McCulloch 1990, 60).

It would be an exaggeration nevertheless to suggest that a firestorm of protest and cries for reform by the public at large had emerged by the early to mid 1980s. However, education got caught up in campaigns waged by the two main political parties to capture the "high-ground" of public opinion. After Labour came to power in July 1984, the Minister of Education promoted wide-ranging consultative reviews of national curriculum. As Labour's first term progressed, pressures grew for a more fundamental change. A Parliamentary Education and Science Select Committee's enquiry into the quality of teaching initially developed a bipartisan approach in examining the professional status and performance of teachers

(New Zealand Parliament 1986). It identified an outdated and complicated administrative structure with limited accountability procedures as factors ultimately undermining the quality of teaching. The Committee also claimed (without providing anything much in the way of supporting evidence) that "provider-capture" had occurred, whereby the providers of education (via, teachers) had captured the terms of their service. The Committee's report initially made little impact on the public. But during the 1987 election campaign, the opposition spokesperson on education departed from the bipartisan approach and used educational issues effectively to put the Government on the defensive.

After Labour's election in 1984 the Treasury "confidently saw itself as the expert not only in the economy but on everything else as well" (Snook 1989, 5). In 1987 the Treasury produced its second volume of *Government Management* for the incoming government. The report (The Treasury 1987) was subtitled "Educational Issues," reflecting the new importance now to be given to education. The 94-page report on education is an extraordinarily thorough study of trends and issues in education well documented by a wide range of research studies and reports although interpreted from a clear rightist ideology. The Treasury's analysis and proposals continue to be influenced by the minimal state theorist, Robert Nozick, and by the American economist, James Buchanan, a leading figure of the "public choice" school, with a strong anti-socialist, anti-welfare state commitment, who argues that the state is prey to the ambitions of special interest groups and of the state's own employees. Buchanan's argument was reproduced in the second volume of *Government Management* in the notion of "capture," with The Treasury arguing that the state (including the education system) was in danger of capture from lobby groups and its own bureaucracy (Jesson 1989). According to Grace (1990, 17), "an ideological agenda derived from New Right Principles" was evidenced in the Report's thesis that (1) education has been misunderstood to be a public good when in fact it is a commodity of the marketplace; (2) the important relationship between the education service and its participants is that of provider and customer/consumer; and (3) the state is not the best mechanism for the provision of education services either on the ground of equity or efficiency--such services would be better provided through the operation of a free market system.

The Treasury's discussion of teacher unions centered around its view of central control, which it opposed and saw as being partly based on "the history of strong pressure by teacher associations to seek a national system of appointments, assessments, grading and promotion. Clearly this national system has positive aspects . . . however, uniformity can lead to rigidity and slowness to react to changing demands" (The Treasury 1987, 10). Teacher unions were viewed as pressure groups that intervened in the "ideal" or "sector neutral" relationship between the "providers" and "consumers" of education, thereby interfering with basic free market principles. Pressure for change also came from the National Party and its members in Parliament who formed the Opposition. National's education manifesto for the 1987 election (*A Nation At Risk*) borrowed both the title and a considerable amount of its content from the 1983 United States Commission on Excellence in Education report of the same name. New Zealand, like the United States, was viewed as losing out in terms of economic competitiveness and faring badly on international comparisons of academic achievement. Illiteracy was a major problem and more emphasis was needed on "basic" school subjects, higher academic standards, and assessment of student achievement. There had to be a new "striving for excellence" (National Party 1987, 5).

The National Party claimed in *A Nation at Risk* that it would ensure better management by entrusting schools with "greater responsibility for their own management." (National Party 1987, 6). Each school would be required to "publish its individual plans and subject them to regular review" by an "Education Audit Team" with education auditors independent of the Department of Education working in the areas of teacher appraisal, school assessment and the maintenance of curriculum and professional standards. *A Nation At Risk* described the central Department of Education's management style as "highly centralized and interventionist" (National Party 1987, 6). Decisions on the employment of teachers needed to be decentralized to the managing bodies of schools, and all teachers holding positions of responsibility should be put onto performance contracts. The National Party (1987, 7) also affirmed its belief that parents should have the choice of public or private schools and would "work to achieve fairer funding to facilitate that choice."

Vouchers were advocated as the best mechanism for achieving a number of these goals.

The media also criticized aspects of the existing education system, focusing illogically, but with considerable impact, on the apparent inability of the system to solve wider economic and social problems such as unemployment amongst school leavers. One article in particular, "The Lost Generation" (DuChateau 1987), which appeared in the mass circulation *Metro* is credited with a considerable impact prior to the 1987 election. It attacked what it described as low academic standards and "liberal" approaches to the curriculum (including "Peace Studies" and "Maori Studies"), which it attributed to radical teachers. Education was "producer led and dominated," and people must "seize back control of the education system from education's vested interests, particularly the liberal and feminist dominated teacher unions" (DuChateau 1987, 32). Much of this critique echoed that in *A Nation At Risk*, which had appeared in the same month. Grace (1990, 21-22) analyzed the conjunction of these influences and their effects:

> The language and the style of the *Metro*'s expose, "The Lost Generation," taken together with National's Education manifesto, *A Nation at Risk*, have all attributes which Cohen (1983) has suggested are connected with the creation, or attempted creation, of a "moral panic." New Zealand in 1987 witnessed an attempt to generate a moral panic about the effectiveness and efficiency of the education system by a lurid and dramatic presentation to the public of deficiencies in the system. "Vested interests" in education, education bureaucracies per se and professional organizations of teachers were, as part of this attempt, cast in the role of "folk devils", i.e., as the root cause and agent of the crisis situation in education. . . . Teachers, once regarded as committed public servants, were now represented as a vested interest group with dangerous and in some cases potentially subversive ideas. Educational bureaucracies and organized teacher power were being targeted in the

New Zealand of the 1980s as being deeply
implicated in the crisis of education at the school
level.

THE REFORMS

Labour's re-election in August 1987 created considerable
interest in whether it would fulfill an election promise and turn its
attention to social policy. Would social policy be used to ameliorate
some of the painful individual and community costs of deregulation
and a restructured economy or would a "user-pays" approach also be
applied to others areas like health and education? Prime Minister
Lange had involved himself closely in a movement for educational
reform, just as President Reagan and Margaret Thatcher had in the
United States and Britain, respectively. However, Lange went even
further, he took the highly significant and symbolic step of
appointing himself Minister of Education in the new Cabinet which
immediately added prestige to the position and was widely viewed
as signaling the Prime Minister's and the government's
determination to put education reform high on the agenda. Such
reform was, Lange said, "a political challenge in that I am certain
the government prospects for re-election in 1990 will depend to a
very great extent on our performance in education" (Lange 1988, 5).
Just prior to the general election a Task Force to Review
Education Administration had been announced. Its chair, Brian
Picot, was a prominent supermarket magnate, a background that
created nervousness amongst many educationists regarding the likely
direction of reform.
A concern to give much greater responsibility to individual
schools and local governing bodies was evident in the Taskforce's
terms of reference: to examine the functions of the central
Department of Education with a view to "delegating responsibility
as far as it's practically possible" and to redefine the work of
governing bodies of primary and secondary schools, teachers
colleges, polytechnics, and community colleges "to increase their
powers and responsibilities" (Taskforce to Review Educational

Administration 1988, ix). The Taskforce was also to consider changes in the "territorial organization" of public education with reference to the future roles of education boards, regional offices of the Department of Education, and other education authorities. Administrative reform, according to the Taskforce would result in an education system where every learner gained "the maximum individual and social benefit from the money spent on education" and one which would be "fair and just for every learner regardless of their gender, and of their social, cultural or geographic circumstances" (Taskforce to Review Education Administration 1988, ix). This was, according to McCulloch (1990, 64), an "appealing prescription for change that appeared to meet Lange's requirements. It set a novel and far reaching agenda that sought to respond to the criticisms of both left and right."

The concepts of devolution, efficiency, choice, and excellence appear throughout the Commission's Report. It begins with a very strong criticism of aspects of the existing system, which is described as "overcentralized," "overly complex," and having too many decision points (Taskforce to Review Education Administration 1988, ix). Effective management practices were lacking, and the information needed to make informed choices at the local level was seldom available. As a result most people felt powerless to bring about change. The Taskforce criticized the fact that in New Zealand "virtually all power and decision-making comes from the center and very few decisions are made at the local level; when they are they are heavily influenced by rules and procedures determined centrally" (Taskforce to Review Education Administration 1988, 22). The result was seen to be that in primary schools "no important administrative decision is made close to the school. In fact, major decisions regarding spending are made furthest away at the Department of Education's head office in Wellington" (Taskforce to Review Education Administration 1988, 13). Negative outcomes of such a system included slow decision-making and excessive involvement by the Minister of Education in school matters that were essentially local. Each individual school should become "the basic unit of educational administration" (Taskforce to Review Education Administration 1988, 45) and the people who actually work in the institution should make most of the decisions affecting it.

The Taskforce concluded that "radical change" was required

to overcome these defects, and if its recommendations were implemented, they would represent "the most thorough-going change to the administration of education in our history" (Taskforce to Review Education Administration 1988, xi). This claim was undoubtedly justified, but whether the changes had equally significant importance for the location of power is much more problematic as I shall shortly discuss.

Most of the Task Force's major recommendations were approved for implementation by the government and were published in August 1988 in *Tomorrow's Schools: The Reform of Education Administration in New Zealand* (New Zealand Government 1988). The same strong devolution theme was carried through into *Tomorrow's Schools* and even extended. Chapter One, "Administering at the Local Level," opens with a quotation from Thomas Jefferson:

> I know of no safe depository of the ultimate power
> of the society but the people themselves and if we
> think them not enlightened enough to exercise their
> control with a wholesome discretion, the remedy is
> not to take it from them but to inform their
> discretion. (New Zealand Government 1988, ii)

This new local emphasis was not confined to education but was to be part of a broad policy for other government departments, including Health and Maori Affairs. Prime Minister Lange in a speech to the Annual Conference of the Education Boards Association in June 1988 stated that "New Zealanders want decision-making as close as possible to the point of implementation. This is at the heart of the government's reforms, social and economic" (Lange 1988, 2). Lange also constantly emphasized that equity was a central and non-negotiable aim of the educational reforms. At their very heart, he said, "are two principles--equality and equity . . . equity is one of the driving forces behind our reforms" (Lange 1989). The concept of school charters was developed to help ensure institutions remain committed to following and achieving equity goals.

School charters include compulsory, nondiscretionary requirements laid out as National Education Guidelines by the

Ministry of Education. These set out principles on national curriculum, the Treaty of Waitangi (signed by the Crown and Maori tribes in 1840 and symbolizing a spirit of partnership between Maoris and Europeans), and other equity issues, including equal employment opportunities for men and women teachers. Parents and teachers determine for each school what to include in the charter, such as the main characteristics of the school and its community or the kinds of ideal educational outcomes to be worked towards. Each charter is then approved by the Minister and the Board of Trustees. Charters are intended to symbolize the new spirit of partnership between each school and its community as well as the central Ministry of Education. They are also viewed as an accountability mechanism. Maurice Gianotti, Executive Officer to the Taskforce suggested in *The Impact of American Ideas on New Zealand's Educational Policy and Thinking* that many American schools were more successful than their New Zealand counterparts in setting "clear, specific objectives which state the intended outcomes" (Gianotti 1989, 192).

In the section of *Tomorrow's Schools* dealing with "National Issues Impinging at Local Level" equity issues are stated first as underpinning all policy elated to the reform of education administration. Equity objectives would attempt to ensure that:

> a new system of education administration promotes and progressively achieves greater equity for women, Maori, Pacific Islanders, other groups with minority status; and for working class, rural and disabled students, teachers and communities; equity issues are integrated into all aspects of changes in education administration and not treated as an optional extra. (New Zealand Government 1988, para 3.1.1.)

New boards of trustees for primary and secondary schools gave 5 elected parent representatives numerical dominance and extended to primary school trustees the right to appoint (and fire) principals and other staff. The number of parents who subsequently offered themselves as candidates for the new boards in May 1989 was unprecedented in the history of school government in New Zealand, reflecting the extent to which parents' expectations had been raised that they would now be involved in real decision-making affecting their school. The principal, another staff member, and a student representative (in high schools) were also made board members with voting rights. To ensure that trustees adequately reflected the composition of the community, if board elections did not produce a satisfactory ethnic, gender, or socio-economic balance, a board could co-opt up to four new members from the community. This replaced the former system whereby outside bodies appointed members to secondary schools with schools themselves unable to exercise control over such appointments and appointees often had little connection with the school. The new school boards emerged with more demanding responsibilities, including a number of those previously performed by local education authorities.

Funding to each new Board of Trustees now comes in the form of a bulk grant based on a formula calculated by the Ministry and weighted for equity considerations. Schools with a large enrollment of Maori, Pacific Island or "new settler" children, rural schools, and schools in economically depressed areas, get extra funding. Overall responsibility for deciding how the general bulk grant is allocated lies with the board. *Tomorrow's Schools* provided one example of how this new local discretion must operate:

> The board may decide that an extra teacher is a priority, and may use funds from the operational activities grant to create another teaching position-- or to subsidize two part-time positions. Similarly, it may decide that, given the objectives set out in its charter, it should forego a teacher position and instead use funds to buy a computer or other high technology teaching aids (New Zealand Government 1988, 13).

As part of its deliberations over the need for greater "choice" in education, the Taskforce considered the concept of vouchers (which the National Party had said it would introduce if elected in 1987) but concluded that vouchers "did not promote choice at all for most parents. . . . [P]arents would be better served, and so would society in a social cohesion sense, by being given the power to change their local school into what they wanted it to be rather than having the power to shop around until they find a school which offers what they want" (Gianotti 1989, 192). Therefore, other measures, designed to promote greater empowerment of parents and local communities, were introduced. Community Forums can now be established at the initiative either of a local community or the Minister, and their purpose is to help make education more responsive to the community. A Forum could be convened to consider an important local issue, such as the educational needs of Maori students, a proposed school closure, zoning, or the development of early childhood services.

Tomorrow's Schools also included an opting-out provision. Under this provision groups of parents representing at least 21 children could withdraw from an existing school and establish their own institution, still within the public school framework, if they feel that the educational needs of their children are not being adequately met. The government has the concerns of Maoris in mind here. During the 1980s a tremendously successful growth of community-based Kohanga Reo ("language nests") or early childhood centers for Maori children occurred and their emphasis on bi-lingualism has been viewed as being of crucial importance in maintaining and expanding the Maori language in the future. But problems arise when bilingual Maori children leave the Kohanga Reo and enter local primary schools where little or no provision may be made for Maori language, an omission that has understandably fuelled the dissatisfaction of many Maori parents. A national independent Parent Advocacy Council has been established to deal with this kind of issue by mediating between schools, parents, and the Ministry.

The 10 Regional education boards, which had administered primary schools since 1877, were abolished after being identified by the Taskforce to Review Education Administration (1988, xii) as contributing to the duplication of services, inefficiency, and slow response to educational needs at the local level. Each local Board of Trustees would now be free to "choose their own services."

The Taskforce considered the role the central department should play in the new arrangements. It concluded that "because the (central) state provides the funds and retains a strong interest in educational outcomes there must be national objectives" (Taskforce to Review Education Administration 1988, xi). It also referred to the need for

> an appropriate balance of responsibilities between
> the local level and central government. We
> acknowledge that complete devolution carries
> certain dangers. New Zealand . . . has a small but
> highly mobile population which makes a certain
> amount of standardization desirable; and it is also
> worth noting that one of the main reasons for
> establishing a central Department of Education in
> 1877 was the prevention of parochialism. As well,
> some matters are the concern of the state."
> (Taskforce to Review Education Administration
> 1988, 5)

Increases in the numbers of women appointed to senior
positions in primary schools and the introduction of *Taha Maori* (the
Maori way of doing things) into schools were cited as two examples
of the benefits of central influence and policies in recent years
(Taskforce to Review Education Administration 1988, 37). However
the Taskforce recommended the replacement of the Department of
Education by a "smaller and leaner" organization, renamed the
Ministry of Education, and stripped it of its former role as a direct
provider of education services. It would now concentrate on policy
advice. To promote greater accountability and to ensure that equity
provisions are maintained, there is an Education Review Officer
with independent multi-disciplinary review teams with expertise in
curriculum, financial and management support, and equity
provisions. A team is to visit each school periodically to evaluate its
performance against its charter and produce a report that will be
made available to parents as well as teachers. The creation of the
Education Review Officer is partly attributed to the influence of the
Director of the University of London Institute of Education (Denis
Lawton) who met the Taskforce in February 1988 and emphasized
the importance of regaining a form of school inspection through an
agency independent of the Ministry of Education.

There were likely to be important implications for principals
and teachers in the new proposals. Changes to their conditions of

employment need to be seen in the wider context of changes affecting the whole New Zealand public service, where former permanent heads of all government departments, for example, have now been renamed Chief Executives and placed on contracts. Each Board of Trustees as the legal employer of all staff will determine starting salaries within a salary range established nationally. Principals will be appointed on a contract negotiated between the board and the principal. The reforms strongly challenge the role of teachers unions in policy development and implementation and in professional matters at the local level (Capper and Munro 1990). Changed conditions of employment for principals and teachers were one of the major issues in the reform, and this would likely affect the relationship between the state and organized teachers (Grace 1990).

The Taskforce reported in April 1988 and *Tomorrow's Schools* was published in August. The new system was implemented during 1989. Two particular aspects of the implementation process are worthy of comment here: the international influence and the new management approach adopted. In addition to the international influences mentioned above, one should note that an Australian academic, Dr. Brian Caldwell, co-author of the internationally widely read *The Self-Managing School* (1988) and advisor to a number of school systems worldwide about local school-based reform efforts, was invited by the Government of New Zealand to run training seminars throughout the country for the trustees and teachers who would be directly concerned with implementation. With respect to the management approach, a new Chief Executive was appointed to the Ministry of Education on a two-year contract as a "change-agent" to oversee the changes. His background in forestry, with no previous employment history in education, was a radical departure from the tradition of experienced educationalists in Ministry positions. It was widely viewed as an attempt to break with the past and overcome any resistance to the changes from the educational bureaucracy.

ANALYSIS AND OUTCOME OF THE REFORMS

Reactions to the reforms were mixed. Bodies representing parental interests, such as the School Committees Federation and the New Zealand Secondary School Boards Association, welcomed greater decentralization of authority to school governing bodies. Support also came from employers; the Employers Federation saw the reforms as providing "a good blueprint for the reform of primary and secondary education" (*Evening Post* 11 May 1988, 2). The main criticism came from the primary teachers union (NZEI), the secondary school teachers' union (PPTA), and lecturers in university departments of education. NZEI expressed fears that the professionalism of teachers could be destroyed unless a nationally determined system of appointment, evaluation, discipline, and promotion of teachers was maintained (Gordon 1988). The secondary teachers' union viewed the reforms as involving an attempt to weaken the influence of teachers as an organized group with the PPTA President describing 1989 as a year in which the union had "been subjected to the most sustained and bitter attack in its history" (quoted in Grace 1990, 47). PPTA's membership was extremely apprehensive about responsibilities for setting salaries being delegated to each local board and viewed the policy of placing principals on contract as likely to drive a wedge between them and teachers as professional colleagues engaged in a common task.

Interviews with a large number of agencies, principals, and members of boards of trustees identified widespread enthusiasm for the decentralization of responsibility amongst an overwhelming majority of schools that reported having successfully completed a "major transition from an excessive dependence on the education boards and the Department of Education . . . to a position where they have far greater autonomy" (Government of New Zealand 1990, 16). But difficulties were also identified. A perception existed that central bureaucratic control had actually increased. There was concern about the speed of change, and some schools were obviously struggling to cope with increased and burdensome administrative tasks often without adequate increases in resources.

There was confusion and uncertainty about respective roles of trustees, chairpersons of boards, principals, and administrative officers under the new arrangements. A national survey of primary schools carried out by the New Zealand Council for Educational Research in September 1989, *The Impact of Tomorrow's Schools in Primary Schools and Intermediates* (Wylie 1989), revealed the concern of many trustees that funding would be inadequate under the new bulk funding arrangements to individual schools. School principals also emerged as a group particularly affected by the changes with an increase in workloads, a feeling that their role was changing from that of professional leader to manager, and the fact that two-fifths of principals still had not received any training for their new roles. A study of primary school principals carried out in September 1989 confirmed this view (Barrington 1989).

Codd (1990, 91) raises the questions as to whether the reforms were part of an ideological takeover by the New Right and whether Rogernomics had "finally caught up with the educational system." Alternatively, one could ask whether the Labour government was returning to its ideological roots by implementing genuine democratic reform at the "grassroots" or whether this was merely a case of "pragmatists exercising greater control over a major area of state spending" (Capper and Munro 1990, 150).

While represented as devolution or decentralization, the new system hardly involved any large scale rush to devolution in the sense of a genuine transfer of real power from a national to a subnational level. The changes could be described as devolution in appearance but not in substance. There has been some devolution of administrative responsibility, but dominant authority in most decision-making areas remains overwhelmingly with central government and the new Ministry of Education. In some instances, power at the center has been increased and not just because of the extent to which greater local responsibility exists within the framework of nationally mandated guidelines. For example, the Minister now has the power not only to remove a board of trustees if it fails to perform adequately but also to appoint a statutory manager to manage the school until new Board elections can be held. Some other decision-making has also become more centralized, including decisions about school buildings, based on the argument of greater expertise and efficiency of operation as in the newly established property division of the central government. According to Nash (1989, 119) "the clear object of this restructuring for the state is to achieve greater control of essential functions and to withdraw from intervention where it cannot be successful."

The importance attached to maintaining a strong central influence is also evident in other ways and the school charter provides a good example. Many parents were undoubtedly surprised when they realized just how many of the charter requirements for their school were mandatory and nondiscretionary and included, in addition to those mentioned earlier, such matters as finance, property, enrollments, and board meetings. Even when discretionary initiatives by boards were possible (such as in non-core curriculum subjects), it was clearly laid down that all discretionary items of the school's charter must take into account the national guidelines. The ultimate retention of control centrally undoubtedly lies in the area of funding, for it will still be central government that can turn the financial tap on or off whenever it chooses. According to Snook (1989, 8) a "system sold to the electorate as a decentralizing measure is becoming more centralized and bureaucratic than ever before. . . . The charters, seen originally as giving freedom are now clearly sources of further control." Bates (1990, 46) views the charter as providing a "mechanism of control greater than that to which schools have been subjected to previously." Although the reforms may have changed the relations between parents and state, they likely also increased the power of the Treasury, which had promoted the strategy of removing layers of bureaucracy. As Grace (1990, 39) explains it:

> The new education settlement was being founded upon a relation with parents and community rather than with intermediate or central levels of bureaucracy. . . . The replacement of a mediated relation between the state and the school by a direct relation raised large questions about exactly who had become empowered as a result. A diffuse collection of Boards of Trustees and Community forums throughout New Zealand were unlikely to constitute a significant power bloc which the Treasury would have to deal with in future struggles over education policy or resources. While

the new relation with parents and community might
serve the purposes of the Labour government's new
education settlement, it also had the potential to
serve the Treasury's agenda for public policy.

Overall, New Zealand's reforms are more typical of the
"early stage of the 'Great Debate' in Britain, rather than of a full-
blown Thatcherism. Lange has more in common with Callaghan
[Labour Prime Minister of Britain, 1974-1979] then with Thatcher
[Conservative Prime Minister of Britain, 1979-1990]" (McCulloch
1990, 66). We should remember, however, that Callaghan's
intervention and the 'Great Debate' was a "prelude to and
legitimation of Thatcher's later radical reforms" (McCulloch 1990,
66). And despite good intentions, the New Zealand changes may
well go in the same direction.

REFERENCES

Barrington, J. 1985. Secondary school governors and their boards. (Report to the New Zealand Secondary School Boards Association, Wellington).

Barrington, J. 1989. Tomorrow's schools: How are principals feeling? *New Zealand Journal of Educational Administration*, 4 (November): 31-35.

Bates, R. 1990. Educational policy and the new cult of efficiency. In *New Zealand educational policy today*, edited by S. Middleton, J. Codd, and A. Jones. Wellington: Allen Unwin.

Blyth, C. 1987. The economist's perspective of economic liberalisation. In *Economic liberalisation in New Zealand*, edited by A. Bollard and R. Buckle. Wellington: Allen Unwin.

Caldwell, B., and Spinks, J. 1988. *The self-managing school*. Lewes, UK: Falmer Press.

Capper, P., and Munro, R. 1990. Professionals or workers? Changing teachers' conditions of service. In *New Zealand education policy today*, edited by S. Middleton, J. Codd, and A. Jones. Wellington: Allen Unwin.

Codd, J. 1990. Educational policy and the crisis of the New Zealand state. In *New Zealand education policy today*, edited by S. Middleton, J. Codd, and A. Jones. Wellington: Allen Unwin.

Dakins, J. 1973. *Education in New Zealand*. Newton: David and Charles.

Department of Education. 1987. *The curriculum review*. Wellington: Government Printer.

Du Chateau, C. 1987. The lost generation. *Metro* (November): 32-47.

Employers support educational reforms. 11 May 1988. *Evening Post*, 2.

Gianotti, M. 1989. Educational administration: Reflection on the Picot Report. In *The impact of American ideas on New Zealand's educational policy, practice and thinking*, edited by G. Lealand, G. McDonald, and D. Phillips. Wellington: New Zealand-United States Educational Foundation.

Gordon, L. 1988. After the Picot Report: What will happen to teachers and teacher unions? (Proceedings of the first Research into Educational policy Conference, Wellington, NZCER).

Government of New Zealand. 1988. *Royal commission on social policy*. Wellington: Government Printer.

Government of New Zealand. 1990. *Today's schools*. Wellington: Government Printer.

Grace, G. 1990. Labour and education: The crisis and settlement of education policy.In *The fourth Labour government*, edited by M. Holland and J. Boston. Auckland: Oxford University.

Harper, D. and Karacaoglu, G. 1987. Financial policy reform in New Zealand. In *Economic liberalisation in New Zealand*, edited by A. Bollard and R. Buckle. Wellington: Allen Unwin.

Holdaway, T. 1989. An outsider's views of tomorrow's schools. *New Zealand Journal of Educational Administration*, 4 (November): 35-40.

Holmes, F.W. 1974. *Directions for educational development*. Wellington: Government Printer.

Holmes Group 1986. *Tomorrow's teachers: A report of the Holmes Group*. East Lansing, Michigan: Holmes Group Inc.

Ingle, S.J. 1967. The politics of education. Doctoral dissertation Victoria University of Wellington, New Zealand.

Jesson, Bruce. 1988. *Revival of the right, New Zealand politics in the 1980s*. Wellington: Heinemann Reid.

Jesson, Bruce. 1989. *Fragments of labour*. Auckland: Penguin.

Lange, D. 1980. Address to New Zealand Education Boards Association Conference (June).

Lange, D. 1989. Press Conference (23 August).

Lauder, H. 1990. The new right revolution and education in New Zealand. In *New Zealand educational policy today*, edited by S. Middleton, J. Codd, and A. Jones. Wellington: Allen Unwin.

McCombs, T. 1976. *Towards partnership*. Wellington: Government Printer.

McCulloch, G. 1990. The ideology of educational reform. In *New Zealand educational policy today*, edited by S. Middleton, J. Codd, and A. Jones. Wellington: Allen Unwin.

McLaren, I.A. 1989. Equity by compulsion: A feature of current New Zealand educational reform. A paper delivered to Australian and New Zealand History of Education Conference, Melbourne New Zealand.

McLaren. I.A. 1974. *Education in a small democracy: New Zealand*. London: Routledge and Kegan Paul.

Munro, R.S. 1989. *The Munro Report: Research into personnel provisions of tomorrow's schools*. Wellington: Post Primary Teachers' Association.

Nash, R. 1988.   Tomorrow's schools: State power and parent participation. *New Zealand Journal of Educational Studies*, 24, 2: 113-127.

National Commission on Excellence in Education. *A nation at risk: The imperative for education reform*. Washington, DC: United States Government Printing Office.

National Party. 1987. *A nation at risk*. (Election Manifesto). Wellington.

New Zealand Government. 1988. *Tomorrow's schools: The reform of education administration in New Zealand*. Wellington: Government Printer.

New Zealand Parliament. 1986. *The quality of teaching: Report of the education and science select committee*. Wellington: Government Printer.

New Zealand Secondary School Boards Association. 1976. *Statistical report*. Wellington.

Nordmeyer, A. H. 1974. *Organization and administration of education*. Wellington: Government Printer.

The President's Lecture. 1989. Christchurch School of Medicine, New Zealand.

Prime Minister. 1988. Press Conference (20 May).

Snook, I. 1989. Educational reform in New Zealand: What is going on? New Zealand ARE Conference, Trenthem.

Taskforce to Review Education Administration 1988. *Administering for Excellence*. (Commonly referred to as the Picot Report after the Taskforce's chairperson, Brian Picot). Wellington: Government Printer.

Thompson, M.A. 1989. Equity issues in the New Zealand education system: An overview. Ministry of Education, Economics of Education Seminar.

The Treasury. 1984. *Government management.* Wellington: Government Printer.

The Treasury. 1987. *Government management: Brief to incoming government, Vol 2 Education Issues.* Wellington: Government Printer.

Wilson, M. 1987. *Labour in government.* Wellington: Allen Unwin.

Wylie, C. 1989. *The impact of Tomorrow's Schools in primary and intermediate schools. 1989 Survey Report.* Wellington: NZCER.

GLOBAL RHETORIC, LOCAL POLICY: A CASE STUDY OF ISRAELI EDUCATION AND TEACHER TRAINING

Esther Gottlieb

Prestigious educational reforms such as those occurring in the pace-setting countries of the world (e.g., the United States and Great Britain) often function as a source model for national educational reform programs elsewhere in the world. What makes certain nations pace-setting sources and exporters of educational reform programs and other nations followers and importers of such programs is their relative positions in a world system of knowledge production and circulation. While advanced industrial nations are mainly involved in the *production* of knowledge, Third-World nations are mainly still concerned with the *distribution and consumption* of knowledge. In the "post-modern condition," according to Lyotard (1979, 6), knowledge behaves analogously to money: "[T]he pertinent distinction would no longer be between knowledge and ignorance, but rather, as in the case of money, between 'payment knowledge' and 'investment knowledge.'" In advanced industrial nations, the role of institutions of higher education is to create new skills ("investment knowledge"), whereas in the Third World educational institutions continue to supply the skills needed to fulfill the society's present needs and to maintain its internal cohesion ("payment knowledge").

Linkages, both formal and informal, keep educational systems in the periphery tied to those in the center. Legitimation of education institutions, structures, curricula, academic standards, policies, approaches, and levels of funding for research programs and educational reform are determined and approved in the metropolitan centers. One need not assume a linear notion of transfer within a functionalist tradition of "development-education" in order to regard this process as instrumental not only in determining educational reforms and their implementation in periphery countries but also in the continuing dominance of the United States in the international knowledge system (Altbach 1988, 137-142).

Lyotard helps us understand the relative positions of central and peripheral nations within a world system of knowledge, but he adds nothing to our understanding of the processes of *transfer* of knowledge from center to periphery. For a better understanding of the processes of diffusion of cultural models in general, of which educational reform is a particular case, the present study sets out to examine not only what knowledge is being transferred but what rhetorical strategies serve as vehicles of such transfer. Identification of pertinent rhetorical strategies is more than merely descriptive; in each case, these rhetorical strategies will be shown to contribute to the construction of specific knowledge.

Traditionally, interference between cultures in contact has been understood in terms of "influence" of one culture (supposedly the "superior" one) on the other (the "inferior" one). Thus, in world-system models purporting to explain educational reform transnationally, the flow of educational reform is directly from center to periphery (Arnove 1980, 48-62; Ginsburg, Cooper, Raghu 1989). By contrast, Even-Zohar (1990) argues the usefulness of first examining the models already in place in the periphery before trying to establish what exactly has been transferred from the "source" culture (i.e., the **transferring** culture) to the "target" culture (i.e., the culture being **transferred to**), and how the transfer took place.

The analysis of teacher education reform in Israel will be conducted against the background of local history and in the light of transnational transfer of educational models and reform movements. The immediate objects of analysis will be educational reform documents, which will be subjected to a discourse analysis designed to bring to light not only what these documents *say* but *how they say it.*

ANALYSIS OF DISCOURSE

This study treats the educational reform documents as a "discursive event" (Foucault 1977, 199-200). This analysis differs from other studies in that its focus is not only on the *content* of the reform documents but also on the form of the *discourse.* In undertaking the concrete analysis of a text, this study demonstrates how educational reform discourse actually operates, instead of remaining at the level of the abstract recognition that rhetoric (or discourse) matters, or, on the other hand, dismissing it as mere decoration ("just rhetoric"). The knowledge that these documents construct is analyzed not from the point of view of its truth (or falsity) or its consistency (or inconsistency) with the data collected or with reality as experienced by the actors but from the point of view of its ability to persuade or even to coerce (Gottlieb 1989, 131-144).

The basic theoretical orientation of this approach is that of the renewal of interest in rhetoric in the social sciences (Nelson, Meghill, and McClosky 1987). Taking their inspiration from accounts of discourse and text by Wittgenstein, Foucault, Derrida, and others, sociologists such as Richard H. Brown (1977 and 1987) have undertaken to read social construction through language, historians such as Hayden White (1973) have given rhetorical accounts of historiography, and anthropologists (Clifford 1988; Marcus and Cushman 1982, 25-70; Rosaldo 1989) have experimented in ethnographic writing, exploring the poetics of cultural accounts. Analyzing successive drafts of an article on quantum theory of the scattering of X-rays, Charles Bazerman (1986) has been able to demonstrate what kinds of pressures and choices constrain and shape the final textual object in the natural sciences. Similarly educationists (Wexler 1987, 185) have striven to synthesize elements of formalism, structuralism, post-structuralism, and semiotics into a "post-new sociology of education. Reinterpreting Foucault and Derrida, these "poststructural investigations in education" undertake the deconstruction of concepts such as construct validity and Bloom's taxonomy of education objectives (Cherryholmes 1988).

    What the studies in these various fields have made clear is that the rhetorical forms which a writer chooses (consciously or otherwise) and those which become institutionalized through the history of publishing in each field determine what kinds of things we consider to be contributions to knowledge. To unpack what kind of thing constitutes a contribution to knowledge in the case of a reform policy such as the academization of teacher education we need to treat form as (relatively) binding. Through a discourse analysis of this kind it will be possible to study what has happened in Israeli teacher education and identify specific items of the international teacher education repertoire used to legitimatize a local policy.

EDUCATION AND TEACHER
EDUCATION IN ISRAEL

    The starting point of a modern Jewish education system in the beginning of the twentieth century precedes the establishment of the State of Israel in 1948.[1] The Teachers Union was the first independent Jewish organization in the Holy Land itself outside the Zionist Congress and other organizations operating from Europe. From both its founding charter in 1903 and 10 years of protocols, it is clear that its major aim was to organize power to unify the educational work around a national Hebrew character (Elboim-Dror 1986, 211).

Teacher education in the first half of the twentieth century
was run by the main ideological organizations within the Jewish
settlers in Palestine, most of them religious organizations supported
by Jewish philanthropic foundations. The structure and content of
the first three teachers seminaries were based on European
(especially German) models. Only in 1940 was the first secular
seminary, Seminary Hakibbutzim, established in Tel-Aviv. Its
founder and first principal (M. Segal) studied in the United States
and was influenced by Dewey, and under his leadership the
Seminary Hakibbutzim was the first to introduce developmental and
social psychology as well as educational philosophy in its innovative
academic curriculum. However, teacher education continued to be
carried out in high-school institutions. The opening of a pedagogical
department by Hebrew University in Jerusalem in 1936 and the
establishment of a post-secondary professional degree in teaching,
reflecting the American influence in training teachers, aroused
political opposition. This led the Department of Education to
establish a committee to investigate teacher's training. While
recommending that teacher's education be lengthened by two years,
the committee recognized and approved the existence of two kinds
of institutions, side by side, secondary and post-secondary teacher's
education (Ben-Peretz and Dror 1990). This duality, on the one
hand, maintaining the Germanic education philosophy because of its
supposed superiority, while, on the other hand, admitting the new
British and American influence, typifies later institutional thinking
and educational planning, including the new policy, the subject of
this paper.

In 1953 the State took over the provision of free mandatory
eight years of schooling and cancelled the existing separate
ideological school boards. Public schooling was divided into three
sectors: Jewish secular, Jewish-religious (not including the ultra-
orthodox, who kept their own independent education), and Arab.
The teaching force (in the Jewish sectors) grew from 15,300 in 1953
to 32,128 elementary schools teachers in 1986 in order to
accommodate a student population that expanded from 139,000 in
1948-49 to 1.2 million students in 1986, amounting to 29 percent of
the population of the state (Shprintzak and Bar 1988, 30-54).

The Ministry of Education and Culture took over the
educational system from the pre-state Department of Education,
leaving only the provision of the physical plants and their care to

local municipalities. By 1987 the Ministry of Education controlled
the education of 93.5 percent of all kindergarten and elementary
school students, 96.5 percent of all high-school students, 86 percent
of all students preparing to be elementary school teachers (68
percent for secular schools and 20 percent for religious-state
schools), and 44 percent of the students preparing to teach in
secondary education (mainly junior high school) (Shprintzak and
Bar 1988, 29).

These statistics only partially explain the power and
political attractiveness of the education ministry. Education is a
central issue in Israel both socially and politically. For a Jewish
society with traditional high regard for education ("the people of the
Book"), which defines itself as a non-class society, depending for
growth on Jewish immigration, under constant threat and external
pressure, dependent on external economic and military aid,
education serves as a major state apparatus, more so perhaps than
in other developing countries (Eisenstadt 1985, 415-427). Education
is considered the main tool for economic development and for
preparing an able military and work force as well as an instrument
for the transmission of Euro-Israeli values and norms to the new
immigrants.

The weight given to education as a main state apparatus
and a major tool for legitimation of the local political and economic
elite was sustained in Israel as the Ministry of Education during the
first two decades remained firmly in the hands of prominent Labor
Party ministers. The Ashkenasi-dominated Labor Party's control
over resource allocation in education and their paternalistic ideology
increased conflict with the new growing majority of Sephardic
immigrants[2] and eroded their legitimacy to represent the working
class. To this the Labor party answered with educational reforms.

By the end of the 1950s the provision of universal primary
schooling was achieved, and the attention of the Ministry and others
in the system turned to coping with internal educational problems.
Educational achievements were not felt to be proportional to the
volume of investment in education. In particular, students of
Sephardic background were perceived as not receiving their fair
share of education.[3] These educational research findings exposed
the fact that, far from closing the socio-economic gap between the
Sephardic and Ashkenazi populations, the educational system
perpetuates that gap. The 1959 demonstrations by Sephardic

immigrants in the slum neighborhood of Wadi Salib in Haifa focused the political elite's attention on the dissatisfactions of the Sephardic population and their emerging political power. Central educational administration moved from a formal-egalitarian approach to a differential-compensatory approach during the period 1958-1968 (Schmida 1987). The educational reforms included remedial reading programs, an extended school day, secondary-level vocational education programs, etc.

In order to codify and implement the new reforms, a new rhetoric was required, organized around a newly-coined term, *t'unei-tipuach*, to designate the target population for the reforms. Routinely translated into English as "underprivileged," "disadvantaged," or "deprived," *t'unei-tipuach* was actually intended by its coiners to replace such terms with one that is more optimistic and progressive in its connotations (*Megamot* 1967, 229-246). *T'unei-tipuach* literally means "in need of cultivation" and thus focuses on *what is needed* rather than on what the target population *is*. Nevertheless, it is clearly an organic metaphor relating to the same root metaphor of biological growth and evolution from which the metaphors of "development" and "underdevelopment" also derive (Gottlieb 1988). Once "objective" criteria for membership in *t'unei-tipuach* were defined, education funds could be channeled according to the numbers of *t'unei-tipuach* students in a school; curricula could be commissioned specifically for this group of students; teachers and counsellors could be trained to address the "special" needs of this group, and so on. Twenty years later, the existence of *t'unei-tipuach* students continues to be taken for granted by policy-makers, academic researchers, and journalists; its socially-constructed nature has been effectively forgotten. During the 1980s the social rejection of the term by administration and educational researchers renewed the controversy over how to define a *t'unei-tipuach* student and how to end the use of the term as a synonym for students of Sephardic background. The term itself is less frequently used and tends to be replaced by alternatives such as "students from socially weak groups" (Yogev 1988).

Ten years of *Tipuach* has not yielded the expected results. Along with the educational policy intended to close the social-economic gap, the system continued to cultivate highly selective-elite high-schools in the urban centers and the elite kibbutz schools.

Symbolic homage was paid to equality, whereas in fact high achievement and excellence were the national goals. By 1988 the gap between Ashkenasi and Sephardic groups (defined by place of father's birth) in obtaining 11-12 years of school had indeed been closed. But this statistic is misleading, since the gap reappears if one examines the statistics for obtaining higher education. In other words, now that the system approaches universal attainment of twelve years of schooling, it is at the higher education level that intergroup inequalities are manifest.[4]

After a protracted public and political struggle, the Israeli parliament (the Knesset) in July 1968 approved the first major structural educational reform since 1953. The proposed change of the educational structure from the 8-4 year system to a 6-6 year system met with great opposition from the Elementary School Teachers Union, which saw in it a threat to their power as the largest union. Their opposition was not sufficient to deflect a parliamentary committee, which recommended the changes (Rimalt Committee 1971). The committee recommended changes shaped both by the Minister of Education and by Ashkenazi academics' appropriation of relatively liberal ideas from the United States, such as integration and busing rather than community control or more equitable ways of distributing economic and political power.

The abolition of standardized testing at the end of grade 8 for selective entrance to high school and the two-year extension of compulsory education, from age fourteen to age sixteen, paved the way for universal free schooling from age four to age eighteen. To form the new junior high schools, school districts were to be re-zoned in such a way as to include a mixture of Sephardic and Ashkenazi students from various socioeconomic strata. Thus in the implementation phase the Ministry of Education has emphasized that the most important implication of the school reform was ethnic integration.

To overcome political opposition, mainly from the religious sector whose constituency is mostly Sephardim living in integrated neighborhoods and settlements and parents who organized against busing, the mode of implementation in one community was not identical to that in another. The school reform was to have been completed in eight years; now, twenty years later, only two-thirds of the local communities have actually changed the structure of the schools. Between 1971 and 1976, 52 percent of all education districts implemented the structural reform, but between 1976 and 1986 only an additional 12 percent implemented it (Chen 1988).

Local governments run by the Labor Party were the first ones to launch the reform encouraged by the Ministry of Education. The deceleration in implementation of reform can be explained by the dramatic political turnover of 1977, when the right-wing opposition block (Likud) was able to form the first non-Labor government since the establishment of the Israeli state. Key leadership positions in the Ministry of Education were taken over by the Religious Party for the next eight years. The emergence of the urban Sephardic "Black Panther" movement as an organized political force to be reckoned with in the run-up to the 1981 election prompted the established politicians to set up the "Prime Minister's Committee for Troubled Youth," which launched massive social and housing development projects. Finally, it was recognized by the Ashkenazi political establishment that education alone could not address poverty and social inequalities. The educational budget was reduced, and funds were channeled to neighborhood renewal programs rather than to educational reform programs. This marked a new symbolic action by the Likud government to improving the collective standard of living of their Sephardic working-class constituency instead of continuing Labor's commitment to individual upward mobility.

The changes in teacher education needed to accommodate the school reform program were carried out in the state-controlled teacher education institutions (the seminars), rather than in the independent universities, thus reasserting central government control over the new teacher education programs. From 1948 to the late 1960s the same division of labor in education had prevailed: the majority of teachers were prepared in two-year seminar programs culminating in teaching certification, while high school teachers first obtained a B.A. or B.S. in one or two major disciplines and then went on to obtain a postgraduate teaching certificate from one of the five university Schools of Education. The continuing wish of Schools of Education to open elementary school training programs met with absolute refusal from the Ministry of Education, which argued that the academic and research-oriented university, based on a German Model, was ill-suited to preparing teaching craftsmen/women. Not incidentally, the Ministry thus reasserted once again the state's economic and political power over teachers.

Once the school reform program was accepted, the Teachers Union cooperated in its implementation, since they saw it as contributing to their effort towards professionalization and the satisfaction of higher salary demands. Although the universities were called upon to help upgrade teachers education programs, which were extended from two to three years, culminating in a new, higher certificate (the "senior teacher" certificate), and Schools of Education were carrying out major research projects planning, implementing, and assessing the school reform, the Ministry of Education's Office of Teacher Training was the sole planner and overseer of teacher education reform. This process culminated in the closing of the smaller and academically weaker seminaries, as defined by the administration, so that by 1987 only 29 of the original 62 state institutions were still in operation.

There were two related unresolved problems yet to be addressed, as far as the administration was concerned, namely, that of recruiting able students into the teacher-training programs and the fact that the Israeli universities did not recognize courses in teacher education programs as post-high school credit toward a B.A. degree. Many able students have been dissuaded from attending teacher education seminaries by the fact that teacher education was not part of the process of accumulating "academic capital," which is "the coin of the realm in universities" (Ginsburg 1988, 19). This means that certified teachers wishing to go on to obtain a university degree would have to start their B.A. studies from the beginning. To find a solution to this problem and to resolve the growing conflict over the "professionalization" of teaching and what is called in local terms "the academization of teaching," the Ministry of Education asked the Commission of Higher Education to appoint a committee to develop a framework for "academizing" teacher education. This committee, headed by Professor Yosef Dan, presented its recommendations in 1981. The "Dan Document" (Committee for Higher Education 1981) recommends the inauguration of a B.Ed. program and the conversion of a small number of the teacher education seminaries into colleges granting an academic first degree to teachers.

The common denominator of reform rhetoric in Israel is similar to that in the United States: the assumption that education would improve if teaching were improved. The United States school reform reports, like the British governmental documents (Tickle

1987, 7-37), presume a relationship among teacher education and
training, student teaching, and eventual classroom practice
(Cornbleth 1989). Moreover educational practice and achievements
are related to national development and economic productivity in the
Israeli case or economic competitiveness in the United States case.
This by itself does not prove the existence of a
transnational cultural transfer, of course. In order to trace the
transfer of items of teacher educational reform from the center of
the knowledge system in the English language (the United States
and Britain) to Israel on its periphery and to see how these
transferred items have served local policy, we turn to the reform
documents themselves.

THE RHETORIC OF TEACHER EDUCATION REFORM

The model for institutes wishing to establish a course of
study leading to the new "Boger Hora'a" (B.Ed.) degree is outlined
in a document by the Committee for Academizing Teacher Training
Institutions entitled "Provisional Model of the Curriculum for
'Boger Hora'a' (B.Ed.)," commonly referred to as the "Dan
Document" (Commission for Higher Education 1981). Over half the
Document is devoted to listing courses. According to the Document,
disciplinary studies for junior high school teachers are to be
concentrated in two major disciplines, while those for elementary
teachers should cover a "great number of subjects." The Document
strictly allocates time among subject studies, professional studies,
and classroom practice, allowing for very few electives and little
personal freedom in choosing a course of study. A number of
courses and an entire fourth year of study, constituting the academic
tier on top of the teacher training program, are added, potentially
reinforcing the Israeli high school institutional arrangement,
whereby students are locked into a program for three years. The
education disciplines of psychology, sociology, and philosophy are
given pride of place as constituting the "theoretical" foundations of
education. Yet these foundations are to be studied only after the

prospective teacher has experienced teaching in a classroom, so that these disciplines will have "direct relevance to educational practice." The tension between teaching as a craft transmitted through first-hand practical experience and education as a codified science founded on strong disciplinary principles runs right through the Dan Document's rationale for the new curriculum. The Document is strongly slanted toward viewing teaching as professional training and not another discipline that could be taught like any other university discipline.

The Dan Document is a "factual," plain-style piece of writing, sounding about as rational, low-key, and "unrhetorical" as it is possible for a piece of writing to be (which of course is itself a form of rhetoric). In order to see more clearly the kind of rhetoric that sustains and animates teacher education reform in Israel, we need to examine other, more openly rhetorical genres, such as the article by Yosef Dan himself (Dan 1983) describing the process of conversion to a teachers college or his conference paper on the same subject delivered at a symposium on "Possible Directions in Teachers Education" (Dan 1988).

Dan's article has a double rhetorical strategy. First, it mounts an offensive against the universities' basic model of teacher preparation, a model which disconnects academic disciplinary studies from teacher preparation. This model, in which a prospective teacher undertakes teacher preparation after or during the final year of B.A. studies in a disciplinary department, is common in Israeli universities and in some states in the United States, where students enter teacher education programs only in their last year of study or after having completed a B.A., and is also similar to the British Postgraduate Certificate in Education.

Dan's second rhetorical strategy is a defense of the teacher education college model leading to the B.Ed., which he helped engineer. This model, he tells us, is "common in several educational systems abroad" (Dan 1983, 23). According to this model, Dan claims, "teaching is a profession," like medicine or law: "Like the doctor[s] or lawyer[s] who go through academic training which grants [them] the license to practice [their] profession, so the teacher[s] [have] to have an academic degree which reflects [their] success in academic studies and grants [them] the license to teach" (Dan 1983, 23)

Thus, on the one hand, Dan advocates an academic course of study for teachers based on a transnational model developed in the pace-setting countries (the United States and Britain); on the other hand, he admits that it would be "completely unrealistic" in the Israeli context to require every teacher to have an academic degree "as in several places abroad and as in the case of doctors and lawyers in Israel" (Dan 1983, 43). Since Dan and his committee were commissioned to make practical recommendations suitable to Israeli conditions, they had to negotiate a construct somewhere between the "ideal model" of teacher professionalization imported from abroad and the local situation. This situation is above all characterized by an urgent need to increase the number of institutes of higher education and by a quest on the part of teachers and the work force in general to accumulate "academic capital" university degrees or their equivalent.

This demand was not so much voiced by teachers organizations as initiated in the form of a policy resolution by the centralized governance of education, which noted the potential for conflict in the mounting demands for post-secondary education on the part of groups, which until recently would not have been expected to complete secondary education. These demands and the conflict they have generated are thus a side-effect of the school reform effort and the extension of free schooling to age eighteen. In 1985, 92 percent of the fourteen to seventeen year age cohort were still in educational institutions; in 1986, 82.2 percent of the students who had completed eight years of schooling in 1982 were still continuing their secondary education, compared to 40.2 percent in 1970. Thus, the Israeli education system is approaching the point of universal attainment of twelve years of schooling. At this point, according to Green (1980, 90), "if there is a level within the system that everyone completes, then completing that level can have no bearing whatsoever upon any social differences . . . whose source is traceable to completing that level." Under this "law of zero correlation" the Israeli system is approaching the point where most of the members of an age-cohort will complete high school. For that age-cohort a high school certificate will cease to be a criterion for job entry, job placement, or job security.

As unemployment has risen in Israel, from 4.8 percent in 1980 to 6.4 percent in 1988, the demand for education has increased, since unemployment is higher for those with less schooling (in 1988, 8.3 percent for those with nine to twelve years of schooling, compared with 4.3 percent for those with thirteen or more years (Central Bureau of Statistics 1989). Thus, more than anything else, political reality dictates educational expansion in post-secondary education, since twelve years of free schooling has already been enacted. Education, as Carnoy (1985, 157-171) has pointed out, is a cheap way to secure political value or legitimacy compared to structural changes in the economy to redistribute income and wealth. The educational change by itself is likely to be ineffective as it was in the case of French reforms studied by Weiler (1988, 265): "The idea, it seems, is to maximize the political gain to be derived from the design of educational reforms and to minimize the political cost of implementing them."

A similar observation can be made about the newly drafted national teacher education policy, which aims to maximize social and political gain through a reform with minimal economic investment and no loss of control. The "academizing" of six post-secondary institutions owned by the state (with an enrollment of 12,000 students in 1987) and more recently (1990) the decision by the Ministry of Education to "academize" the entire educational work force (about 37,000 teachers in 1987), are compensatory strategies on the part of central government in the face of challenges to the legitimacy of its control of access to higher education. This strategy also reinforces the symbolic role of education in the modern welfare state as the means to individual upward mobility.

Dan and his committee had a charter to resolve the contradiction between the competing claims of the ideal transnational model (where teacher education is academic) and local practical realities by proposing a "mixed" teacher education system. University teacher education programs (B.A. followed by teaching certification) would coexist side by side with teacher education college programs (teaching certification followed by B.Ed.). Moreover, university postgraduate programs would now be open to holders of the new B.Ed.

Dan (1983, 26) seeks to convince his audience that the proposed solution is not merely a "technical solution" to the basic questions of length, content, and status of teacher education. Indeed, it is not a technical solution; it is a rhetorical one, accomplished by constructing the new "Boger Hora'a" degree in a way that makes use of the underlying "teaching is doctoring" metaphor. The medical profession is a common basis for comparisons among professions; its code of ethics, its training program, and its status frequently serve as an example for aspiring professions. So common is its use that its metaphorical function is often overlooked and its implications taken for granted. The medical metaphor, not surprisingly, is also dominant in United States teacher education reform rhetoric.

Both in the article (Dan 1983) and in the Dan Document (Commission for Higher Education 1981), the Hebrew name of the degree, "Boger Hora'a," is explicitly equated with the "B.Ed." (supplied parenthetically in Latin letters in the Hebrew text). Nevertheless, as Dan himself observes, "Boger Hora'a" is not an exact translation of "Bachelor of Education." A literal translation of "Boger Hora'a" would be "teaching graduate." The structure of the Hebrew word *hora'a* (instruction) is parallel to that of *refu'a* (curing, doctoring); thus, the "Boger Hora'a" degree grants a teacher the right to practice instruction just as the medical degree grants a doctor the right to practice medicine. The metaphoric transfer of semantic materials from the medical frame of reference to the pedagogical one is much easier in Hebrew, thanks to the grammatical parallelism between the words for "curing" and "instructing."

Up till now, according to Dan, a teacher was "a history teacher" or "a math teacher" or "an elementary school teacher"; now, for the first time, "a person will receive an academic degree for being a *teacher*, period" (Dan 1983, 47). That is, people will now be awarded a degree on the strength of their ability to teach not for their mastery of a discipline or age group: "A doctor doing pediatrics or geriatrics, from the point of view of his or her academic standing is a doctor regardless of his or her specialty. The same with a lawyer . . . and the same should be true in the case of teaching" (Gottlieb and Cornbleth 1989, 3-5).

As in the case of the Holmes Group report in the United States, Dan falls back on a nineteenth-century model of the medical and legal professions, conveniently overlooking the highly-specialized structure of the late twentieth-century professions, where doctors or lawyers *are* identified by their specialties ("neurologist," "corporate lawyer," etc.). As in the use of the medical metaphor in teacher education discourse in the United States, the metaphor is used in Israel without being problematized (Gottlieb and Cornbleth 1989, 3-15). Its use suppresses recent changes in the medical profession as well as the potentially dangerous implications of this unexamined medical metaphor for education.

The fact that the medical metaphor is used in an uncritical way both in the reform discourses of the pace-setting countries and in Israeli reform discourse (and even in a different language) is only one indicator pointing to the existence of a transnational reform discourse. The strategy of calling for school reform or for the academizing of the teaching force rather than undertaking radical structural changes (such as more equitable distribution of economic and political power) is easily traced to the strategies modern advanced capitalist states resort to in the face of increased conflict and "chronic deficit of legitimacy" (Weiler 1988, 265).

Israel is not different in this respect, having to resort to the legitimating potential of symbolic action such as imported educational reforms in order to ease pressure on the state to close the socioeconomic gap between the Ashkenasi and Sephardic groups of the Jewish population. The legitimacy of the state has also needed shoring up against erosion from other directions, though not necessarily the expected ones. Neither the political crisis arising from the Lebanese incursion of 1982, nor the economic problems (an inflation rate 373 percent in the consumer price index in 1984, 304 percent in 1985), nor, so far, even the Palestinian uprising (or *intifada*) in the Occupied West Bank and Gaza (from 1987) has substantially affected the national consensus. The major threat to legitimacy of the state and political elites is the continuing political deadlock between the Labor and the Likud blocs, which are so finely balanced that neither can form a government except by means of an intrinsically unstable coalition between the two blocs (as in 1984-1988 and again in 1988-90) or by ceding disproportionate power and influence to tiny minority parties in exchange for their crucial handful of votes (as in the case of the June 1990 Likud coalition with religious and extreme right-wing parties). The higher education reforms address these other challenges to the state's legitimacy only indirectly, while they directly address (if only symbolically) the challenge to legitimacy represented by the socioeconomic gap within the Jewish population.

CONCLUSION

The Israeli reform documents advocate the importation of an international model, the B.Ed., which is symptomatic of the more recent cultural penetration from the United States and Great Britain, by contrast with the long-standing Continental (Germanic) influence on the model of Israeli higher education. This new repertoire has been introduced by translational and transformational procedures that serve to legitimize, to empower, and to lower opposition to the local policy. The center of the knowledge system, namely the pace-setting countries for teacher education reform (Britain and the United States) exports "packaged knowledge" (e.g., educational reform reports) to countries on the periphery, such as Israel, as part of a world knowledge network (Altbach 1987), while Israeli academics also import such knowledge, either by being personally exposed to United States or British models in their own careers or as participants in reviewing foreign innovations as part of drafting national policy.

This United States model of teacher education was not imposed on Israel by United States government officials, consultants hired by bilateral agencies, or representatives of international organizations. Rather this model has been "informally" exported by United States academics and "freely" imported by Israeli academics and government officials because they viewed them to be worthy of consideration (even if critically). The model has been fairly smoothly incorporated into the Israeli scene at least in part because it has the legitimating potential to accommodate local political, economic, institutional, and linguistic contexts. A case in point is the importation and diffusion of the United States reform reports to Israel. The author of this paper distributed the Holmes Group report to deans of two teachers colleges and one university school of education in August 1987. The recommendations of the Carnegie Forum were translated by a professor of education and published in the Teachers Association journal *Hed-Hachinukh*, (22 [1], 1987). A United States professor delivered a critical review of the United States reform reports at a Ministry of Education symposium (21 January 1988). Most of the foreign educational journals that have reviewed and criticized the reform reports are available in college and university libraries.

The present analysis shows that the local discursive practices determine how imported models will be perceived and used. The concept of *"Boger hora'a"* is a good example of this process. Thus, when Dan inserts the Latin letters "B.Ed." in a Hebrew text in the context of *"Boger hora'a"* he legitimizes the *"Boger hora'a"* by assimilating it to the transnational model of "B.Ed." However, the transnational transfer in the Israeli case differs from the imitative pattern of knowledge which Lee, Adams, and Cornbleth (1988, 233-246) found in the Korean case of center-periphery transfer of knowledge in education. In the case of the recent Israel teacher educational reforms, we witness the use of indigenous language and local educational repertoires to carry out a new function, that of "academizing" the teaching work-force--in itself a concept transferred from the pace-setting cultures. This case study shows that the behavior of the system is *not* explicable in terms of the national system alone but that the context of a larger system and that of transnational cultural transfer must also be taken into account.

My interest in the discursive practices of educational reform can be seen as part of the broader exploration of the "rhetoric of inquiry." Such an inquiry takes us beneath the masks of methodology. This paper is by no means an exercise in what Wexler (1987, 190) denounces as "textualism [that] denies its own social/ historicity." Rather the present study takes seriously the form of educational documents as constraining and shaping, in their social context, the production of institutional knowledge and the making available of that knowledge for policy decisions. This case study is offered as a possible model for further discourse analysis of educational reform, of local and national policy documents, and indeed of discursive practices in other subfields of education and policy in general.

NOTES

1. (14) It should be made clear from the start that this paper deals exclusively with secular education in the Jewish sector in the State of Israel. This is a methodological necessity, since the education systems among the Jewish and Arab sectors of the State are separate as are the secular and religious Jewish sectors. (There are, in addition, Jewish religious schools independent of any of the State systems.) Nor does this paper address the education system in the territories occupied by Israel after the 1967 war (the West Bank and Gaza Strip), which are not administered by the Israeli Ministry of Education.

2. The term "Sephardic" (some authorities prefer "Oriental" or "Eastern") is used here to designate Jewish immigrants and descendants of immigrants from North African and Asian countries. "Ashkenazi" designates Jewish immigrants and descendants of immigrants from European countries and the Americas. Ashkenazi Jews constituted the bulk of the Israeli population before 1948 and have continued to function as the political and economic elite until very recently.

3. Only 57 percent of Sephardic students attended ninth grade in 1962; in 1961, only 6.1 percent who had entered first grade passed the high school matriculation exam ("Bagrut") that controls entrance to higher education, compared to 30 percent of students of Ashkenazi background. In higher education the picture was even grimmer: only 2.4 percent of the age groups (twenty to twenty-nine year-olds) who attended universities were of Sephardic origin, compared to 14.2 percent of Ashkenazi origin (Peled 1982).

4. In 1988 only 13 percent of the Sephardic population had obtained thirteen to fifteen years of schooling, and only 5 percent sixteen or more years, compared to 26 percent and 23 percent, respectively, for the Ashkenasi population (Central Bureau of Statistics 1989).

REFERENCES

Altbach, P. G. 1988. International organizations, educational policy, and research: A changing balance. *Comparative Education Review* 32, 2: 37-142.

Altbach, P. G. 1987. *The knowledge context: Comparative perspective on the distribution of knowledge.* Albany: State University of New York Press.

Arnove, R. F. 1980. Comparative education and world systems analysis. *Comparative Education Review* 24: 48-62.

Bazerman, C. 1986. *Shaping written knowledge: The genre and activity of the experimental article in science.* Madison: University of Wisconsin Press.

Ben-Peretz, M., and Dror, Y. 1990. Critical issues in teacher education in Israel. In *Educating the world teachers: Global perspectives, issues, policies & problems*, edited by H. Leavytt. Westport: Greenwood Press.

Brown, R. H. 1977. *A poetic for sociology: Toward a logic of discovery for the human sciences.* Cambridge: Cambridge University Press.

Brown, R. H. 1987. *Society as text: Essays on rhetoric, reason, and reality.* Chicago: University of Chicago Press.

Carnoy, M. 1985. The political economy of education. *International Social Science*, 37: 157-171.

Central Bureau of Statistics 1989. *Statistical abstracts of Israel, No. 40.* Jerusalem: Keter.

Chen, M. 1988. The impact of ecological factors on education reform. Paper presented at the annual meeting of the Comparative and International Education Society, Atlanta, Georgia, March.

Cherryholmes, C. H. 1988. *Power and criticism: Poststructural investigations in education.* New York: Teachers College, Columbia University.

Clifford, J. 1988. *The predicament of culture: Twentieth-century ethnography, literature, and art.* Cambridge, MA and London: Harvard University Press.

Commission for Higher Education 1981. Committee for Academizing Teacher Training Institutions, "Provisional model of the curriculum for 'Boger Hora'a'(B.Ed.)." Jerusalem: Commission for Higher Education. [In Hebrew]

Cornbleth, C. 1989. Cries of crisis, calls for reform, and challenges of change. In *Crisis in teaching*, edited by L. Weiss, et al. Albany, NY: SUNY Press.

Dan, Y. 1983. The process of becoming a teacher education college. Mahalachim: The Levinsky Teachers College Annual: 22-32. [In Hebrew]

Dan, Y. 1988. Possible directions for teachers education. Unpublished minutes of symposium, Jerusalem: Ministry of Education and Culture. [In Hebrew] (21 January).

Eisenstadt, S.N. 1985. The Israeli political system and the transformation of Israeli society. In *Politics and Society in Israel*, edited by E. Krausz and D. Glanz. Vol 3, 415-427. New Brunswick: Transaction Books.

Elboim-Dror, R. 1986. *Hebrew education in Eretz Israel. Vol.I, 211.* Jerusalem: Yad Ben-Zvi Institute.

Even-Zohar, I. 1990. *Polysystem studies: Papers in historical poetics and semiotics of culture*. Tel-Aviv: Poetics Today.

Foucault, M. 1977. *Language, counter-memory, practice: selected essays and interviews*, edited by D. F. Bouchard. Ithaca, NY: Cornell University Press.

Ginsburg, M.B. 1988. *Contradictions in teacher education and society: A critical analysis*. London: The Falmer Press.

Ginsburg, M.B., Cooper S., and Raghu R. 1989. National and world-system explanations of educational reform. Paper presented at the Comparative and International Education Society, Boston, March.

Gottlieb, E.E. 1989. The discursive construction of knowledge: The case of radical education discourse. *Qualitative Studies in Education* 2, 2: 131-144.

Gottlieb, E.E. 1988. Development education: How knowledge is constructed by and through discourse in intellectual paradigms. Paper presented at the annual conference of the Comparative and International Education Society. Atlanta, Georgia, 1988.

Gottlieb, E.E., and Cornbleth, C. 1989. The professionalization of tomorrow's teachers: An analysis of United States teacher-education reform rhetoric. *Journal of Education for Teaching*, 13, 1: 3-15.

Green, T.F. 1980. *Predicting the behavior of the educational system*. Syracuse: Syracuse University Press.

Lee, J.J., Adams, D., and Cornbleth, C. 1988. Transnational transfer of curriculum knowledge: A Korean case study. *Journal of Curriculum Studies*, 23, 3: 233-246.

Lyotard, J.F. 1979/84. *The postmodern condition: A report on knowledge*. Minneapolis: University of Minnesota Press.

Marcus, G., and Cushman, D. 1982. Ethnographies as texts. *Annual Review of Anthropology*, 11: 25-70

Nelson, J.S., Megill, A., and McCloskey, D.N., eds. 1987. *The rhetoric of the human sciences*. Madison: University of Wisconsin Press.

Peled, E. 1982. The educational reform in Israel--the political aspect. In *Educational administration and policy making*, edited by E. Ben-Baruch and Y. Neumann. Herzlyia: Unipress

Rimalt Committee. 1971. *Report of the parliamentary committee for the examination of the primary and secondary educational system of Israel*. Jerusalem: The Governmental Press.

Rosaldo, R. 1989. *Culture and truth: The remaking of social analysis*. Boston, MA: Beacon Press.

Schmida, M. 1987. *Equality and excellence: Educational reform and the comprehensive school*. Ramat-Gan: Bar-Ilan University. [In Hebrew].

Shprintzak, D., and Bar, A., eds. 1988. *Ministry of Education and Culture*, 30-54. Jerusalem: Ministry of Education and Culture. [In Hebrew].

Smilansky, M. 1967. A social analysis of the educational structure in Israel. *Megamot*, 8, 3: 229-246. [In Hebrew].

Tickle, L. 1987. *Learning teaching . . . teaching teaching . . .: A study of partnership in teacher education*. London: The Falmer Press.

Weiler, H.N. 1988. The politics of reform and nonreform in French education. *Comparative Education Review*, 32, 3: 251-265.

Wexler, P. 1987. *Social analysis of education--after the new sociology*. New York: Routledge & Kegan Paul.

White, H. 1973. *Metahistory: The historical imagination in nineteenth-century Europe*. Baltimore: Johns Hopkins University Press.

Yogev, A. 1988. Israeli educational policy for the advancement of students from weak social groups. A Policy Paper presented to the Pedagogical Secretariat of the Ministry of Education, Jerusalem, June. [In Hebrew].

THE POLITICAL ECONOMY OF SCHOOL REFORM IN THE UNITED STATES

Don T. Martin

The general public in the United States has traditionally viewed the schools as institutions that are created, maintained, and controlled by "the people." With some notable exceptions, conventional wisdom has it that schools have somehow escaped the socially damaging effects of corrupt politics. This view persists despite the many trenchant critiques made of public education in the past. During the Progressive Era an outpouring of social commentary on the political, economic, and social uses and misuses of schools was made, and such criticism of the social effects of schooling has continued to the present. Thus, even a cursory examination of our past and present reveals that the local, state and federal governments--and the various dominant group interests they serve--have been and continue to be an active and indeed a crucially significant force in the historic reform of public schooling.

341

The reform of schools in the United States in the 1980s was thrust onto the public scene in dramatic fashion. A report, *A Nation At Risk* (National Commission on Excellence in Education 1983), sounded the alarm that drastic measures needed to be taken to rescue the nation's schools from their alleged abysmal condition. But *A Nation At Risk* was only one of many national reform reports of what the architects of these reports claimed to be the direct relationship between a deteriorating United States school system and a declining United States economy (see also Carnegie Corporation of New York 1983; Task Force on Education for Economic Development 1983; Twentieth Century Fund Task Force 1983). These government and corporate foundation reports were preceded by sensationalist reporting in the mass media of schools' and teachers' failings (e.g., Williams 1981a, 1981b).

HISTORICAL CONTEXT

By implication these reports convey the notion that their call for educational reform was somehow a unique national experience, but an examination of the past reveals that efforts to reform education in the United States date from the earliest years of the Republic. The most notable "progressive" reform movements have been the Common School Movement of the 1830s and 1840s, the Land Grant Acts of 1862 and 1890, and the Progressive Education Movement of the 1920s, 1930s, 1940s and its re-emergence in the 1960s and 1970s. Although these reform movements were considered progressive, their overall effect tended to be conservative in that none of them sought to significantly alter the political and economic structure of the then prevailing social system.

There were also more explicitly conservative reform movements, usually focused on the development of vocational education in public schools. In the early 1900s concern was expressed in a series of reports about the United States' competitiveness with other industrialized nations, especially Germany. The report of the Committee on Industrial Education stated: "Technical and trade education for youth is a national necessity, and the . . . nation must train its youth in the arts of production and distribution" (National Association of Manufacturers 1905). Germany then, like Japan today, was both feared and admired for its industrial might and educational system, respectively. Much attention was given to the German trade and vocational schools, and many believed that the United States should copy German vocational education in order to improve the nation's international competitiveness. For example, the Comittee on Industrial Education report in 1905 stated: "The German technical and trade schools are at once the admiration and fear of all countries. In the world's race for commercial supremacy we must copy and improve upon the German method of education" (National Association of Manufacturers 1905). The Committee on Industrial Education's 1912 report called for the development of human capital through vocationally trained secondary students in response to the fear of foreign competition. The report maintained that there were two types of capital: land, machinery and money--as well as human capital. The charge was made that the development of the latter, human capital, had been overlooked in the United States. Schools were therefore viewed as the logical setting to develop human capital, and they were called upon to do so by this report through increased efforts in vocational education. The 1912 report also sounded the alarm that: "We should act at once because of the stress of foreign competition. We are 25 years behind most of the nations that we recognize as competitors. We must come nearer to the level of international competition" (National Association of Manufacturers 1905).

Established by the Congress, the Commission on National Aid to Vocational Education issued a report in 1914 that became one of the most significant documents in the early vocational education movement. Its recommendations were incorporated into the nation's most important vocational education legislation, the Smith-Hughes Act of 1917. Besides outlining all the major arguments for vocational education, the members of the Commission also maintained that vocational education would reduce discontent among workers: "Industrial and social unrest is due in large measure to a lack of a system of practical education fitting workers for their calling" (United States Congress 1914). The report warned, furthermore, that the United States could not continue to draw indefinitely on Europe for cheap labor nor would such cheap labor meet the demand for more intelligent workers. According to the Commission, therefore, vocational education was needed to help solve economic problems then facing the United States.

Yet there were some in the United States who were highly skeptical of the Vocational Education Movement. Labor unions in general and especially the Congress of Industrial Organizations were critical of the vocational emphasis in schools. This was not because they opposed vocational training per se, but because they feared that a new non-organized youthful workforce would cause a surplus of workers, a suppression of wages, unemployment, and a general lowering of union members' standard of living.

Some educators, most notably John Dewey (1916), opposed the movement to create separate vocational schools in part because of the concern that this could lead to the furthering of a class system. Dewey and other opponents of separate vocational and academic schools argued for a comprehensive school where vocational, general, and academic curricula would be housed under the same roof. A similar stance was adopted by the National Education Association, which in 1913 appointed the Committee on the Reorganization of Secondary Education. The Committee's final report in 1918 on *The Seven Cardinal Principles of Secondary Education* helped to curb the movement to create separate vocational schools and aided in establishing the comprehensive high school.

Conservative reform movements, such as vocational education, the administrative centralization and efficiency movements of the early twentieth century, the back-to-basics, accountability, competency-based movements of the 1970s, and the vocational and career education movements of the 1960s and 1970s contrasted sharply with the progressive reform movements. Although each of the major conservative educational reform movements had distinct characteristics that formed a particular history, they all were oriented toward shaping schooling to correspond to the emerging interests of the larger social system, particularly the economy. In the 1970s for instance, Leon Lessinger, the architect of the accountability movement, in *Every Kid a Winner* (1970) called for schools to be modeled after the space industry just as schools in the 1920s were to be modeled after the steel industry (Martin et al. 1976).

The progressive and the conservative reform movements were similar in one important respect, that is, how they based their proposed educational changes on the perceived "needs" of the capitalist economy. Conservative educational movements have corresponded with the changing structures of the capitalist economic system, and conservatives looked to the schools to provide a lockstep, stratified educational experience that explicitly prepared students for a changing workplace. Students (at least the males) from varying racial, ethnic, and socio-economic levels were to be efficiently sifted and sorted so as to better fit them into an increasingly hierarchically structured workplace. However, as Bowles and Gintis (1976) argue, progressive reform movements early in the century also were partly oriented to accommodate and correspond to the changing needs of a developing corporate capitalist economic structure.

At the same time we should note that there were pedagogical divisions and major ideological struggles within the progressive and conservative camps. For example, there were the child-centered, social reconstruction, and scientific divisions within the Progressive Movement (Cremin 1961). And there was a split between the essentialist or Great Books proponents and the vocational/career education movements within the conservative camp.

There also have been examples of radical educational reform movements that took place outside the public domain of education. Opening in 1932 and continuing until today, the Highlander Folk School in New Market, Tennessee, has been devoted to providing nonformal educational programs designed to serve the economically and politically dispossessed residents of the historically depressed Appalachian Region. Another prominent example of a nonformal, radical educational reform movement involved the labor colleges that flourished in the first half of the twentieth century. Most notable among them were Brookwood Labor College, Work People's College, and Commonwealth College. The main objective of labor colleges was to prepare their students to become more sympathetic and understanding about working class struggles and, more specifically, to prepare their students to become labor organizers. The objective was formulated in the context of the belief by promoters of the labor college concept that public schools by and large favored business and industry and were anti-union (Altenbaugh 1990).

A more recent neo-progressive movement, the free school, open classroom reform movement of the late 1960s and early 1970s, did not accommodate capitalism as did most earlier progressive movements. On the contrary, it arose out of political and social crises and proceeded to criticize the rigidities and structures of a bureaucratic corporate system associated with schools and work organizations under capitalism. The ultimate effect of the free school movement, nevertheless, did little to alter the educational system, let alone the economic and political systems. However, it did help to promote a cultural revolution, and the vestiges of its effect remain until the present.

POLITICAL ECONOMIC CONTEXT OF THE 1980s REFORM MOVEMENT

The arguments for the reform of education in the earlier part of the century to meet international competition were renewed in the 1980s. But the effort to restore the hegemony of the United States in the world's economic and political order had been rendered more difficult by the legacy of Vietnam as well as the youth rebellion in the 1960s and early 1970s against the social and cultural status quo. Certainly, the military and political dominance in the world by the United States was diminished by its involvement in the Vietnam War. The post-World War II prosperity that continued into the 1960s was disrupted in part because of the excessive costs of the war as well as the strategic policies of the Organization of Petroleum Exporting Countries (OPEC) in the 1970s.

Economic dominance, however, was most affected by major structural changes in the world economic order. These changes were evidenced mainly by corporations moving their manufacturing plants to non-union, lower-waged regions of the United States and to a number of "developing" nations where wages were even lower and where the work force was more docile and non-unionized. For example, U.S. Steel, rather than making ongoing reinvestments in plant equipment renewal and modernization, let its steel mills deteriorate to the point where they became outmoded and contributed to U.S. Steel not being able to compete in the world markets. Using the latter as a rationale, U.S. Steel accelerated its closing of mills in the United States, while exporting steel-making to low-wage Third World countries, especially Brazil.

Moreover, the process of deindustrialization also contributed to major disruptions in the social system that had to be dealt with by various social institutions--not least of which were the schools. The civil rights, environmental, and women's movements, coupled with the counter-cultural and the free school/open classroom education movement, significantly challenged prior sets of relationships.

SCHOOL REFORM DISCOURSE IN THE 1980S

What assumptions underlie the reform debate and what is the nature of the criticisms directed at present reform proposals? When conservative values emphasizing private interests and individual competition were dominant in the 1920s, 1950s, and 1980s, reform efforts were oriented to having schools stress higher academic standards, efficiency, orderliness, and achievement. When liberal political values, emphasizing equality of opportunity for male and female children of different social class and racial/ethnic groups, generally prevailed in the 1930s and the 1960s, educational reforms were concerned more with issues of promoting access and reducing institutional biases. The 1980s have also witnessed voices from a radical perspective. Although not as influential as the conservative or liberal reform discourse, the radical discourse does pose an alternative framework for analyzing the contemporary scene of schooling and society.

Conservative Voices in Reform Discourse

In the 1980s the reform of schools once again came to the forefront. A relatively small group of educators, politicians, business leaders, media representatives, parents, and other members of the community vigorously debated the quality of our present educational system and the goals and strategies around which it should be organized. The debate was launched and fostered by a series of reports, which drew attention to the sharp decline since the 1960s of standardized achievement test scores. This was used as a rallying cry in spite of the fact that between 1980 and 1983, the period just before the national reports emerged, there were some gains in standardized test scores. It is also noteworthy that the mobilization of the reform movement by conservative critics took place during a period marked by the highest level of parental satisfaction with the public schools (Hodgkinson 1982).

On a more fundamental level the conservative reports gave special emphasis to the lack of correspondence between the education of youth in the United States and their later fit into the workplace. While attention was devoted to the continuing high dropout rates, especially among minority youth in urban areas, what seemed to have most alarmed conservative critics was their perception of the relationship between the decline of educational test scores, standards, and discipline and the decline of economic productivity in the United States. There was an economic and identity crisis because of the United States' failure to compete economically and technologically with the Japanese and other industrialized societies. To rectify this crisis, the local, state, and federal levels of government were once again called upon to intervene in the affairs of schooling to rearrange educational priorities so as to restore the dominance of the United States in the world political and economic order.

What appears to be an attempt in the conservative reports to gain some national consensus about reform is not directed so much at remedying the multifarious problems confronting the nation's schools as it is an attempt to create a better fit between training in the school and the perceived needs of a changing national and world economy. For example, the report of the Committee for Economic Development, *Investment in Our Children* (1985), contended that the schools, and particularly vocational education programs, in the United States have been failing to educate the nation's children, and this undermined the nation's international competitiveness because industry has been forced to spend large sums of money to train high school graduates in the basic skills necessary to perform on-the-job tasks. The report recommended that the schools should set as their priorities the teaching of academic skills and improved behavioral attitudes toward work (Committee for Economic Development 1985, 3-6). Although the report called upon the business community to become active in schools, it freed the business community of any additional responsibility for financing the schools (Committee for Economic Development 1985, 30-35).

Revealing his support for the reform of education for competitive purposes, President Reagan asked a six-member task force of leading corporate and university executives to investigate how the nation's international competitive position could be improved through more creative technology and corporate productivity. This group of executives, the Business and Higher Education Forum, prepared a report entitled *America's Competitive Challenge: The Need for a National Response* (1983). Their report contained specific and detailed recommendations designed to strengthen the competitiveness of United States based corporations in world markets. The report recommended that "our society must develop a consensus that industrial competitiveness on a global scale is crucial to our social and economic well-being" (Business and Higher Education Forum 1983, 2). To achieve this goal, the report maintained workers would need continued skill training in order to keep up with the changing competitive demands of a multinational corporate environment. Workers were described as "the essential ingredient in the process of technological innovation and economic competitiveness" but were viewed as having "antiquated functional skills and deficient academic skills" (Business and Higher Educational Forum 1983, 21). Thus, workers were seen as poorly prepared and trained and capable of making only substandard contributions to productivity. Workers, therefore, needed to be better trained in the skills to increase productivity. Much emphasis was also placed on socializing students to "self-discipline," "reliability," "team work," and "responsibility." In the end, it was thought that the goals of educators and employers for improving schools must be more closely linked together.

Liberal Voices in the Reform Discourse

It should be noted here that these conservative voices for reform were countered by more moderate or liberal reformers, such as Boyer (1983), Goodlad (1984), and Sizer (1984). In sharp contrast to the conservative reports, the more liberal reform reports were based on extensive research in the schools, analyzing the links between student achievement and the schools' organizational structure, pedagogical practices, and curricula. These three liberal reports promoted educational reforms, but they did not call for a restructuring of schools or society so as to eliminate prevailing social and educational inequalities persistent in the United States today.

John Goodlad's (1984) *A Place Called School: Prospects for the Future* covers the broadest aspects of public schools dealing with both elementary and secondary education. Goodlad deals extensively with teachers in their workplace and describes their 37-50 hour work week as "a combination of the inflexible schedule normally associated with blue-collar jobs and a little of the flexibility associated with a profession" (Goodlad 1984, 169). Moreover, Goodlad (1984, 170) reports that salaries are so low that at least 29 percent of teachers are forced to "moonlight," to work other jobs in addition to teaching.

Ernest Boyer's (1983) *High School: A Report of Secondary Education in America* and Theodore Sizer's (1984) *Horace's Compromise: The Dilemma of the American High School* treat a broad range of issues and practices confronting the schools. Boyer found that teachers perform numerous menial, demeaning tasks, while Sizer saw the instructional work of teachers devoted largely to the frustrating chore of motivating uninterested students; coping with trivial administrative, clerical, and record keeping tasks; supervising extra-curricular activities; and assuming student counseling burdens. The poor working conditions for teachers was also evidenced by supply shortages, dingy and antiquated facilities, and the threat of violence. According to Boyer (1983, 159), "One-third of New York City [high school] teachers and one-fourth of those elsewhere said they had been assaulted. Forty percent reported that violence is a daily concern."

Goodlad and Boyer portray teachers work as insular, fragmented, isolated, and lonely, which contributes to a sense of alienation and powerlessness. And Sizer (1984, 1985-87) emphasizes teachers' relative economic deprivation: there has been a "13 percent drop in public school teachers salaries from 1970 to 1980, and a 16 percent real reduction in the compensation for independent school teachers." But in spite of their criticisms of their poor pay and working conditions for teachers, Boyer, Sizer, and Goodlad fail to call for a radical change in the corporate structure of public schools; their liberal reform proposals reflect a consensus outlook rather than a radical conflict-oriented one (Altenbaugh 1989, 170).

Liberals, although concerned as well about the loss of the United States's competitive edge, argued for the well-rounded and more balanced reform of education rather than a narrow emphasis on the basics. Liberal reformers (and some of their conservative counterparts) did not promote a narrow technical or vocational education programs but stressed the importance of literacy and computation skills and sought to socialize youth more effectively to assume available positions in what was taken for granted as a stratified society.

Radical Voices in the Reform Discourse

There has been a relatively small core of contemporary "left" critics who have made penetrating analyses of contemporary schooling--for example, Apple (1982), Apple and Weis (1983), Giroux (1983), Giroux and Aronowitz (1985), Bowles and Gintis (1976), Carnoy and Levin (1985), Shapiro (1985), Ginsburg (1988). Although radical educational theorists have provided varying critical interpretations of the nature of present-day schools there is a crisis in critical theory as it moves into the twenty-first century. As Giroux and Aronowitz have perceptively stated, "the rise of the new right and its economic and ideological attacks on the schools [and] . . . the failure of radical educators to match neo-conservative politics with a corresponding set of visions and strategies" has contributed to this crisis.

Social, economic, and cultural reproduction theories based on a political-economy model have formed the basis of most radical theories of schooling. The work of radical educators might be summarized around the following concepts. First, schools contribute to the process of capital accumulation in a capitalist economy by preparing graduates who will fit into an unequal workforce and social system. Schools sort and select students into a credential market that tends to reproduce a hierarchically arranged workforce. Second, schools have become significant agencies for the legitimation of a social, economic, and political ideology. And, finally, the totality of schooling constitutes an important agency for economic and knowledge production and cultural control.

As for the conservative contention that schools are to blame for the United States's declining world economic competitiveness, radical educators argue that the decline in production and the loss of millions of jobs in steel, autos, rubber, electronics, and other major industries in the so-called "rust belt" in the past decade or so is much more a result of the lack of proper management and foresight in planning as well as the self-interested and greedy investment policies of large corporations than it is the incompetence of teachers and the general failure of the schools.

According to radical educators, poor management practices and avarice-oriented investment polices, however, can be viewed as secondary to capitalism's structural response to the economic crisis of the 1970s and 1980s. The problem of declining profits, exacerbated by increased "competition" from abroad, particularly Japan, has caused capitalists to seek new ways to increase "productivity" and profitability. One major strategy has been to reduce the cost of labor, thus extracting more surplus value from an already exploited labor force, who for the past century or more helped to build giant economic empires and produced so many personal fortunes for others. The suffering that has been experienced by millions of laid-off industrial workers is in large part due to the fact that multinational corporations and giant financial institutions have exported labor intensive industries and have virtually abandoned the workers for more profitable ventures in the non-union sunbelt of the United States and the sweat shops of Third World countries.

The radical educators acknowledge that many of the

conservative reform reports, although giving absolute priority to restoring the United States's world economic dominance, express a rhetorical commitment to the ideology of equal education opportunity. But equal educational opportunity, radical educators argue, is quite different than equal education. Even a cursory observation of the educational system in the United States reveals significant differences in state and local provision for education, and even if equal educational resources were provided on a national scale, such equality would do little to counteract other social, economic, and political inequalities throughout the larger social system.

As it stands, the rhetoric of the ideology of equal opportunity is encapsulated into the ideology of "excellence." Indeed the ideology of excellence has become a keystone to many of the reform proposals. The concepts of equal educational opportunity and excellence are juxtaposed in the reports and are blended together so that the separate meanings of these two ideas are blurred and left unclear. In the reports excellence becomes the code word for the creation of a new class of technocratic and managerial elite, with the vast majority of students, consisting largely of the poor, especially minorities, thus being "legitimately" relegated to positions with less status, power, and wealth.

If the Conservatives proposed reform agenda were to become reality, radical educators have argued, most lower-class students would experience even greater failure, higher dropout rates, and further social decline. The reforms would benefit mainly those advantaged students, especially those whose parents own and control a disproportionate share of the wealth in the United States and the world and who are destined for higher levels of education and employment. By elevating the requirements to achieve excellence while not providing any compensatory educational programs for the poor, these conservative reform proposals of the 1980s, if successfully implemented, would merely widen inequalities in the present unequal social and educational structures in the United States

Finally, radical discourse has focused on the conditions of the teachers' work. Unlike their liberal counterparts, though, radical educators see the teachers' situation as fundamentally linked to processes within capitalist economies. For instance, Apple's (1983) analysis shows how curricula embody forms of technical control that results in a deskilling of the work of teachers. Teachers, thus, are seen to be undergoing a process of proletarization similar to that of other skilled workers in industry organized within the capitalist mode of production. More specifically, pre-packaged curricula reduce teachers to the status of a mere technician and devalue their importance as the central figure in the classroom. Skills central to effective teaching are no longer essential. With the growth of prepackaged materials, curricular planning is done at the level of production, and its execution, separated from planning, is carried out by the teacher. Based on a similar critique of teachers' work in the United States, Giroux (1983) calls for teachers to become transformative intellectuals, working actively and collectively with other workers and citizens to reorganize schools and restructure society to serve democratic and egalitarian goals.

EFFECTS OF THE 1980s SCHOOL REFORM PROPOSALS

The national reform reports have sparked numerous legislative efforts to reform schools in all 50 states. These efforts have focused on reforms that call for direct action by state governments, such as increased core academic requirements for graduation, career ladders, merit pay and increased teacher salaries, and instructional supervision or teacher evaluation systems to improve learning and teaching in the classroom. The state-driven reforms have, in effect, resulted in some state legislatures becoming super school boards that have mandated strict rules for teachers and students. More recently some reform efforts have favored school-site councils, school-based management, and plans that would give teachers a much greater voice in managing schools.

An important trust of the present reform reports is designed to create more business and education cooperation through alliances. However, business and industry's interest in public schooling is not new. The Chamber of Commerce, National Association of Manufacturers, and similar organizations have for many years consistently sought to influence the schools. Their successful involvement has risen and declined in relationship to their own vested interests. Business owners, industrialist, professionals, and other "elites" have, throughout much of the century, played significant roles on school boards and on the state and local levels.[1] Schools have long been modeled after industry and business, and school administrative policies have often been heavily influenced by leaders in business, industry, and the professions.[2] However, in recent years, local and state policy makers have increasingly appropriated the ideological perspectives and the language of corporate board rooms (Cuban, 1990).

Although there are varying economic and political interests within business and industry, their impact on the present reform movement is evident by the fact that most panels or state commissions on education frequently include many prominent business and industry leaders, and these panels and commissions often use them as consultants as well. Many conventions of educators feature speeches and workshops on the need to expand and strengthen "partnerships" between business and education. And few communities have failed to launch projects to build cooperation and understanding between business leaders and educators.

Several of the national reform reports claim that high technology will be a key source of new jobs in the 1990s and thus there is a need to reform the education system to promote the acquisition of higher levels of technical skill. Many technical forecasts that attempt to show the impact of new high technologies paint a rosy picture of future growth and development, i.e., higher productivity, greater flexibility and response to market demand, and improved quality control (Lund and Hansen 1986; National Academy of Sciences 1983; National Science Board Commission in Mathematics, Science, and Technology 1983; Servan-Schreiber and Crecine 1986). The Third Industrial Revolution is predicted to fuse design, manufacturing, and marketing into one combined form of information that will enable industry to automate nearly all tasks presently done by humans (Draper 1985, 48). These same optimistic forecasts also predict that new technologies will restructure work and reorganize the workplace to produce more creative and satisfying jobs demanding ever-higher skill levels. A 1986 report funded by Congress' Office of Technological Assessment states that employment opportunities are changing from physical, "hands on" type of work to work that is based on an abstract understanding of the production processes (Lund and Hansen 1986, 95).

The contention of reformers that the development of a high technology will require large numbers of highly educated, highly trained workers is contradicted by several studies of the nation's future labor force needs (Levin 1984; Little 1982; Rumberger 1984). Levin (1984) argues that there are two fallacies in the reform reports. First, the jobs expected to grow most rapidly in the future are fast food workers, guards and doorkeepers, and kitchen-helpers-- with high-tech jobs far down the list. The second fallacy, according to Levin (1984), is the belief that high-tech jobs require higher education and highly complex skills, while in reality microprocessors and robotics have deskilled many jobs traditionally requiring high levels of skill. Rumberger (1984) points out that cashiers no longer need math skills, secretaries are being displaced by word processors, and similar changes are occurring with workers in auto repair, industrial design, and drafting.

Computer literacy programs are justified on the basis of preparing secondary students for high-level computer jobs (Douglas and Bryant 1985). However, the computer industry requires only a small number of specialists and offers to most of its workers low-paying unskilled jobs. Moreover, computer literacy programs tend to emphasize the technical dimensions of computer literacy, thus deflecting attention from social and cultural issues. This tends to subordinate a broader-based educational experience to the job-oriented demands of the business sector (Robins and Webster 1985). Therefore, the reform proposals seem destined to continue the widening gap between an elite, highly educated technocratic minority and the mass of lower status marginally employable students.

REFORMING TEACHER EDUCATION

The question of how to attract and train high quality teachers has taken on a new urgency given the predictions of a major teacher shortage by the mid-1990s. The assumption in the early 1980s seems to have been that despite the significant reform efforts made by teacher training institutions in the 1970s, especially the development of competency- or performance-based programs as part of the accountability movement, much remained to be done to improve teacher training. The Holmes Group, made up of deans of education, initially from large research universities but later comprised by a wider range of institutions, identified three major goals in its initial report, *Tomorrow's Teachers* (1986): (1) the elimination of the undergraduate education degree replacing it with a five-year program, with emphasis on the liberal arts; (2) bolstering research activities to improve education and teacher education practices as well as to enhance the prestige of schools of education; and (3) converting some elementary and secondary schools into "professional-development schools" and making them the educational counterpart to teaching hospitals. In May 1987 the Carnegie Corporation's Forum on Education and the Economy published a report, *A Nation Prepared: Teachers for the 21st Century*. Like the Holmes Group, it called for the end to undergraduate degrees in education and announced plans to create a teacher dominated National Board for Professional Teaching Standards so as to begin offering certification to teachers much like medical boards presently certify medical doctors.

A power struggle is shaping up in the 1990s over issues such as who will train teachers, how long it will take to train them, and, in the final analysis, who will be the gatekeeper to the classroom. There is a conflict among teacher educators as most education deans in research universities support a pattern of the four-year liberal arts plus one year of professional training, while nearly all education deans from four-year liberal arts colleges prefer four-year programs during which academic and professional education coursework is taken. Complicating an analysis of this struggle is the fact that the heads of both historically antagonistic unions of schools teachers--the (organized labor affiliated) American Federation of Teachers and the (larger) National Education Association--have participated actively and amicably in the deliberations of both the Holmes Group and the Carnegie Forum. The political struggle over certification is made even more complex because some state legislatures are moving in a different direction. For example, New Jersey, Texas, and approximately 30 other states have implemented alternative certification programs that allow teachers, after they have earned a bachelor's degree, to be certified through programs run by local school districts rather than by university-based education programs.

Further complicating the power struggle over certification is the way reform-minded groups outside the public school domain, such as the Carnegie Forum, are pressuring educators to reform teacher training by circumventing their present certification procedures. What is most significant about this development is the threat posed by these external forces to the very legitimacy of state governments and the educational establishment in their traditional role as certifiers of teachers. Indeed, the long-established power of state educational bureaucracies (Katz 1968, 1971; Karier 1976; Kaestle 1983) is presently being challenged by new and powerful groups from business, industry, the professions, and others from the community as well as by national leaders of the American Federation of Teachers and National Education Association.

Presently, most teachers are certified through four-year university-based programs accredited by the National Council for Accreditation of Teacher Education (a private organization composed of educators' organizations) and approved by one of the 50 state education departments. An increasing number of states also require new teachers to pass the National Teachers Exam, developed and administered by the Educational Testing Service (a private corporation), or a similar type of a standardized test consisting of general and pedagogical knowledge.

Reform movements in a growing number of states, according to critics, are requiring culturally-biased, state-mandated teacher tests that adversely affect the hiring, retention, and morale of teachers from black and other racial/ethnic groups.

The Holmes and Carnegie reform proposals and the initiatives of state governments seem directed toward a major restructuring of the teaching force into a rather rigid hierarchy (Ginsburg 1988). Varying levels of status would accrue to teachers based initially on their performance on standardized tests and on the type of program in which they were prepared. At the top would be a minority of an elite corps of teachers, while the majority would be somewhere in the middle ranges, and those at the bottom would be stigmatized as marginally prepared.

CONCLUSION

The United States is a highly regionally, racially, and ethnically diverse society with the long tradition of decentralization in the educational system. Because of this ideological work has often played a key role in efforts to mobilize disparate groups to support a wide range of educational goals. The struggle between groups over the control of policies affecting the development of education has involved ideological battles. For example, educational issues related to the concept of equal educational opportunity have been the focus of heated and contracted debate during different historical periods.

It seems clear by now that the reform reports of the 1980's reflect a turning point in the history of public education in the United States that parallels a major shift in the nation's economic order and, indeed, the world economic order. In the name of "excellence" these reforms would produce a new, even less observable and more "accepted" tracking system. While accommodating the changing international economic order, the public school system, as the mainstay of the ideological state-apparatus, would assist in the restoration, legitimation, and maintenance of a class based hierarchical social system. This hardening of the stratification system involves changes in the lives of both students and teachers.

The reform reports also reflect a radical shift away from the "discredited" liberal reforms of the 1960s and 1970s. And the 1980s reforms are likely to reinforce existing inequalities in the 1990s. The reforms, I believe, are destined to reinforce further alienation and resistance from working class and racial ethnic minority students. We should not be surprised, however, if these students' resistance, particularly if individualized and not connected with broader political struggles, results in more student academic failure and more school leaving--ensuring them a lifetime of reduced employment opportunities and a lifetime of lower social ranking (see also Willis, 1977). The very act of resistance on the part of students from subordinate groups would deny them the skills and attitudes that might enable some of them to escape their social condition. Social class structure and the racial formation would be reproduced as mostly those advantaged students, predisposed to comply with the new school requirements, would find positions at the upper rungs of the social ladder.

The stage has been set for the 1990s by the reform agenda of the 1980s. The probable end result will be that the reforms of the 1980s, responding to a crisis in the economy and the state and through the aid of the most effective ideological state-apparatus, the schools, will assist in the 1990s in the continuation and expansion of the production/reproduction and the legitimation of a class-based, hierarchical social system. Historical processes, however, should not be conceived of as determined. The dynamics in the 1990s and into the twenty-first century will also be shaped by the ideological work and political action of educators and other workers and citizens, both in the United States and abroad. How such groups will align and pursue the struggle to achieve what kind of schools and society are the unanswered questions.

NOTES

1.   Elite membership on school boards was dramatically revealed in George Count's (1927) study of the social composition of the Chicago Board of Education. Although most boards of education in the United States have generally been composed disproportionally of white male business owners and professionals (Charters 1953), there are regional variations--with southern states having the most elite school boards. In recent years the percentage of elites has declined, and the number of women on boards of education have steadily increased, although school boards members still do not constitute a representative sample of adults. For example, national figures reveal that between 1982 and 1983 women on boards increased from 28.3 percent to 37.1 percent while professional and managerial board members declined from 66.6 percent to 55 percent (Spring 1989).

2.   Raymond Callahan's (1962) historical work on the school/business nexus in the 1920s analyzes how school administrators sought to model public schools after business and industry. The "Cult of Efficiency" in the 1920s, with guidance from a newly emerging educational administration that Callahan wrote about, seems to have reemerged as a dominant force in much of the reform agenda of the 1980s.

REFERENCES

Altenbaugh, R. 1990. *Education for struggle: The American labor colleges of the 1920s and 1930s.* Philadelphia: Temple University Press.

Altenbaugh, R. 1989. Teachers, their world and their work: A review of the ideas of professional excellence in school reform reports. In *The new servants of power*, edited by C. Shea, E. Rahane and P. Sola (167-175). Westport: Greenwood Press.

Apple, M. 1982. *Education and power.* Boston: Routledge and Kegan Paul.

Apple, M., and Weiss, L. (Eds.) 1983. *Ideology and practice in schooling.* Philadelphia: Temple University Press.

Apple, M., and Giroux, H. 1985. *Education under siege: The conservative and radical debate over schooling.* South Hadley, MA: Bergin and Garvey Publishers.

Bowles, S., and Gintis, H. 1976. *Schooling in capitalist America: educational reform and the contradictions of economic life.* New York: Basic Books.

Boyer, E. 1983. *High School: A report of secondary education in America.* New York: Harper and Row.

Business and Higher Education Forum, American Council on Education 1983. *America's competitive challenge: The need for national response.* Washington, DC: American Council on Education.

Callahan, R. 1962. *Education and the cult of efficiency: A study of the social forces that have shaped the administration of public schools.* Chicago: University of Chicago Press.

Carnegie Corporation of New York 1983. *Education and economic Progress: Toward a national educational policy.* New York: Carnegie Corporation.

Carnegie Corporation Forum on Education and the Economy. 1986. *A nation prepared: Teachers for the 21st century.* The report of the Taskforce on Teaching as a Profession of the Carnegie Forum on Education and the Economy. New York: Carnegie Corporation.

Carnoy, M., and Levin, H. 1985. *Schooling and work in a democratic state.* Stanford, California: Stanford University Press.

Charters, W. 1953. Social Class Analysis and the Control of Public Schools. *Harvard Educational Review* 23, Fall: 268-79.

Committee for Economic Development 1983. *Productivity policy. Keys to nation's economic future.* New York: Committee for Economic Development.

Committee for Economic Development 1984. *Strategy for United States industrial competitiveness.* New York: Committee for Economic Development.

Counts, G. 1927. *Social composition of boards of education: A study in the social control of education.* Chicago: University of Chicago Press.

Cremin, L. 1962. *The transformation of the school: Progressivism in American education, 1876-1957.* New York: Knof.

Cuban, L. 1990. Reforming again, again and again. *Educational Researcher*, 19, 1: 3-13.

Dewey, J. 1916. *Democracy and education.* New York: Macmillan.

364 The Political Economy

Douglas, E., and Bryant, D. 1985. Implementing computer-assisted instruction: The Garland way. *[T.H.E.] Journal*, 13 (September): 21-30.

Draper, R. 1985. The golden rains. *New York Review*, 32, (28 October): 46-49.

Ginsburg, M. 1988. *Contradictions in teacher education and society: A critical analysis*. Philadelphia: Falmer Press.

Giroux, H. 1983. *Theory and resistance in education: A pedagogy for the opposition*. South Hadley, MA: Bergin and Garvey Publishers.

Goodlad, J. 1984. *A place called school: Prospects for the future*. New York: McGraw-Hill Book Co.

Hodgkinson, H. 1982. What's still right about education? *Phi Delta Kappan*, (December): 231.

Holmes Group 1986. *Tomorrow's teachers*. East Lansing, Michigan: Michigan State University.

Kaestle, C. 1983. *Pillars of the republic: Common schools and American society, 1780-1860*. New York: Hill and Wang.

Karier, C. 1976. *Shaping the American educational state*. New York: Free Press, Macmillan Publishing Company.

Katz, M. 1986. *The irony of early school reforms*. Cambridge, Mass: Harvard University Press.

Katz, M. 1971. *Class bureaucracy and schools: The illusion of educational change in America*. New York: Praeger.

Kitter, B. 1983. The declining middle. *Atlantic*, 25 (July): 26-31.

Lazerson, M., and Grubb, W. 1974. *American education and vocationulism: A documentary history, 1870-1970*. New York: Teachers College Press.

Lessinger, L. 1970. *Every kid a winner: Accountability in education*. New York: Simon and Schuster.

Levin, H. 1984. Jobs: A changing workforce, a changing education? *Change*, 16, 7.

Little, J.W. 1982. Norms of collegiality and experimentation: workplace conditions of school success. *American Educational Research Journal*, 19, 3: 325-346.

Lund, R. and Hansen, J.A. 1986. *Keeping America at work: Strategies for employing new technologies*. New York: John Wiley and Sons.

Martin, D., Overholt, G., and Urban, W. 1976. *Accountability in American education: A critique*. Princeton, NJ: Princeton University Press.

National Academy of Sciences 1983. *Education for tomorrow's jobs*. Washington, DC: National Academy Press.

National Association of Manufacturers 1905. Report of the Commission of Industrial Education, 1905. In *American education: A documentary history, 1870-1970*. (1974). New York: Teachers College Press.

National Association of Manufacturers 1912. Report of the Commission of Industrial Education, 1912. In *The American school: 1642-1985*. (1988). New York: Longman.

National Commission on Excellence in Education 1983. *A nation at risk: The imperative for educational reform*. Washington, DC: United States Government Printing Office.

National Education Association 1918. *Cardinal principles of secondary education: A report of the Commission on the reorganization of secondary education*. Washington, DC: United States Government Printing Office.

National Science Board Commission of Precollegiate education in Mathematics, Science and Technology 1983. *Educating Americans for the 21st century*. Washington, DC: National Science Foundation.

National Society for the Study of Education 1982. *Education and work*. 21st Yearbook. Chicago: National Society for the Study of Education.

Robins, K., and Webster, F. 1985. Higher education, high tech, high rhetoric. In *Compulsive technologies: Computer as culture*, edited by T. Solomonides, and L. Levidrus. London: Free Associations Books.

Rumberger, K. 1984. The growing imbalance between education and work. *Phi Delta Kappan*, 65, 5.

Servan-Screiber, J., and Crecine, B. 1986. *The knowledge revolution*. Pittsburgh: Carnegie Mellon Press.

Shapiro, S. 1985. Capitalism at risk: The political economy of the education reports of 1983. *Educational Theory*, 35 (Winter): 21-26.

Sizer, T. 1984. *Horace's compromise: The dilemma of the American high school*. Boston: Houghton Mifflin.

Spring, J. 1988. *The American school: 1842-1985*. New York: Longman.

Task Force on Education for Economic Growth 1983. *Action for Excellence: A Comprehensive Plan to Improve Our Nation's Schools*. Denver: Education Commission of the States.

Twentieth Century Fund Taskforce 1983. *Making the grade. Report of the Twentieth Century Fund Taskforce on Federal Elementary and Secondary Education Policy.* New York: Twentieth Century Fund.

United States Congress, House, 63d Congress, 2nd session 1914. Report: Commission on national aid to vocational education. In *American education.* (1974). New York: Teachers College Press.

United States Congress, House, 63d Congress, 2nd session 1914. Report: Commission on national aid to vocational education. In *The American School 1942-1985.* (1988). New York: Longman.

Williams, D. 1981a. Why public schools fail? *Newsweek* (20 April): 62-65.

Williams, D. 1981b. Teachers are in trouble. *Newsweek* (27 April): 78-84.

Willis, P. 1977. *Learning to labour: How working class kids get working class jobs.* Westmond, UK: Saxon House Press.

EDUCATIONAL REFORM, THE STATE, AND THE WORLD ECONOMY: UNDERSTANDING AND ENGAGING IN IDEOLOGICAL AND OTHER STRUGGLES[1]

Mark B. Ginsburg and Susan Cooper

In the work represented in this volume we and our colleagues have sought to understand why particular kinds of educational reform rhetoric and action have occurred in diverse societies, what role educators have played in the reform debates and efforts, and what impact these reform movements have had on the work and lives of educators.

The first chapter reviews conceptual issues related to understanding educational reform from equilibrium and conflict perspectives focusing on national and world system level dynamics (see also Ginsburg et al. 1990). The national case studies of Australia, Côte d'Ivoire, England, Hungary, Israel, Mexico, New Zealand, Nicaragua, Spain, Tanzania, and the United States are then presented in the intervening chapters. The historical and contemporary data presented in these chapters provide a basis for us in this chapter to reconsider a number of the conceptual issues raised in the initial chapter.

As noted in the first chapter, however, our project is concerned not only with understanding why and how educational reform occurs. It is focused on developing strategies as part of what could be called critical praxis (Ginsburg 1988), aimed at effective collective action for progressive social change. Thus, in this final chapter we will also identify some issues related to such a program of political action, drawing on what we have learned from the experiences of educators and other citizen/workers analyzed in the national case studies.

REFORM RHETORIC VERSUS REFORM ACTION

To begin our discussion we need to return to some basic questions about the concept of educational reform. We should note that what is sometimes labelled "educational reform" is better understood as reform rhetoric that is not necessarily associated with any real, sustained efforts to bring about changes in education. Sometimes the lack of correspondence between rhetoric and action is the result of an elite group lacking commitment to change. In such cases educational reform rhetoric functions as a "placebo" giving the appearance of elite concern about as well as commitment and competence to address problems in education and society (see Campbell 1982). In Côte d'Ivoire, for instance, Assie-Lumumba and Lumumba-Kasongo indicate that we are still waiting to see implementation of reforms that were initially proposed by a Commission in 1972 and adopted as government policy by the National Assembly in 1977. This occurred, they argue, partly because the dominant class did not perceive it to be in their interest to alter existing institutional arrangements in education or society. Lack of elite commitment also seems to account for the neglible response by university and government officials to the demands made during the 1986-87 student movement in Mexico (see Torres chapter). And in Hungary in the latter 1970s and most of the 1980s, state and party elites' rhetoric about reforming the education system was generally unconnected from any real commitment to bring about these changes (see Darvas chapter).

Reform proposals are at times not implemented because the society and the state suffer from an economic and fiscal crisis. In the above-noted cases of Hungary, Côte d'Ivoire, and Mexico, there were insufficient resources to even begin implementing the educational reform plans, or at least this is what was claimed by state elites.[2] In other cases reforms were implemented but fiscal problems were cited as the reason for changing the direction of the reform or halting its full implementation. For example, Urch informs us that in Tanzania economic and fiscal crisis had a double dampening effect on reforms promoted under the banners of "self reliance" and "African socialism." On one hand, state and party elites were hard pressed to fund key elements of the proposed reform, eventually radically changing the direction of educational (and other) reform efforts in order to obtain loans and project funds from the International Monetary Fund, the World Bank, and the United States government. On the other hand, the reversal of initial, post-independence economic growth contributed to the decision by many parents and students in the rural areas to resist the reforms and pursue individualist, private strategies for obtaining education and improving their lives.[3] In Nicaragua the efforts in the 1980s to expand schooling opportunities, increase literacy, and refocus university science to deal with practical problems were similarly undermined by economic problems, not to mention the United States-funded Contra war (see Paulston and Rippberger chapter).

Other times reform rhetoric is not followed by the implementation of reform because educators and others resist the change efforts of elites (see also Plank 1987). Curricular reforms during the 1960s in the United States provide an example of this (see Martin chapter) as does the Ashkenazi population's resistance to the school integration and busing program in Israel in the 1960s and 1970s, which was designed to deal with the problem of lower achievement among Sephardic children (see Gottlieb chapter). Additionally, Torres notes that the 1986-87 student movement in Mexico was somewhat successful in deflecting or delaying the implementation of some of reforms at the National Autonomous University even though the students were not able to set in motion an alternative agenda. Also relevant here is the resistance by village dwellers in Tanzania to state and party efforts to shift education from an individualistic, academic, and urban orientation to one that embodied collectivistic, practical, and rural values and skills (see Urch chapter). And as Martin tells us, the conservative vocational education reforms in the early decades of the twentieth century in the United States were to some extent successfully resisted by educators and labor unions, although the compromise organizational concept--the comprehensive high school--can be seen as merely instituting a mental/manual hierarchy into a tracking system within (rather than between) schools.

However, in other situations, for example, in the current era in Australia, England, New Zealand, and the United States, reform rhetoric and proposals have been associated with dramatic restructuring of policy-making or administrative structure, curriculum, funding, etc. That such reforms were implemented in the face of resistance by teachers and other groups is worthy of note here as well. The relative powerlessness of teachers and a whole range of individuals and groups in England to resist or modify the 1988 Education Act is illustrative (see Miller and Ginsburg chapter) as is the limited effectiveness of teachers and other radical intellectuals to challenge the rhetoric or action of conservative reformers in the United States during the 1980s (see Martin chapter).[4]

CONFLICTING EVALUATIONS OF REFORM

We should not conceive of educational or other "reforms" as necessarily "change for the better," as many dictionaries and equilibrium theorists (e.g., Merritt and Coombs 1977; Simmons 1983) define it. Instead, from a conflict perspective (see Apple 1986; Carnoy 1976; Carnoy and Samoff 1990; Paulston 1977), social relations in education and other sectors should be seen as characterized by conflict and contradictions. Thus, what might be viewed as constructive change by one group may be viewed by others as either tokenism or destructive or regressive change (see also Altbach 1974). This can be illustrated by recent "reforms" undertaken by labor, liberal, and conservative governments in Australia, England, and New Zealand. The "reforms" have been celebrated by industrialists and centrist and right-wing parties but have been strongly criticized by organized teachers and leftist parties.

It is apparent from most of the national case studies presented in this volume that reforms have been and will continue to be evaluated differently by different groups in a given society. Martin documents with reference to the United States, both historically and currently, the competing conceptions--conservative, liberal, and radical--of what the problems in schooling and society are and what changes need to be implemented to solve these problems. In Mexico Torres identifies the conflicting visions and strategies for educational reform associated with groups he terms "modernizing technocrats," "controlling patrimonialists," and "democrats." Darvas provides considerable details of the varying analyses of and proposals for education by the different educator groups and political parties in Hungary. Conflicting proposals for and assessments of educational reform were also evidenced in the cases of Côte d'Ivoire, Israel, and Tanzania.

The major effort required by the Socialists in Spain to forge a consensus around the recent reforms provides another example of the conflicting perspectives on educational reform (see Morgenstern de Finkel chapter). The Spanish case, along with the cases of Australia and Mexico, represents different forms of *corporatism*. In the case of Spain, corporatism is historically rooted in civil society, although it was reinforced by the Francoist bureaucracy. In Mexico and Australia corporatism was instituted by governing elites to reduce the amount of conflict that surfaces at any point in time. While the leadership (and sometimes the rank and file) of the mass organizations connected to the dominant party benefit as well by having some influence on government policy, it is also clear that at least dissident groups within the mass organizations, not to mention groups which are not included in the corporatist arrangement, are often disenfranchized.

Although not discussed in terms of corporatism, the dynamics in Hungary and Côte d'Ivoire, at least until the late 1980s, could be usefully analyzed in this way. We should also note that, at least in England and New Zealand, alliances between dominant parties and educators, which had characterized politics of education in these countries during the 1940s through 1970s, were broken in the 1980s as governing elites sought closer and more explicit links with business owners and industrialists. This not only indicates conflicting stances on needed educational reform but also that corporatist-type arrangements may be established and reconfigured depending on the perceived interests of elite groups.

The applied science university reform in Nicaragua discussed by Paulston and Rippberger is also relevant here. In this case all but one of the major stakeholders reported positive evaluations of the collaborative effort between the United States and Nicaraguan governments, universities, and other organizations. Significantly, however, the Reagan administration in the United States decided not to continue, let alone expand, the project; instead, in line with its criticisms of and attempt to overthrow the Sandinista-led government of Nicaragua, the Reagan administration sought to punish the Nicaraguans by killing the project.

PROBLEMS IN EDUCATION, ECONOMY, OR THE STATE

Educational reform rhetoric and action are not necessarily targeted fundamentally on "problems" in education but may have more to do with national and global economic crises and/or crises of legitimation of the state. This is not to argue that reform occurs in the absence of real problems needing attention in education. Indeed, we assume that there are always aspects of the organization, content, and processes of education in any society that are perceived to be problems for one or more internal or external groups. The point is, however, that reform rhetoric and action only arise on a grand scale at certain times, while these "problems" exist before and after educational reform is on the local, national, or global agenda.

In this light one can examine the case of England in the mid-1970s during a Labour Party government headed by James Callaghan or that of Hungary in the late-1970s in a state dominated by the Socialist Workers Party led by Janos Kadar. In these cases, as well as in Australia, Côte d'Ivoire, New Zealand, and Tanzania, educational reform rhetoric and action can be seen as attempts to deal with economic and legitimation crises experienced in different ways by different nations. The critiques of and proposals for changes in education that were promulgated pre-existed the period of educational "reform," and thus the timing of the reform movement appears to have more to do with responding to or deflecting attention from economic and political crises than with dealing with educational problems.

Torres argues that a recurring theme in the Mexican context is that educational policy making reflects attempts by economic and state elites to deal with legitimation crises of the state (see also Weiler 1988), at least in part brought on by economic and fiscal crises. The case of Spain is specific in the sense that both the educational reform of the 1970s and the present one, were planned in a context of remarkable economic growth. But, while in the 1970s there was a clear attempt to achieve political legitimacy, given the challenge posed by the workers and the student movements, the ongoing reform is the result of a consensual agreement of most of the political parties (see Morgenstern de Finkel chapter).

The fact that in the United States a National Commission for Excellence, with the initially reluctant support of a Republican President, Ronald Reagan, helped to launch an educational reform movement in 1983 is also indicative that education may not be the main focus of concern. The Commission's (1983) report, bemoaning the "rising tide of mediocrity" in schools in the United States, was issued one year after Scholastic Achievement Tests scores had begun to move upward after several years of decline and one year after Phi Delta Kappa's national survey of parents showed schools receiving the highest favorable rating ever (see Martin chapter).

NATIONAL VERSUS WORLD SYSTEM EXPLANATIONS

In attempting to explain the timing and focus of educational reform one might be tempted to restrict one's analysis to dynamics and actors within nation-states or their subunits. That this volume is built on a series of national case studies might seem to encourage such a view. The various chapters indicate that attention must be focused on the local and national states that often constitute the sites of debates and struggles over what education should be, what ends it should serve, and in whose interests it should function. Certainly, historical and contemporary political, economic, and cultural features of a given society must be taken into consideration (see also Amin 1985; Therborn 1978).

However, a national level focus deflects attention from the equally important global or world system level cultural, political, and economic developments (see also Simmons 1983; Wirt and Harmon 1986). Thus, we need to include in our analysis of the timing and focus of educational reform the contradictory dynamics of the world capitalist economic system and the activities of multinational corporations, philanthropic foundations, international organizations, bilateral agencies, and universities (e.g., Berman 1983; Meyer and Hannan 1979). To reiterate the discussion begun in the first chapter, we view existing global or international relations in terms of a dynamic capitalist system, including, even before recent changes in Eastern Europe and the Soviet Union, both "capitalist" and "socialist" societies, which are stratified into "core," "semi-periphery," and "periphery."[5]

The importance of understanding educational reform in global context is evidenced by the fact that since the mid-1970s we have witnessed educational reform movements in so many different countries during the period of global recession or crisis in the world economic system. Thus, there seem to be parallel dynamics in education occurring in various countries at approximately the same time and in relation to volatile movements within the world economic system. It is also instructive that fiscal and other educational policy reforms were made in Hungary and Mexico but also England under conditions set by the International Monetary Fund (IMF) for obtaining loans.

Tanzania had a similar experience with the IMF. Urch informs us that state elites, who assumed power in the mid-1980s, also pursued certain types of programs in order to obtain funding from bilateral agencies, such as the United States Agency for International Development. The Tanzanian case is particularly important because during the 1960s and 1970s Tanzania represented a much celebrated alternative mode of development for Third World societies, one that stressed self-reliance and a locally interpreted and adapted form of socialism. To see Tanzania reverse itself on both fronts, moving toward dependent and subordinated capitalist relations, is a strong reminder of the force of dominant actors and processes in the world system. Similarly, changes in economic and educational policy both in China since the death of Mao and in the Soviet Union under the leadership of Gorbachev illustrate that it is very difficult, if not impossible, for societies to remain immune from the effects of the world capitalist system.

We should also mention the retrenching and regressive changes in education that occurred between 1983 and 1989 in Nicaragua under the Sandinistas in the face of an economic embargo and the Contra war organized by the United States government. And, of course, whatever reforms are talked about and/or pursued by the Chammoro-led UNO coalition government elected into power in 1989 in Nicaragua must be seen in the context of a particular set of imperialist or neo-colonial international relations. Paulston and Rippberger also note that the type and limited provision of education organized in Nicaragua during the pre-Sandinista period can be understood at least in part as occurring in the context of subordinated and dependent development in relation to the United States.

With respect to global cultural dynamics, we highlight Côte d'Ivoire's penchant in the two decades after its political independence for reforming its educational system to reflect changes implemented by its former colonizer, France (see chapter by Assie-Lumumba and Lumumba-Kasongo). Gottlieb's analysis provides the example of Israeli academics and political elites appropriating the rhetoric of teacher education reform from reports of the Holmes Group (1986) and Carnegie Task Force on Teaching as a Profession (1987) published in the United States. In the case of New Zealand,

Barrington documents how government policies were framed based on the decentralization and minimal state ideas of neo-liberals imported by New Zealand's economic and political elites from the United States and England; even the titles and texts of reports pointing the way to educational reform explicitly borrowed from similar documents in the United States.

CONTRADICTIONS AND SOCIAL STRUGGLE

Educational reform, thus, should be seen as the rhetorical and other activities by individuals involved in a process of struggle among social groups on a terrain of contradictory economic, political, and cultural dynamics at the local, national, and world system levels. The dynamics at these various levels occur through social struggles, involving conflict and cooperation within and among state elites, international organizations, capitalists, workers, political parties, and gender and racial/ethnic/religious groups. There is thus a dialectical relation between structural dynamics and human action--people's educational reform rhetoric and activity are both constituted by *and* constitive of social structure (see also Giddens 1979). Both human struggle and systemic contraditions are sources of movement and change.

While many of the chapters in this volume have stressed economic-based divisions between social classes, we also want to highlight struggles in terms of both racial/ethnic group relations (see Hawkins and LaBelle 1985) and gender relations. For instance, gender relations constitute a significant focus given that in almost all societies today the vast majority of teachers are women, while top educational administrators and union leaders tend to be males (e.g., see Apple 1988; Connell 1985; Cortina 1989; Ginsburg 1990; Schmuck 1987; Strober and Tyack 1980). Thus, debates and struggles between teachers and political and economic elites over the organization, process and content of education (e.g., in England, Côte d'Ivoire, and New Zealand) or to alter the existing structure and processes in teachers' unions (e.g., in Hungary and Mexico) must be understood not only in terms of social class but also gender struggles.

We also need to pay more attention to the implications of educational reform rhetoric and action for male and female students and for male and female adults, particularly as there are calls for more parental involvement. As David (1989) observes, the concept of parental involvement in schooling often implies mothers volunteering time to fulfill functions determined by others. Further investigation is required to see whether if mothers or fathers come to exercise any real power at the local school level as is being promised by the rhetoric of parental participation in Australia, England, New Zealand, and the United States. Also, how are patriarchal relations reproduced or challenged by curricular or other reform efforts? What do male and female students learn about gender relations from the reformed formal and hidden curricula of schooling? And do students and their teachers internalize or resist these "new" messages?

The relations within and among the various groups involved in struggles in and about education are characterized by inequalities in membership size, wealth, and power (including control of the economy, the state apparatus, the military, and the media), and thus the struggles are not among equals. Furthermore, as discussed in the first chapter, these struggles take place on what can be conceived of as dynamic terrain of contradictions, so that even if one could factor in the relative weights of membership size, wealth, and power, it would not be possible to predict in a straightforward manner exactly what the outcome of such struggles would be for reforming education. In a sense, contradictions both provide space for and serve to constrain the possibilities of counter-hegemonic ideological work and other forms of action (see also Ginsburg 1988).

One of the contradictions that requires our attention is what Hopkins and Wallerstein (1982, 58) term the economy--polity contradiction of the world system, that "the economy is primarily a world structure, but [union and other forms of] political activity takes place primarily within and through [nation]-state structures." Another important contradiction can be termed accumulation--legitimation, that to sustain extant social relations there are contradictory structural imperatives, on one hand, to foster capital accumulation (or profits) and other forms of exploitation, alienation, and oppression, and, on the other hand, to sustain the legitimacy of, capitalist relations of production, patriarchy, racial/ethnic/religious group formations, political parties, social organizations (such as unions), and nation-states themselves.

Major eruptions of reform rhetoric and/or action are more likely to arise when contradictions within and between the economy, the state, the family, and education are not being successfully mediated by existing ideological and structural arrangements at these various levels. The focus of reform rhetoric and action develops as a result of the ideological work and other strategies undertaken by the social groups involved in struggle. And we should remember that it is not just dominant groups that shape the struggle.

For instance, recently in Hungary, Côte d'Ivoire, and Mexico the mobilization of dissident teacher groups and opposition political parties have set in motion political and educational reform projects by political and union elites, although it seems that more fundamental changes have occurred so far only in Hungary and the Côte d'Ivoire as a result. Morgenstern de Finkel's analysis of the Spanish case also illustrates the centrality of the concept of struggle, both in the 1970s, in the context of efforts to overthrow Franco and his attempt to maintain state power, and in the 1980s, with respect to the conflict between the Socialist government and secondary school students, school teachers, other workers.

The Spanish case also illuminates the contradictory terrain on which such struggles take place. We witness the Socialist government's efforts to foster capital accumulation, increasingly in relation to a European and global economy, while at the same time seeking to reproduce the labor force and to legitimate the economy and the state. These efforts occur in the face of teachers and other workers demanding that they not continue to bear personally and disproportionately the cost of economic growth and increased state provision in education and other sectors. To the extent the Socialist government moves to meet these demands through increased wages and business taxes, it will retard capital accumulation. To the extent that the state and the party ignore these demands, their legitimacy is undermined and the institutional arrangments for reproducing the labor force become less effective (see Morgenstern de Finkel chapter).

The contradictory nature of the terrain on which struggles over education occur between state elites, economic elites, educators, workers, parents, and other citizens is also evidenced in the cases of Australia, Mexico, Tanzania, Hungary, Côte d'Ivoire, and New Zealand, and the United States. In the English case, perhaps, we can see most clearly how the accumulation-legitimation contradiction renders problematic the notion of correspondence between economy and education; the contradictions provide space for defining educational policies and practices that do not match the preferences of economic and political elites. Miller and Ginsburg show how in the case of "Midland County" middle schools Conservatives' efforts to legitimately reproduce the social relations of production (by more explicitly stratifying students and establishing stronger boundaries between curriculum subject areas) were undermined not only by some teachers' resistance but also by Conservatives' efforts to foster accumulation (by reducing educational expenditures). Similar dynamics seem to be occurring in the context of the development of city technology colleges in England.

THE STATE AND IDEOLOGICAL WORK

Educational reform rhetoric and action, however, should not be conceived of as a sort of functional response to the needs of the world capitalist system. We need also to examine the economic, political, and cultural dynamics at the national and local level. In particular, we need to analyze the state and its relation to the national and global economy. The state is a site of struggle, and, to varying extents in "capitalist" and "socialist" societies, the state embodies the contradictions of capitalism but also patriarchy and racist social relations. The state comes to embody the contradictions of capitalism, for example, because in the capitalist world economy the state is driven (and not automatically but with the intervention of international and domestic agencies) to reproduce a particular set of social relations, to foster accumulation, and to legitimate the capitalist mode of production, because the revenue (via taxation, loans, etc.) that sustains the state's continued operation (and its own legitimacy) depends directly or indirectly on the profits extracted (see Dale 1982; Ginsburg, Wallace, and Miller 1988; Offe and Ronge 1981). Here we can note the strong influential role of the Treasury in shaping administrative and other educational reforms in New Zealand (see Barrington chapter). The contradictory (as opposed to a simple correspondence or dependency model) nature of state-world economy relations was also discussed above with reference to the fact that in England and other nations the state's efforts to establish and maintain its own and capitalism's legitimacy, the state is likely to siphon off part of the capital from the accumulation process.

The contributions of the state to the processes of accumulation and legitimation, though, are not always fully appreciated (Young 1980). Indeed, through the use of nationalism, populism, and other ideologies, state and economic elites may seek to conceal the state's capitalist functions and represent it as "the incarnation of the popular will of the people/nation" (Poulantzas 1975, 173). It is thus important to attend to ideological struggles among various social groups, who have greater or lesser control over and access to public and private modes of mass producing and distributing ideas at local, national, and global levels. The use of mass media, reports of governments, political parties, business/industry and labor groups, philanthropic foundations, bilateral agencies, and international organizations should be understood as part of the process of giving and denying voice (see Smith 1988).

Gottlieb emphasized that rhetoric is not merely abstraction or decoration in political struggle, but that it functions to persuade and coerce, to define the problem and focus attention toward (and away from) certain possible solutions. In England, Hungary, Côte d'Ivoire, and New Zealand, we saw the important role that ideological work played in educational reform movements. In these cases economic and political crises were, at least for a time, redefined as problems in education. Economic problems were not ignored in the reform proposals and debates--indeed, quite the contrary--but they were discussed as being rooted in the shortcomings of the educational system, which needed reforming, rather than in the basic structure of the national and global economy. Martin's analysis of the ideological work of conservative, liberal, and radical writers in the United States perhaps brings this point home most strongly.

CENTRALIZATION/ DECENTRALIZATION AND TEACHERS' POWER

Another issue that emerged in the context of this collaborative research project represented by this volume concerns centralization/decentralization. Here, we would mention the examples of Australia, England, and New Zealand, where there have been moves to strengthen the participation of parents in decision-making at the school level and either reducing or (in the case of New Zealand) eliminating the role of intermediate level units (state ministries, local education authorities, or regional boards). While this might be interpreted initially as a form of decentralization, when we look closer we see an associated increase in control over education at the national level, which for Australia and England is a fairly dramatic shift. In all three cases the national state increasingly placed fairly clear boundaries on the action of school-level decisions, so that rather than devolving power, the process seemed to involve delegating responsibility to implement centralized curricular and other policies. Similar developments have been identified in the United States (Plank 1987) and in a range of societies that have undergone radical political and social transformations (La Belle and Ward 1990).

This complex strategy of devolving responsibility to the local school level, while concentrating decision-making power at the national government level may be motivated by desire to shift the blame for failure of reforms to schools and communities. They can be blamed for incorrect or inefficient implementation of the policies.

Additionally, local school communities may have been seen as more likely to be in accord with the assumptions and direction of the reform than were actors operating at the intermediate levels. Centralization and decentralization must be understood, then, not as technical adjustments to enhance the efficiency of achieving goal upon which there is general agreement. Centralization and decentralization must also be seen as political strategies to implement certain curricular or other reforms by one group faced with opposition or resistance to its reform agenda. Therefore, the real issues may not be the degree of centralization or decentralization but the extent to which the governance structure enables and encourages participation by citizens in real decision-making (McGinn 1991).

What is also significant about these cases of societies in which English is the dominant (but not the only) spoken language is the way the power of teachers and their organizations have been affected by such moves to centralize authority and decentralize responsibility. In all four cases the reform movements were fueled by government or other commission reports and mass media-disseminated criticisms of educators. Teachers were blamed for schools' graduates being unemployed or unskilled and uncooperative (read not subservient) workers, all of which were portrayed as the major explanation for the respective country's economic problems.

Teachers and their organizations were also portrayed as being too strong and influential, having the "unfortunate" ability to shape the education system so as to serve their own "narrow" occupational group interests. For example, in New Zealand, the claim was frequently made that the "providers" of education had "captured" the system (see Barrington chapter). Following these attacks on teachers and not unrelated to teachers' resistance to some of the initially proposed reforms, strategies were developed by economic and state elites to all but remove teachers from effective participation in the politics of education generally and even in the processes of determining teachers' salaries, benefits, and working conditions. We thus observed a process of proletarianization or deskilling and depowering of teachers, whereby they become the implementors of policy and practice conceived and controlled by others (see Ginsburg, Wallace and Miller 1988).

EDUCATORS' ALLIANCES WITH OTHER GROUPS IN STRUGGLES

It is also salient that in these cases teachers had few solid links to either parent groups or other workers. For example, in

England during a major confrontation between the teachers' unions and the Thatcher government (1984-86), the state was able to undermine the support that parents were beginning to provide to the teachers' demands because there was not a strong history of teachers and parents working together for common purposes (see Miller and Ginsburg chapter). More often historically teachers had pursued a strategy of professionalization, an occupational group project involving negotiations with the state for remuneration, status, and power as well as a distancing of "professional" educators from the "nonprofessional" or lay community, including parents. As teachers' past strategy of professionalization was undermined by recent efforts by state elites to proletarianize the work of teachers and teachers responded by militant "trade union" action, parents often became further alienated from teachers. Thus, the possibility of an alliance between teachers and parents became more remote.

We should also note that during this same period in England the powerful mine workers union was challenging the Thatcher government, but no real alliances were formed between the two groups of workers. One block to such an alliance was the differences in ideology and strategy between teachers, perceived as "professionals," and mine workers, perceived as militant trade unionists (see also Ginsburg, Meyenn and Miller 1980). That both the teachers and the mine workers were soundly defeated, even though at one point they both appeared to be on the verge of victory, suggests that an opportunity was missed to reinforce each other's struggle and thus provide a different outcome. Educators seeking to forge an occupational group strategy in isolation of other social groups may succeed for a while in their struggle with economic and state elites but perhaps only as long as the educators are perceived to be serving the elites' interests (see Miller and Ginsburg chapter).

The university student movements in Mexico are also relevant here. Torres documents the differences between the 1968 and the 1986-87 movements, with the former, even despite the brutal, repressive response from the Mexican state, having a much more significant impact on educational and other policies. While there are alternative explanations of the differences, the fact that in 1968 students formed alliances with workers and other groups as part of a broader social movement has to be seriously considered.

It is in this sense that mass participation (as opposed to

decentralization of responsibility or administrative functions) provides the promise of progressive educational as well as political and economic change. These dynamics in Mexico as well as more recent struggles in Hungary and Côte d'Ivoire provide a basis for hope. Urch's discussion of Tanzania, though, somewhat deflates this hope. We saw masses of Tanzanians opt for conservative, individualist, privatized solutions to shared problems and resist efforts by "leaders" to implement policies of "self-reliance" and "African socialism." However, in this case we must ask whether the Tanzanian masses were really involved in conceptualizing and executing policies or whether, especially as the global economic dynamics placed severe constraints on Tanzania's options, they were asked (and forced) to carry out centrally determined directives. Similarly, we should question whether the "leaders" were true to their collective rhetoric or whether they themselves modeled individualist, privatized strategies for achieving greater benefits for themselves.

Let us end with another note about strategy for struggle in relation to educational reform movements that must be understood to operate within global and well as local and national context. We as gender, racially/ethnically, and social-class stratified educators (and other worker-citizens and family members) need to develop ways to work together across national boundaries to intervene in dynamics, including those that are called "educational reform," in order to further a collective project to create a more just, equitable, environmentally sound, and peaceful world system.

In the context of educational reform movements we need to develop more effective forms and means of communication to counter the ideological work of those seeking to serve the interests of elites. We need to talk and write in a manner and in places that ease access by educators and other citizen/workers. Given the domination of mass media channels by economic and political elites, though, we must find creative alternative channels of communication, which will allow dialogue among the large majority of people all over the world who are committed to progressive social change. And we need to figure out better ways to exploit the space created by contradictory ideologies and social structures.

However, we cannot be satisfied with only speaking and listening or writing and reading; we must also engage in strategic action in concert with others. We cannot just discuss and debate about the problems (and their solution) in education, the economy, and politics. Rhetoric and theorizing are important, but they must be fused with action. It is this joining of theory and action constructed from a critical or conflict-oriented perspective that is at the heart of critical praxis (see Ginsburg 1988). Such critical praxis would involve working with educators and others around the world to resist efforts to "reform" education in anti-progressive directions. It would also entail seeking with other to implement progressive reforms in education--reforms that serve the interests of the majority of people who suffer under existing forms of social relations at the local, national, and global levels.

As Morgenstern de Finkel emphasizes in her analysis of the Spanish case, such efforts will require technical and organizational skills and not just progressive goals and commitments. Limited financial resources place enormous constraints on what can be undertaken. Thus, questions of efficiency need to be considered very seriously. However, especially given the contradictory dynamic in relation to which we seek to conceive and implement changes in education, we need to be critically reflective of our own and others' ideas and actions. We cannot simply identify what appears to be a efficient strategy for achieving a given long-or short-term goal. We need to clarify how this goal may or may not be compatible with or contradictory to other goals in education or more generally. We also need to monitor the process to make sure the means for achieving a desired end do not contradict the values of participation, justice, and equity.

Our critical praxis must extend beyond a focus on education (see Ginsburg 1987). As we have noted, much of what is defined in the interest of elites as educational problems are at a more fundamental level economic and political problems. We should not be deceived into putting all of our time and energies into debating and seeking change in education, however important such activity may be. Recall that many of the constraints that limit far-reaching reforms in education derive from the existing relations of power and the existing distribution of wealth in nations and the world system. We need to dialogue with those who are disadvantaged by existing social relations and work together with them to challenge unjust, inequitable, environmentally unsound, and oppressive social policies and practices. We need to align with other people all over the globe to construct a future that works in the interest of the vast majority of inhabitants of this globe and not just a small privileged and powerful group.

Such cross-national collaboration will not be easy. It will require empathy for others' situation, dialogue, clarification of mutual interests, creative resolution of conflicting interests, and a pragmatic, though principled orientation to developing strategies. However, as the analyses presented this volume suggest, national and global economic and political elites have found ways to cross national boundaries in pursuing their interests, whether that be in education or other domains of human experience. Thus, we need to find means to meet the challenge of struggle in the global context.

NOTES

1. This is a revised version of a paper presented by Mark
    Ginsburg to the Encuentro Internacional de Trabajadores de
    la Educación on "Estado, Sociedad y Educación en el Marco
    de las Transformaciones Contemporaneas," organized by the
    Sindicato Nacional de Trabajadores de la Educación,
    Mexico City, 9-13 July 1990.

2. We should distinguish between the reality of economic and
    fiscal crisis experienced by all three of these countries and
    the ideological work that translates fiscal crisis into a
    situation that "requires" cutbacks or in at least limits for
    education and social services, while maintaining or
    increasing government expenditures in other areas. It is also
    important to note that the fiscal crisis of the state, although
    related to national and global economic crisis (O'Connor
    1973), also stems from taxation and other government
    policies that allow a continuation or increase in the
    concentration (nationally and globally) of private wealth,
    which might otherwise be used in education and other
    public service areas.

3. In the Tanzanian case--as well as in the cases of nominally
    "socialist" or "revolutionary" societies of Hungary, Mexico,
    and Nicaragua--the legitimacy of the states and their
    educational and other reforms was undermined not just by
    their inability to sustain economic growth (see chapters by
    Darvas, Torres, and Paulston and Rippberger). That wealth,
    power, and status were inequitably distributed in the favor
    of party and government leaders was not lost on many
    workers and peasants, even as they experienced real gains
    compared to previous eras, and this perceived reality served
    to undermine the legitimacy of party and state elites.   In
    Hungary and Nicaragua the legitimation crisis (with some
    help from international intervention) resulted in changes in
    governments, while in Mexico and Spain, thus far, the
    dominant party and the government have been able to

maintain power.

4.   It is noteworthy that the arguments of radical scholars from
         the United States and England were used by conservative
         groups in New Zealand in developing their critique of
         schooling and in justifying the less than progressive reforms
         they proposed (see Barrrington chapter).

5.   Hence, rather than discussing societal changes only in terms
         of national "development," we also focus on processes of
         reproducing and transforming these unequal global
         relations. Moreover, we do not think the current
         transformations, for example, in the Soviet Union or in
         Eastern and Western Europe have much to do with radically
         changing these unequal international relations. The
         reduction of east-west conflict and the opening of economic
         relations between east and west may engender a climate in
         which north-south relation become more unequal. We would
         also note that, with the exception of developments within
         the European Economic Community (EEC), the process of
         globalization and regionalization of economic relations has
         involved breaking down borders to facilitate the flow of
         capital and commodities but not the movement of labor
         (i.e., liberalizing immigration law). Moreover, although
         labor within the EEC will be able to be mobile
         transnationally, there has been no serious discussion of
         opening European or other northern countries' borders to
         the flow of labor from Africa, Asia, or Latin America.
         Indeed, there are increasing political pressure to restrict
         immigration, both from the continents as well as from
         Eastern Europe and the republics of the Soviet Union.

REFERENCES

Altbach, P. 1974. Comparative university reform. In *University reform: Comparative perspectives for the seventies*, edited by P. Altbach, 1-14. Cambridge, MA: Schenkman.

Amin, S. 1985. *Delinking: Towards a polycentric world*. London: Zed Books.

Apple, M. 1986. Ideology, reproduction and educational reform. In *New approaches to comparative education*, edited by P. Altbach and G. Kelly, 51-71. Chicago: University of Chicago Press.

Apple, M. 1988. *Teachers and text*. New York: Routledge.

Berman, E. 1983. *The influence of the Carnegie, Ford, and Rockefeller Foundations on American foreign policy: The ideology of philanthropy*. Albany: State University of New York Press.

Campbell, D. 1982. Experiments as arguments. *Knowledge: Creation, Diffusion, Utilization*, 3, 3: 327-37.

Carnegie Task Force on Teaching as a Profession 1987. *A nation prepared: Teaching for the 21st century*. Hyattsville, MD: Carnegie Corporation of New York.

Carnoy, M. 1976. International educational reform: The ideology of efficiency. In *The limits of educational reform*, edited by M. Carnoy and H. Levin, 245-68. New York: Longman.

Carnoy, M., and Samoff, J. 1990. *Education and social transition in the Third World*. Princeton: Princeton University Press.

Connell, R. 1985. *Teacher's work*. Sydney: Allen and Unwin.

Cortina, R. 1989. Women as leaders in Mexican education. *Comparative Education Review*, 33, 3: 357-76.

Dale, R. 1982. Education and the capitalist state: Contributions and contradictions. In *Cultural and economic reproduction in education: Essays on class, ideology and the state*, edited by M. Apple, 127-61. Boston: Routledge and Kegan Paul.

David, M. 1989. Schooling and the family. In *Critical pedagogy, the state and cultural struggle*, edited by H. Giroux and P. McLaren, 50-65. Albany: State University of New York Press.

Giddens, A. 1979. *Central problems in social theory.* Berkeley: University of California Press.

Ginsburg, M. 1987. Contradictions in the role of Professor as Activist. *Sociological Focus*, 20, 2: 111-22.

Ginsburg, M. 1988. *Contradictions in teacher education and society: A critical analysis*. New York: Falmer Press.

Ginsburg, M. 1990. El proceso de trabajo y la accion politica de los educadores: Un analisis comparado (The labor process and political action of educators: A comparative analysis). *Revista de educación* (August).

Ginsburg, M., Cooper, S., Raghu, R., and Zegarra, H. 1990. National and world system explanations of edcuational reform. *Comparative Education Review*, 34, 4: 474-499.

Ginsburg, M., Meyenn, R., and Miller, H. 1980. Teachers' conceptions of professionalism and trades unionism: An ideological analysis. In *Teacher strategies*, edited by P. Woods, 178-212. London: Croom Helm.

Ginsburg, M., Wallace, G., and Miller, H. 1988. Teachers, economy and the state: An English example. *Teaching and Teacher Education*, 4, 4: 317-37.

Hawkins, J., and La Belle, T. 1985. *Education and intergroup relations*. New York. Praeger.

Holmes Group 1986. *Tomorrow's teachers*. East Lansing, MI: Holmes Group, Inc.

Hopkins, T., and Wallerstein, E. 1979. *World-systems analysis: Theory and methodology*. Volume 1. Beverly Hills: Sage.

La Belle, T., and Ward, C. 1990. Education reform when nations undergo radical political and social transformation. *Comparative Education*, 26, 1: 95-106.

McGinn, N. 1991. Reforming educational governance: Centralization/decentralization. In *Emergent issues in education: Comparative perspective*, edited by R. Arnove, P. Altbach, and G. Kelly. Albany: State University of New York Press.

Merritt, R.,and Coombs, F. 1977. Politics and educational reform. *Comparative Education Review*, 21, 2/3: 247-73.

Meyer, J., and Hannan, M. 1979. National development in a changing world system: An overview. In *National development and the world system: Educational, economic and political change, 1950-70*, edited by J. Meyer and M. Hannan, 3-16. Chicago: University of Chicago Press.

National Commission on Excellence in Education 1983. *A nation at risk: The imperative for educational reform*. Washington, D.C.: United States Department of Education.

O'Connor, J. 1973. *The fiscal crisis of the state*. New York: St. Martin's Press.Offe, C. & Ronge, V. 1981. Theses on the theory of the state. In *Education and the state: Volume 1. Schooling and the national interest*, edited by R. Dale, G. Esland, R. Ferguson, and M. MacDonald, 77-86. Sussex: Open University Press.

Paulston, R. 1977. Social and educational change: conceptual frameworks. *Comparative Education Review*, 21, 2/3: 370-95.

Plank, D. 1987. Why school reform doesn't change schools: Political and organizational perspectives. In *The politics of excellence and choice*, edited by W. Boyd, and C. Kershner, 143-52. New York: Falmer Press.

Poulantzas, N. 1975. *Classes in contemporary capitalism*. London: New Left Books.

Schmuck, P. 1987. Introduction. In *Women educators: Employees in schools of western countries*, edited by P. Schmuck, 1-17. Albany: State University of New York Press.

Simmons, J. 1983. Reforming education and society: The enduring quest. In *Better Schools: International Lessons for Reform*, edited by J. Simmons, 3-19. New York: Praeger.

Smith, D. 1988. Femininity as discourse. In *Becoming feminine: The politics of popular culture*, edited by L. Roman, L. Christian-Smith, and E. Ellsworth, 37-59. New York: Falmer Press.

Strober, M., and Tyack, D. 1980. Why women teach and men manage? *Signs*, 5, 31: 494-503.

Therborn, G. 1978. *What does the ruling class do when it rules?* London: New Left Books.

Weiler, H. 1988. The politics of reform and nonreform in French education. *Comparative Education Review*, 32, 3: 251-65.

Wirt, F., and Harman, G. 1986. The editors: A view from across the board: The international recession and educational policy. In *Education, recession and the world village: A comparative political economy of education*, edited by F. Wirt and G. Harman, 163-80. Philadelphia: Falmer Press.

Young, T. 1980, August. The public sphere and the state in capitalist society. Paper presented at the American Sociological Association annual meeting. New York (distributed by the Red Feather Institute).

INDEX

Accord, 95-97
accumulation, 21-22, 90, 117, 154, 379-381, 382
accumulation-legitimation contradiction, 90, 117, 172, 379, 381
adult education, 183, 210
AFT, 357
African socialism, 205, 371, 377, 386
A Nation At Risk, 295, 297-298, 342
Arusha Declaration, 205-206
Assisted Places Scheme, 61, 66
Australia, 85-114, 285, 372-375, 379-381, 383

Boyson, Rhodes, 60
British Council, 223
Buchanan, James, 296
bureaucratic restructuring, 98-99
Burnham Committee on Teachers' Salaries, 52, 65

Callaghan, James, 50, 57-58, 66, 310, 374
Canada, 285
Carnegie Foundation, 333, 357-358, 377
Chamorro, Violeta, 195, 377
China, 377
city technology colleges, 67, 71-72
class analysis, 154
class relations, 15, 153-154, 386
class struggle, 232, 379
CNTE, 119, 130-132, 134, 136
cold war, 232
colonialism, 203, 263-264, 270
conflict paradigm, 8-9, 10-12, 26-27, 369, 373
conflict theories of education, 295, 351-352, 390
contradictions of capitalism, 22, 378, 381
contradictions of world system, 16, 19, 28, 379, 387
core problems of capitalism, 10, 86